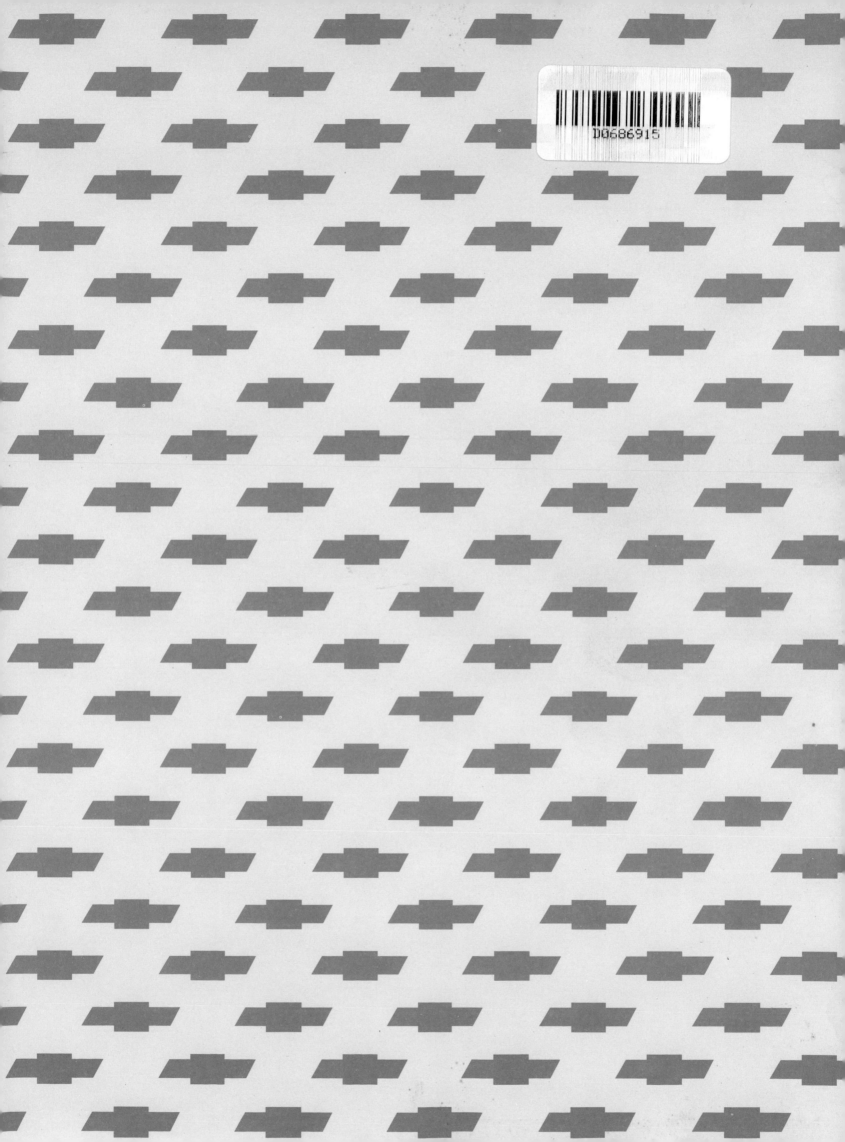

CHEVROLET

CHRONICLE

THE COMPLETE & COLORFUL STORY OF CHEVROLET FROM 1904

BY THE AUTO EDITORS OF CONSUMER GUIDE®

Publications International, Ltd.

ISBN: 0-7853-5566-9

Library of Congress Control Number: 2001096915

Very special thanks to:
Chevrolet Public Relations; M.G. "Pinky" Randall.

Production figures for years 1912-29 courtesy: Jerry Heasley, *The Production Figure Book for US Cars*, Motorbooks International

PHOTO CREDITS
The editors would like to thank the following people and organizations for supplying the photography that made this book possible. They are listed below, along with the page number(s) of their photos:

Orazio Aiello: 127; **Roger D Barnes:** 227; **Scott Baxter:** 162; **Ken Beebe:** 183; **Scott Brandt:** 124; **Chan Bush:** 66, 151, 169, 173; **Gary Cameron:** 134; **Champion Spark Plug:** 192; **Cooke Photographic:** 119; **Des Plaines Historical Society:** 159; **Charles Dupree:** 177; **E.T. Satory Collection:** 165; **Al Ferreira:** 119; **Roland Flessner:** 292, 293, 310; **Jim Frenak:** 122; **Mitch Frumkin:** 312, 317, 319; **Ron Grantz, National Automotive History Collection-Detroit Public Library:** 7, 8, 9, 40, 42, 45; **Thomas Glatch:** 118, 157, 158, 178, 184, 213, 237; **David Gooley:** 56, 57, 104; **Sam Griffith:** 17, 22, 23, 70, 97, 103, 105, 106, 107, 113, 118, 125, 130, 133, 139, 140, 141, 142, 145, 148, 161, 181, 184, 187, 191, 203, 239, 308, 316, 324, 331, 332, 333, 334, 335; **Jerry Heasley:** 140, 170, 176, 192, 214; **Don Heiny:** 204; **Ron Hussey:** 60; **Hutchinson Photo:** 142; **Jeff Johnson:** 88, 155, 186; **Bud Juneau:** 37, 61, 67, 85, 86, 96, 104, 107, 163, 198, 202; **Milton Kieft:** 89, 97, 168, 178, 179, 182, 198, 296; **Lloyd Koenig:** 153; **Walt Kuhn:** 242; **Parker Little:** 18, 29; **Dan Lyons:** 16, 82, 86, 98, 100, 129, 130, 161, 178, 184, 204, 208, 234, 239, 243, 244, 253; **Vince Manocchi:** 16, 19, 24, 25, 26, 30, 43, 44, 52, 55, 56, 58, 59, 73, 76, 99, 102, 109, 111, 115, 116, 118, 123, 124, 126, 134, 143, 145, 149, 152, 153, 156, 158, 169, 170, 171, 177, 178, 188, 193, 194, 197, 203, 207, 208, 209, 214, 215, 217, 232, 238, 246, 258, 262, 267, 287, 289, 291, 312, 326, 332; **Michigan State Police:** 112, 151; **Minnesota Historical Society:** 112; **Doug Mitchel:** 54, 58, 59, 78, 79, 103, 109, 112, 119, 122, 131, 138, 140, 148, 149, 150, 154, 158, 159, 160, 165, 166, 167, 177, 178, 183, 186, 188, 189, 193, 195, 197, 199, 200, 209, 215, 226, 246, 287, 338; **Steve Momot:** 145; **Ron Moorhead:** 160, 204; **Mike Mueller:** 124, 137, 138, 165, 183, 191, 204, 206, 214, 218, 242; **NHRA Archives:** 167; **Robert Nicholson:** 180; **Neil Nissing:** 355; **Owens-Corning:** 196; **Nina Padgett:** 36, 84, 91, 93, 131, 216, 336, 342, 343; **Jay Peck:** 152, 225; **Jeff Rose:** 193, 198; **David Ryan:** 147; **Tom Shaw:** 146; **Gary Smith:** 14, 15, 38, 39, 201, 232; **Richard Spiegelman:** 120, 166, 231; **Tom Storm:** 229; **David Temple:** 109, 151, 172, 217, 253, 319; **Bob Tenney:** 194; **Susan E. Teubert, Motor Vehicle Manufacturers Association:** 17, 33, 34, 48, 61, 65, 68, 71, 74, 79, 80, 87, 92, 106, 114, 126, 155; **Phil Toy:** 94, 142, 161, 193, 201, 312; **Chris Trame, Illinois State Police:** 166; **W.C. Waymack:** 50, 51, 53, 64, 68, 69, 70, 72, 75, 76, 82, 96, 101, 107, 108, 109, 113, 132, 139, 140, 146, 148, 151, 154, 158, 159, 164, 167, 173, 176, 178, 183, 184, 186, 187, 194; 202, 204, 205, 210, 218, 219, 222, 228, 233, 238, 244, 249, 251, 277, 284; **Joseph H. Wherry Collection:** 10, 156, 163; **White Eagle Studios:** 148; **Hub Wilson:** 145, 147; **Nicky Wright:** 32, 40, 46, 47, 58, 85, 98, 100, 118, 144, 145, 151, 187, 194, 196, 203, 309.

Owners:
Special thanks to the owners of the cars featured in this book for their enthusiastic cooperation. They are listed below, with the page number(s) on which their cars appear:

Robert and Diane Adams: 153; **Kirk Alexander:** 217; **John B. Albert:** 68, 69; **Mike Allen:** 219; **Gary Almeida:** 160; **Homer Altevoght:** 151; **Norman Andrews:** 195; **Jim and Mary Ashworth:** 96; **Carolyn and Mark Badamo:** 165; **Orville L. Baer:** 249; **Howard L. Baker:** 179; **Michael Bancroft:** 67; **Ray and Dolores Banuls:** 204; **Dennis Beauregard:** 145; **Steve Bergin:** 112; **Chuck Bernecker:** 115; **Les Bieri and John Angwert:** 118; **Bill Bodnarchuk:** 144; **Pete Bogard:** 141, 142; **Bill Borland:** 201; **James and Patricia Boyk:** 148; **Jeanine and Don Brink:** 228; **Dave Bristol:** 169; **Roy and Sandi Brookshire:** 156; **Dan Brown:** 164; **Robert Bruggeman:** 64; **Jerry and Carol Buczkowski:** 203, 309; **Donald A. Burkholder:** 59; **Bill Bush:** 194; **Jim Cahill:** 130; **Jerome Cain, Fred Gaugh, Terry Sheafer:** 138; **Clay and Judy Campbell:** 158; **Frank Capolupo:** 203; **Daniel Carr:** 220; **Cars of San Francisco, Inc.:** 142; **David Chance:** 151; **John L. Clark:** 113; **Lew Clark:** 46, 47; **Gordon and Dorothy Clemmer:** 118, 246; **Marilyn Cliff:** 204; **Bob and Cindy Cohn:** 119; **James E. Collins:** 204; **Contemporary and Investment Automobiles:** 225; **Dr. Randy and Freda Cooper:** 209; **Kenneth A. Coppock:** 122; **Corvette Mike:** 258, 262, 312; **Donald R. Crile:** 198; **Thomas and Mae Crockett:** 197; **Dr. Mike Cruz:** 207; **Allen Cummins:** 193; **Ed Cunneen:** 203; **Rick Cybul:** 218; **Charles Davis:** 147; **David Dawes, Bob Painter:** 178; **Charles and Cathy Deaubl:** 54; **"T" and Ed DeCamp:** 196; **Ken Dedic, Levy Venture Management:** 17; **John DeLoach:** 319; **Dick Dennis:** 58; **Richard DeVecchi:** 86; **Ronald L. Diebold, Sr.:** 210; **Dave Diedrics:** 193; **Thomas H. Dietz:** 166; **Bruce Dockery:** 138; **Richard and Joyce Dollmeyer:** 186; **Greg Don:** 214; **George Don-Pedro:** 312; **Jeff Dranson:** 137; **Jerry and Robin Driemeier:** 251; **Keith Duncan:** 182; **Bill Edman:** 284; **Rob Embleton:** 191; **Douglas Englin:** 167; **Greg Englin:** 159; **Ernie's Wrecker Service:** 105; **David Ertel:** 146; **Don Essen:** 154; **Harold D. Evans:** 96; **Margaret Evans:** 186; **Rex and Justin Fager:** 70; **Fairway Chevrolet:** 36, 84, 91, 93, 131; **David L. Ferguson:** 123, 134; **Al Ferreira:** 119; **Don Ferry:** 192; **Gordon Fenner:** 217; **Dennis Fink:** 44; **Robert G. Finley:** 184; **Christina Finster:** 188; **Jeanne C. Finster:** 188; **Sam Fittante:** 109; **Bob Flack:** 144; **Theodore Freeman:** 124; **Tom and Christine French:** 218; **John L. Fuller:** 176; **John Gales:** 107; **Mr. and Mrs. Raymond Garcia:** 66; **George W. Gass:** 187; **Margaret A. Geib:** 237; **Denny R. Geiler:** 164; **Jim Geraghty:** 131; **Jack Gersch:** 203; **William Giembroniewicz:** 82; **Fred Gildner:** 59, 60; **Gary Girt:** 168; **Dave and Mary Glass:** 184; **Elmer Goehring:** 37; **Eric Goodman:** 150; **Bill Goodsene:** 85, 37; **Barbara Ann Grafton:** 139, 140; **Bill Grathic:** 229; **Jack Gratzianna:** 162; **Peter Guide, Jr.:** 78; **Howard Gumbel:** 109; **Harry Hadley:** 161; **Whitney and Diane Haist:** 94; **Bill Halliday:** 104; **Dan and Carol Hansen:** 40; **Charles M. Havelka:** 133; **William T. Hayes and Sons:** 105; **Orren "Spike" Headley:** 173; **Dennis Helferich:** 296; **Chuck Henderson:** 165; **Pete Henneberger:** 177; **Budd Hickey:** 196; **Bill Hoff:** 192; **Les Huckins:** 169; **Robert Ingold:** 152; **Chesley Jacobs:** 127; **J. Bruce Jacobs:** 171; **John E. and Barbara E. James:** 216; **K.D. James:** 170; **Roger A. James:** 88, 155, 186; **Blaine Jenkins:** 98; **Gary Johns:** 138; **Stephen M. Johnson:** 127; **Bill Jones:** 163; **Richard Kalinowski:** 129; **Arnold Kaplan:** 149; **Bill Kaprelian:** 109; **Robert Kleckauskas:** 184; **Donald A. Klein:** 122; **Larry Knebel:** 75, 76; **Terry Knight:** 101; **Larry Koetting:** 233; **Edward S. Kuziel:** 137; **Robert Landers:** 183; **Chris Lapp:** 89; **Donald Laraway:** 86; **Tony Leopardo:** 193; **Charley Lillard:** 202; **Ed Lojac:** 147; **Phillip and Sandy LoPiccolo:** 170; **Terry Lucas:** 158; **Dan and Joyce Lyons:** 208; **Joseph and Suzanne Lysy:** 158; **Jim MacDonald:** 183; **Bob Macy:** 176, 214; **Bill and Rita Malik:** 145; **Larry Martin:** 238; **Rich Mason:** 143; **Richard Matzer:** 242; **Mike and Kay Maxson:** 172; **Raymond L. May:** 140; **Dick McKean:** 100; **Michael D. McCloskey:** 149; **Keith C. McDaniel:** 242; **Michael P. McFarland:** 187; **Paul McGuire:** 191; **Ken McMullen:** 202; **Keith W. Meiswinkel:** 234; **Tom Meleo:** 16, 19, 24, 25, 26, 27, 30, 43, 99; **Andrew J. Mesrausras:** 188; **Ed Milas:** 213; **Harry J. and Carol S. Miller:** 194; **Jim Miller:** 232; **Paul Miller:** 56, 57; **Connie and Larry Mitchell:** 180; **Albert Mitchell:** 146; **Ralph Moceo:** 107; **Bob Moore:** 154; **Fred Morgan:** 148; **Robert and Carole Morin:** 204; **John Murray:** 115; **Dennis Murry:** 76; **National Automobile Museum:** 32; **Don Nelson:** 50, 51; **Burt and Lynda Neuner:** 177, 193; **Carl Noll:** 121; **Louis and Inez Noose:** 97; **Northern Illinois Classic Auto:** 209; **Dan J. Obele:** 58; **D.R. Ogsberger:** 198; **Karl Oliver:** 152; **John Olsen:** 215; **Edward E. Ortiz:** 267; **Ray Ostrander:** 124; **Steven S. Pasek:** 239; **John W. Petras:** 139, 140; **Allen Petroskey:** 177; **Sam Pierce:** 178; **Bill Pierson:** 167; **Ronn Pittman:** 138; **David and Terry Plunkett:** 126; **Kenneth Pool:** 178; **Bruce Powell:** 166; **Pro-Team Corvette Sales:** 160; **Steve Provart:** 184; **Ramshead Automobile Collection:** 198; **M.G. "Pinky" Randall:** 14, 15, 38, 39, 201, 232; **Greg Reynolds:** 187; **Robert F. Richards:** 103; **Wayne Rife:** 145; **Vivian Riley:** 158, 161; **LuAnne and Rodney Rinne:** 189; **Kenneth H. Rufkahr:** 124; **Jim and John Russell:** 209; **Ron Ryan:** 157, 158; **Joseph F. Salierno:** 109; **Chuck Sarges:** 187; **Herb Saul:** 55; **Bob Schaffhauser:** 82; **Tom Schay:** 52, 171; **Stan Scheitler:** 227; **Allen Scherler:** 214; **William and Joseph Schoenbeck:** 22, 23, 70, 125; **Bill Schwelitz:** 154; **Robert and Esther Seely:** 200; **Ralph Segars:** 253; **Dale Shetley:** 287; **Jerry Shumate:** 244; **Gerald Sichel:** 16; **Eugene R. Sinda, Jr.:** 138; **Raymond Silva, Jr.:** 102; **Fred A. Smith:** 215; **Steve Smith:** 159; **Ron Snyder:** 61; **Roy L. Spencer:** 194; **Frank Spittle:** 183; **Jack Stevens:** 178; **Charles E. Stinson:** 183; **Tom and Nancy Stump:** 194; **Andrew Surmeier:** 108; **Ernest R. Sutton, Jr.:** 226; **Larry and Loretta Swedberg:** 199; **Steve Sydell:** 181; **Rusty Symmes:** 167, 173; **Wayne Thuenemann:** 277; **Phil Trifaro:** 194; **Ron and Marie Troyer:** 98, 100; **Sam Turner:** 104; **Bill Ulrich:** 145, 147; **Bruce Valley:** 134; **Marion and Lindy Van Wormer:** 161; **Charles A. Vance:** 208; **Charles F. Vander Velde:** 119; **Carlos and Sherry Vivas:** 179; **Earl Vogel:** 164; **John R. Vorva:** 116; **Barry Waddell:** 206; **Marvin Wallace:** 151; **Donald Walkemeyer:** 132; **Glen Warrick:** 140; **Glen Weeks:** 72; **Ron Welch:** 132; **Leo Welter:** 204; **William Whitney:** 151; **Bobby Wiggins:** 97, 103, 106, 107, 113, 118, 130, 145, 148; **Leroy and Judy Williams:** 222; **Rosanne Winney:** 238; **Dennis G. Wise:** 118; **Thomas J. Wilt:** 142; **Henry Woodrow:** 173; **Al Worms, Jr.:** 53; **Bill Worthington:** 183; **Mike and Laurie Yager, Mid-America Designs, Inc.:** 197; **Peter Zannis:** 243; **Gordon Zinser:** 178.

FOREWORD

Chevrolet Motor Company was incorporated on November 3, 1911, and for much of its history since, Chevrolet has claimed the honor of "USA-1"— the most popular nameplate in the land. To those who have followed the company's progress (or more likely, its *products*), the achievement comes as no surprise.

Ironically, the phenomenal success enjoyed by the Chevrolet Motor Company did not carry over to its founders. William C. "Billy" Durant, the ambitious industrialist who not only started Chevrolet but General Motors as well, was forced out of both companies, lost his fortune, and died in meager obscurity in 1947 at the age of 86.

A similar fate befell the company's namesake, Louis Joseph Chevrolet. The Swiss-born mechanic and notable race-car driver left in a huff less than two years after production began. He went on to a series of failed ventures, and from 1934-38 worked as a line mechanic in a Chevrolet plant. He retired due to ill health in 1938, and quietly passed away on June 6, 1941. He was buried in Indianapolis, home of the Indy "500" and site of his greatest racing victories, although none of them came behind the wheel.

Many other colorful individuals have also had a hand in shaping Chevrolet's future, particularly during the company's formative years. While we cannot mention them all, we do highlight several who were long-time officers of the company or involved in what proved to be momentous events.

The story behind Chevrolet's remarkable success is chronicled within these pages in a unique format of photographs with informative captions. Also included in each year's coverage is a "Model Breakdown" chart providing weights, prices, and production figures for most vehicles. Starting in 1960 with the introduction of the Corvair, engine offerings became so diverse as to justify the inclusion of a separate "Engine Availability" chart.

It should be noted, however, that some information wasn't readily accessible or was sketchy at best. Particularly in the early years, accurate records were often not kept; changes that affected a vehicle's weight or price were often incorporated in a haphazard fashion, and some production figures were recorded based on *calendar* year rather than *model* year—or sometimes even on sales rather than production. Also, trucks were occasionally counted in the total figure, particularly in the beginning when they were little more than cars with a cargo bed in the back. Prices often changed during the course of a year (just as they do today), so we've usually listed the price quoted at the start of the model run.

These problems occur less frequently in later years, though the breakdown of some body styles within a model line may not be available. Furthermore, we have not included specifications for trucks, sport utility vehicles, or cars made outside of the U.S. (such as the Japanese-built Sprint) even though they might be mentioned in the text. Vehicles marketed under the Geo nameplate are not included at all.

Sprinkled throughout the pages are photos of Chevrolet's more famous and prophetic show cars. Some are merely customized versions of production cars, others carry styling themes later seen in the showroom, a few were built to test new technology, and a couple represent far-out designs that seemingly served little purpose other than to spark the imagination.

One way or another, nearly everyone has memories of a Chevy in their past. And whether it was the car you vacationed in, the car you learned to drive in, or the car that you took to prom, you will likely find it pictured in this book. Chevrolet has, since its inception, been as much a part of Americana as…well …baseball, hot dogs, and apple pie. Chevrolet has been building cars for almost a century, and will likely continue to produce vehicles that create memories (in whatever form they may take) for many generations to come.

– The Auto Editors of Consumer Guide®

CONTENTS

1904-1911

NINETEEN FOUR TO NINETEEN ELEVEN NINETEEN FOUR TO NINETEEN ELEVEN

• The story of General Motors and Chevrolet has more twists and turns than a best-selling mystery novel, and more colorful individuals in its cast of characters than many a television soap opera.

Louis Joseph Chevrolet

It all began with William Crapo Durant, the prominent carriage-builder and onetime cigar salesman who purchased control of Buick in 1904, then founded General Motors four years later after acquiring Oldsmobile. Soon the Cadillac and Oakland (forerunner of Pontiac) Divisions were added, along with a number of lesser properties. Before long, however, the fledgling company was in serious financial trouble.

The amalgamation of several automotive firms was not a new idea for Durant. As early as 1907, he had modestly confided to associates that his goal was to control the entire automobile

industry! His first attempt at an automotive combine involved Buick, Ford, Maxwell, and Reo, but Henry Ford wanted cash for his company, as did Ransom Olds, so the deal fell through.

But Durant was out to conquer the world. As head of General Motors he worked long hours, often with little or no sleep. It wasn't unusual for him to schedule important business meetings for the wee hours. His acquisition of Olds Motor Works, for instance, was finalized at dawn after a meeting that started at 3 A.M.

This relentless drive explains the overly ambitious expansion that caused GM's early money troubles. Stretching his credit to the limit, Durant bought numerous properties like Welch, which built a high-quality $7000 automobile that proved almost impossible to sell. He also acquired many other dubious prospects including the Randolph, the Rainier (later replaced by the ill-fated Marquette), the two-cycle Elmore, the friction-drive CarterCar, and the Ewing taxicab. All were losers.

By mid July 1910, General Motors was $7 million in hock to the First National Bank of Boston, which soon cut off loans. Creditors thought Buick worth saving, but recommended that everything else be liquidated. Then wizened Henry Leland, founder of Cadillac (and later Lincoln), convinced the bankers to supply GM with needed capital—at exorbitant rates, of course—provided Durant stepped down. He did.

As ever, though, Durant was undeterred. Though he remained on GM's Board of Directors, he soon teamed with William Little, former general manager of Buick, to form the Little Motor Company. Its first car, bowing in 1912, was a $690 roadster, $100 more than a comparable Model T Ford.

But it was also in 1911 that Durant helped form Chevrolet Motor Company, incorporated on November 3. Its first car was developed in a Detroit workshop by one of his partners in the enterprise, world-famous racing driver Louis Joseph Chevrolet. Louis and his brother, Arthur, had been the principal drivers on Buick's 1907 racing team.

Born in LaChaux-de-Fonds, Switzerland, on Christmas Day 1878, Chevrolet had grown up in France. His family was poor, so Louis received little formal education. He worked for a time at a wine cellar, then taught himself to repair motorbikes. Eventually he became an automotive mechanic. Emigrating via Canada, he arrived in the United States in 1900, finding work as a me-

William C. Durant

James J. Storrow

chanic. He started racing five years later, establishing a reputation as a daredevil driver.

Meanwhile, back at General Motors, banker James J. Storrow had taken over temporarily as president, charged with straightening out the tangle of affairs left behind by Billy Durant. Certain Durant acquisitions, such as Rainier and Welch, were summarily jettisoned. But Cadillac was thriving and Storrow believed Olds had a future—as indeed proved to be the case.

Though Durant had undoubtedly envisioned it, few people in those days could have foreseen that beleaguered General Motors would become the world's largest automotive empire. Nor could many have imagined that the fortunes of this giant corporation would be built on the phenomenal success of an automaker that was once deemed a liability—Chevrolet.

6

1911

- **Louis Chevrolet completes the first Chevrolet prototype**

- **Chevrolet Motor Car Company incorporated under William C. Durant**

- **Former Detroit lamp factory site chosen for first Chevrolet manufacturing plant**

◄ Though Billy Durant was the founder and guiding genius of General Motors during its early years, the company's first president was George E. Daniels, shown here in a 1908 photograph. But Daniels held the position for only a month, September 22 to October 20, 1908, before being replaced by William M. Eaton, who served concurrently as president of the Buick Division. Daniels later served as president of Oakland Division, then manufactured a luxury V-8 automobile under his own name in 1916-24.

► Billy Durant instigated the Chevrolet Motor Company as the core of a "new GM" that he undoubtedly hoped would put his old company out of business. But Louis Chevrolet himself, here at the wheel of one of his racing cars, only had the title of Consulting Engineer and was not even an officer. William H. Little was the company's first president, with Durant son-in-law E. R. Campbell as vice president.

◄ Like other early car builders, Louis was evidently inclined to test his racing machines on public streets, something the local authorities no doubt disliked. Indeed, "horseless carriages" were still deemed a public menace in many locales.

▼ Louis Chevrolet photographed at the wheel of one of his early racers, accompanied by a riding mechanic. Louis, who had beaten the legendary Barney Oldfield in at least three races, entered the Indianapolis 500 four times, but never managed to win. His brother Gaston, however, won the 1920 Indy contest driving a Monroe that Louis had built.

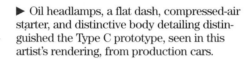

▲ After first tinkering for a time with a high-speed four-cylinder auto, Louis Chevrolet got busy on a prototype of a much larger six-cylinder car. Here, he takes it out for a spin.

▶ Oil headlamps, a flat dash, compressed-air starter, and distinctive body detailing distinguished the Type C prototype, seen in this artist's rendering, from production cars.

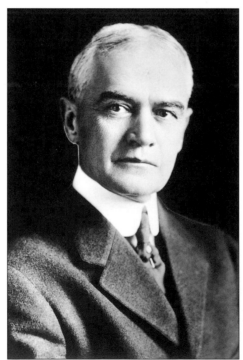

▲ Though conventional in design, Chevrolet's six-cylinder touring car was a 3350-pound machine on an expansive 120-inch wheelbase.

▲ Jim Storrow held the presidency of GM for only a couple of months before turning the office over to Thomas Neal, manager of the Acme Lead and Color Works. Neal served as president during most of 1911 and 1912, a tumultuous time in the corporation's history. Storrow, meanwhile, held the critical position of chairman of GM's powerful finance committee.

8

▲ The Type C used a cone clutch connecting to a three-speed transmission mounted on the rear axle. Its engine, designed with help from Etienne Planche, a French engineer formerly with the Walter Automobile Company, displaced 299 cubic inches—the largest powerplant used by any Chevrolet until the 348-cid big-block V-8 arrived for 1958. A six-cylinder of T-head configuration (intake and exhaust valves mounted in the block on opposite sides of the cylinders), it produced 35-40 horsepower.

1912

- Republic Motors formed to manufacture and market Little and Chevrolet cars

- Republic produces 2299 cars, but virtually all are Little Fours

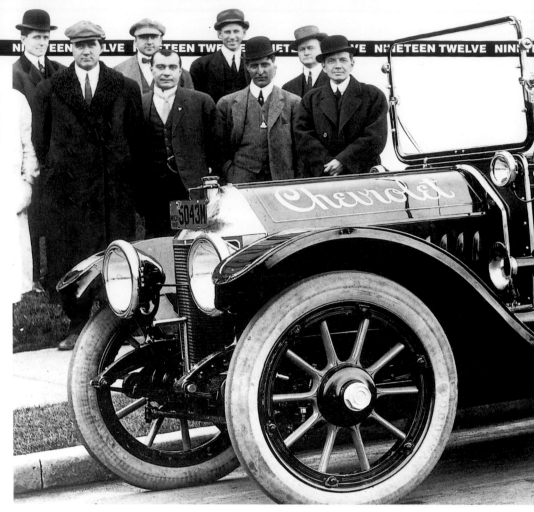

▲ By this time, Jim Storrow had nearly finished straightening out General Motors' tangled affairs, and he wanted to get back to the banking business. This led to something of a reorganization, resulting in the appointment of Charles W. Nash (shown) as GM's new president. Earlier, as president of the Buick Division, Nash had established a fine reputation for frugal management as well as for spearheading more efficient production methods.

▼ Preceding Chevrolet's famous "bow tie" emblem was this signature logo, used on the Classic Six.

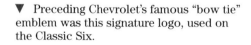

▲ Chevrolet production per se did not begin until very late in 1912, so Billy Durant's new Republic Motors Company sold the Little Four, based on the defunct Whiting automobile. The Four, with a 20-horsepower Mason engine, came only as a $690 roadster with right-hand steering. In the works for the 1913 season was a Little Six touring car with a Sterling-built powerplant.

◄ Unlike many of its competitors in the early days, the Chevrolet used left-hand drive from the start. Featuring a low-slung chassis, the Classic Six had something of a European look. The compressed air starter was replaced by a Gray and Davis electric unit. Lighting was electric and even included a lamp to illuminate the speedometer—a most unusual feature for the time. Reportedly, the first Classic Six was driven off the assembly line by Billy Durant's son, Clifford. Young Durant and his wife drove an early Type C (possibly the flat-dash prototype fitted with a windshield) from Detroit to San Francisco, which would have been quite a motoring adventure when cars were hardly refined—and most roads were even less so!

► The first Chevrolet was formally unveiled in January 1913 as the Type C, but was known as "Classic Six" by midyear. A few were built in late 1912.

▼ The oldest known surviving Chevrolet (now believed to be a '13) is this Classic Six, purchased by the Industrial Mutual Association and donated to the Alfred P. Sloan Panorama of Transportation, located in the College and Cultural Center in Flint, Michigan.

1913

- **Production shifts to Flint, Michigan**

- **Series L Light Six and Series H Four bow in July for 1914**

- **Sales reach 5987**

- **A. B. C. Hardy named vice president and general manager; Louis Chevrolet quits in dispute with Durant**

▲ Introduced in mid 1913, the 1914 Series H Four was evolved from the soon-to-be-dropped Little Four but had a 24-horsepower 171-cubic-inch overhead-valve engine. It came as a roadster and as this touring model, called "Baby Grand," which was priced from $875.

▶ Billy Durant began consolidating Chevrolet operations in 1913 with an eye to entering the lucrative low-priced field, a decision that moved Louis Chevrolet to quit. By year's end, Chevrolets were being built in Flint, Michigan, at a much larger plant than the Detroit facilities the company had been using.

▼ The Type C Classic Six was sold throughout 1913 with few changes from Louis Chevrolet's prototype. The windshield was more securely braced and bolted to a new swept-back cowl instead of to the dashboard, a revision made soon after production began. A list price of $2500 put the new Chevrolet in the fairly small, but highly competitive, "quality car" market of the day. In fact, the Type C weighed half-a-ton more than that year's largest Buick and cost nearly twice as much. Calendar-year sales were accordingly modest. The Classic Six came only as a four-door touring model. Standard tread width was 56 inches, but a 60-inch "southern" tread was available on special order.

▲ Called "Royal Mail," the 1914 Series H roadster listed for $750, including top, side curtains, windshield, speedometer, magneto ignition, and Presto-O-Lite lamps. An electric starter and lights were available for $125 on both H-models, which introduced Chevrolet's now-familiar "bowtie" emblem.

◄ This Chevrolet Royal Mail piled up 216,000 miles, almost unbelievable for a car of that era. The door legend is in error, though; production didn't begin before mid 1913. Chevrolet/Little production for calendar 1913 also included the interim Chevrolet Special Little Six tourer, which was replaced at midyear by the 1914 Series L Light Six. The latter made 35 horsepower from its 271-cid engine; strode a six-inch longer, 112-inch wheelbase; and cost $1475.

Model Breakdown

Series C Classic Six	Wght	Price	Prod
tour 5P	na	2,500	5,987*

*Production total was the total for Chevrolet and Little.

1914

- **Sales slip to 5005; Series H accounts for almost 80 percent**

- **Type C phased out**

- **Durant wheels and deals to position Chevrolet for taking on the Ford Model T**

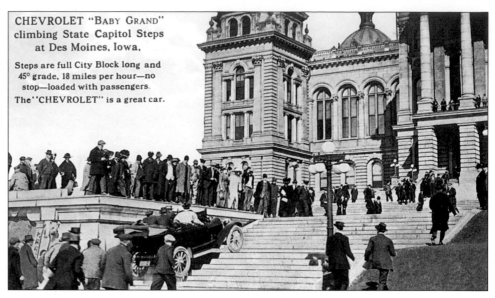

CHEVROLET "BABY GRAND" climbing State Capitol Steps at Des Moines, Iowa.

Steps are full City Block long and 45° grade, 18 miles per hour—no stop—loaded with passengers.
The "CHEVROLET" is a great car.

▲ This ad pretty much explains itself. Chevrolet and other early automakers staged such stunts to prove their products' performance, reliability, and durability at a time when cars were not known for those qualities. Many people still agree with the ending statement here.

▲▶ Having debuted early as 1914 models, the Series H Chevrolets carried on into the calendar year with only one notable change: a one-piece windshield to replace the original two-piece "zig-zag" type. This Baby Grand touring is finished in the plum main body color normally reserved for the Royal Mail roadster, but its black hood, fenders, and chassis are factory correct.

▲ The vertical windshield also identifies this Royal Mail as a true 1914 Series H. Research indicates the change was made by chassis-number 470. Based on serial numbers, 6243 Series H cars were built through the end of 1914, but actual production was probably lower.

▲ Though it no longer appeared on the radiator, Louis Chevrolet's signature still adorned the floorboard plate of Series H models in 1914.

Model Breakdown

		Wght	Price	Prod
H-2	rdstr 2P	1,975	750	*
H-4	tour 5P	2,500	875	*
L	tour 5P	3,050	1,475	490
C	tour 5P	3,750	2,500	*

*Total production was 5,005 Chevrolets of all models.

▲ The Type C Classic Six was phased out by early 1914, leaving the Series L Light Six as the "senior" Chevrolet. It continued as a single six-passenger touring model priced at $1475 and finished in your choice of dark blue (shown) or gray body paint.

▼ A rear-mount spare tire was standard equipment for the 1914 Light Six. Tires were 34×6 balloon types on demountable "artillery-spoke" rims. Also included were a full electrical system, which cost extra on Series H models, and a tool kit.

◄ Billy Durant later claimed that the design of the Chevrolet bow tie emblem was inspired by the wallpaper pattern he observed in his hotel room during a 1908 visit to Paris. His wife, however, said he found it in a Sunday newspaper supplement.

1915

- Series L Light Six dropped after a final 500 are built as 1915 models

- New "Amesbury Special" roadster adds exclusive style to the Series H line

- Chevrolet unveils a new Model T fighter in April: the 1916-model 490; orders pour in

- Durant declares $50 dividend on Chevrolet common stock

▲ Though not much changed at first glance, the Series H rode a two-inch longer, 106-inch wheelbase for 1915. A fifth wheel rim became standard—though not the spare—but the four road tires were now two sizes larger at 32×3½ inches. This is the $750 Royal Mail roadster.

◄ "Styling" wasn't yet part of the automotive lexicon in 1915, but Chevrolet showed how it could be used to perk up interest in a familiar car by offering a snazzier Series H roadster. Designated Model H-3, but better known as the "Amesbury Special," it had its own body, typically finished in "Chevrolet French Gray," with contrasting windshield frame and a color band at the cowl suggesting an old-fashioned firewall. (Chassis were painted black at the factory.) Price was $985 with the standard wood-spoke wheels shown here, though most buyers seem to have opted for the $125 Houk wire wheels. The folding fabric top could be positioned to act as a dust shield, and the windshield could be removed or folded down.

Model Breakdown

		Wght	Price	Prod
H-2	rdstr 2P	2,000	750	*
H-4	tour 5P	2,500	850	*
H-3	Spl. rdstr 2P	2,100	985	*
L	tour 5P	3,050	1,475	500

*Total production for calendar 1915 was 13,605 Chevrolets including 313 cars built in Canada.

Note: Model H-2 also called "Royal Mail," Model H-4 also called "Baby Grand," Model H-3 also called "Amesbury Special."

▼ Standard amenities for the rather natty Series H interior included a mohair top and top boot, speedometer, buffed pleated leather upholstery, and side curtains. Hidden door hinges were a modern touch. A black top and a painted dash were originally supplied.

▲ This Royal Mail roadster has the accessory electrical kit, down-priced to $110 for 1915. This again amounted to electric ignition and headlights. When new, the Royal Mail came with a Brewster Green or Gunmetal body and black hood, fenders, and radiator.

▲ After qutting his namesake company in 1913, Louis Chevrolet turned to designing and building race cars in Indianapolis under the Frontenac banner. That's him behind the wheel of a small 1915 machine called the Cornelian. Brothers Arthur and Gaston look on at the upper right. The Chevrolets turned out a variety of racers through the late Teens, but scored only two major wins: in the 1920 Indianapolis 500, with Gaston driving; and the 500 of 1921, with Tommy Milton at the helm. Gaston's tragic death during a November 1920 race in Los Angeles prompted Louis and Arthur to retire from racing and pursue less dangerous ventures.

1916

- **Billy Durant regains control of General Motors by trading Chevrolet stock for GM stock**

- **Chevrolet output in the U.S. soars to near 63,000 cars, led by new low-priced 490**

- **Series H returns for its final year**

▲ In the "good old days," a mechanic could practically walk into the engine compartment and parts were more often repaired than replaced. Note the foundry at left, useful for making those last-minute "adjustments," as on this Series H Baby Grand tourer.

▲ Named for its base price, Chevrolet's new 490 outflanked Ford's Model T with a cone clutch and three-speed sliding-gear transmission versus a tricky pedal-operated two-speed planetary gearbox. Available as a roadster and this touring model, the 490 also one-upped the Tin Lizzie by offering electric starter and lights for $60.

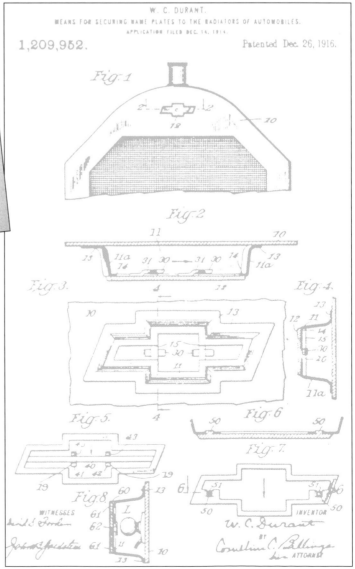

Model Breakdown

		Wght	Price	Prod
490	rdstr 2P	1,820	490	*
490	tour 5P	1,910	490	*
H-2	rdstr 2P	2,000	720	*
H-4	tour 5P	2,500	720	*
H-2	Spl. rdstr 2P	2,100	750	*

*Total production was 70,701 Chevrolets including 7,721 cars made in Canada.

Note: Model H-2 also called "Royal Mail," Model H-4 also called "Baby Grand," Model H-2 Special also called "Royal Mail" Torpedodeck.

▲ The "490" started at $490 in either touring (shown) or roadster form. Not coincidentally, that price was exactly what Ford charged for comparable Model Ts. By 1917, Chevy standardized the $60 electrical kit, which raised advertised price to $550 but wasn't available on Ford's Flivver at any price.

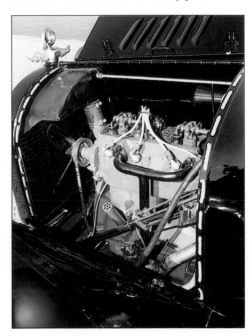

▲ Like its Model T rival, the 490 touring had only one door on the left—at the rear. The companion roadster also lacked a left-front door. Colors? Again like Ford, anything you like so long as it was black.

▶ The 490 carried a simplified version of the 171-cubic-inch Series H four-cylinder engine. Rated horsepower was 20, same as the Model T's, but it didn't quite match the Ford mill for "bulletproof" reliability.

1917

- **New Series F introduced, replacing the Series H**

- **Electric starter and lights now standard on all Chevrolets**

- **Series D V-8 debuts as early 1918 model**

- **Production totals 125,000, placing Chevrolet fourth in the sales standings**

▲ Chevrolet's 1917 Series F was mechanically much like the Series H it replaced, but rode a new 108-inch wheelbase and looked more like the 490 apart from a smoother hood and cowl and slightly different fenders. The $800 touring (shown) was again called Baby Grand.

▶ An instant sales success from its mid-1915 debut, the 490 saw some 57,900 copies in 1917 despite virtually no change. The majority were built in Flint, Michigan, but Chevy still had plants in Tarrytown, New York; St. Louis, Missouri; Oakland, California; and Ft. Worth, Texas.

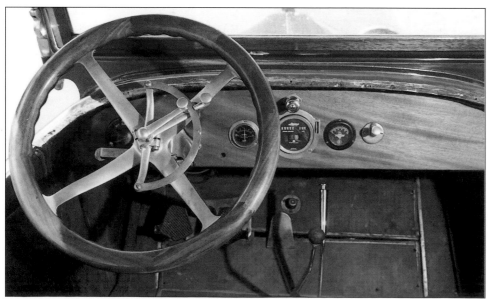

◀ Before the mid Thirties, car bodies were built around wooden frames, a practice carried over from carriage makers, with a wood dashboard a vital part of the structure. That's why even inexpensive early cars had real-wood instrument panels, though many cars of the day still didn't have much in the way of instrumentation, as the Chevrolet Series D in this photo shows. Note the "courtesy lamp" to the right of center, and a similar light above the speedometer. Closed body styles had begun to appear by 1917, and Chevrolet offered one for the 490 this year. Called the All-Season Tourer, it had a fixed solid roof instead of folding fabric and four side windows that could be raised into the roof for breezy semiopen motoring. Though few of these cars were built (even original factory photographs are hard to come by), Chevrolet was evidently eager to embrace most any new feature, especially if it meant a competitive advantage over Henry Ford's seemingly unchangeable Model T.

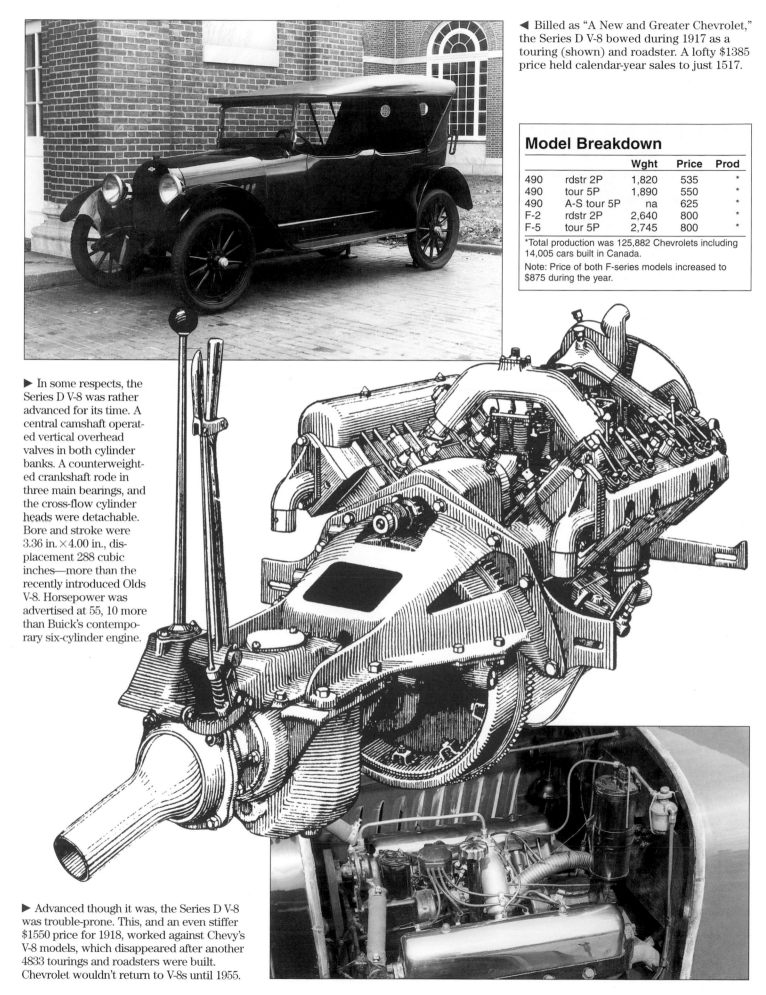

◄ Billed as "A New and Greater Chevrolet," the Series D V-8 bowed during 1917 as a touring (shown) and roadster. A lofty $1385 price held calendar-year sales to just 1517.

Model Breakdown

		Wght	Price	Prod
490	rdstr 2P	1,820	535	*
490	tour 5P	1,890	550	*
490	A-S tour 5P	na	625	*
F-2	rdstr 2P	2,640	800	*
F-5	tour 5P	2,745	800	*

*Total production was 125,882 Chevrolets including 14,005 cars built in Canada.

Note: Price of both F-series models increased to $875 during the year.

► In some respects, the Series D V-8 was rather advanced for its time. A central camshaft operated vertical overhead valves in both cylinder banks. A counterweighted crankshaft rode in three main bearings, and the cross-flow cylinder heads were detachable. Bore and stroke were 3.36 in. × 4.00 in., displacement 288 cubic inches—more than the recently introduced Olds V-8. Horsepower was advertised at 55, 10 more than Buick's contemporary six-cylinder engine.

► Advanced though it was, the Series D V-8 was trouble-prone. This, and an even stiffer $1550 price for 1918, worked against Chevy's V-8 models, which disappeared after another 4833 tourings and roadsters were built. Chevrolet wouldn't return to V-8s until 1955.

21

1918

- To no one's surprise, Billy Durant folds Chevrolet into General Motors

- Chevy offers its first commercial vehicles

- Series F replaced by Series FA with larger, improved engine and new sedan model

- 490 adds coupe and sedan, receives detail engine upgrades

- Despite government-ordered production curbs in support of World War I, Chevrolet leapfrogs Buick to claim third place in the U.S. auto industry behind Ford and Willys-Overland.

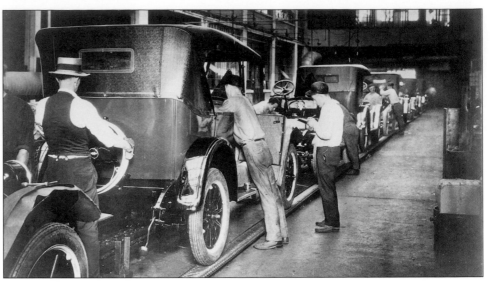

▲ Chevrolet photographers would capture many scenes like this over the years. Here, a bevy of 1918 models near completion at the company's main plant in Flint, Michigan. The "dress code" even for line workers was obviously a lot more formal in those days.

▲ Chevrolet's "quality" four-cylinder car for 1918 was the Series FA, built on the same 108-inch wheelbase as the Series F it replaced. A stroked, 224-cubic-inch engine with 37 horsepower boasted an improved cooling system (shared with 490s), with a centrifugal pump replacing the outmoded thermo-siphon system. Besides the usual touring and roadster models, the FA offered this new fully enclosed two-door sedan, priced at $1475-$1825. Its center posts could be removed with the windows lowered, and the right-side door was centrally located to ease rear-seat entry and exit. Also unusual was a right front-seat backrest that could be swung over, permitting the passenger to face either forward or backward.

Model Breakdown

		Wght	Price	Prod
490	tour 5P	1,890	685	Note 1
490	rdstr 2P	1,820	660	Note 1
490	A/W cpe 3P	2,040	1,060	Note 1
490	A/W sdn 4P	2,160	1,060	Note 1
FA-2	rdstr 2P	2,640	935	Note 1
FA-5	tour 5P	2,680	935	Note 1
FA-4	A/W sdn 4P	2,950	1,475	Note 1
D-4	rdstr 4P	3,150	1,550	Note 2
D-5	tour 5P	3,200	1,550	Note 2

Note 1: Total production of the 490 was 86,200 including 12,250 made in Canada. Total production of the FA was 11,403 including 1,275 in Canada.

Note 2: Total production of the Series D (V-8) was 1,517 in 1917 and 4,833 in 1918 (71 of which may have been sold in 1919). Prices in 1917 were $1,385 for both models.

▶ The 490 roadster and touring (shown) benefited from a new gear-driven oil pump, replacing a plunger type, as well as water-pump instead of thermo-siphon cooling. New for 1918 were a two-door sedan, mimicking the FA Series, plus a two-door coupe. Here, too, removable center roof posts provide a breezy preview of the post-World War II "hardtop." Prices spanned a broader range of $620-$1185.

◄▲ The owner of this 490 touring has added an earlier "signature" logo to the radiator, plus an accessory front bumper. (The original paint scheme for all 490s was all black with black wheels.) Open 490s retained a gravity fuel feed, but the new closed models boasted rear-mounted gas tanks and vacuum feed. An oil pressure gauge became standard. Production rose to 86,200, versus 11,403 for the costlier FAs. Also, Chevy added a 490-based commerical chassis and its first truck—ironically dubbed Model T—a one-ton job using modified FA mechanicals.

1919

- **Improved Series FB replaced FA**

- **Series D dropped**

- **490 little changed but remains popular**

- **Car sales reach nearly 150,000 as Chevrolet moves up to number-two**

▲▶ Though again little changed, the 490 stayed on a strong upward sales track in 1919, orders rising 47.5 percent to 127,231. Inflationary pressure from America's involvement in World War I was pushing prices higher for all consumer goods, and these Chevrolets were no exception. This roadster remained the most affordable 490, but now cost $715. The touring was up to $735, the coupe to $1100, the sedan to $1185. The derivative Model T truck, also little changed, now started at $1460 in basic cowl/chassis form, up from $1245 in debut 1918. But as with the 490, Chevy truck sales kept rising, though this year's total of 3356 is miniscule by today's standards. As before, the 490 roadster provided a small rear storage compartment—a sort of embyronic trunk—and could be ordered with wire wheels instead of the regular "artillery" wood rims. This restored beauty is also equipped with the an accessory water-temperature gauge atop the radiator, a period device generally known as a "Moto-Meter." (Moto-Meters bearing the Chevrolet trademark weren't offered until 1923, however.) As ever, the 490's little four-cylinder engine wasn't much for speed; rugged reliability and easy maintenance counted for a lot more in those days, and these Chevrolets delivered.

▲ Two of Durant's most significant and profitable moves took place during 1919. The first of these was the purchase of a 60-percent interest in Fisher Body. And the second was the incorporation of the General Motors Acceptance Corporation, founded for the twin purposes of assisting dealers in "flooring" their cars, and making it possible for individuals to purchase new cars on "time payments."

Model Breakdown

		Wght	Price	Prod
490	rdstr 2P	1,820	715	Note 1
490	tour 5P	1,890	735	Note 1
490	sdn 4P	2,160	1,185	Note 1
490	cpe 3P	2,040	1,100	Note 1
FB-20	rdstr 2P	2,640	1,110	Note 1
FB-30	tour 5P	2,880	1,235	Note 1
FB-50	cpe 3P	2,820	1,635	Note 1
FB-40	sdn 4P	2,950	1,685	Note 1
FB-40	sdn 4P*	2,950	1,685	Note 1

*This was the FB sedan using the old FA body with a center door on passenger side.

Note 1: Total production was 149,904 including 17,431 cars made in Canada.

▲ With the costly, slow-selling Series D V-8 discontinued, the four-cylinder Series FB was Chevy's best for 1919. Basically, it was the predecessor FA with a two-inch longer wheelbase (110) and stylish "reverse-curve" fenders. Reflecting the growing interest in closed cars, a coupe was added as an early 1920 model alongside the roadster and touring (shown). The "center-door" sedan was dropped at mid 1919 after a brief run of 1514 units. Replacing it was Chevrolet's first true four-door sedan, notable for having crank-type window winders instead of pull-up straps. Considering its evolutionary nature, the Series FB was a fair success, attracting 14,516 sales for the calendar year.

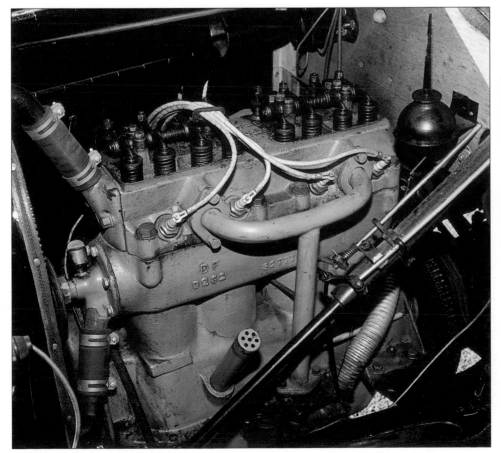

- **Durant, under fire, leaves Chevrolet and GM**

- **Pierre S. duPont becomes new GM president**

- **Karl W. Zimmerschied installed as president of Chevrolet**

- **Prices drop in response to postwar depression**

- **The 490 models get appearance updates**

▲ With GM staggering under a mountain of debt and stuck with $209 million worth of unsold cars, Billy Durant resigned under pressure on November 30, 1920. Pierre S. duPont, who had supported him when he recaptured control of the company four years earlier, but had been allied with the bankers this time in engineering his departure, succeeded him as president of General Motors.

▲▼ The 1920 Chevrolet 490 bore the marks of simplicity that characterized early cars, especially in the low-price field. Rudimentary safety equipment included a single taillight and stop lamp mounted on a bracket that fit between the spare tire rim. The tire itself cost extra, by the way. Meanwhile, the 171-cid four-cylinder engine showed off its exposed overhead-valve rocker arms. An underhood oil can stood ready to keep things limber.

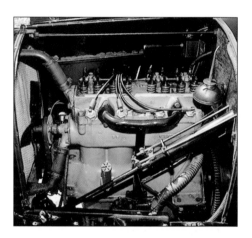

▲ Undoubtedly the best of Durant's moves during this period was the creation of United Motors, a consolidation of parts and accessory manufacturers. He also commissioned the construction of the world's largest office complex. Planned as the Durant Building (and the initial "D" can still be seen at corners of the structure), the huge, 15-story edifice later became known as the General Motors Building.

▼ The most substantial changes to any Chevrolet product in 1920 were appearance modifications made in the 490 line. Fenders, which had previously descended toward the running boards in straight, flat panels, became modern flowing units that more closely traced over the wheels. Splash aprons were revised and running boards were widened, as well. Open cars adopted twin "portholes" for rearward vision with the top up. Headlights were attached directly to the fenders and the cross bar between them was eliminated.

Model Breakdown

		Wght	Price	Prod
490	rdstr 2P	1,820	795	*
490	tour 5P	1,895	810	*
490	sdn 5P	2,160	1,285	*
490	cpe 3P	2,040	1,210	*
FB	rdstr 2P	2,160	1,270	*
FB	tour 5P	2,800	1,355	*
FB	sdn 5P	2,950	1,885	*
FB	cpe 3P	2,820	1,855	*

*Total production was 150,226 Chevrolets including 18,847 cars made in Canada.
Note: Prices dropped about $100 during 1920 model year.

- Chevy drops from third to fifth in industry sales

- Chevrolet losses amount to $8.7 million

- Model G truck, rated at ¾-ton, introduced

▼ Chevrolet lost $8.7 million in fiscal 1921, and ended up with 150,000 unsold 490s. In part, the problem had to do with the reputation of the product; the public had come to realize that the Chevy 490 was by no means as tough an automobile as Henry Ford's Model T. The most expensive 490 was the five-passenger sedan, a two-door with a central door on the right side.

▼ Alfred Sloan, acting as a special advisor to Pierre duPont, hired a firm of industrial engineers to study GM's properties and make suggestions for corporate restructuring. Their report seems incredible to us today: They saw the Chevrolet Division as hopeless and advised its liquidation! But Sloan, recognizing Chevy's potential, ignored the recommendation.

Model Breakdown

		Wght	Price	Prod
490	chassis	na	na	*
490	rdstr 2P	1,820	795	*
490	tour 5P	1,890	820	*
490	cpe 3P	2,040	1,325	*
490	sdn 5P	2,160	1,375	*
FB	rdstr 2P	2,640	1,320	*
FB	tour 5P	2,780	1,345	*
FB	cpe 3P	2,820	2,075	*
FB	sdn 5P	2,950	2,075	*

*Total production was 76,370 Chevrolets including 8,187 cars made in Canada.
Note: Prices reduced in late 1921 due to recession.

1922

- **Chevy enacts dramatic price cuts to stimulate sagging sales**

- **Sales triple, moving Chevy once again to second place**

- **Radio first offered as an option**

- **William S. Knudsen hired as vice president of manufacturing**

- **Utility Coupe and four-door sedan join 490 lineup**

▲ One of the most significant personnel moves in all Chevrolet history took place on February 22, 1922, when William S. Knudsen was hired to oversee production. An immigrant from Denmark, he was head of manufacturing for Ford before leaving the company in the wake of disagreements with Henry Ford. Before the year was out, he was elevated to vice president for operations at Chevrolet and aggressively set about improving the product. Before his service to GM was done, Knudsen would rise to the corporation's presidency.

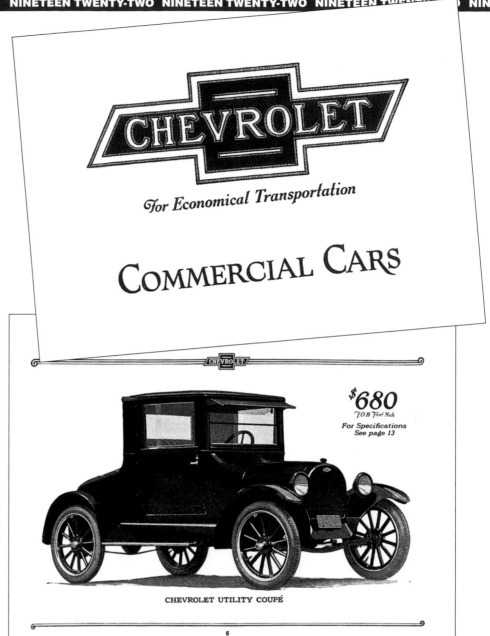

For Economical Transportation

COMMERCIAL CARS

$680
F.O.B. Flint Mich.
For Specifications
See page 13

CHEVROLET UTILITY COUPÉ

6

▲ Chevrolet ads often proclaimed that the new 490 Utility Coupe was perfect for the traveling salesman, as it "carries him to the customer in the physical and mental condition best adapted to successful sales contacts." A bit of hyperbole perhaps, but a positive marketing approach at a time when open styles were the order of the day for low-cost company cars.

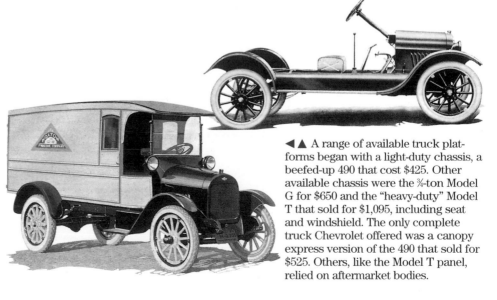

◀▲ A range of available truck platforms began with a light-duty chassis, a beefed-up 490 that cost $425. Other available chassis were the ¾-ton Model G for $650 and the "heavy-duty" Model T that sold for $1,095, including seat and windshield. The only complete truck Chevrolet offered was a canopy express version of the 490 that sold for $525. Others, like the Model T panel, relied on aftermarket bodies.

29

◄▲ Aside from the new two-passenger Utility Coupe, Chevrolet continued to offer a four-passenger coupe in the 490 series. The latter was little changed from the previous two model years. Hayes-Iona Body Company continued to build bodies for the four-seat coupe and sedan. (Fisher bodies were used for the utility model.) The sedan did see a major change, however, becoming a four-door vehicle in place of the offset two-door car of years past. All 490s were newly outfitted with a lever-activated parking brake. FB model changes were confined to technical details.

Model Breakdown

		Wght	Price	Prod
490	chassis	1,435	na	*
490	rdstr 2P	1,725	510	*
490	tour 5P	1,770	525	*
490	cpe 4P	2,015	850	*
490	utl cpe 2P	1,945	680	*
490	sdn 5P	2,150	875	*
FB	rdstr 2P	2,310	865	*
FB	tour 5P	2,595	885	*
FB	cpe 4P	2,735	1,325	*
FB	sdn 4P	2,890	1,395	*

*Total production was 243,479 Chevrolets including 19,895 cars made in Canada.

- **Production of 1-millionth Chevrolet takes place on February 22**

- **Introduction of ill-fated "Copper Cooled" model**

- **Superior model debuts, replacing both the 490 and FB**

- **Two-door Sedanette with small, removable trunk is new body style**

- **New Series D truck chassis takes over from discontinued Models G and T**

- **Additional assembly plants open in Ohio, Wisconsin, and New York**

- **Pierre duPont steps down as GM president; replaced by Alfred Sloan**

▶ There was a new one-ton truck chassis for 1923. The Series D replaced the ¾-ton Model G and one-ton Model T. With the demise of the Series FB passenger cars, production of the 224-cid engine also used for trucks ceased, leaving only the 171-cube Superior for use in the truck line. Bodies continued to be the province of specialty builders.

▲ Advertising from 1923 for the new Superior series attempted to reach a broad spectrum of potential customers. The then-radical notion of the "girl in business" was steered toward the two-seat coupe, with its combination of low purchase price and closed-car comfort. Meanwhile, the four-door sedan was touted as an ideal accoutrement for any family, regardless of social rank.

▲ The technical sensation of the '23 Chevy lineup may have been the Copper Cooled cars with their air-cooled engine, but the "normal" water-cooled cars were newly refined, too. Twenty-five pounds heavier than its predecessor and an inch longer in wheelbase, the Superior featured a tall radiator and restyled hood. However, mechanical components were nearly identical to those of the 490.

▲ Engineering wizard Charles Kettering was the force behind the air-cooled engine program, but he was seriously embarrassed by its failure—one of his very few blunders. Pre-ignition detonation aggravated by insufficent flow of cooling air, problems that couldn't be licked, did in "Boss Ket's" baby.

◄▲ Though Copper Cooled cars looked almost identical to more conventional Superiors, their louvered grilles heralded Chevrolet's gamble on the unknown. Smaller than the water-cooled job at only 134.7 cubic inches and rated at 22 horsepower, the new engine was cooled by means of copper fins bonded to the separately cast cylinders.

Model Breakdown

		Wght	Price	Prod
M	rdstr 2P	na	710	Note 1
M	tour 5P	na	725	Note 1
M	sdn 5P	na	1,060	Note 1
M	coach 5P	na	1,050	Note 1
M	utl cpe 2P	1,700*	880	Note 1
M	Del tour 5P	na	725	Note 1
B	chassis	1,390	na	Note 2
B	rdstr 2P	1,715	510	Note 2
B	tour 5P	1,795	525	Note 2
B	utl cpe 2P	1,915	680	Note 2
B	S'net 4P	2,055	850	Note 2

*Based on *Special Interest Autos* "Drive Report" Sept.-Oct. 1975. Indicated that Copper Cooled was 215 lbs. lighter than conventional Chevrolet.

Note 1: Total production: 739; total sales: 100.

Note 2: Total production was 480,737 Chevrolets including 25,751 cars made in Canada. Prices for Deluxe models slightly lower than prices for 1924 Deluxe models.

◄ "Big Bill" Knudsen's first year at Chevrolet had been a difficult baptism by fire. Originally hired for his manufacturing expertise, he very soon assumed a greater role in divisional affairs when President Karl Zimmerschied suffered a nervous breakdown. Promoted to vice president for operations, Knudsen was squarely in the middle of the launch of the problematic Copper Cooled cars. Of the 759 made, only 500 made it to dealers and just 100 were ever sold.

1924

- Knudsen promoted to president and general manager of Chevrolet

- Superior models continued in an updated Series F

- Running changes include straightened front axle and rods in place of brake cables

- DeLuxe versions of the touring, coupe, and four-door sedan are cataloged

- Sales drop; stagnant product line is blamed

- At Chicago dealer meeting, Knudsen issues his famous challenge to someday match industry leader Ford "one for one" in sales

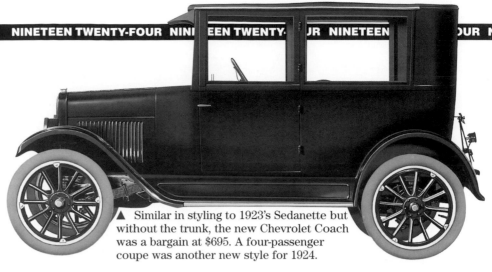

▲ Similar in styling to 1923's Sedanette but without the trunk, the new Chevrolet Coach was a bargain at $695. A four-passenger coupe was another new style for 1924.

◄ The slogan "For Economical Transportation" was continued in Chevrolet advertising and would be prominently featured for several more years. Ads credited the company's numerous production facilities for keeping prices low. The four-door sedan, pictured in this ad, continued to gain favor. Still, at $795, this model cost $300 more than the best-selling touring car.

▼ Leading the popularity parade once again was the touring car, priced at $495— or $640 with DeLuxe equipment (as shown here), which included disc wheels; nickeled radiator shell, headlamps, and bumpers; running board step plates; cowl lights, and a Boyce Moto Meter.

Model Breakdown

		Wght	Price	Prod
F	rdstr 2P	1,690	490	*
F	tour 5P	1,875	495	*
F	sdn 5P	2,070	795	*
F	cpe 2P	1,880	640	*
F	cpe 4P	2,005	725	*
F	coach 5P	2,030	695	*
F	Del tour 5P	1,955	640	*
F	Del sdn 5P	2,240	940	*
F	Del cpe 2P	2,050	775	*

*Total production was 307,775 Chevrolets including 20,587 cars made in Canada.

◄ The lighter of Chevrolet's two commercial chassis was the ½-ton Series F. It used the passenger-car wheelbase of 103 inches and sold for $395. Available aftermarket bodies included the panel delivery style seen here being used for grocery delivery. The one-tonner for 1924 was the Series H, essentially the '23 Series D with a new name. It was built on a 120-inch wheelbase and used 30×3.5 tires in front and 30×5s in the rear.

33

- **Superior Series K introduced with improved engine and running gear**

- **Duco colors offered**

- **Sales increase by 70 percent**

- **2-millionth Chevrolet produced**

▲ Though the Series K looked quite similar to the previous Series F, its mechanical improvements were many. Displacement remained at 171 cubic inches, but the engine was completely revised with a newly designed block, heavier crankshaft, and drop-forged connecting rods with larger bearings. New, too, was an enclosed flywheel.

This is the **100,000TH CHEVROLET** MADE IN JANESVILLE, JUNE 3, 1925

100,000.Th.

◄ Just two years after having been converted from the production of the ill-fated Samson trucks and tractors, the Janesville, Wisconsin, plant yielded its 100,000th Chevrolet. The historic vehicle was this Series M one-ton commercial chassis. Series M trucks used Series K running gear and front bodywork.

▼ Chevrolet's 2-millionth car, a Coach, was built in 1925. Closed models came equipped with a windshield wiper and a windshield that could be raised slightly for ventilation. Calendar-year production totaled 519,229; about a quarter of Ford's total, but nearly 70 percent ahead of Chevy's 1924 output.

▲ This photo depicts the body drop station in a Chevrolet assembly plant. Wood artillery wheels were standard equipment on Chevy's open cars in 1925, while the closed coupes and sedans came with steel disc wheels.

▼ Series K Chevrolets stream out of the factory on their maiden voyage to await shipment. Early '25s were produced without a tie bar between the headlights, but these cars from later in the season all have the lamp braces.

◄► One of the reasons for the Chevy's increasing popularity was its new Duco finish, replacing the old-fashioned enamel. The sedan was finished in Aqua Marine Blue; the coupe in Sage Green; the roadster, touring, and coach all came in dark blue. Not surprisingly, 1925 marked the first time Chevrolet ran ads in color. Passenger cars now all came with nickeled radiator shells, but commercials had painted shells.

Model Breakdown

K Superior		Wght	Price	Prod
K	rdstr 2P	1,690	525	*
K	tour 5P	1,855	525	*
K	cpe 2P	1,880	715	*
K	sdn 5P	2,070	825	*
K	coach 5P	2,030	735	*

*Total production was 519,229 Chevrolets including 30,968 cars made in Canada.

◄▲ This Series K Light Delivery has been fitted with a "C-cab" panel body, a style that was becoming a bit outdated by the mid Twenties. Instrumentation on all Series K Superiors was simple and centrally grouped. As the year wore on, spark and throttle controls in the cars were moved to the dash, but trucks retained these levers on the steering column. Other 1925 truck chassis included the short-lived Series M and new Series R.

◄ The Coach quickly gained favor as a family car. Weighing 2,030 pounds and selling for $735, it came with wood-spoke wheels and balloon tires. Chassis improvements on all Series K cars included a single dry-plate clutch (replacing the miserable leather-faced cone), strengthened transmission and universal joints, and adoption of semielliptic springs.

▲▼ Chevrolet's price leader, as usual, was the two-passenger roadster. An unbeatable value at $525 (without optional bumpers), it was pro-viding growing competition for the Model T, and even stubborn old Henry Ford was becoming aware of the ominous trend.

1926

- **GM purchases remaining stock in coach builder Fisher Brothers**

- **Series V introduced at midyear**

- **Dressy Landau Sedan joins lineup**

- **Sales of Ford's Model T drop for third year in a row; Chevy production climbs past 730,000**

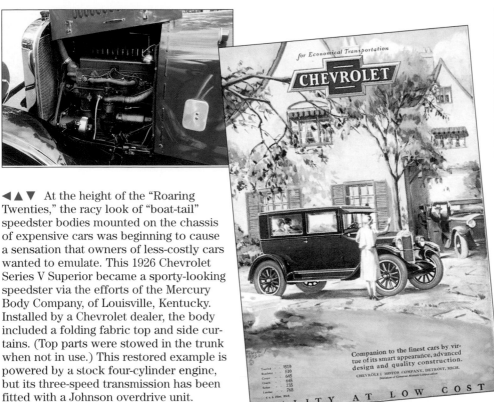

Model Breakdown

V Superior		Wght	Price	Prod
V	rdstr 2P	1,790	510	*
V	tour 5P	1,950	510	*
V	cpe 2P	2,035	645	*
V	sdn 5P	2,225	735	*
V	coach 5P	2,150	645	*
V	Lan sdn 5P	2,220	765	*

*Total production was 732,147 Chevrolets including 39,967 cars made in Canada.

◀▲▼ At the height of the "Roaring Twenties," the racy look of "boat-tail" speedster bodies mounted on the chassis of expensive cars was beginning to cause a sensation that owners of less-costly cars wanted to emulate. This 1926 Chevrolet Series V Superior became a sporty-looking speedster via the efforts of the Mercury Body Company, of Louisville, Kentucky. Installed by a Chevrolet dealer, the body included a folding fabric top and side curtains. (Top parts were stowed in the trunk when not in use.) This restored example is powered by a stock four-cylinder engine, but its three-speed transmission has been fitted with a Johnson overdrive unit.

◀ While its cars were aimed primarily at those of modest means, Chevrolet also pursued a more elite clientele by running ads in upscale magazines. This full-color promotion in *Country Life* declared that its vehicles were "companion to the finest cars." The two-door Coach pictured was the sales leader among closed models. Finished in Bloomfield Gray, it sold for $645.

1926

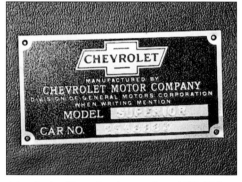

▲▶ Series K production ran into 1926. This restored coupe's accessories include step plates, front bumper, and Moto-Meter (essentially a thermometer atop the radiator cap).

▲ Production of Ford's Model T fell for the third year in a row during 1926, though the figure was still well ahead of Chevrolet's output. The Ford's styling was updated slightly and at long last there was even a limited choice of colors, but the Model T was plainly doomed—in no small part due to the popularity of this Chevy roadster.

▲ A new body style was the Series V Landau Sedan—at $765 Chevrolet's most expensive car. Dummy landau irons were featured, along with a rubberized fabric roof. Yet both the fabric and the landau irons were for appearance's sake only; it was not possible to lower the top. Landau Sedans were finished in Arizona Gray.

▲ Arguably the best looking of this year's Chevrolets was the two-passenger coupe, which sported dummy landau irons. Wood-spoke artillery wheels were optional; steel discs were standard equipment on this and other closed body styles. Coupe prices started at $645. Series V Superiors adopted a belt-driven generator and larger brakes.

- **Capitol Series AA introduced with updated styling and technical features**

- **Ford shuts down production lines for five months for Model A changeover; Chevy outsells Ford for the first time**

- **Coupe with rumble seat debuts**

- **Closed cars garner top three sales positions in Chevy's line**

▶ The $715 Capitol Series AA Sports Cabriolet, featured here in a *Country Life* magazine ad, was built to look like a convertible, but it actually had a fixed-position roof. Supplied in Royal Oak Green with a tan top, it was the first Chevrolet (and in fact, the first low-priced car of any make) to be furnished with a rumble seat.

Model Breakdown

AA Capitol		Wght	Price	Prod
AA	rdstr 2P	1,960	525	41,313
AA	tour 5P	1,895	525	53,187
AA	cpe 2P	2,090	625	124,101
AA	spt cabr 2-4P*	2,135	715	41,137
AA	coach 5P	2,190	695	239,566
AA	sdn 5P	2,275	695	99,400
AA	Imp Lan 5P	na	na	37,426
AA	Lan sdn 5P	2,270	745	42,410

*The Sports Cabriolet (spt cabr) was a closed car—not a convertible.

▶ By this time, the popularity of open cars had faded drastically. In fact, the favorite Chevrolet for 1927 was this Coach, which outsold that year's second and third most popular models—the Coupe and the Sedan—put together! Priced at $695, production hit 239,566. Among four-doors, an Imperial Landau sedan with blank rear quarters replaced the Landau Sedan during '27.

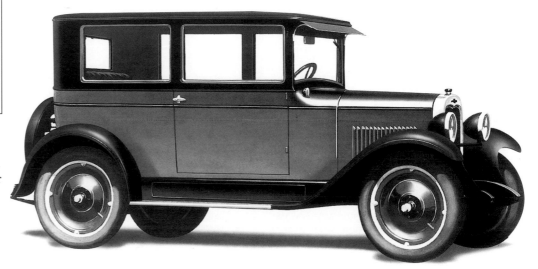

1928

- **National Series AB introduced on longer wheelbase**

- **5-millionth Chevy produced**

- **Chevy offers its first convertible**

- **Pierre duPont steps down as GM chairman; replaced by brother Lammont**

- **Despite introduction of Ford's new Model A, Chevy still leads sales race**

▲ A bargain at $585—$110 less than the corresponding 1927 model—the popular Coach accounted for nearly half of Chevrolet's 1928 sales. Fittingly, it was a Coach that in September garnered recognition as the 5-millionth Chevy produced.

▲ The taunt "Get a horse!" endured by early motorists had long faded from their ears by 1928. Still, horses were just the ticket to get a sled-borne caravan of new Chevys to dealers in wintery Montana.

▲▶ With Ford still trying to get production of its highly anticipated new Model A series up to full capacity, Chevrolet prospered in 1928. That fact was not lost on the company's promotional department. Advertising, created by the Campbell-Ewald agency, was more colorful and stressed the car's ease of operation (when aimed at the growing female market), as well as its overall popularity.

▲ There were solid reasons for the "Bigger and Better" logo in Chevrolet ads. The National—as Chevrolet called its range of 1928 cars—rode a 107-inch wheelbase that was four inches longer than before, most of the new length situated at the front of the car. There was more horsepower from the four-cylinder engine and four-wheel brakes were adopted, too. Furthermore, the model lineup was revised at midyear when the Convertible Sports Cabriolet, a true convertible, replaced the rumble-seat coupe. Consumers liked what they saw and demand was up—except for traditional body styles like this touring car, orders for which were nearly halved from 1927.

Model Breakdown

AB National		Wght	Price	Prod
AB	rdstr 2P	2,030	495	39,809
AB	tour 5P	2,090	495	26,973
AB	cpe 2P	2,235	595	150,356
AB	cabr 2-4P	2,270	665	na
AB	cabr conv 2-4P	2,265	695	38,268
AB	coach 5P	2,360	585	346,976
AB	sdn 5P	2,435	675	127,819
AB	Imp Lan 5P	2,405	715	54,998

▼► Once again the Imperial Landau was Chevy's most impressive four-door car. At $715, it cost $40 more than the regular sedan. To the style-conscious, that small premium was money well spent, for the car looked more expensive than it really was.

◄▲ Dealerships of the period weren't as elaborate as they are today—but neither were the cars. Potted plants and some patriotic flourishes on the windows dressed up this otherwise austere showroom. Back in the shop, simple handtools and a lift sufficed to service Chevys of the day.

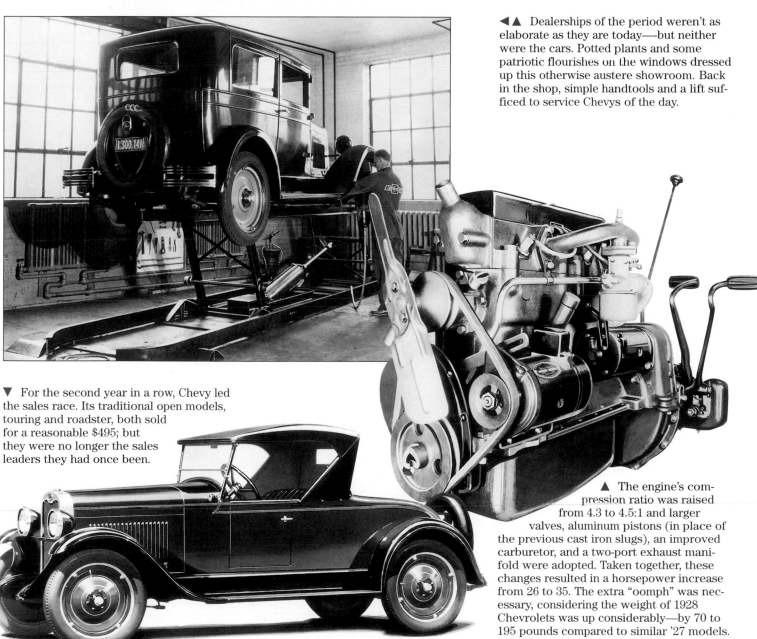

▼ For the second year in a row, Chevy led the sales race. Its traditional open models, touring and roadster, both sold for a reasonable $495; but they were no longer the sales leaders they had once been.

▲ The engine's compression ratio was raised from 4.3 to 4.5:1 and larger valves, aluminum pistons (in place of the previous cast iron slugs), an improved carburetor, and a two-port exhaust manifold were adopted. Taken together, these changes resulted in a horsepower increase from 26 to 35. The extra "oomph" was necessary, considering the weight of 1928 Chevrolets was up considerably—by 70 to 195 pounds compared to similar '27 models.

1929

- "Stovebolt Six" introduced

- International Series AC cars wear freshened styling

- Among new models is Landau Sedan with folding rear roof section

- Series LQ truck, Chevy's 1½-tonner, stretches wheelbase

- Chevrolet sells 600,000 cars in first five months

- 6-millionth Chevy rolls out on June 25, but Ford retakes the lead in sales

- October 29 stock market crash cripples nation's economy

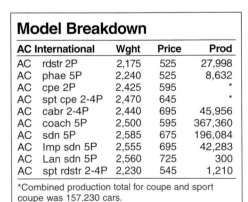

Model Breakdown

AC International	Wght	Price	Prod
AC rdstr 2P	2,175	525	27,998
AC phae 5P	2,240	525	8,632
AC cpe 2P	2,425	595	*
AC spt cpe 2-4P	2,470	645	*
AC cabr 2-4P	2,440	695	45,956
AC coach 5P	2,500	595	367,360
AC sdn 5P	2,585	675	196,084
AC Imp sdn 5P	2,555	695	42,283
AC Lan sdn 5P	2,560	725	300
AC spt rdstr 2-4P	2,230	545	1,210

*Combined production total for coupe and sport coupe was 157,230 cars.

◄▲► The reason for the extra length built into the 1928 Chevrolets was revealed in 1929, when the six-cylinder Series AC International was introduced. Not only did Chevy offer "a six for the price of a four," it put it in a tidier, lower package featuring a revised grille and bodyside moldings, and smaller-diameter wheels. Coupes, such as this rumble-seat-equipped model, did away with fabric roof coverings and landau irons. But the star of the show was certainly the new engine. As usual, it was an overhead-valve design. It displaced 194 cubic inches and generated 46 horsepower. Pistons were made of cast iron and lubrication was via a combination of splash and gravity. The six was the first Chevy engine with a fuel pump.

▶ A 1929 Chevrolet Coach undergoes a speedometer accuracy test at the General Motors Proving Grounds, in Milford, Michigan. A precise speedometer would have been welcomed by law-abiding drivers; the new six-cylinder engine could propel a Chevy at more than 60 mph. Ormond E. Hunt's Chevrolet engineering team had been working on sixes since the mid Twenties. It was sales chief Richard Grant who insisted the new engine have overhead valves. Both men won corporate promotions in '29.

▼ Fun in the sun! Chevrolet's success continued into 1929 when, as it says in this *Literary Digest* ad, the make sold a record 600,000 cars in less than five months. However, the sun was about to set; as a result of the October market crash, it would be many years before Chevrolet would sell so many cars in so short a time.

for Economical Transportation
CHEVROLET

Scoring another sensational success · · over 600,000 new Six Cylinder Chevrolets in less than five months !

The COACH $595

A SIX IN THE PRICE RANGE OF THE FOUR

▲ Touted as a new safety feature for '29 were twin-beam headlamps. The driver could change the angle of the beam by stepping on a floor-mounted button.

▶ Rarest of all 1929 Chevrolets was the Landau Sedan, a smartly styled $725 car featuring a convertible rear quarter. Only about 300 were produced before Chevy managers, worried that it might be too fancy a car for their customers, had it replaced by the similarly handsome, fixed-roof Imperial Sedan. (Chevy wasn't alone in offering an upscale body in the low-price field; at the same time, Ford cataloged a $1400 open-front town car in its Model A lineup.) The $625 Imperial Sedan featured blank rear quarters, a fabric-covered top, and dummy landau irons, much like the Imperial Landau of 1927-28. It drew more than 42,000 orders. The restyled coupe again came two ways, the Sport Coupe style with rumble seat having been reinstated after disappearing midway through the '28 model year. There was a new roadster, too, a rare sport model with rumble seat.

1930

- 7-millionth vehicle produced

- Production slumps due to economic conditions

- Convertible Cabriolet dropped

▲ Once again, the Coach was Chevrolet's most popular body style, with 255,027 copies produced. The price was cut $30 to $565.

▲ The Sport Coupe, featured in this ad and priced at $615, came standard with wire wheels, rumble seat, and a rear window that could be lowered in order that those in the front seat could communicate with those in back. (That feature was also an aid to ventilation, of course.)

▲ The Sport Roadster, equipped with rumble seat and wire wheels, was far more popular than the standard roadster—27,651 were sold at $515.

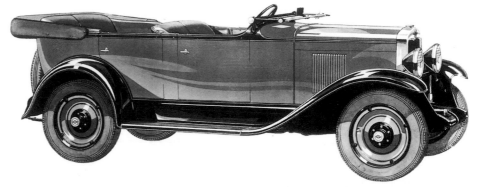

▲ For many years, the touring car had been America's (and the world's) most popular body style, but its days were numbered by 1930. Chevrolet changed to the fancier "phaeton" title and priced the car attractively at $495, but only 1713 examples were produced—about two-tenths of one percent of the model year's total output. Ironically, the phaeton and roadsters were the only open models cataloged for the year as a result of the temporary cessation of the stronger-selling cabriolet convertible. Horsepower was up slightly (from 46 to 50) thanks chiefly to the use of larger intake valves. Also, the rear axle was strengthened.

Breakdown Chart

AD UNIVERSAL	Wght	Price	Prod
rdstr 2P	2,195	495	5,684
spt rdstr 2-4P	2,250	515	27,651
phtn 5P	2,265	495	1,713
cpe 2P	2,415	565	100,373
spt cpe 2-4P	2,525	615	45,311
coach 5P	2,515	565	255,027
club sdn 5P	2,575	625	24,888
sdn 5P	2,615	675	135,193
Special sdn 5P	2,625	685	35,929
cpe 2-4P	2,540	na	9,211

◄▲ "Smoother, faster, better" was Chevy's 1930 slogan, and on May 28, the company produced its seven-millionth vehicle, a Series AD Universal Coach, much like the one seen here. Rumble-seat-equipped "sport" models came outfitted with wire wheels, but the purchasers of other Chevrolet models could order them at extra cost. Other accessories visible on this well-maintained survivor include bumpers, running-board step plates, rearview mirrors (of a later period, however), a rack-mounted detachable trunk, and an under-dash heater. Listed options also included wood-spoke wheels, sidemount spare tires, spare-tire covers, and a cigar lighter.

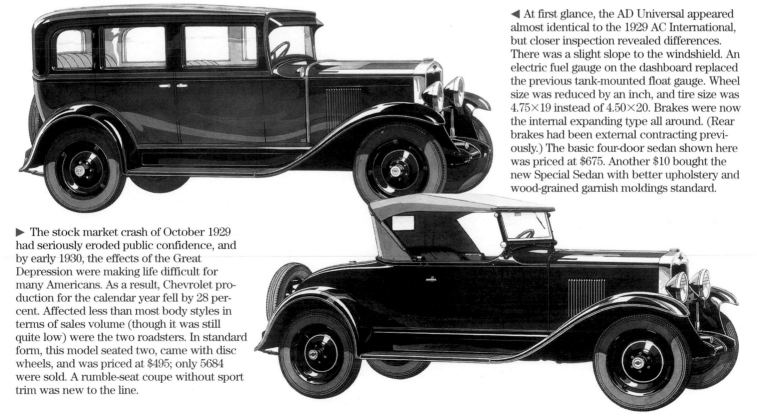

◄ At first glance, the AD Universal appeared almost identical to the 1929 AC International, but closer inspection revealed differences. There was a slight slope to the windshield. An electric fuel gauge on the dashboard replaced the previous tank-mounted float gauge. Wheel size was reduced by an inch, and tire size was 4.75×19 instead of 4.50×20. Brakes were now the internal expanding type all around. (Rear brakes had been external contracting previously.) The basic four-door sedan shown here was priced at $675. Another $10 bought the new Special Sedan with better upholstery and wood-grained garnish moldings standard.

► The stock market crash of October 1929 had seriously eroded public confidence, and by early 1930, the effects of the Great Depression were making life difficult for many Americans. As a result, Chevrolet production for the calendar year fell by 28 percent. Affected less than most body styles in terms of sales volume (though it was still quite low) were the two roadsters. In standard form, this model seated two, came with disc wheels, and was priced at $495; only 5684 were sold. A rumble-seat coupe without sport trim was new to the line.

- **Independence Series AE bows with longer wheelbase, more body styles**

- **Eight-millionth Chevrolet built**

- **First factory-bodied trucks introduced**

▲ Functional top irons quickly distinguished Chevrolet's cabriolet from the similar-looking Sport Roadster. Both were four-passenger models with standard rumble seat. All 1931 Independence Series AE models boasted a wheelbase lengthened two inches, to 109, plus new styling highlighted by a taller, larger radiator and more hood louvers. This cabriolet started at $615, but wears numerous factory accessories including bumpers, whitewall tires, trunk and rack, and sidemount spare. The interior was quite dressy for a period low-priced car.

◄▲ Chevrolet billed its Independence models as "the Great American Value." They certainly were by the pound, considering curb weights were up by some 75 pounds while prices were down. This $650 Special Sedan was one of two four-door sedans in this year's line. The other was a less fancy $635 standard sedan. The headlight buckets and tie bar now came chromed for all Chevy passenger cars.

▼ A different rear-end contour and built-in trunk identified this $595 five-passenger coupe, one of three new Chevy body styles for 1931. The others were the revived rumble-seat cabriolet and a two-door five-passenger convertible Landau Phaeton at $650.

Model Breakdown

AE Independence	Wght	Price	Prod
rdstr 2P	2,275	475	2,939
spt rdstr 2-4P	2,330	495	24,050
Deluxe phtn 5P	2,370	510	852
cpe 2P 3W	2,490	535	57,741
spt cpe 2-4P	2,565	575	66,029
cpe 2P 5W	2,490	545	28,379
coach 5P	2,585	545	228,316
sdn 5P	2,685	635	52,465
Special sdn 5P	2,725	650	109,775
cpe 5P	2,610	595	20,297
cabriolet 2-4P	2,520	615	23,077
conv sdn 5P	2,610	650	5,634

▲ With the Depression refusing to lift and new-car sales weak, Chevy stressed durability in one 1931 ad (*left*). Others, however, extolled the style and sturdiness of Chevrolet's Fisher bodies (*right*), which still used wood framing. But that was actually a plus. Though other manufacturers had switched to all-steel bodies, many buyers were wary, preferring the older style of construction.

▲ The coach remained Chevy's most popular single model in 1931 with 228,316 built. A $20 price cut, to $545, no doubt helped. Despite the Depression, Chevy model-year car sales eased by only three percent to 619,554. Ford dropped much further and finished second by about 4100 units.

▶ Like the previous year's Universal line, the 1931 Independence series included a rumble-seat Sport Roadster and this basic two-passenger version, now listing at $475. As it happened, the price-leader had the honor of being the 8-millionth Chevrolet built, coming off the line on August 25. Inspecting the milestone car in this press photo are (*from left*), Chevrolet president William Knudsen, vice president and sales manager Harry Klingler, manufacturing manager C. E. Wetherald, and chief engineer James Crawford.

▼ Also expanding Chevy's 1931 lineup was this two-passenger "five-window" coupe, so called because the extra panes behind the doors made for five windows, excluding the windshield. The rumble-seat Sport Coupe also adopted this roofline, too. Respective starting prices were $545 and $575. The earlier "three-window" style contined, but in a single model priced from $535.

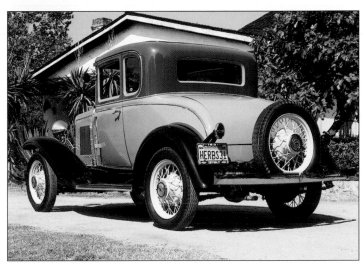

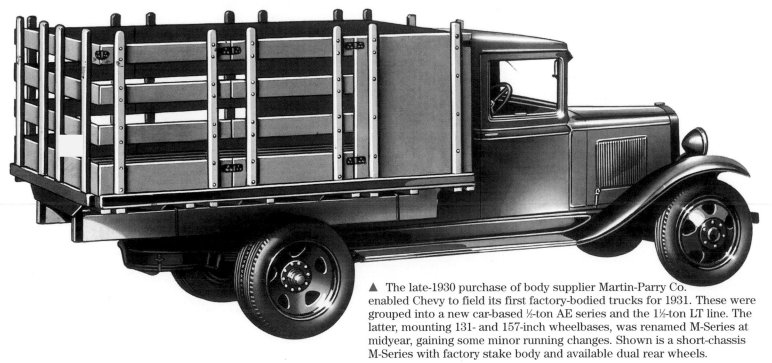

▲ The late-1930 purchase of body supplier Martin-Parry Co. enabled Chevy to field its first factory-bodied trucks for 1931. These were grouped into a new car-based ½-ton AE series and the 1½-ton LT line. The latter, mounting 131- and 157-inch wheelbases, was renamed M-Series at midyear, gaining some minor running changes. Shown is a short-chassis M-Series with factory stake body and available dual rear wheels.

1932

- **Depression deepens; Chevy car sales drop nearly 50 percent**

- **New Confederate line offers two trim levels, handsome Cadillac-like styling**

- **"Cast-Iron Wonder" adds 10 horsepower**

- **"Silent Second" transmission arrives**

- **Freewheeling offered for the first time**

- **Numerous mechanical upgrades for all models**

- **Factory employment down by 18,610 at year's end**

▲▶ All previous Chevy body styles continued for 1932 (*opposite page, bottom*), but with a choice of DeLuxe as well as Standard trim on most models. Priced about $15 higher, DeLuxes included twin trumpet horns and chromed cowl lamps and hoodside doors. There were few differences inside, but all '32 Chevys now featured a tiltable windshield and a fore/aft-adjustable front seat. The picture above provides a peek inside the $505 DeLuxe five-window sport coupe (also shown *opposite page, top*).

▶ Chevrolet's 1932 lineup was designated Confederate Series BA. A more efficient downdraft carburetor boosted the sturdy "Stovebolt" six to 60 horsepower, a gain of 10, and a new "Silent Second Synchromesh" transmission virtually eliminated gear-grinding shifts. Other mechanical changes included a stiffer crankcase, a heavier crankshaft newly counterbalanced for smoothness, a quieter four-blade engine radiator fan, more effective diamond-pattern rubber engine mounts, and a 5.25×18 wheel/tire package. The last enhanced handsome new styling, shown to good effect on this DeLuxe cabriolet equipped with trunk, trunk carrier, and other official and unofficial accessories.

1932 Body Styles

Standard Coach

Standard Sedan

DeLuxe Convertible Cabriolet

Standard Five Window Coupe

Standard Coupe

DeLuxe Sport Roadster

Special Sedan

DeLuxe Five Passenger Coupe

Standard Phaeton

DeLuxe Sport Coupe

DeLuxe Convertible Landau Phaeton

Standard Roadster

1932

▶ Pretty but not very popular was the 1932 five-passenger coupe, shown here in $590 DeLuxe trim but also available in Standard form for $575. They cost $75-$80 more than comparable coaches, which sold far better—141,455 units versus 7566—despite lacking the convenience of a built-in trunk.

Model Breakdown

BA Confederate	Wght	Price	Prod
roadster 2P	2,410	445	1,118
sport rdstr 2-4P	2,480	485	8,552
Dlx sport rdstr 2-4P	2,530	500	
cabriolet 2-4P	2,540	595	7,066
Dlx cabriolet 2-4P	2,590	610	
Landau phaeton 5P	2,700	625	1,602
Dlx Landau phtn 5P	2,750	640	
phaeton 5P	2,520	495	419
coupe 2P 3W	2,580	490	8,874
Dlx coupe 2P 3W	2,630	510	
coupe 2P 5W	2,580	490	34,796
Dlx coupe 2P 5W	2,630	505	26,623
sport coupe 2-4P	2,645	535	2,226
Dlx sport cpe 2-4P	2,695	550	
coupe 5P	2,700	575	7,566
Deluxe coupe 5P	2,700	590	
coach 5P	2,665	495	132,109
Deluxe coach 5P	2,715	515	9,346
sedan 5P	2,750	590	27,718
Special sedan 5P	2,800	615	52,446
Dlx Special sdn 5P	2,850	630	

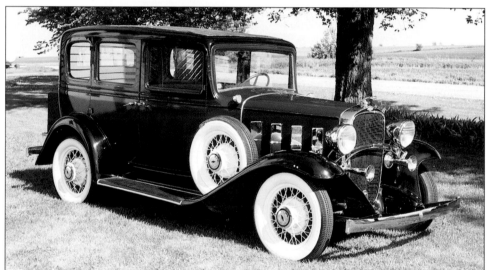

▶ Bearing a head-turning resemblance to this year's Cadillac, the Confederate BA is widely regarded as one of the best-looking Chevys ever. Shown here is the Special Sedan, which came as a DeLuxe for $630.

▲ The year-old Landau Phaeton, here in DeLuxe trim, attracted only 1602 customers for '32. That was far too few for "hard times," so the model would not return.

▶ Production of the phaeton came to only 419, making it the rarest domestically built Confederate model by far. But more of the tourers were manufactured for markets outside the U.S. This Holden-bodied right-hand-drive version was native to Australia.

1933

- Chevy car sales rise 55 percent as America gets a "New Deal"

- Car line receives lower, more stream-lined styling in new Eagle and midseason Mercury series

- "Stovebolt Six" adds five more horsepower in Eagle models

- Closed cars feature Fisher Body's new "No-Draft" ventilation

- "Starterator" auto-matic starter adopted

- Marvin Coyle named general manager

◄▲ A slightly sloped radiator, raked wind-shield and deeper "skirted" fenders comple-mented an inch-longer, 110-inch wheelbase for Chevrolet's redesigned 1933 Eagle line. The number of model offerings was cut back and offered in a single trim level, not two. With the two-passenger model axed, this $485 rumble-seat version was the sole roadster in the line.

The leader in sales presents a new leader in style
THE NEW CHEVROLET TOWN SEDAN

New
CHEVROLET SIX
$445 to $565

◄ Reflecting a growing buyer preference for more secure cargo space was the Eagle line's new $545 two-door "trunkback" Town Sedan, here in a color ad from *Collier's* magazine. It scored a healthy 30,657 sales. All Eagles used an enlarged "Stovebolt" with 206.8 cubic inches and a claimed 65 horses, 10 fewer than Ford's year-old V-8. At midyear, Chevy added three price-leader Mercury models with a new short-stroke, 181-cid version of the familiar six, with the same 60 bhp as the previous 194-cid engine.

▲ The Eagle two-seat five-window coupe was a $495 bargain that drew 60,402 orders, third best among 1933 Chevys. Highlighting this year's PR effort was the demonstration assembly line at Chicago's Century of Progress Exhibition, where visitors could watch Chevrolets being built from start to fin-ish. Capitalizing on the fair's popularity were ads proclaiming "Again Chevrolet leads the Parade of Progress."

1933

▲ Master eventually replaced Eagle in popular 1933 parlance and became official for '34. Name aside, these were the only '33 Chevys with Silent Synchro-Mesh transmission, as well as the new "Starterator," which linked the starter motor with the accelerator through a vacuum unit for starting when no engine vacuum was available. Mercury models did without these conveniences. This rumble-seat Eagle/Master Sport Coupe came only with three-window styling at a $535 starting price. Production was 26,691.

▲ With an over-the-shoulder look at a new six-cylinder rival from Plymouth, Chevrolet advertised itself in 1933 as having "the only proved six-cylinder engine in the low-priced field."

▼ The phaeton (seen in pre-production form) remained the least-popular Chevy. A $515 Master/Eagle model, it saw just 543 orders.

Model Breakdown

CA Eagle	Wght	Price*	Prod
sport roadster 2P	2,675	485	2,876
phaeton 5P	2,715	515	543
coupe 2P	2,715	495	60,402
sport coupe 2-4P	2,780	535	26,691
coach 5P	2,820	515	162,629
Town sdn 2d 5P	na	545	30,657
sedan 5P	2,880	565	162,361
cabriolet 2-4P	2,715	565	4,276
*All models $15 extra with 6-wire wheel equipment.			
CC Mercury			
coupe 2P	2,335	445	8,909
coupe 2-4P	2,395	475	1,903
coach 5P	2,425	455	25,033

◄ The 1933 Chevrolet line was the first in 11 years to span two wheelbases. This four-door sedan, downpriced $25 from the previous year, was exclusive to the mainstay Eagle series, which posted 450,435 total sales. A shorter 107-inch chassis and matching bodies marked the Mercury series that debuted at midyear with two-passenger and rumble-seat coupes and a five-passenger coach. Despite prices of just $445-$475, the Mercurys drew only 35,845 customers in this deep Depression year.

▼ A new double-drop chassis took a rakish three inches off the overall height of 1933 Chevys. This ad photo attempted to show the new design's prowess on a Belgian block road in a "routine test" at the General Motors Proving Grounds in Milford, Michigan.

► Chevy's 1933 trucks got a new hood with louvers instead of costlier vent doors, but other front end components were carried over from '32, even on more carlike models like this smart Sedan Delivery. Beneath that hood was the new 206.8-cid six. A four-speed transmission, previously reserved for 1½-ton models, was now available in the ½-ton line, which was redesignated Series CB.

▼ Despite its low starting price, only 2876 Master/Eagle Sport Roadsters were built. The sidemount spare was a $15 accessory. Another extra was the pretty eagle radiator mascot often seen on restored '33 Chevys. Other add-ons include the trunk rack, sidemount mirrors, and bright wheel trim.

1934

- **Streamlining more evident on new Master and Standard models**

- **Independent "Knee-Action" front suspension, more powerful "Blue Streak Six"**

- **Trucks restyled with unique body panels**

- **Chevrolet builds its 10-millionth car**

▲ A redesigned cylinder head, improved lubrication, and other changes transformed the Chevy six into 1934's more potent "Blue Streak" engine (later renamed "Blue Flame"). Exclusive to Masters, it delivered "80 mph from 80 hp," one of the few times Chevy ads had stressed speed. Standards used the smaller 60-hp version from 1933.

▶ Besides much more power, 1934 Master models like this $580 coach trumped their Standard-trim sisters with a new 112-inch-wheelbase chassis. Available at extra cost for all models was "Knee-Action" independent front suspension. Based on a design by Andre Dubonnet, of French *aperitif* fame, Knee-Action greatly improved ride and handling. But it was not as sturdy as the traditional solid front axle, which would persist at Chevrolet through 1940.

▲ A Standard-trim coach body meets its chassis in this 1934 production line photo.

▲ Chevy's 1934 ads encouraged buyers to drive a new Knee-Action Master "only five miles and you'll never be satisfied with any other low-priced car." This flyer claimed "The same old roads—but a brand new ride" for Knee-Action and also extolled the Master's new looks and greater power.

▲ Chevrolet styling was even more streamlined for 1934, enhanced by inch-smaller 17-inch wheels and matching 5.50 tires. All models came with a rear-mount spare, but sidemounts remained a $30 extra. Chevy built more than 551,000 1934-model cars. This $540 Master Sport Roadster attracted a slim 1974 sales.

◄ Exclusive to the Master line in 1934, the familiar three-window rumble-seat Sport Coupe (*shown*) was waning in popularity, drawing some 18,000 orders at its $600 starting price. The $560 two-seat five-window version found three times as many buyers. The Standard series listed but one coupe, a three-window model for two passengers, starting at just $485.

◄ Again trying to position itself as a maker of affordable yet elegant cars, Chevrolet placed many ads in upscale magazines during 1934. This one, appearing in *House Beautiful*, was rather snooty for the period.

◀▲ Besides a smart new dashboard (*bottom left*), the 1934 Master line offered sedans with and without integral trunks, which were larger this year. The "trunkback" versions were a $615 two-door Town Sedan and new $675 four-door Sport Sedan. This trunkless four-door priced from $640.

Model Breakdown

DA Master	Wght	Price	Prod
sport roadster 2-4P	2,815	540	1,974
coupe 2P	2,935	560	53,018
sport coupe 2-4P	2,995	600	18,365
cabriolet 2-4P	2,990	665	3,276
coach 5P	2,995	580	163,948
sedan 5P	3,080	640	124,754
Town sedan 2d 5P	3,020	615	49,431
Sport sedan 4d 5P	3,155	675	37,646
DC Standard			
sport roadster 2-4P	2,380	465	1,038
phaeton 5P	2,400	495	234
coupe 2P	2,470	485	16,765
coach 5P	2,580	495	69,082
sedan 5P	2,655	540	11,840

*all DA/DC models except DC sedan $30 extra with six-wire wheel equipment.

1935

- **New styling graces all-steel "Turret Top" Master DeLuxe bodies**

- **Chevy again trails Ford in car sales**

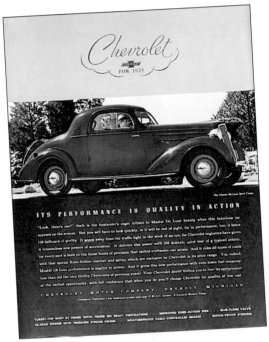

▲ Chevrolet president Marvin E. Coyle (*left*) and Charles E. Wetherald, divisional vice-president and general manufacturing manager, inspect the 10-millionth Chevrolet, a 1935-model Standard four-door sedan that came off the line on November 13, 1934.

▲ Abandoning its somewhat snobbish approach of recent years, Chevy advertising in 1935 targeted average middle-class consumers, the brand's core buyer group. Knee-Action suspension was again touted, but safer new all-steel bodies and smoother styling got at least equal emphasis. This ad, appearing in *The Saturday Evening Post* of June 1, 1935, spotlights the rumble-seat three-window Sport Coupe in the uplevel line, which was now titled Master DeLuxe.

▲ Where 1935 Master DeLuxes were redesigned on a new 113-inch wheelbase, Standards like this $550 four-door sedan were again basically 1933 Mercurys with a 107-inch chassis and a smaller, less-powerful six. Frontal styling of Standards maintained a family resemblance with Masters, but bodies still had fabric roof inserts, not all-steel "Turret Tops."

Model Breakdown

EC Standard	Wght	Price	Prod
sport roadster 2-4P	2,430	465	1,176
phaeton 5P	2,495	485	217
coupe 2P	2,540	475	32,193
coach 5P	2,645	485	126,138
sedan 5P	2,700	550	42,049
ED/EA Master DeLuxe*			
coupe 2P 5W	2,910	560	40,201
sport cpe 2-4P 3W	2,940	600	11,904
coach 5P	3,010	580	102,996
sedan 5P	3,055	640	57,771
Town sedan 2d 5P	3,055	615	66,231
Sport sedan 4d 5P	3,130	675	67,339

*ED had no Knee-Action. EA Knee-Action cars add 60 pounds and $20 to listed weights and prices.

◀ Chevy touted the 1935 Master DeLuxes as "a new expression of modern styling," but some judged them a bit dull. This may partly explain why the old-look Standards took nearly 37 percent of total car sales, versus some 18 percent in '34. Making a fuel stop here is the Standard two-passenger coupe, which continued its three-window styling and priced from $475. Chevy car sales eased to 548,215 units while Ford soared past 820,000.

◄▲ Another look at the 1935 Standard four-door sedan, this one beautifully restored. Its two-door companion, the $485 coach, was Chevy's most popular single model this year, bringing in 126,138 orders, but the $550 four-door managed a relatively weak 42,049. Unlike the equivalent Master DeLuxe, this model retained front-hinged front doors and a 1933-style instrument panel (*above left*), but also nice interior fittings for such a low-priced car and good rear seat room (*left*) considering the fairly short wheelbase.

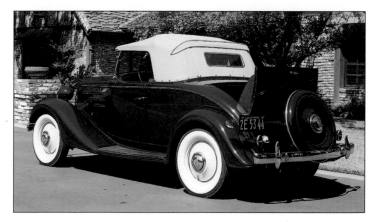

▲ With their clumsy side curtains and higher noise levels, roadsters and touring cars had been on a long sales decline by 1935. Chevy would abandon both altogether after a brief early season run in this year's Standard line. The $465 Sport Roadster (shown) managed only 1176 sales, the $485 four-door phaeton a paltry 217. Independent Knee-Action front suspension was no longer available for any '35 Standard.

▲ This Master DeLuxe Town Sedan was part of a line that Chevy ad makers described as the "Aristocrat of the Low-Priced Field." The steel "Turret Top" was a genuine class exclusive in 1935, made possible by the advent of larger sheetmetal dies and stamping machinery. Engineers worked hard to eliminate unwanted "drumming" from the one-piece roof.

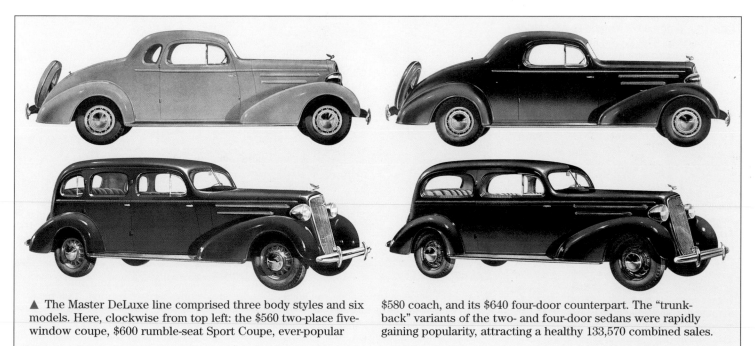

▲ The Master DeLuxe line comprised three body styles and six models. Here, clockwise from top left: the $560 two-place five-window coupe, $600 rumble-seat Sport Coupe, ever-popular $580 coach, and its $640 four-door counterpart. The "trunk-back" variants of the two- and four-door sedans were rapidly gaining popularity, attracting a healthy 133,570 combined sales.

1936

- Passenger-car sales rebound to 918,278

- Four-wheel hydraulic brakes debut

▲ Foreshadowing a trend that wouldn't become common until the Fifties, some 1936 Chevy ads, like this one from *House Beautiful*, painted rosy pictures of multiple car ownership. The theme may have been inspired by signs of a more robust national economy in '36, though full pre-Depression prosperity was not yet achieved.

Model Breakdown

FC Standard	Wght	Price	Prod
coupe 2P	2,645	495	59,356
cabriolet 2-4P	2,745	595	3,629
coach 5P	2,750	510	76,646
sedan 5P	2,775	575	11,142
Town sedan 2d 5P	2,775	535	220,884
Sport sedan 4d 5P	2,805	600	46,760
FD/FA Master DeLuxe*			
coupe 2P 5W	2,895	560	49,319
sport coupe 2-4P	2,940	590	10,985
coach 5P	2,985	580	40,814
sedan 5P	3,060	640	14,536
Town sedan 2d 5P	3,030	605	244,134
Sport sedan 4d 5P	3,080	665	140,073

*FD had no Knee-Action. FA Knee-Action cars add 50 pounds and $20 to listed weights and prices.

▲▼▶ Four-wheel "Perfected Hydraulic Brakes" were standard for all 1936 Chevys, a feature Ford wouldn't match for another three years. Here, the $590 Master DeLuxe Sport Coupe, this year's only closed rumble-seat model.

▲ All '36 Chevys sported a "fencer's mask" radiator carrying headlamps moved up from the fenders. Standards moved closer to Master DeLuxes, gaining Turret-Top bodies on a new 109-inch wheelbase, plus a trunkback Sport Sedan (shown) and two-door Town Sedan. Though still denied Knee-Action suspension and synchromesh transmission, the Standard line improved its sales to 418,417, nearly half of Chevy's model-year car total.

◄ With Knee-Action still a Chevy class exclusive, ads proclaimed the '36 Master DeLuxe "The Only Complete Low-Priced Car!" Here, the $560 two-passenger five-window coupe displaying the standard-equipment 17-inch-diameter pressed-steel artillery-style wheels.

▼ After a year's absence, a cabriolet returned to the Chevrolet line, somewhat surprisingly as a member of the Standard series. It was Chevy's only open model for '36, versus Ford's six distinct ragtops. Despite a bargain $595 price, the revived cabriolet drew only 3629 orders, leaving Chevy barely ahead of Plymouth in convertible sales among the "Low-Priced Three."

69

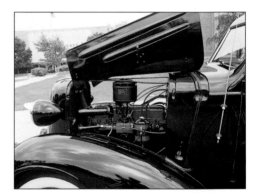

▲ It took a second look to distinguish 1936 Standards from Master DeLuxes, though the former's shorter wheelbase was apparent. This is the $535 Standard Town Sedan, the line's most popular model with 220,884 sales, second only to the $605 Master DeLuxe version's 244,134. Accessory white-wall tires and contrasting wheel paint here were more common on Masters, but provided welcome visual zip for any '36 Chevy.

► Chevy trucks began 1936 as virtual carryovers, then received a midyear redesign with new round-corner all-steel cab that reduced overall height by some two inches. Half-ton models arrived with standard hydraulic brakes in the Series FB, while the 1½-tonners were tagged RA, RB, RC, or RD depending on wheelbases, which were unchanged. This FB pickup wears wire wheels, though steel rims were standard for the revised models.

1937

- **Cars and trucks redesigned with related styling themes**

- **"Blue Flame" six gains size, power**

- **Chevy again bows to Ford in car sales**

▲ After four years of fielding two distinct car lines, Chevrolet consolidated all 1937 models around a new 112.3-inch-wheelbase chassis and "Diamond Crown" styling by General Motors designer Jules Agramonte. Also shared was a larger-bore Blue Flame six making 85 horsepower from 216.5 cubic inches. Here, the $721 Town Sedan in upper-echelon Master DeLuxe trim. Master replaced Standard as the name for this year's lower-priced models.

▶ This $788 Master DeLuxe Sport Sedan started just $18 above the "trunkless" four-door and outsold it by 65-to-1 at 144,110 units. Reflecting the improved economy, the Master DeLuxe line outsold the Master series by almost 2-to-1, but total Chevy car sales dropped by some 103,000 units, so Ford remained the industry sales champ.

▼ This illustration aimed to paint the '37 Chevys as fast, but despite a larger engine with five more horsepower and four main bearings instead of three, speed in the low-priced field still meant Ford, not Chevy, to most buyers.

71

◀▲ As in '36, Chevrolet had but one open model for '37, again exclusive to the lower-priced series. But this year's Masters were larger, peppier, and better furnished than the previous Standards, and the rumble-seat cabriolet reflected that with a price hiked by a substantial $130 to $725. This beauty is one of a mere 1724 built, the lowest output for any 1937 Chevy model.

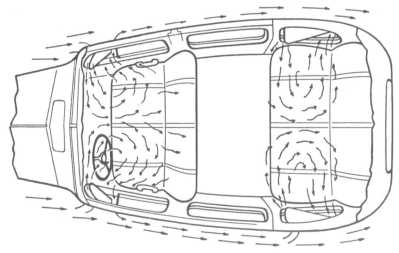

◀ Fisher Body's "No-Draft" ventilation remained a Chevy talking point in 1937. This diagram shows how air flowed through a four-door sedan via the front-door vent windows and the small swing-out panes aft of the rear doors. The idea was to eliminate the draftiness and noise from cranking down door windows—and it worked. Not illustrated here, but just as important for interior comfort, was the tilt-up ventilator door atop the cowl for admitting air to the footwells.

▲ Expanding Chevy's truck line was a "forward-control" chassis with the engine moved inside, to the driver's right, for maximum cargo space within a more urban-friendly size. This tall Metropolitan Body van was typical of applications on the new platform.

▲ Chevy ads continued to press the safety and comfort of optional Knee-Action independent front suspension, which was still reserved for top-line cars. Other 1937 appeals touted standard safety plate glass, "Super-Safe" shockproof steering, and hydraulic brakes. Wheel diameter was reduced an inch, matched by 6.00×16 tires. DeLuxes upstaged Masters with better upholstery; a front-passenger armrest; and dual taillights, wipers, and sunvisors.

▶ The '37s were the first Chevys with full all-steel bodies, which helped trim weight on Master DeLuxes by 55-125 pounds. Lightest of all were the coupes, now a trio of five-window models: $619 two-seat Master, $724 rumble-seat DeLuxe Sport Coupe, and this two-passenger $685 Deluxe (with accessory fender skirts). Also offered was a Master Coupe Delivery with a removable pickup box in place of a lidded trunk.

Model Breakdown

GB Master	Wght	Price	Prod
business coupe 2P	2,770	619	54,683
cabriolet 2-4P	2,790	725	1,724
coach 5P	2,800	637	15,349
Town sedan 2d 5P	2,830	655	178,645
sedan 4d 5P	2,845	698	2,755
Sport sedan 4d 5P	2,885	716	43,240
GA Master DeLuxe			
coupe 2P	2,840	685	56,166
sport coupe 2-4P	2,870	724	8,935
coach 5P	2,910	703	7,260
Town sedan 2d 5P	2,935	721	300,332
sedan 4d 5P	2,935	770	2,221
Sport sedan 4d 5P	2,960	788	144,110

1938

- Car sales drop nearly 50 percent in an unexpected recession, but Chevy again tops the industry

- Only minor changes in both the car and truck lines

Model Breakdown

HB Master	Wght	Price	Prod
business coupe 2P	2,770	648	39,793
cabriolet 2-4P	2,790	755	2,787
coach 5P	2,795	668	3,326
Town sedan 2d	2,825	689	95,050
sedan 4d	2,840	730	522
Sport sedan 4d	2,845	750	20,952
HA Master DeLuxe			
business coupe 2P	2,840	714	36,108
sport coupe 4P	2,855	750	2,790
coach 5P	2,900	730	1,038
Town sedan 2d	2,915	750	186,233
sedan 4d	2,915	796	236
Sport sedan 4d	2,940	817	76,323

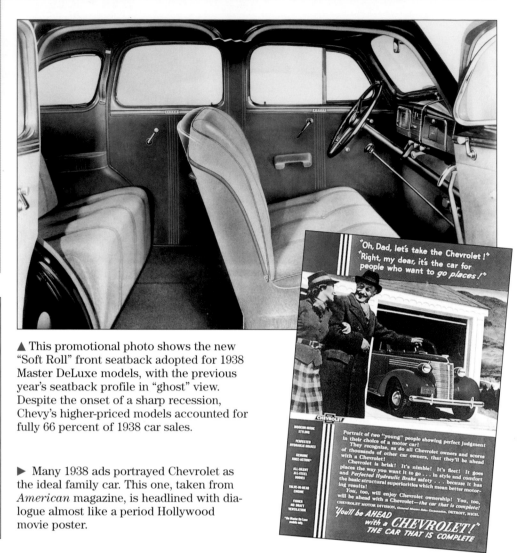

▲ This promotional photo shows the new "Soft Roll" front seatback adopted for 1938 Master DeLuxe models, with the previous year's seatback profile in "ghost" view. Despite the onset of a sharp recession, Chevy's higher-priced models accounted for fully 66 percent of 1938 car sales.

▶ Many 1938 ads portrayed Chevrolet as the ideal family car. This one, taken from *American* magazine, is headlined with dialogue almost like a period Hollywood movie poster.

Chevrolet Accessories Sampler

74

◄ Retaining its crown as Chevrolet's top-selling model, the Master DeLuxe Town Sedan drew 186,233 orders in 1938. Priced from $750, it cost $61 more than its Master series counterpart, yet outsold the cheaper version by nearly 2-to-1. The whitewall tires on this restored beauty were still a relatively rare extravagance, especially in the sharp economic downturn of 1938 that some New Deal opponents branded the "Roosevelt Recession." Save minor cosmetic and technical changes and a few new features, this year's Chevy cars and trucks were close copies of the 1937 models.

▼ Chevy's 1938 truck line comprised ½-ton HC, ¾-ton HD, one-ton HE, and 1½-ton T-Series models. Shown is a farming-oriented HE with stake bed.

▲ Chevy produced a seven-passenger taxi on a special 127-inch-wheelbase in 1937-38. GMC Truck dealers sold this 1938 version, but under the General Cab nameplate. The taxis shared regular passenger-Chevy updates, but were discontinued after this year.

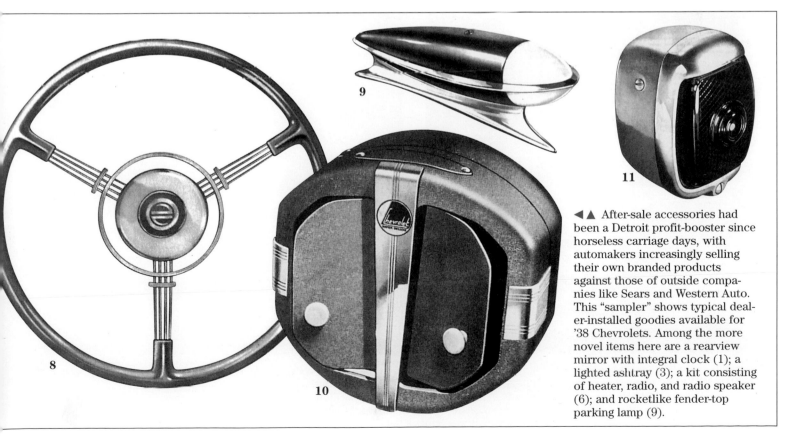

◄▲ After-sale accessories had been a Detroit profit-booster since horseless carriage days, with automakers increasingly selling their own branded products against those of outside companies like Sears and Western Auto. This "sampler" shows typical dealer-installed goodies available for '38 Chevrolets. Among the more novel items here are a rearview mirror with integral clock (1); a lighted ashtray (3); a kit consisting of heater, radio, and radio speaker (6); and rocketlike fender-top parking lamp (9).

1938

◄▲ As before, low-priced Chevy Masters for 1938 were less lavish than DeLuxes, equipped with just a single taillight (*far left*) instead of two, less brightwork, and a painted instead of wood-grained dashboard (*left*). Such "decontenting," to use the modern term, naturally enabled Masters to sell for less: $689 for this Town Sedan versus $750 for the counterpart DeLuxe.

▲ Chevy's biggest 1938 visual change was a barrellike grille with horizontal rather than vertical bars. It was penned by Frank Hershey, who created Pontiac's 1935 "Silver Streak" hood trim and would go on to supervise the design of Ford's 1955-57 Thunderbirds. A downsloped bodyside "speedline" continued from '37 Chevys. As before, the Master DeLuxe price-leader was the $714 two-passenger Business Coupe, this year drawing 36,108 buyers. A larger midmounted gas tank was unique to both Business Coupe models.

1939

- **Trunkless sedans are phased out during the year, but Chevy catalogs a station wagon for the first time**

- **Chevrolet builds its 15-millionth vehicle as car sales inch up to 577,278 units**

- **Optional steering-column shift debuts**

- **Truck line adds cab-over-engine models**

▲ The first factory-authorized Chevrolet station wagons bowed for 1939 with wood-framed bodies supplied mainly by Hercules and Iona, though Mid-States Body Corporation was the builder of record. This wagon was part of a lower-priced series renamed Master 85. It was priced from $848 and drew just 430 orders. Its $883 DeLuxe sibling sold 989 copies. A sidemount spare tire was standard on wagons.

▼ Chevy trucks were basically unchanged for 1939, though a restyled grille was noticeable. More significant was the arrival of 1½-ton V-Series cab-over-engine (COE) models in six basic chassis/payload versions. This stake-body "conventional" was part of 1939's ¾-ton JD Series. Half-ton trucks were designated JC.

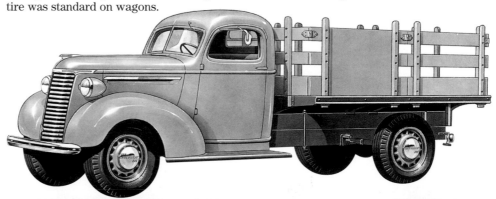

▲ Each year from 1931 through the early Fifties, Chevrolet ran at least one full-color, two-page ad with a brochurelike "lineup" in *The Saturday Evening Post*. This display, appearing in the March 25, 1939, issue, lays out the year's volume-selling Master DeLuxe line.

77

Master DeLuxe for 1939

Two-Door Town Sedan

Four-Door Sport Sedan

Four-Passenger
Sport Coupe

Two-Passenger
Business Coupe

Two-Door Coach

Four-Door Sedan

▲ Chevy ads and sales catalogs still often shared artwork, as this 1939 display attests. A major facelift on the basic 1937-38 bodies moved headlamps outboard and lower on the "cat-walks" between radiator and fenders. Trunkless coach and sedan models were phased out this year due to poor sales.

▼ Again Chevy's volume-leader model, the Master DeLuxe Town Sedan improved its sales to 220,181 for 1939. Its Master 85 sibling was number-two at 124,059. This DeLuxe wears several popular period Chevy accessories including "cadet" windshield visor, rear fender skirts, winged hood ornament, bumper guards, side mirrors, and whitewall tires.

▲ General Motors design chief Harley Earl likely passed on some of Bill Mitchell's Cadillac sketches to Chevy stylist Jules Agramonte, as the '39 Chevy bore a definite resemblance to that year's Cadillac Sixty-One. This Master DeLuxe Sport Sedan sold for $766 without acccessories and was the year's third most popular Chevrolet model with 110,521 sales.

◄ In something of a surprise, Chevrolet dropped its convertible for 1939, but offered a new DeLuxe Sport Coupe with interior rear jump seats. Also known as the four-passenger coupe, this model won far more acceptance than the wind-blown rumble-seat style it replaced, nearly matching the sales of the 1936-38 Sport Coupes put together. Even so, the figure was not that high: 20,908.

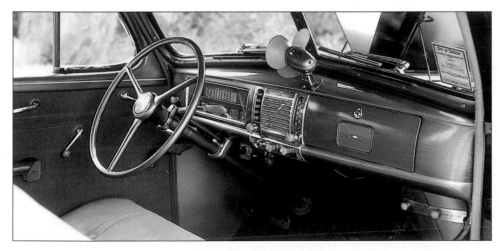

▲ Air-conditioned Chevys were still many years off in 1939, but that year's dashboard was the most elaborate yet. An accessory clock was mounted in the rectangle on the glovebox

Model Breakdown

JB Master 85	Wght	Price	Prod
business coupe 2P	2,780	628	41,770
coach 5P	2,795	648	1,404
Town sedan 2d	2,820	669	124,059
sedan 4d	2,805	689	336
Sport sedan 4d	2,845	710	22,623
station wagon 4d	3,010	848	430*

*229 with folding end gates, 201 with rear door.

JA Master DeLuxe	Wght	Price	Prod
business coupe 2P	2,845	684	33,809
sport coupe 4P	2,845	715	20,908
coach 5P	2,865	699	180
Town sedan 2d	2,875	720	220,181
sedan 4d	2,875	745	68
Sport sedan 4d	2,910	766	110,521
station wagon 4d	3,060	883	989

1940

- **"Royal Clipper" styling for fully redesigned bodies**

- **Convertible returns in new top-line Special DeLuxe series**

- **Sealed-beam head-lamps adopted**

- **Chevy remains "USA-1" as car sales improve to 764,616**

▲ A four-door Sport Sedan appeared in all three 1940 Chevrolet series. Most popular was the new top-line Special DeLuxe version with 138,811 sales, followed by this Master DeLuxe, which cost a modest $36 less and drew just 40,924 orders. The Master 85 model, with solid front axle, sold just 11,468 copies.

▼ Chevrolet's premium wagon for 1940 shifted up to that year's new Special DeLuxe line and was the year's priciest offering at $934. It drew a modest 2493 sales. The bare-bones Master 85 edition listed for just $31 less, which partly explains why only 411 were sold.

▼ William "Big Bill" Knudsen (at microphone), GM president since 1937, heralds the corporation's 25-millionth passenger car, a 1940 Chevy Master DeLuxe Town Sedan. At his right is M. E. Coyle, Chevy president since 1933. To Knudsen's left are GM chairman Alfred P. Sloan, Jr. and, to his left, Charles "Engine Charlie" Wilson, who would take over as GM president in 1941.

▲ A convertible returned to the Chevy line as this 1940 Special DeLuxe, billed as being "At home in the smartest company." Priced from $898, it sold far better than any Chevy ragtop since 1931 at 11,820 units. A first-ever power soft top was standard.

▶ With the economy more robust than at any time since 1929, the new Special DeLuxe line outsold the less-costly Master DeLuxe nearly 2-to-1, the low-end Master 85 by more than 4-to-1. Specials looked much like Master DeLuxes, but were better equipped. This Special Town Sedan was the year's top-selling model with 205,910 units.

▶ Chevy extended its sales lead over Ford from just under 100,000 in '39 to more than 222,000 for 1940, making "Chevrolet's first again!" an apt advertising headline. New "Royal Clipper" styling included a smoother front with a lower, wider grille, seen here on the $750 Special DeLuxe Sport Coupe.

Model Breakdown

KB Master 85	Wght	Price	Prod
business coupe	2,865	599	25,734
Town Sedan 2d	2,915	699	66,431
Sport Sedan 4d	2,930	740	11,468
stn wagon 4d, 8P	3,106	903	411
KH Master DeLuxe			
business coupe	2,920	684	28,090
sport coupe	2,925	715	17,234
Twn Sedan 2d	2,965	725	143,125
Sport Sedan 4d	2,990	766	40,924
KA Special DeLuxe			
business coupe	2,930	720	25,537
sport coupe	2,945	750	46,628
convertible coupe	3,160	898	11,820
Town Sedan 2d	2,980	761	205,910
Sport Sedan 4d	3,010	802	138,811
stn wagon 4d, 8P	3,158	934	2,493*

*367 with double rear doors.

▲▶ Though little changed in specifications or appearance, most 1940 Chevy trucks (save cab/chassis and school-bus applications) sported a new, carlike instrument panel (*right*), though the industry was still decades away from producing trucks that would rival cars for handling, performance, quietness, and style. Another model year meant new series designations: ½-ton KC conventionals and KP cab-overs, ¾-ton KD/KE conventionals, one-ton KFs, and 1½-ton WA/WB conventionals and WD/WE/WF cab-overs. A conventional cab and 133-inch-wheelbase chassis are the foundations for this restored WA stake-body.

▼▶ A fixture in the Chevy truck line since 1928, the sedan delivery broke ranks with other 1940 commercials by adopting the car line's new "Royal Clipper" styling. It was still trimmed and equipped to Master 85 level, but was newly available with independent front suspension. This restored example has been owner-personalized with steel wheels in the old "artillery" style. The steering-wheel "necker's knob" (*right*) was a factory extra.

▲ Former Chevy chief William S. "Big Bill" Knudsen resigned as GM president in 1940 to serve as director of war production programs. President Franklin D. Roosevelt had personally recruited Knudsen considering his vast GM experience with manufacturing processes and factory management.

1941

- A vintage year for Chevrolet cars brings eye-catching new styling, a three-inch longer wheelbase, and numerous technical improvements

- Blue Flame Six becomes 90-horse-power "Victory Six"

- 16-millionth Chevrolet rolls off the assembly line

- Car sales soar beyond one million

- Fully redesigned trucks boast modernized styling and a larger, more potent engine

▲ Division chief Marvin Coyle (*left*) and sales manager William Holler inspect the 16-millionth Chevrolet, a new 1941 Special DeLuxe Sport Sedan. Though clearly evolved from 1940, this year's Chevys sported a more sharply raked windshield, in-fender headlamps, and a definite "big car" look overall. Indeed, many still regard the '41 as a sort of scaled-down Buick.

◄ Lurking behind the fetching foursome and other golf club denizens in this ad for U.S. Royal tires is a 1941 Chevrolet. All passenger cars were equipped with a set of five 6.00×16 tires. Blackwall tires were standard, but extra-cost whitewalls were available from the factory. So were bright wheel trim rings and discs. Sedans bore their spares upright in the trunk, coupes carried them horizontally under the cargo floor, and wagons held theirs on the tailgate.

▼ Call it a "Hollywoody": *Friends*, the Chevrolet owners magazine, conducted a poll to determine the public's favorite celebrity of 1941. Film star Spencer Tracy won the most votes—and a new Special DeLuxe station wagon. This publicity photo pairs the actor (*left*) with his well-optioned prize. Looking on is Chevy assistant sales manager W. G. Lewellen.

83

▲▶ America was out of the Depression by 1941, largely due to increased military production prompted by an alarming new war in Europe. Industry heeded President Roosevelt's call to become an "arsenal of democracy," which all but eliminated unemployment but brought on inflation. Higher car prices were but one result. This '41 Special DeLuxe Sport Sedan started at $851, $49 (six percent) above the '40 model.

▼ Even with a smaller, two-series lineup for 1941, Chevrolet increased its sales lead over runner-up Ford by more than 300,000 units and set a model-year production record of 1,008,976. Handsome styling helped, as did a thoroughly reworked six-cylinder engine boosted to 90 horsepower. Joining the cause at midyear was this Special DeLuxe Fleetline sedan with a formal, Buick-like "blind quarter" rear roofline. Despite a premium $877 price, sales were quite respectable at 34,162.

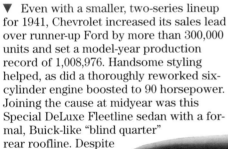

◄▲ Like all '41 Chevys, the five-passenger Special DeLuxe coupe, a.k.a. club coupe, looked brighter than ever—and impressively larger on a new 113-inch wheelbase. A new symmetrically styled dash (*top*) continued the theme inside, and most models boasted more trunk space (*above*) as well as passenger room. Note the newly concealed running boards, achieved by flaring out the lower door sheetmetal. Special club coupe sales jumped more than threefold for 1941 to 155,889. Prices started at $800.

▼ Reflecting its previous year's sales superiority, the Special DeLuxe wagon was Chevrolet's only such car for 1941. Even so, sales slid nearly 18 percent to an even more modest 2045 units. The body again accommodated eight passengers and was a lovely piece of carpentry, but Chevy's 1941 dimensional increases added more than 250 pounds to curb weight. As in prior years, the wagon was Chevy's costliest '41 model, priced from $995. Today it's worth many times that as a highly coveted "woody."

◄ Chevy's 1941 business coupes comprised a budget-friendly $712 Master DeLuxe and a fancier $769 Special DeLuxe. Respective sales were 8089 and a mere 1716. This Special is atypically dressed for a "commercial" vehicle with its whitewall tires, two-tone paint (increasingly popular in the immediate prewar years), "wing-tip" bumper guards, and bright-metal "washboard" front fender trim. As usual, business coupes came with a package shelf instead of a normal three-passenger back seat.

Model Breakdown

AG Master DeLuxe	Wght	Price	Prod
business coupe	3,020	712	48,763
coupe	3,025	743	79,124
Town Sedan 2d	3,050	754	219,438
Sport Sedan 4d	3,090	795	59,538
AH Special DeLuxe			
business coupe	3,040	769	17,602
coupe	3,050	800	155,889
convertible coupe	3,285	949	15,296
Town Sedan 2d	3,095	810	228,458
Sport Sedan 4d	3,127	851	148,661
stn wagon 4d, 8P	3,410	995	2,045
Fleetline sedan 4d	3,130	877	34,162

◀ Chevrolet's redesigned 1941 trucks also boasted in-fender sealed-beam "safety" headlamps. The standard engine was the same 90-horsepower six used in cars. Here, the mainstay ½-ton pickup in the AK series.

▲ Again diverging from other Chevy trucks, the 1941 sedan delivery got the same new styling as its passenger car parents. It also adopted sturdier independent front suspension , vacuum-assisted gearshift, and hydraulic shock absorbers (replacing friction-type) as standard.

▲ Also returning for '41 as a car-based Chevy "truck" was the Master DeLuxe coupe pickup, essentially the business coupe with a small cargo box set into the trunk. The bed could be removed and a normal decklid installed. Despite this versatility and a low price, the model drew only 1135 sales this season.

◀ Ferrying refrigerators made by General Motors-owned Frigidaire is a 1941 YS-Series conventional, a 1½-tonner on a 160-inch wheelbase, Chevy's longest standard truck chassis. "Aerodynamic" lower-body skirts were included on the deluxe stake-bed job.

1942

- **America enters World War II in December 1941**

- **"Blackout Specials" mandated after January 1**

- **Civilian production ends on February 9 as U.S. industry gears up to defeat Axis powers**

- **Chevy car output stops at 254,885 units**

▲ Although America had been preparing for war for some two years before the Japanese bombed Pearl Harbor, the country still officially hoped to stay neutral. Detroit thus rolled out its 1942 models in an almost "business as usual" atmosphere that ended abruptly on December 7, 1941. Among the most striking of these final prewar cars was Chevrolet's new Fleetline Aerosedan, a sleek two-door fastback coupe priced from $880.

Model Breakdown

BG Master DeLuxe	Wght	Price	Prod
coupe 2P	3,055	760	8,089
coupe 5P	3,060	790	17,442
Town Sedan 2d	3,090	800	41,872
Sport Sedan 4d	3,110	840	14,093
BH Special DeLuxe			
coupe 2P	3,070	815	1,716
coupe 5P	3,085	845	22,187
convertible coupe	3,385	1,080	1,182
Town Sedan 2d	3,120	855	39,421
Sport Sedan 4d	3,145	895	31,441
stn wagon 4d, 8P	3,425	1,095	1,057
BH Fleetline			
Aerosedan 2d	3,105	880	61,855
Sportmaster sdn 4d	3,165	920	14,530

► Most 1942-model Chevrolet ads ran before December 1, 1941, generally black-and-white displays making the usual appeals to value-conscious consumers. Though the industry didn't cease advertising after Pearl Harbor, messages naturally turned patriotic. This January 10, 1942, ad, for example, declared how "Chevrolet aids national defense" less than a month before all civilian production was suspended for the duration of World War II.

▼ The Fleetline Aerosedan was as much an instant hit as the fastbacks introduced by General Motors's senior makes for '41. An adept facelift gave all 1942 Chevys a still lower and wider grille, plus fully integrated headlamps, but triple chrome fender strips were exclusive to the Aerosedan and its four-door Fleetline sister, now called Sportmaster. Despite a fairly high price, the Aerosedan was Chevy's most popular 1942 model, attracting 61,855 orders.

1942

▲▼► America declared war on Japan the day after the Pearl Harbor raid and on Nazi Germany a few days later. With the nation soon on a total war footing, the government ordered that as of January 1, 1942, strategic materials such as rubber, gasoline, plastics, and most metals be diverted from civilian use to military production as much as possible. For Detroit, this meant switching from chrome-plated to painted trim pieces, among many measures. The result was the "blackout special," named for the air-raid drills conducted in many cities requiring that all lights be "blacked out" so as to minimize the possibility of a nighttime aerial attack. This Fleetline Aerosedan is typical of the "blackouts" built through early February 1942. Intriguingly, Washington had warned industry as early as August 1941 that the country might have to go to war and had already limited civilian production and non-military use of many materials.

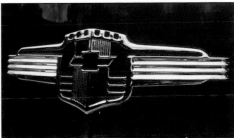

◄▲ After the previous year's many improvements, the 1942 Chevys saw little technical change. However, Special DeLuxe models got new full dashboard woodgraining (*left*), and the convertible, now priced from $1080 (*top*), added rear quarter windows for improved visibility.

► The advent of war shortened Detroit's 1942 model year, resulting in much lower car production. Chevy's total was 254,885, though that still topped the industry. Here, the Special DeLuxe Sport Sedan, which repeated as Chevy's fourth most popular model with 31,441 sales. The two-door Special DeLuxe Town Sedan finished number-three, while the Master Deluxe Town Sedan was runner-up to the new Fleetline Aerosedan. Though all '42 American cars were short lived, they would return with minor changes for a time after the war.

• **General Motors, Chevrolet, and all of American industry become an "Arsenal of Democracy" for winning World War II**

• **Chevrolet speeds the return of peace by manufacturing aircraft engines, artillery shells, armored scout cars, and over a million trucks and cars**

• **Chevrolet resumes civilian truck production in summer 1945**

• **Chevy builds 12,776 1946-model passenger cars in October-December 1945**

▲▼ With all civilian production halted in favor of war matériel, Chevrolet joined the rest of American industry in running patriotically themed magazine ads intended to bolster home-front morale with the promise of speedy victory through mass production. Most Chevy ads used illustrations instead of photographs, and were typical in urging readers to buy War Bonds. Several months after V-E Day in May 1945, Chevy returned to civilian truck production and was soon advertising the fact.

▼ Besides being a prime supplier of the government's all-purpose four-wheel-drive G7, Chevy built thousands of World War II military trucks based on 1942 civilian models, with the same wide array of configurations and ½- to 1½-ton payload ratings. Starting in mid 1944, a few trucks—½-ton pickups first, then heavier rigs like this long cab/chassis—were released for private use, but full-scale reconversion to civilian manufacturing did not begin until July 1, 1945.

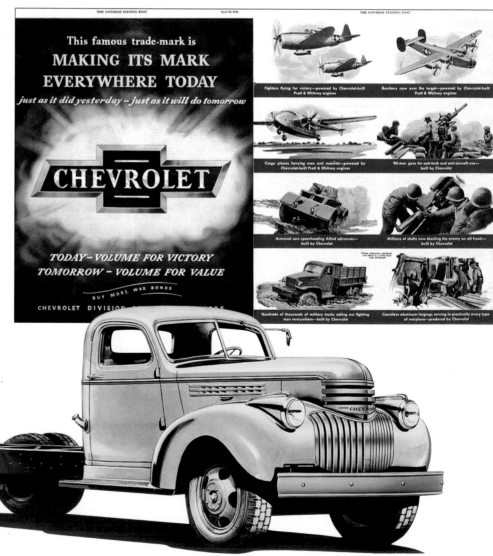

▲ With America's entry into World War II after Pearl Harbor, the government ordered that chrome and other strategic materials be diverted to military use. Cars built in January-February 1942 thus left factories with painted, instead of chrome-plated, trim. Because chrome-reflected light is easily seen at night, and with most U.S. cities preparing for possible nighttime attacks by conducting "blackout" drills (all lights turned off everywhere), these final '42s were called "blackout specials." While some such cars—and a few thousand more built after February—saw military and government service, this '42 Fleetline Sportmaster, olive-drab paint nothwithstanding, is likely a re-creation; most all official-use cars had "blackout" trim. Chevy resumed civilian car output on October 3, 1945, building 12,776 of the 1946 models through year's end.

▲ Chevrolet's proud production record during World War II included not only a half-million military cars and trucks, but also 60,000 Pratt and Whitney aircraft engines; wing sections and fuselage components as a contractor to Grumman Aircraft Company; T17 "Staghound" and T28 armored scout cars; 2000 90mm guns; 200 million pounds of aluminum forgings; 5.7 million pounds of magnesium castings; and two *billion* pounds of grey-iron castings.

◄ The size and "can-do" spirit of Chevrolet's plants played a vital role in America's war effort. Though the division began producing some military goods as early as 1940, it did not adopt an all-out war footing until January 1942. This photo shows a few of the eight million shells produced in Chevrolet factories during the war.

1946

- Autoworkers' strike hits all of General Motors, holds 1946-model Chevrolet output to 398,028

- 1946 Chevys are essentially '42s with minor styling changes

- Nicholas Dreystadt moves from Cadillac to become Chevrolet Division general manager

▲ Like most Detroit makes after World War II, Chevrolet reprised its 1942 models for 1946 with minor appearance changes. Three series continued, but Master DeLuxe was retitled Stylemaster and Special DeLuxe was now Fleetmaster. The latter group included Chevrolet's lone convertible, which at $1476 cost 28 percent more than its '42 counterpart, the result of postwar inflation. Other '46s went up by as much as 64 percent. Despite huge pent-up demand for all cars, Chevrolet struggled against shortages of certain materials and a crippling strike that hit all of General Motors just as civilian production resumed, resulting in artificially low output for both the calendar and model years.

▲ Chevy's 1946 brochure proclaimed, "You put it first in sales, we keep it first in value," but Ford finished first in production. Specifications were the same as in '42 save a different carburetor and slight gains in weight. This Fleetmaster Town Sedan saw 56,538 copies for the '46 model year. It sold from $1225 versus $855 in prewar trim. Two-tone paint returned as an extra-cost factory option.

▲ In contrast to the somber tone of its wartime advertising, Chevy's campaign was back to its old colorful self by 1946—both in pictures and words—typically blending photography with artwork. This *Collier's* ad, illustrated by Fred Ludekins, emphasized "Big-Car Roadability" and "Big-Car Quality at lowest cost!" Reflecting the nation's relief at war's end is the boxed text at the lower right headlined "Thank you for waiting for your new Chevrolet." Another line here says ". . . enter your order today!"

▲ Fleetline kept its prewar name and the same two models for '46. This $1249 fastback Aerosedan was the year's fourth best-selling Chevy with 57,932 built. Triple chrome fender strips again distinguished the Aerosedan and its four-door Sportmaster companion; the latter returned starting at $1309, but only 7501 were produced. After nearly four years of war, people stood in line ready to buy most any car in 1946, so long as it was new, but Chevy couldn't begin to meet demand until late in the year, by which time the GM strike was settled and certain necessary materials were becoming more readily available.

▼ You almost had to look twice to tell a 1946 Chevrolet from a '42, though a new, more upright hood medallion was easily spotted. The grille was simplified, losing its vertical center bar and substituting four horizontal bars for the five thinner bars previously employed.

▼ A prewar pioneer of two-tone paint jobs and bright colors in the low-priced field, Chevrolet offered more of the same for 1946. This catalog page illustrated a few of the possibilities for the Stylemaster Sport Sedan. It also touts "Beauty-Leader" styling, which was a bit much to claim for the relatively minor cosmetic changes made that year to an older design.

▲ Leading Chevrolet's 1946 production parade was the four-door Stylemaster Sport Sedan with 75,349 units. Close behind, at 73,746, was this uplevel Fleetmaster version priced from $1280, a $75 premium over the Stylemaster. Like their prewar predecessors, both these series also listed two-door Town Sedans and Sport Coupes. A business coupe was exclusive to the Stylemaster line, while a convertible and four-door eight-passenger wood-bodied wagon were reserved for Fleetmaster. Not surprisingly under the circumstances, all 1946 Chevys relied on the division's trusty overhead-valve six-cylinder engine with the same 216.5-cubic-inch displacement introduced way back in 1937. Horsepower was 90, unchanged from 1941-42. Also as in those late prewar years, both Stylemaster and Fleetmaster four-door sedans used "six-light" roof styling with a separate window aft of each rear door. The top-shelf Fleetline Sportmaster retained a more formal-looking "four-light" configuration with closed rear roof quarters.

The New 1946 CHEVROLET STYLEMASTER Sport Sedan

New Beauty-Leader Styling Enhanced by Sparkling Colors Distinguishes Every New 1946 Chevrolet

▲ Detroit's first order of business after World War II was getting back *to* business, and that applied to trucks as well as cars. It's no surprise, then, that Chevrolet and others made few changes to their prewar trucks for 1946. Chevy's mainstay ½-ton pickup still had an opening windshield, fender-top headlights, and a no-frills interior. After May 1, chrome grilles returned as standard.

Model Breakdown

DJ Stylemaster	Wght	Price	Prod
Sport Sedan 4d	3,175	1,205	75,349
Town Sedan 2d	3,170	1,152	61,104
spt cpe	3,130	1,137	19,243
bus cpe	3,105	1,098	14,267
DK Fleetmaster			
Sport Sedan 4d	3,225	1,280	73,746
Town Sedan 2d	3,190	1,225	56,538
spt cpe	3,145	1,212	27,036
conv cpe	3,445	1,476	4,508
wgn 4d, 8P	3,465	1,712	804
DK Fleetline			
Sportmaster sdn 4d	3,240	1,309	7,501
Aerosedan 2d	3,165	1,249	57,932

▲▼ Chevrolet got back to civilian truck production on August 20, 1945, shortly before World War II ended with Japan's surrender on V-J Day. By 1946, most of the broad prewar lineup was again available, including tractors and cab/chassis units for "upfitting" with cargo van, dumper, and other special-use bodies. Most of the heavier rigs still offered a choice of conventional cab or cab-over-engine styles.

1947

- Car production gets back up to speed, rising to 671,543 units

- New or expanded plants in four cities

- Cadet compact developed, but is quickly shelved as unnecessary

▲ The 1947 Chevys were little changed from the '46 models save a bolder grille and a revived winged hood medallion. This year's Fleetline Sportmaster (shown) started at $1371, only $26 more than the four-door Fleetmaster Sport Sedan. Yet with production of only 54,531, it was outsold by its cheaper linemate by nearly two-to-one.

▲ Runner-up to the Fleetline Aerosedan in 1947 Chevy sales was this Fleetmaster four-door Sport Sedan with 91,440 orders. Stubborn, strong, postwar inflation made the '47s costlier than similar '46 models—by 12.6 percent in this case. But Chevy production was back to normal as anything that was built could be sold in a still car-hungry "seller's market."

Model Breakdown

EJ Stylemaster		Wght	Price	Prod
1503	Sport Sedan 4d	3,130	1,276	42,571
1502	Town Sedan 2d	3,075	1,219	88,534
1524	spt cpe	3,060	1,202	34,513
1504	bus cpe	3,050	1,160	27,403
EK Fleetmaster				
2103	Sport Sedan 4d	3,185	1,345	91,440
2102	Town Sedan 2d	3,125	1,286	80,128
2124	spt cpe	3,090	1,281	59,661
2134	conv cpe	3,390	1,628	28,443
2109	wgn 4d, 8P	3,465	1,893	4,912
EK Fleetline				
2113	Sportmaster sdn 4d	3,150	1,371	54,531
2144	Aerosedan 2d	3,125	1,313	159,407

▶ At $1286, the Fleetmaster Town Sedan two-door was Chevy's third best-selling '47, though its 80,128-unit volume paled next to the top-dog Fleetline Aerosedan's 159,407. Many publicity photos this year pictured cars with available two-tone paint—but not whitewall tires, which were still in short supply. Placid suburban scenes like this were increasingly evident, too.

▼ The State of Idaho must have had money to burn in '47, as it chose a $1313 Fleetline Aerosedan, Chevy's most expensive two-door sedan, as a highway patrol car. Perhaps officials felt that the fastback's evidently superior "aerodynamics" would come in handy for high-speed chases.

1947

▲▶ Chevy's 1947 styling update erased the upper-body beltline moldings, a change some felt made the cars look shorter. This Fleetmaster Sport Coupe, priced new from $1281, is one of 59,661 built. It wears several popular period accessories including rear fender skirts, spotlamp, "cadet" windshield visor, and those hard-to-get whitewalls.

▶ A record 28,443 Chevy ragtops rolled off the lines for 1947, all Fleetmasters starting at $1628. This example is dressed in a "Country Club" trim kit then marketed by Engineered Enterprises of Detroit. Priced at $148.50 (plus installation), it was a Chevy-owner's aftermarket answer to the factory-built Ford Sportsman "woody" convertible, a surprise 1946 debut that continued into '47, albeit with few sales. Country Club Chevys were doubtless just as rare, though sales figures aren't available. (A few 1947-48 Fleetline Aerosedans also got this treatment.) The paneling was not structural as on "real" woodies of the day, but was bolted on to the sheetmetal. Most Chevy dealers apparently chose not to bother with the kit; they were just too busy selling cars.

▲▶ The Fleetmaster convertible remained Chevy's glamour queen for 1947, even though it was still only the second costliest model in the line. At $1628, its price was up a steep $152 from 1946. The '47 Chevys were late to reach showrooms, delayed until February 8. Not that it mattered much in the booming seller's market of the early postwar years, where "fresh from the factory" counted for far more than fresh styling or features. Even so, Chevy was already hard at work on its first new postwar car designs.

▼ Again holding the top-rung on Chevrolet's price ladder was the Fleetmaster station wagon, an eight-passenger four-door with structural-wood body, priced at $1893 in '47. It also remained the least popular model, with 4912 built. A rear tire carrier was standard issue, but not the whitewall tires.

1948

- **New "Advance-Design" trucks enter first full sales year**

- **Car production rises to 696,449 units**

- **Thomas H. Keating takes over as general manager after death of Nicholas Dreystadt**

Model Breakdown

FJ Stylemaster		Wght	Price	Prod
1502	Town Sedan 2d	3,095	1,313	70,228
1503	Sport Sedan 4d	3,115	1,371	48,456
1504	bus cpe	3,045	1,244	18,396
1524	spt cpe	3,020	1,323	34,513
FK Fleetmaster				
2102	Town Sedan 2d	3,110	1,381	66,208
2103	Sport Sedan 4d	3,150	1,439	93,142
2109	wgn 4d, 8P	3,430	2,013	10,171
2124	spt cpe	3,050	1,402	58,786
2134	conv cpe	3,340	1,750	20,471
FK Fleetline				
2113	Sportmaster			
	sdn 4d	3,150	1,492	64,217
2144	Aerosedan 2d	3,100	1,434	211,861

▶ Though Chevrolet was still hardly a hot performer in 1948, this Fleetmaster convertible was chosen pace car for that year's Indianapolis 500 racing classic. Chevy ragtop volume declined to 20,471 for the model year, perhaps because persistent postwar inflation prompted another price hike—this time a $122 increase to $1750.

▲ A revived vertical grille bar was one of the few visual changes for 1948 Chevrolets. That year's Fleetmaster Sport Coupe (shown) started at $1402, $21 more than the roomier two-door Town Sedan. Fleetmaster coupe production was 58,786. Fifteen-inch wheels with 6.70 tires were newly optional for all '48s in lieu of the standard 6.00×16 rolling stock.

▶ Fleetmaster interiors again sported "woodgrain" paint on the top of the dash, plus a deluxe steering wheel with horn ring. The accessory in-dash clock shown here was spring-wound and thus had a "fast-slow" adjustment knob.

◀ Chevy's veteran "Stovebolt six" got precision main bearings for '48, but was otherwise unchanged. Note the old-fashioned sediment bowl and oil-bath air cleaner.

▲ The 1948 Fleetline Sportmaster retained the "four-light" roofline styling introduced on more expensive GM four-door sedans back in 1940, and the "premium-brand look" remained part of its appeal. Priced at $1492, the model garnered 64,217 orders this year, 18 percent more than the '47. Again enhancing the Sportmaster's "low-priced luxury" aura were such standard rear-compartment amenities as dual assist straps, coat hooks, arm rests, robe cord, ashtray, and foot rest. Wartime gas rationing was by now a fast-fading memory and Americans were again hitting the road for vacations. In 1946, a new travel magazine appeared called *Holiday,* and Chevrolet reached out to its young, upscale readership with a series of special advertisements that paved the way for the soon-to-be-famous "See the USA in Your Chevrolet" ad campaign.

▲ Decked out with windshield visor, side window sunshades, twin spotlamps, whitewalls, and other typical period accessories, this 1948 Fleetline Aerosedan started at $1434, up $121 (9.2 percent) from '47. This remained Chevy's single best-selling model, but by an even wider margin, as production reached 211,861 units.

▲ Though Chevrolet car production was up for a second straight year in 1948, the total was actually less than the 1935 tally. Still, most models posted satisfying increases over 1947. Among the more spectacular gainers was the Fleetmaster station wagon, demand for which more than doubled to 10,171 units. It sold from $2013, the first Chevrolet since the pioneering Classic Six to list above two-grand. Iona and Cantrell continued to supply wagon bodies of mahogany with ash framing.

▲ Former Chevrolet president M. E. Coyle was a General Motors vice president by 1948. For one of that year's publicity photos, he posed with a sign comparing the 1948 Chevy to a 1929 Buick for overall customer value. Why the seemingly odd matchup? To "prove" that GM was offering more car for the money than it had 20 years before. The claim was rather weak, however, considering that the nearly identical '42 Chevys had cost about one-third less than the '48 models.

▶ Looking rather plain, save for an accessory "cadet" windshield visor, is this basic Stylemaster coupe. Chevy again offered the body style in two low-end models: a six-passenger Sport Coupe, priced from $1323 this year, and a three-passenger business coupe with no back seat, tagged at $1244. In uplevel Fleetmaster trim, only the Sport Coupe was offered. As before, Fleetmasters and Stylemasters were much alike outside, but the latter came without bright windshield surrounds and were less "deluxe" inside. Rear quarter windows on all coupes could still be slid open for ventilation.

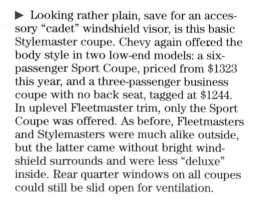

▲ The greatest improvements in Chevy's "Advance-Design" trucks centered on cabs that were modernized for more comfort. But appearance wasn't ignored, either. This 1948 ½-ton DeLuxe Panel Delivery came with more brightwork than usually seen on most trucks.

▼ Though still basically prewar in engineering, Chevy "Advance-Design" trucks were moderately innovative—for trucks—with new features like a fixed windshield, cowl-mount wipers, cowl ventilation, and a carlike face with in-fender headlamps.

▲ The first examples of Chevy's postwar trucks were produced at the company's plant in Janesville, Wisconsin. Here, the "Queen of America's Dairyland," Miss Betty Gardner, christens one of the new models as Wisconsin Governor Oscar Rennebohm and two Chevy executives look on.

▲ Chevrolet's 1948 truck fleet spanned 107 light-, medium-, and heavy-duty models, a wide array of bodies, and eight wheelbase lengths. Bigger rigs now included a four-speed synchromesh transmission, while lighter models adopted a more "modern" column-mount shift lever.

▲ Arriving in summer 1947, Chevy's new-look trucks—and their GMC siblings—were the first GM vehicles designed entirely postwar. The mainstay ½-ton pickup (shown) rode a 116-inch wheelbase and was two inches wider than previous models for extra cargo and cab space.

101

1949

- **Car line receives fresh postwar styling, new series names**

- **Fastbacks multiply**

- **Chevy's first all-steel wagon replaces true "woody" at midyear**

- **Car production soars to a record million-plus, but Ford wins the model-year race by jumping the gun**

▲ Car companies have never been shy about extolling styling, and Chevy was no exception with its new 1949s. "Setting off the striking design . . . a rugged, graceful grille lends a touch of rare distinction," noted a promotional piece. "Sturdy wrap-around bumpers, which protect the sides of the front fenders, and inset parking lamps are luxury treatments new to the low-priced auto field."

▲ With a new Fleetline DeLuxe two-door sedan as its "marquee," this ad from the September 1949 *Better Homes and Gardens* was one of several appeals made to women that year, proclaiming the new Chevys as easy to operate and convenient to drive. This series of illustrations was created by artist John Holmgren.

▶ An expanded 1949 Chevy lineup used the Styleline name for all body styles save fastback sedans, which retained the prewar Fleetline name. Most models offered a choice of Special and upmarket DeLuxe trim. This Styleline DeLuxe four-door Sport Sedan was the year's top seller at 191,357 units. It sold from $1539, exactly the same price as the Fleetline version.

▶ Again for '49, Chevy bore a clear styling kinship to costlier GM cars, something buyers always seemed to appreciate. Proving the point in a corporate family portrait are (from left) that year's Oldsmobile 88, Buick Super, Chevy Fleetline DeLuxe, Pontiac Chieftain, and Cadillac Sixty Special.

▶ This 1949 Fleetline DeLuxe four-door sedan wears accessory headlamp shades, windshield visor, fender skirts, wheel trim rings, and whitewall tires. Despite a wheelbase trimmed one inch to 115, all '49s looked longer and sleeker than previous models. They were also lower with newly standard 15-inch wheels and 6.70 tires.

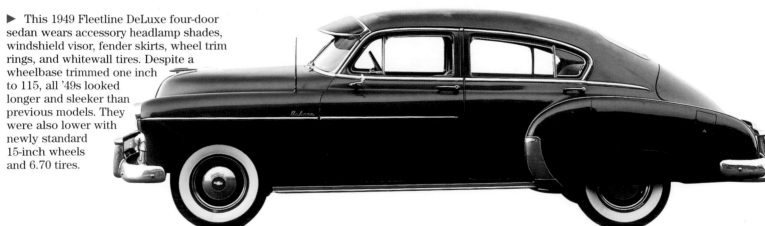

▲► Chevy's new 1949 bodies brought numerous interior improvements, including an asymmetric dash design and wider doors. In addition, all seats were moved forward so that rear passengers no longer rode above the rear axle. This meant more hiproom as well as "a safer, softer, roomier ride that cradles you between the wheels"—plus sensational handling qualities." Shown here is the nifty Styleline DeLuxe convertible, which garnered 32,392 sales at a $1857 starting price.

▼ Americans still had plenty of money in 1949, and Chevy sales proved it, as the nicer DeLuxe-trim models outdrew cheaper Specials by more than three-to-one. This Fleetline DeLuxe four-door sedan was one of 1,037,600 Chevys sold for '49, a new model-year record. But Ford launched its all-new '49s a few months ahead of Chevy to record more than 1.1 million sales.

▲ Chevy's 1949 Sport Coupe was offered in Special and DeLuxe trim. This one is the DeLuxe version. (A business coupe was reserved for the Special series.) Brake-drum diameter was cut one inch to 11 inches this year, and swept area was reduced from 161 square inches to 149. Two-tone paint, unavailable on fastback Fleetlines, was a popular option on nonwagon Styleline models.

Model Breakdown

GJ Styleline Special	Wght	Price	Prod
1502 sdn 2d	3,070	1,413	69,398
1503 sdn 4d	3,090	1,460	46,334
1504 bus cpe	3,015	1,339	20,337
1524 spt cpe	3,030	1,418	27,497
GJ Fleetline Special			
1552 sdn 2d	3,060	1,413	58,514
1553 sdn 4d	3,095	1,460	36,317
GK Styleline DeLuxe			
2102 sdn 2d	3,100	1,492	147,347
2103 sdn 4d	3,125	1,539	191,357
2109 wgn 4d, wood body	3,485	2,267	3,342
2119 wgn 4d, steel body	3,465	2,267	2,664
2124 spt cpe	3,065	1,508	78,785
2134 conv cpe	3,375	1,857	32,392
GK Fleetline DeLuxe			
2152 sdn 2d	3,100	1,492	180,251
2153 sdn 4d	3,135	1,539	130,323

▲ In line with a 1949 industry trend, Chevy offered a true structural-wood wagon through midseason, then replaced it with a simlar-looking all-steel version with wood-look side and rear body panels. Both were eight-passenger Styleline DeLuxe models and had an identical $2267 base price, tops among the new '49s. Production of the true woody (shown) was 3342 units; the the all-steel version saw 2664 copies.

◀▲ With all-new cars taking the 1949 spotlight, Chevrolet's well received "Advance-Design" truck line carried on virtually unchanged. The ½-ton 3100-series pickup (shown) remained the sales mainstay, powered by the division's reliable 216.5-cid "Thrift-Master" overhead-valve six with 90 hp. The same engine again featured in ¾-ton 3600 and one-ton 3800 models as well. An accessory underdash heater (*left*) was a popular extra, but not the fire extinguisher to the far right, installed much later by the owner strictly as a safety precaution.

▼ As ever, Chevy built truck chassis for special applications, like this restored 1949 4400-series with Holmes wrecker body. All 4400 chassis had a nominal 1½-ton payload rating and used the larger 235-cid "Load-Master" six with 90-93 hp; the same engine also powered two-ton 5000- and 6000-series models. This rig originally handled towing chores for a Pennsylvania Chevy dealer.

▲ Another 4000-series '49, here with a farming-oriented stake body for toting produce. Cab comfort again vied with rugged reliability as major talking points in Chevy truck advertising.

1950

- **Optional Powerglide automatic transmission debuts, comes with bigger engine**

- **Bel Air "hardtop convertible" bows**

- **Car sales set a new record at nearly 1.5 million units**

- **Mild styling changes**

▲ A simplified grille was one of the few visual changes setting 1950 Chevrolets apart from their immediate predecessors. Even so, production and sales set new records during 1950, partly because the Korean conflict sparked fears that Detroit might shut down civilian production, as it had in 1942. Chevrolet turned out 1,498,590 cars for the model year, very close to the previous all-time record set in 1927. Meantime, General Motors and the auto workers union signed a new five-year contract providing, among other things, for a new pension plan. GM boss Charles Wilson had worked out a strategy whereby pensions would be funded through stock-market investments, which was criticized on the grounds that it would eventually make workers the company's owners. To this, Wilson replied, "Exactly what they should be!"

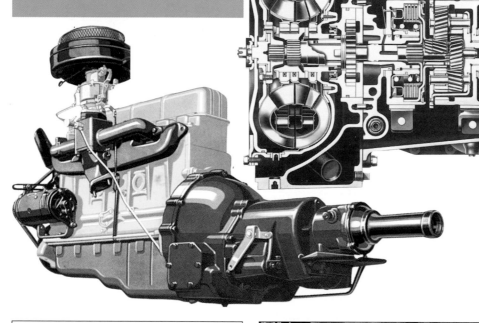

◀▲ Chevy had a big advantage over rivals Ford and Plymouth with its new 1950 Powerglide (*above*), the first fully automatic transmission among "The Low-Priced Three." Destined to endure into the late Sixties, it had a five-element torque converter but only two forward ratios and did nothing for Chevy's already tepid performance. Indeed, though Powerglide-equipped cars came with Chevy's larger 235.5-cubic-inch truck six (*left*), 0-60 mph took some 21.8 seconds, a full two seconds slower than with manual shift. Still, Powerglide was a Chevy sales plus and quickly proved popular.

Model Breakdown

HJ Styleline	Wght	Price	Prod
1502 sedan 2d	3,085	1,403	89,897
1503 sedan 4d	3,120	1,450	55,644
1504 business cpe	3,025	1,329	20,984
1524 sport coupe	3,050	1,408	28,328
HJ Fleetline Special			
1552 sedan 2d	3,080	1,403	43,682
1553 sedan 4d	3,115	1,450	23,277
HK Styleline DeLuxe			
2102 sedan 2d	3,100	1,482	248,567
2103 sedan 4d	3,150	1,529	316,412
2119 station wgn 4d	3,460	1,994	166,995
2124 sport coupe	3,090	1,498	81,536
2134 convertible cpe	3,380	1,847	32,810
2154 Bel Air htp cpe	3,225	1,741	76,662
HK DeLuxe Fleetline			
2152 sedan 2d	3,115	1,482	189,509
2153 sedan 4d	3,145	1,529	124,287

▲ As with exterior styling, Chevy made few interior changes for 1950. Here's a peek inside the convertible, which was again reserved for the Styleline DeLuxe series. Against the fairly plain Specials, all DeLuxe-trim models really lived up to their name inside.

◀▲ This pristine 1950 Styleline DeLuxe convertible (*above*) is mildly "accessorized" with whitewall tires, front-fender stone shields, and winged hood ornament, all available from dealers. Bright rear-fender stone shields remained standard on all DeLuxe models. The 1950 ragtop found 32,810 buyers at a starting price of $1847; only the Styleline wagon cost more. This year's Styleline DeLuxe two-door Town Sedan (*left*) started at $1482 and was Chevy's second best-selling 1950 model with nearly 249,000 orders. As before, this body style carried a longer roofline and shorter rear deck than the sport coupe. Chevy had helped pioneer two-toning, but only the "notchback" Styleline models offered it as a factory extra in this period.

▼▶ As if Powerglide wasn't enough, Chevy had another trump card for 1950 in America's first low-priced pillarless coupe, the new Styleline DeLuxe Bel Air (*below*). Like the senior GM "hardtop convertibles" introduced the previous year, it appealed for combining the comfort of a closed car with the open-air sportiness of a true convertible. Chevy even used convertible-type frame reinforcing to make up for the missing center roof post. The interior (*right*) featured pile-cord and leather upholstery, plus bright ceiling strips simulating a convertible's top bows—all quite plush for a Chevy. Bel Air sales were strong at 76,662, encouraged by an attractive $1741 base price.

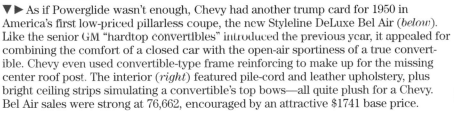

107

▲ Passenger room was still very important to 1950 car buyers, though Chevy, like most manufacturers, most always touted it with illustrations like this, not actual photos.

◄ One of the best series of Chevrolet print ads appeared for the 1950 models. Running mainly in *Collier's*, they were often double-page center spreads showing typical American scenes—a beach, college campus, a country picnic, a suburban railroad station, and here, a city street. These idealized, Norman Rockwell-style visions were largely the work of Detroit-based advertising artist John Osler, who created dozens of illustrations for many car campaigns.

▲ Repeating as Chevrolet's single most popular model for 1950 was the $1529 Styleline DeLuxe Sport Sedan, which attracted a smashing 316,412 orders. America's high postwar prosperity was a big sales boost to all DeLuxe models, especially Stylelines, and they again way outsold their far more spartan Special counterparts. The latter garnered some 261,000 combined 1950-model sales versus a million-plus for DeLuxes, both including Fleetline fastbacks.

▲ Chevy's Suburban Carryall continued as a two-door wagon in the new postwar "Advance-Design" truck series. There was also a panel truck version with blanked-off rear side windows. Both offered more interior room than car-based wagons.

◀ Again part of Chevy's light-commercial fleet, the car-based sedan delivery looked even more attractive with the new postwar styling. Its body was basically that of the steel-bodied station wagon, but with two doors only, no rear side windows, and low-line Special trim and equipment. Orders for the 1950 model came to 23,045; it would prove to be the most ever recorded in the many years Chevy offered sedan deliveries.

▲ The windshield visor became a popular late-Forties add-on for trucks as well as cars. The chrome grille and front bumper on this 1950 Chevy 3100 pickup were available as regular factory options.

▲ Another 1950 3100 wears the optional "Nu-Vue" rear quarter windows introduced with Chevy's postwar "Advance-Design" trucks. They increased glass area by 40 percent over the previous cab style.

1951

- A mild facelift brings a wider, more "important" look

- Dressier "Modern-Mode" interiors bow with new "Safety Sight" instrument panel

- Larger new "Jumbo-Drum" brakes provide shorter, easier stops

- Most Fleetline fastbacks dropped by mid model year due to continued flagging sales

- Total car sales ease to 1.25 million, but Bel Air surges ahead by 35 percent

▲ General Motors photographers had been snapping assembly-plant action since the mid Thirties, and 1951 was no exception. Here, a two-tone Bel Air hardtop nears completion at Chevy's Flint, Michigan, factory. Bel Air sales jumped to 103,356 for the model year.

◄ Later immortalized on TV by singer Dinah Shore, Chevrolet's famous "See the USA" slogan debuted in print ads during 1951. Featured in a *Holiday* magazine series, the new tag line coupled with illustrations of Chevys in famous locations all around the country. This October 1951 piece pictures a Styleline DeLuxe four-door sedan near the Mississippi River. Also for '51, Chevy marketers dropped the Sport and Town monikers from sedan models; only the hardtop Bel Air still denoted body style with a special name. Priced from $1680, the Styleline four-door sedan was again Chevy's top-seller, attracting 380,270 orders.

Model Breakdown

JJ Styleline Special	Wght	Price	Prod
1502 sedan 2d	3,095	1,540	75,566
1503 sedan 4d	3,130	1,595	63,718
1504 business coupe	3,040	1,460	17,020
1524 sport coupe	3,060	1,545	18,981
JJ Fleetline Special			
1552 sedan 2d	3,090	1,540	6,441
1553 sedan 4d	3,130	1,594	3,364
JK Styleline DeLuxe			
2102 sedan 2d	3,110	1,629	262,933
2103 sedan 4d	3,140	1,680	380,270
2119 station wgn 4d	3,470	2,191	23,586
2124 sport coupe	3,115	1,647	64,976
2134 convertible cpe	3,380	2,030	20,172
2154 Bel Air htp cpe	3,225	1,914	103,356
JK Fleetline DeLuxe			
2152 sedan 2d	3,125	1,629	131,910
2153 sedan 4d	3,155	1,680	57,693

▲ Another portrait of the Styleline DeLuxe four-door sedan shows off 1951's revised grille with outboard parking lights, new side trim, and subtly reshaped fenders. The result was a wider, somewhat more "substantial" look for the 1949-50 bodies. Like other Detroit makes, Chevy sales eased in '51 due to government-imposed production curbs for the Korean War.

▲ Chevy's 1951 DeLuxe interiors featured foam-rubber seats covered in attractive striped broadcloth; ads claimed "New smartness and luxury." Among the year's popular accessories were manual or push-button radios, two choices of heater and defroster, windshield and side-window sun shades, front and rear bumper wing tips, and grille guard. This Styleline DeLuxe Sport Coupe sports many of those items, plus whitewall tires. Base price was $1647. Model production totaled 64,976.

◀ Ads declared the '51 Chevys "More beautiful from bumper to bumper." The same might be said for the brighter, jazzier, new "Safety Sight" instrument panel (*left*). It's shown within the Styleline DeLuxe convertible, which remained Chevy's second costliest '51 model—after the station wagon—at $2030. That was $81 above Ford's V-8 Custom ragtop, and partly explains why Chevrolet convertible sales fell more than 38 percent for the model year to 20,172.

▼ This promotional piece hawked not only Chevy's 1951 lineup but the convenience of optional Powerglide automatic transmission, a feature Plymouth didn't have and Ford wouldn't match until late in the year.

111

▲ Buyers were tired of fastback styling by 1951. Chevy took the hint and began phasing out its Fleetline models save the DeLuxe two-door. This DeLuxe four-door, dressed with "cadet" windshield visor and other accessories, priced from $1680 and saw production of 57,693 units. The related two-door pulled in 131,910 orders.

▲ "Aircraft-inspired" dashboards were all the rage after World War II, and even sensible Chevrolet wasn't immune to this new Detroit fad. Its 1951 "Safety Sight" panel was designed to look more "high tech," though the "safety" aspect was questionable what with the protruding steering-wheel hub and so much dazzling brightwork.

▲ Chicago's Midway Chevrolet was one of the bow tie brand's most-successful dealers. Note the rooftop sign touting "36 months to pay." General Motors had pioneered installment purchasing, and in the postwar "baby boom" prosperity, consumer-goods companies of all kinds made it easy for millions of new families to buy "on time."

▲ Though V-8 power kept Ford the low-priced performance leader in 1951, law-enforcement agencies also used sturdy, dependable Chevrolets, at least for tasks that didn't involve high-speed chases. A good example is this Styleline Special two-door sedan outfitted for patrol work with the Michigan State Police.

▲▲ Representing 1951's Special series is this Styleline two-door sedan, which sold new for $1540. The whitewall tires and "cadet" windshield visor here cost extra, of course. Specials again lagged DeLuxes in overall sales by more than 5-to-1. Chevy's elderly, but respected, "Stovebolt Six" soldiered on without change for '51, delivering 92 horsepower from 216.5 cubic inches with manual shift or 105 hp from 235.5 cid with optional Powerglide automatic.

▲▶ Reflecting strong postwar inflation, the Styleline DeLuxe Bel Air hardtop was hiked to $1914 for 1951, a one-year jump of $173, which in those days was a big jump. A wrap-around rear window remained unique to Bel Air, as did upmarket leather/cord fabric upholstery (right), but all nonwagon '51s wore a new emblem on a slightly recontoured trunklid. This beauty sports accessory front-fender gravel guards, fuel-filler trim, and "overriders" on the bumper guards. All were mainly for show, though the accessories catalog said they provided useful protection, especially in parking lots.

1952

- **Car sales drop to 818,142 as Korean War production curbs tighten**

- **Styling touched up, colors and trim choices expand, but no basic change**

▲ The 1952 Chevrolets were very mildly facelifted via a "toothier" grille and minor trim shuffles. This Styleline DeLuxe convertible started at $2128 and found 11,975 buyers. Color and fabric selections expanded to include 10 exterior finishes and five colors for the soft top.

▲ Artwork still dominated Chevy's print advertising campaign in the early Fifties, with very few ads featuring photography. This beach setting was illustrated by Pennsylvanian Harrison Miller, one of many artists who worked on the Chevy campaign during that era.

▲ Priced at $1761 for '52, the Styleline DeLuxe four-door sedan remained Chevrolet's top-seller, but orders fell to 319,736 as Washington tightened curbs on civilian production due to the Korean War. Blackwall tires suggest the year's new austerity in this factory photo.

▲ Like most other Detroit makes, Chevrolet sales declined across the line for 1952. This Styleline DeLuxe wagon saw just 12,756 copies, not quite a quarter of Ford's wagon output. Inflation pushed Chevy's eight-person hauler to $2297, $106 more than the '51 model.

Model Breakdown

KJ Styleline Special	Wght	Price	Prod
1502 sedan 2d	3,085	1,614	54,781
1503 sedan 4d	3,115	1,670	35,460
1504 business coupe	3,045	1,530	10,359
1524 sport coupe	3,050	1,620	8,906
KK Styleline DeLuxe			
2102 sedan 2d	3,110	1,707	215,417
2103 sedan 4d	3,145	1,761	319,736
2119 station wgn 4d	3,475	2,297	12,756
2124 sport coupe	3,100	1,726	36,954
2134 convertible cpe	3,380	2,128	11,975
2154 Bel Air htp cpe	3,215	2,006	74,634
KK Fleetline DeLuxe			
2152 sedan 2d	3,110	1,707	37,164

▲ "More beautiful than ever" was the claim, though the 1952 Chevrolets were outwardly little changed from the '51s. The Bel Air was billed as "the most colorful performer in the low-priced field," but was in its second year of direct competition from Plymouth's Cranbrook Belvedere hardtop. More worrisome for Chevy was Ford's pillarless Victoria. Fully redesigned for '52, it slipped past Bel Air in model-year sales by nearly 2700 units.

▲▶ The Bel Air name would apply to more than Chevy's hardtop after '52, though buyers couldn't know that at the time. Base price was up to $2016; most other models also cost some $100 more than equivalent '51s. Bel Air and the Styleline convertible again sported two-tone interiors (*right*), but with more color and pattern choices (and the availability of optional niceties like the deluxe steering wheel seen here). Sales of Chevy's two-door hardtop model fell to 74,634, reflecting continued government diversion of strategic materials from civilian to military production.

115

1952 Colors

Emerald Green

Saddle Brown

Sahara Beige

Regal Maroon

Birch Grey

Dusk Grey

Spring Green

Admiral Blue

Twilight Blue

Honeydew

Cherry

Bittersweet

Beach White

▲ First seen at Chevy a decade before, "torpedo" styling was dropped after a half-year run of Fleetline DeLuxe two-door sedans, the sole fastback in that year's line. Priced from $1707, the model saw 37,164 final copies, scarcely one-sixth the volume of the "notchback" Styleline two-door sedan. This example shows off a number of available factory dress-up accessories.

◀ Recalling a certain 1942 Mack Truck ad was this 1952 Chevrolet truck concept by the same artist, Peter Helck. One of the best remembered automotive advertising illustrators, Helck portrayed Chevy trucks from 1950 through '59 in many dramatic, true-to-life ads that appeared regularly in *The Saturday Evening Post*, *Collier's*, and *Time*.

◀ ▲ This 1952 Series 3100 pickup recalls the days when one paid extra for fenders painted like the rest of the body—though that time now was long gone at Chevy. It sports factory-optional chrome bumpers, sidemount spare, and "Nu-Vue" cab windows. Pushbutton-type door handles were new to a truck line that was little changed for 1952, in part due to government curbs on civilian production and reallocation of strategic materials to the military, both prompted by the country's involvement in the Korean "police action." Not that truck buyers expected much annual change; that was still decades into the future. As in recent years, Chevy's truck fleet again included 22 series, 10 wheelbases, and two

1953

NINETEEN FIFTY-THREE   NINETEEN FIFTY-THREE   NINETEEN FIFTY-THREE   NINETEEN FIFT

- Chevy surprises the auto world with the Corvette sports car

- Passenger Chevys get a fresh look, new series names, optional power steering, and standard 235.5 six-cylinder engine

- Car sales rebound to near 1.35 million as the Korean War ends in stalemate

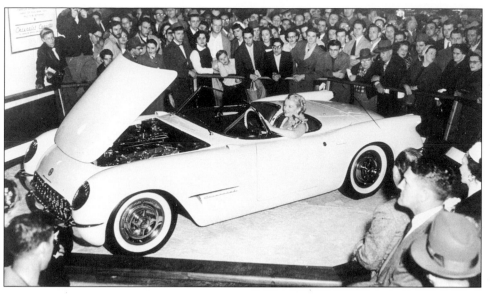

▲ Seeking to reverse an increasingly staid image, Chevy unveiled the flashy Corvette sports car in January 1953 at General Motors's first Motorama show of the year, held at New York City's Waldorf-Astoria hotel. An enthusiastic reception convinced GM brass to put the two-seater into production, which commenced some six months later.

▲ Started in 1951 and developed as project EX-122, the Corvette mounted a novel fiberglass body atop a Chevrolet wagon chassis cut down to a 102-inch wheelbase, though later modifications rendered the frame virtually unique to the new sports car. Triple carburetors, a more radical camshaft, high-compression heads, and other tweaks boosted Chevy's 235.5-cubic-inch six to 150 horsepower. Powerglide automatic was the only transmission.

▲ Except for minor trim changes, Corvette survived to production with its Motorama "dream car" styling fully intact. Price was set at a lofty $3513, but the new sports car wouldn't be readily available to the general public until 1954, and '53-model production was held to a mere 300 units, according to most sources.

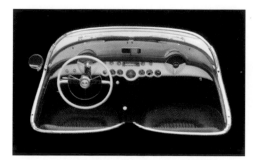

▲ Corvette arrived with a "twin-cowl" dashboard design theme that would later be picked up for Chevy passenger cars. A tachometer was included, but all gauges bar the speedometer were on the lower center dash rail and thus hard to read easily. Cockpit space was only adequate with two European-inspired bucket-type seats.

▲ One of many now-famous photos documenting the start of Corvette production on June 30, 1953. All '53s came off a small line at Chevy's Flint, Michigan, home plant, set up so workers could learn to build the new fiberglass bodies properly without being rushed.

117

▲ Masterminded by legendary GM Styling chief Harley Earl, the '53 Corvette was intended not only to liven up Chevy's image but as GM's reply to the small but intense interest in sporty two-seaters. Even so, many fans of European sports cars chided Corvette for its jazzy Detroit styling, pedestrian powertrain, and gimmicky fiberglass body. The spinner wheel covers here were one of several running changes made during 1953 production. All of that year's 'Vettes were finished in Polo White.

► The first 25 or so Corvettes came with '53 standard-Chevy wheel covers. The manual soft top stowed behind the cockpit under a solid cover—a real "dream car" touch—but was prone to leaks. So were the clumsy clip-in side curtains that substituted for the roll-up windows most Americans expected.

▲ Passenger Chevys were fully restyled for 1953 around the same 115-inch-wheelbase chassis and basic inner bodies of 1949-52. Bel Air was now a four-model top-line series that included this $2175 convertible, of which 24,047 were built.

▲ The '53 Chevys might have turned out completely new if a small-displacement V-8 study earlier in the decade had born fruit; management granted a heavy facelift instead. Still, '53s like this ragtop Bel Air were billed as "Entirely new through and through!"

How Chevrolet's new high-compression horsepower
takes you more places on less gas . . .

MORE PEOPLE BUY CHEVROLETS THAN ANY OTHER CAR!   CHEVROLET

▲ Yet another portrait of the '53 Bel Air convertible, with Chevy's newly redesigned instrument panel just visible. Ad types extolled the dashboard's "rich gleam of heavy chrome." A new option for all models was power steering, another Chevy first in the low-priced field. Its $178 price was rather stiff for the times, so demand was relatively low this year. In another mechanical change, manual-shift Chevys, save a few special-ordered fleet vehicles, were upgraded to the 235.5-cid "Blue Flame Six" previously limited to Powerglide cars, though the latter had slightly higher compression for 115 horsepower versus 108 with stickshift. Chevy car sales rebounded for '53 as the Korean War and government production curbs ended.

▲ Chevrolet was Number One out West— and in the East, South, and North in 1953! Ads still reminded readers that "More people buy Chevrolets than any other car," as it was still the country's best-seller. This Western scene featuring the Bel Air hardtop was painted by California native Fred Ludekins.

◄ Begun under GM designer Ed Glowacke but completed under new Chevy styling chief Clare MacKichan, the 1953 facelift considerably freshened the division's 1949-vintage body design. A "toothy" grille provided a visual link to the new Corvette sports car, and Bel Airs had a lot of new brightwork all around. This four-door sedan started at $1874 and attracted a strong 247,284 buyers.

▼ Contrast the rear roofline of this 1953 Bel Air two-door sedan with the more formal C-pillar treatment of the four-door to the left. All '53 Bel Airs wore rear-fender spears that provided a natural place for repeating the roof color with optional two-tone paint. The top-line two-door sedan started at $1820 and managed 144,401 sales.

119

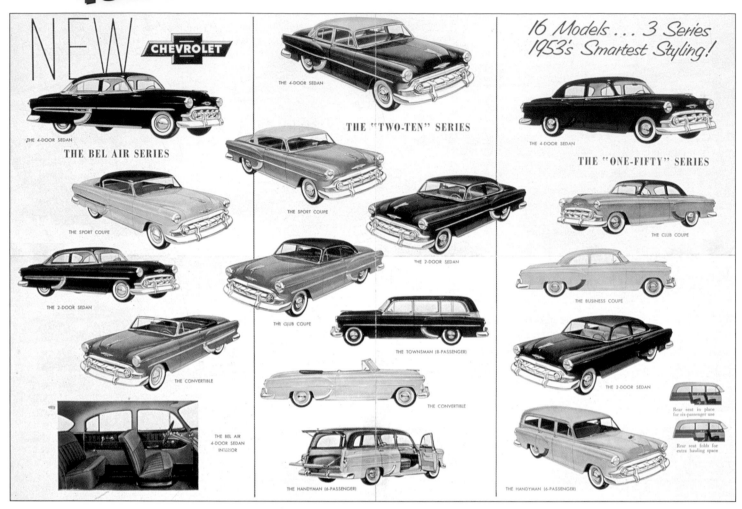

NEW CHEVROLET

THE BEL AIR SERIES

THE 4-DOOR SEDAN

THE SPORT COUPE

THE 2-DOOR SEDAN

THE CONVERTIBLE

THE BEL AIR 4-DOOR SEDAN INTERIOR

THE "TWO-TEN" SERIES

THE 4-DOOR SEDAN

THE SPORT COUPE

THE 2-DOOR SEDAN

THE CLUB COUPE

THE TOWNSMAN (8-PASSENGER)

THE CONVERTIBLE

THE HANDYMAN (6-PASSENGER)

16 Models . . . 3 Series
1953's Smartest Styling!

THE "ONE-FIFTY" SERIES

THE 4-DOOR SEDAN

THE CLUB COUPE

THE BUSINESS COUPE

THE 2-DOOR SEDAN

THE HANDYMAN (6-PASSENGER)

Rear seat in place for six-passenger use

Rear seat folds for extra hauling space

Model Breakdown

150 Special	Wght	Price	Prod
1502 sedan 2d	3,180	1,613	79,416
1503 sedan 4d	3,215	1,670	54,207
1504 business coupe	3,140	1,524	13,555
1509 Handyman wgn 4d	3,420	2,010	22,408
1524 club coupe	3,140	1,620	6,993
210 DeLuxe			
2102 sedan 2d	3,215	1,707	247,455
2103 sedan 4d	3,250	1,761	332,497
2109 Handyman wgn 4d	3,450	2,123	18,258
2119 Townsman wgn 4d	3,495	2,273	7,988
2124 club coupe	3,190	1,726	23,961
2134 convertible coupe	3,435	2,093	5,617
2154 hardtop coupe	3,295	1,967	14,045
240 Bel Air			
2402 sedan 2d	3,230	1,820	144,401
2403 sedan 4d	3,275	1,874	247,284
2434 convertible coupe	3,470	2,175	24,047
2454 hardtop coupe	3,310	2,051	99,028
Corvette			
2934 convertible rdstr	2,705	3,513	300

▲ The 1953 Chevrolets didn't go on sale until just after the New Year. The "family portrait" highlights the newly revamped lineup with three trim levels: a base group called One-Fifty; midlevel Two-Ten, and top-line Bel Air. All had one-piece windshields, another part of '53's heavy styling makeover, plus a key-activated starter switch in place of the old foot pedal. The Powerglide automatic, a $178 option for Two-Tens and Bel Airs (up from $159), now started off in Low range rather than High for faster stoplight getaways.

◄ They might have worn new clothes, but Chevy's 1953 wagons offered the same long, flat load deck as the 1949-52 models. Also retained was a gaping load aperture with drop-down tailgate and separate liftgate. Chrome tailgate "skid" strips were useful for shifting heavy cargo.

▲ Chevy wagon offerings grew from one to three for 1953, all four-doors. Here, the $2123 six-passenger Two-Ten Handyman. Also cataloged were a $2273 eight-seat Townsman and $2010 six-person One-Fifty Handyman. The expanded lineup reflected the era's fast-growing wagon market.

◄ Grouped according to body style and series designation, it seems as though this collection includes scale models depicting every 1953 Chevrolet in every available color combination.

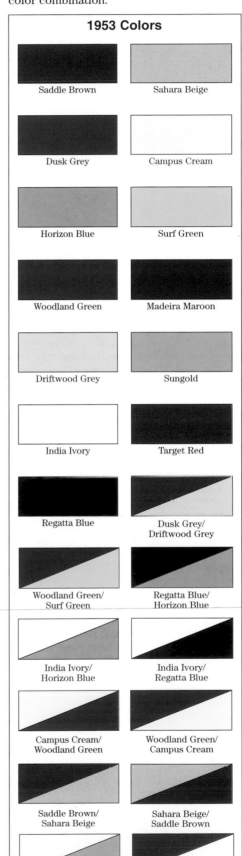

1953 Colors

Saddle Brown	Sahara Beige
Dusk Grey	Campus Cream
Horizon Blue	Surf Green
Woodland Green	Madeira Maroon
Driftwood Grey	Sungold
India Ivory	Target Red
Regatta Blue	Dusk Grey/ Driftwood Grey
Woodland Green/ Surf Green	Regatta Blue/ Horizon Blue
India Ivory/ Horizon Blue	India Ivory/ Regatta Blue
Campus Cream/ Woodland Green	Woodland Green/ Campus Cream
Saddle Brown/ Sahara Beige	Sahara Beige/ Saddle Brown
India Ivory/Sungold	Target Red/India Ivory

▲ Unlike Bel Air and Two-Ten sedans, low-line One-Fiftys lacked wraparound rear windows. This $1670 four-door, shown with optional whitewalls, attracted 54,207 sales.

► Like the Styleline DeLuxe four-door sedan before it, this $1761 Two-Ten was Chevy's top-seller with 332,497 orders for '53. In a show of durability and speed—and one of Chevy's few racing triumphs so far—C.D. Evans drove a Powerglide-equipped Two-Ten to win the Light Stock Car class in that year's grueling *Carrera Panamericana*, the famed Mexican Road Race.

▲ Chevy's 1953 sedan delivery shared the new styling and most mechanical changes of that year's passenger cars, but was still marketed as part of the division's truck line. Now starting at $1648 and trimmed to One-Fifty level, it remained a wagonlike two-door with a swing-out rear load door. Some of the 15,523 built were used as light-duty rescue vehicles.

▲ Promoting Chevy's "Advance-Design" trucks was this ad highlighting the veritable "banquet" of chassis and body styles that again comprised the 1953 lineup.

▲▶ Again on Chevy's truck menu for 1953 was a ½-ton panel delivery, another of the division's "Advance-Design" models. It sold for $1620. The Carryall Suburban, the same rig with rear side windows and seating for up to eight passengers, also returned, newly priced from $1947. Suburbans came with a choice of panel doors or two-piece tailgate.

◀ A sidemount spare tire could be ordered in place of the standard frame-mounted spare for 1953 Chevy pickups like this mainstay ½-ton 3100. The convenient side spare required a specially indented left rear fender. Now priced from $1407, this model again rolled on 16-inch wheels shod with six-ply 6.00 tires.

1954

- **Corvette enters full production, but sales disappoint GM brass**

- **Passenger models get a light restyle**

- **Power brakes, windows, and seats are first-time options**

- **Car sales slip below 1.2 million as Chevy fights a price war with archrival Ford**

▼ Though visually unchanged for 1954, Corvette continued to benefit from numerous running changes, most to correct design flaws and to improve fit-and-finish. In addition, a midyear camshaft revision lifted horsepower by five to 155, and paint choices expanded to include Sportsman Red, Pennant Blue, and black, plus the original Polo White. List price rose a nominal $10 to $3523, but production soared tenfold to 3640, though GM brass had hoped for more.

▲ A star of General Motors 1954 Motorama shows was this special Corvette with a lift-off hard top, a practical feature that would resurface on later production models.

▲ Previewing another future Chevy at the '54 Motoramas was the Corvette Nomad, a six-passenger wagon combining a standard chassis with the sports car's styling.

▲ Where 1953 Corvettes had been doled out to a few GM executives and other VIPs, Chevy shifted production from Flint, Michigan, to a much larger plant in St. Louis with the '54 models, which meant the sports car was at last readily available to the general public. To emphasize the fact, Chevrolet PR issued several "cavalcade" photos like this one, staged at the famous "S-Curve" (since erased) on Chicago's Lake Shore Drive.

1954

▶ Chevrolet executives marked production of the 30-millionth Chevrolet, a new Bel Air convertible, on June 9, 1954. From left: E. W. Ivey, administrative assistant to the general manager; Edward Kelley, general manufacturing manager; William Fish, general sales manager; division general manager Thomas Keating; Chevy chief engineer Edward Cole; and W. J. Scott, executive assistant to the general manager, manufacturing.

▼ "Smooth lines and smarter styling" was how Chevy billed its modestly facelifted '54s. Highlighted in this view of the Bel Air convertible are a revised grille with two extra "teeth," oval outboard parking lamps, and fluted headlight rims. This example also wears an extra pair of bumper guards and an accessory crossbar bridging the stock (inner) guards. Bel Air ragtop production eased to 19,383 even though base price rose only $10 to $2185. In fact, passenger-Chevy sales were down overall this year, in part because a brand-new design was being rumored for '55, but also because of a brutal price war touched off by a "Ford Blitz."

▲ Chevy's option list lengthened again for 1954 with the addition of power brakes ($38), power front windows ($86), and power front seat (also $86). The available power steering was downpriced to $135 to attract more customers. Powerglide automatic still cost $178, but was now available on any standard-size model. Factory-fit whitewall tires ran $27. With Bel Air now denoting top-line models, the original hardtop was renamed sport coupe. Exactly 66,378 were sold at a $2061 starting price.

▲ There were relatively few rear-end changes in Chevy's 1954 facelift, though bumper and taillights were revised. Bel Airs like this ragtop wore slightly more elaborate wheel covers.

▲ The Bel Air two-door sedan returned for '54 with an $1830 starting price. Sales for this model slipped a bit to 143,573. Side trim and two-toning were essentially repeated from 1953.

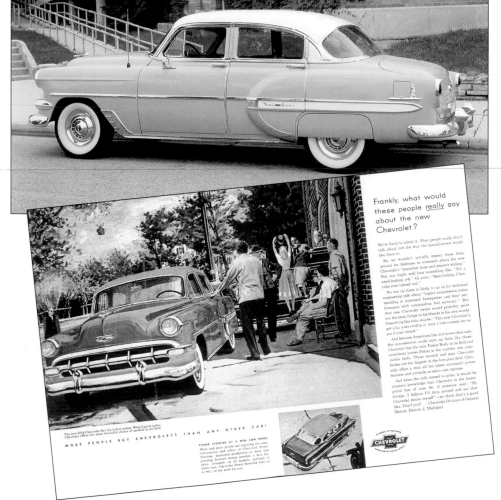

▲ "Powered for *performance*, engineered for *economy*" was the way Chevrolet described its revised Powerglide engine. In an effort to keep up in the performance department with Ford (which had a new 130-hp ohv V-8 for 1954), Chevy's veteran six got higher compression and a "wilder" camshaft that lifted horsepower to 115 with manual shift, 125 with Powerglide. Repeating as the most popular single model, the Bel Air four-door sedan (shown) attracted 248,750 sales with an $1884 starting price.

◄ Much of Chevy's 1954 print advertising portrayed small-town America. This New England setting with a fire station was created by Connecticut artist Austin Briggs.

125

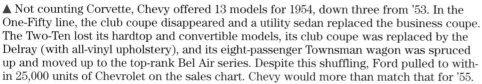

The Bel Air Series   The "Two-Ten" Series   The "One-Fifty" Series

New 1954 CHEVROLET Four-Door Sedans

New 1954 CHEVROLET Two-Door Sedans

New 1954 CHEVROLET
BEL AIR SPORT COUPE
"TWO-TEN" CLUB COUPE
"ONE-FIFTY" UTILITY SEDAN

New 1954 CHEVROLET Station Wagons

New 1954 CHEVROLET Convertible

PICK YOUR FAVORITE '54 MODEL OF AMERICA'S FAVORITE CAR

13 Beautiful Models!
3 Great Series!

This tag means a better buy!

This is an OK USED CAR

Only at Chevrolet Dealers

6 Ways Better

1. Thoroughly Inspected
2. Reconditioned for Safety
3. Reconditioned for Performance
4. Reconditioned for Value
5. Honestly Described
6. Warranted in Writing

Headquarters for OK Used Cars and Trucks

See Your Chevrolet Dealer for All Your Automotive Needs

CHEVROLET

▲ Not counting Corvette, Chevy offered 13 models for 1954, down three from '53. In the One-Fifty line, the club coupe disappeared and a utility sedan replaced the business coupe. The Two-Ten lost its hardtop and convertible models, its club coupe was replaced by the Delray (with all-vinyl upholstery), and its eight-passenger Townsman wagon was spruced up and moved up to the top-rank Bel Air series. Despite this shuffling, Ford pulled to within 25,000 units of Chevrolet on the sales chart. Chevy would more than match that for '55.

▲ Chevrolet courted those unable to afford new cars with ads like this one for dealer-warranted "OK Used Cars."

▲▶ At $2133 to start, the six-passenger Two-Ten Handyman station wagon offered an appealing blend of comfort, practicality, and value, but was hardly the last word in high-fashion styling. Then again, Detroit designers had yet to pay much attention to this utilitarian body style, though they soon would as wagons fast became popular in burgeoning suburban America. Another $150 bought a new eight-seat Bel Air Townsman.

▲ Though outsold by its Bel Air counterpart, the Two-Ten four-door sedan (*above*) sold 235,146 copies at $1771. Two-Ten was again Chevrolet's most popular line for 1954, but its margin over Bel Air narrowed considerably. Totals were 486,240 Bel Airs, 524,222 Two-Tens, and 129,459 for the One-Fifty group. Runner-up in Two-Ten popularity was the two-door sedan (*below*), which started at $1717 and satisfied 195,498 customers. Chevy typically discounted prices this year to match an aggressive, unexpected production and sales "blitz" by archrival Ford.

▲ A bolder grille, one-piece windshield, and optional availability of Hydra-Matic automatic transmission made news for Chevy's 1954 truck line—the first major changes in years for the "Advance-Design" fleet. Light-duty models like this 3100 pickup again relied on six-cylinder "Thriftmaster" and "Loadmaster" engines, but with slightly more power on models up to and including the 1½-ton 4500 series. A DeLuxe Cab option with two-tone upholstery, more ammenities, and added external brightwork was released after the start of the year.

Model Breakdown

150 Special	Wght	Price	Prod
1502 sedan 2d	3,165	1,680	64,855
1503 sedan 4d	3,210	1,623	32,430
1509 Handyman wgn 4d	3,455	2,020	21,404
1512 utility sedan 2d, 3P	3,145	1,539	10,770
210 DeLuxe			
2102 sedan 2d	3,185	1,717	195,498
2103 sedan 4d	3,230	1,771	235,146
2109 Handyman wgn 4d	3,470	2,133	27,175
2124 Delray coupe	3,185	1,782	66,403
240 Bel Air			
2402 sedan 2d	3,220	1,830	143,573
2403 sedan 4d	3,255	1,884	248,750
2419 Townsman wgn 4d	3,540	2,283	8,156
2434 convertible coupe	3,445	2,185	19,383
2454 hardtop coupe	3,300	2,061	66,378
Corvette			
2934 convertible rdstr	2,705	3,523	3,640

1955

- All-new "Motoramic" styling for Bel Air, Two-Ten, One-Fifty

- Landmark "small-block" V-8 makes Chevy "The Hot One"

- Corvette gets the new "Turbo-Fire" V-8

- High-style Bel Air Nomad wagon debuts

- Totally new Cameo Carrier pickup arrives

- Chevrolet builds a record 1.7 million cars

▲ Designed by veteran GM engineers Harry Barr and Ed Cole, Chevrolet's new 1955 "Turbo-Fire" V-8 pioneered an innovative block casting technique that made for uncommon manufacturing precision, especially in the low-priced field. This cutaway view highlights other state-of-the-art features, including lightweight aluminum pistons; a tough forged-steel crankshaft (versus alloy iron); short-stroke cylinder dimensions; and lightweight, independent rocker arms. With the standard two-barrel carburetor shown, the efficient Turbo-Fire offered 162 lively horses from 265 cubic inches and a mild 8.0:1 compression ratio.

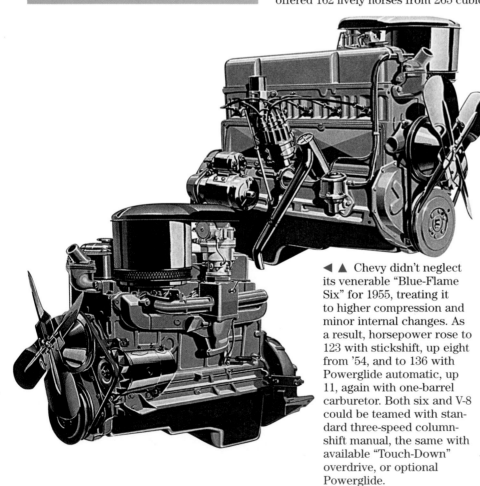

◄ ▲ Chevy didn't neglect its venerable "Blue-Flame Six" for 1955, treating it to higher compression and minor internal changes. As a result, horsepower rose to 123 with stickshift, up eight from '54, and to 136 with Powerglide automatic, up 11, again with one-barrel carburetor. Both six and V-8 could be teamed with standard three-speed column-shift manual, the same with available "Touch-Down" overdrive, or optional Powerglide.

▲ Chevy's first V-8 since since its poor-selling attempt of 1917-18 became the standard for modern Detroit performance. Early engines suffered oiling problems, but Chevy was quick to remedy that. The Turbo-Fire transformed Chevy's image from dull family car to a dynamic performer that ads rightly termed "The Hot One." Available dual exhausts and four-barrel carb boosted horsepower from the stock 162 to 180, and a racing-oriented 195-horsepower setup was added late in the model year.

▲ Clare M. MacKichan, head of the Chevrolet design studio in 1953-62, later said of the '55 development program: "We all had wanted to do a brand new car and the 1955 was new from the ground up. The car was made to do it . . . the engine was made to do it . . . and we did it."

▲ Masterminding Chevrolet's engineering program was Edward N. Cole, who took over as chief engineer. He beefed up the engineering crew from 850 to 2900, and the new V-8 engine, drivetrain, and chassis were designed in just 15 weeks.

▲ Chevy pioneered low-priced hardtops with its 1950 Bel Air. When Bel Air became the top-line series for '53, the body style was renamed sport coupe. The '55 sport coupe was initially offered only as a Bel Air, and was often two-toned like this example, which also wears several period "dress-up" accessories available through dealers. Note the rear fender skirts, chrome fuel-door edging and rocker-panel trim, and front-fender gravel guard.

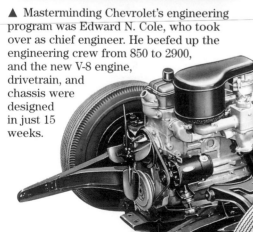

◀ Chevrolet's Bel Air sport coupe looked great from any angle. Press releases called it "an excellent example of smart profile styling." Certainly, the simple Ferrari eggcrate grille, the flat horizontal planes of the fenders, the dip in the beltline, and tasteful application of chrome moldings contributed to its good looks. More than 185,000 of these Bel Air hardtops were produced. Base price was $2067 with standard six.

◀ All '55 Chevys boasted improved handling to match their newfound V-8 sizzle. Chassis highlights included longer, wider rear leaf springs riding outside the frame rails; diagonally mounted shock absorbers to match; and an improved "Glide Ride" front suspension with coil springs, unequal-length A-arms, and new "spherical joint" (ball joint) geometry. Tubeless tires were newly standard too.

129

1955

▲ Chevy billed its '55 models as "Motoramic," playing off General Motors' famous "Motorama" traveling exhibits. This scene, created by Fred Ludekins, places a Bel Air convertible at one of the first Pebble Beach *Concours d'Elegance* classic-car competitions in California—an accurate prediction of the '55 Chevy's high collectible status today.

▲ The exterior "Continental" spare tire was a popular custom touch in the Fifties, but relatively few '55 Chevys were equipped with the factory's dealer-installed "wheel carrier" as is this Bel Air convertible. One possible reason: Unlike some later versions, Chevy's '55 "conti" spare was fixed, thus complicating access to the trunk. By contrast, the chrome tailpipe extension seen here was far more popular. Chevy's '55 accessory book also listed wheel covers, wheel trim rings, backup lamps, locking gas cap, compass, cigarette lighter, nylon/plastic/fiber seat covers, an outside rearview mirror with spot "safetylamp," "traffic light viewer," exterior shades for windshield and side windows, even an electric shaver.

▲ The Bel Air convertible remained queen of the Chevy line for '55, priced at $2206 to start. A power top and electric window lifts were among many factory options offered. Bel Air's chrome side moldings emphasized a racy beltline "notch" behind the doors, a favored idea of legendary GM Styling chief Harley Earl.

▶ The '55 Bel Air convertible looked great even with the top up and no lower-body two-toning. This beauty mates a white roof with Coral paint, one of 15 colors offered that year in both monotone and two-tone combinations.

▲ Mid-Fifties America was wild about wagons, and Chevy offered two in its top-line 1955 Bel Air group. The more conventional of the pair was a four-door called Beauville in the brochure, though it wore no identifying nameplates. At $2262 to start, it was Chevy's second-costliest '55 model. Exactly 24,313 were produced.

▲ Chevy's costliest '55 was the posh $2571 Bel Air Nomad two-door wagon. Its sporty "hardtop" roof styling and chrome "banana" tailgate trim were previewed on a Corvette-based 1954 showcar, but Chevy decided to make the Nomad a last-minute addition to the '55 passenger-car line. Rivals Ford and Plymouth had nothing like it, but the stiff-price, water leak problems with the tail-gate, and a relative lack of wagon practical-ity limited '55 output to just 8386 Nomads.

▶ With a production run of nearly a quarter-million units, the Two-Ten two-door sedan was Chevy's most popular two-door model for 1955. Along with the new body styling came a new dashboard with a symmetrical arrange-ment and adoption of a 12-volt electrical sys-tem. Note here the "cadet" windshield visor.

▲ On November 23, 1954, a '55 Chevy Bel Air sport coupe rolled down the Flint, Michigan, assembly line as General Motors' 50-millionth car. Company photographers were tipped well in advance of the big event, and were on hand to record it.

▲ In its typical fashion, GM got maximum PR mileage from its 50-millionth car. Designers finished the milestone car in Anniversary Gold, then ladled on 716 gold-plated trim parts. Following the celebratory festivities in Flint, GM took the car on the road, displaying it at civic luncheons in 65 cities coast-to-coast and for "open house" events at various GM plants. The car also appeared in numerous parades during 1954-55.

▲ GM president Harlow H. Curtice bids *bon voyage* to the corporation's 50-millionth car. Gathered in the background are a few of the hundreds of guests invited for the historic event, including many journalists and government officials.

▲ Again adding spiff to the midrange Two-Ten line was the six-passenger Delray club coupe, offering a lot of Bel Air style for $1835, just $60 more than the regular two-door. A Two-Ten hardtop coupe was quietly added at midyear, but saw 11,675 copies versus Delray's 115,584.

▲ ▶ The Delray club coupe was dressier inside than the regular Two-Ten two-door sedan on which it was based. Seats, door panels, and the headliner were covered in fancier vinyl. Chevy's dashboard was rather restrained for '55, with a motif like that introduced on the Corvette. (The Delray dash shown at right has been augmented with bright Bel Air trim including 987 tiny embossed bow-tie emblems.) Aiding comfort was new "High Level" ventilation with a mesh-covered air intake atop the cowl.

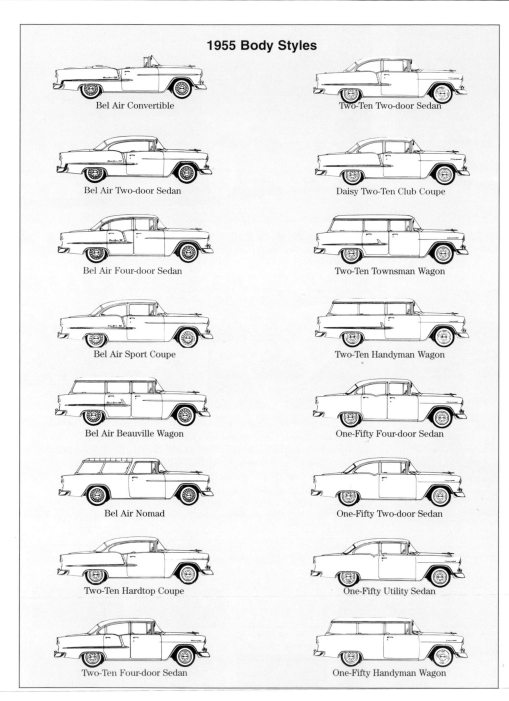

1955 Body Styles

Bel Air Convertible

Bel Air Two-door Sedan

Bel Air Four-door Sedan

Bel Air Sport Coupe

Bel Air Beauville Wagon

Bel Air Nomad

Two-Ten Hardtop Coupe

Two-Ten Four-door Sedan

Two-Ten Two-door Sedan

Daisy Two-Ten Club Coupe

Two-Ten Townsman Wagon

Two-Ten Handyman Wagon

One-Fifty Four-door Sedan

One-Fifty Two-door Sedan

One-Fifty Utility Sedan

One-Fifty Handyman Wagon

Model Breakdown

150	Wght	Price	Prod
1502 sedan 2d	3,145	1,685	66,416
1503 sedan 4d	3,150	1,728	29,898
1512 utility sdn 2d	3,070	1,593	11,196
1529 Handyman wagon 4d	3,275	2,030	17,936
210			
2102 sedan 2d	3,130	1,775	249,105
2103 sedan 4d	3,165	1,819	317,724
2109 Townsman wagon 4d	3,355	2,127	82,303
2124 Delray coupe	3,130	1,835	115,584
2129 Handyman wagon 2d	3,315	2,079	28,918
2154 hardtop coupe	3,158	1,959	11,675
Bel Air			
2402 sedan 2d	3,140	1,888	168,313
2403 sedan 4d	3,185	1,932	345,372
2409 Beauville wagon 4d	3,370	2,262	24,313
2429 Nomad wagon 2d	3,285	2,571	8,386
2434 conv coupe	3,300	2,206	41,292
2454 sport coupe hardtop cpe	3,180	2,067	185,562
Corvette			
2934 conv roadster	2,650	2,934	700

▲ Staged studio shots were often used in the Fifties to glamorize workaday products like the One-Fifty four-door sedan. Chevy's bottom-rangers were vastly outsold by costlier counterparts. This $1728 model posted 29,898 orders against nearly 318,000 for the $1819 Two-Ten four-door and some 345,000 for the $1932 Bel Air version.

▲ Another slightly contrived studio shot, this of a '55 One-Fifty two-door. This happens to be the $1685 "consumer" model, but Chevy also listed a $1593 utility version, *sans* back seat, for commercial users. A lack of trim limited One-Fifty two-toning options.

▲ With its potent new Turbo-Fire V-8, Chevy was not only a much stronger rival to Ford for street performance in '55 but a serious new challenger for police-car business. The one problem was keeping up with the much faster new V-8-powered Corvettes.

▲ For 1955, Chevy's sports car stayed with its 1953-54 styling, but a gold "V" in the Corvette bodyside name script identified the new V-8, fitted to all but a handful of the 700 cars built for the model year.

▲ Tuned for 195 horsepower, the Turbo-Fire V-8 helped keep Corvette alive in '55 while Chevy readied an all-new replacement. Base price was cut $589 to $2934 to spark sales—which didn't.

◄ ▲ Even blue-collar pickups started becoming style-conscious in '55. Leading the way was Chevy's new Cameo Carrier, part of the fully redesigned "Task-Force" truck fleet that bowed on March 25. A unique fiberglass-skinned flush-side cargo box combined with carlike features such as chrome bumpers, colorful two-tone interior—and available V-8. A near-$3000 base price kept sales modest, but the Cameo Carrier set trends in pickup design and packaging that were soon imitated and remain popular to this day.

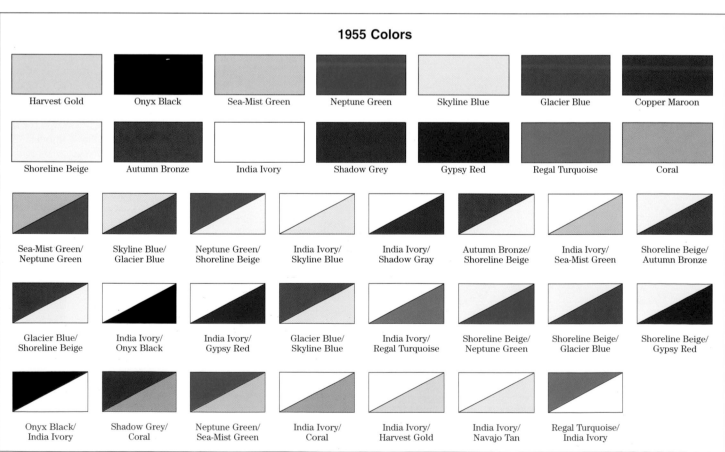

1955 Colors

Harvest Gold	Onyx Black	Sea-Mist Green	Neptune Green	Skyline Blue	Glacier Blue	Copper Maroon
Shoreline Beige	Autumn Bronze	India Ivory	Shadow Grey	Gypsy Red	Regal Turquoise	Coral
Sea-Mist Green/ Neptune Green	Skyline Blue/ Glacier Blue	Neptune Green/ Shoreline Beige	India Ivory/ Skyline Blue	India Ivory/ Shadow Gray	Autumn Bronze/ Shoreline Beige	India Ivory/ Sea-Mist Green	Shoreline Beige/ Autumn Bronze
Glacier Blue/ Shoreline Beige	India Ivory/ Onyx Black	India Ivory/ Gypsy Red	Glacier Blue/ Skyline Blue	India Ivory/ Regal Turquoise	Shoreline Beige/ Neptune Green	Shoreline Beige/ Glacier Blue	Shoreline Beige/ Gypsy Red
Onyx Black/ India Ivory	Shadow Grey/ Coral	Neptune Green/ Sea-Mist Green	India Ivory/ Coral	India Ivory/ Harvest Gold	India Ivory/ Navajo Tan	Regal Turquoise/ India Ivory	

1956

- • "The Hot One is Even Hotter" with a new 205-horsepower "Super Turbo-Fire" V-8

- • All-new Corvette offers slick styling, true sports-car moves

- • Standard Chevys get heavy facelift, new Bel Air and Two-Ten four-door hardtop models

▲ To whet the public's appetite for more powerful '56 models, Chevy sent this prototype Bel Air sport sedan hardtop to Pikes Peak in Colorado for a Labor Day 1955 speed-record assault. Prepared and driven by Corvette engineering wizard Zora Arkus-Duntov, the heavily disguised car scaled the mountain in 17 minutes, 24.05 seconds to set a new American stock-sedan record, besting the previous mark by 2 minutes, 3 seconds. Ads trumpeting the feat appeared just weeks before the '56s reached dealer showrooms. NASCAR officials were on hand to insure that everything was on the up-and-up.

▲ Playing off the success of its all-new 1955 design, Chevy introduced the '56 under the banner "The Hot One's Even Hotter." A "friskier" V-8 was hyped in many ads that year, with top-line Bel Airs the most pictured models. This March 1956 *Holiday* magazine ad was illustrated by Bruce Bomberger, one of the "big three" California-based Chevy advertising artists. The livelier new "Super Turbo-Fire" V-8 packed 205 horsepower with four-barrel carburetor and 9.25:1 compression ratio—Chevy's highest yet. A linewide option, it was joined at midyear by a 225-horsepower twin-four-barrel version lifted from the all-new '56 Corvette.

▲ General Motors mounted another of its periodic Motorama shows for 1956, meaning it was the responsibility of each division to create something special to show off at the traveling extravaganza. Chevrolet's contribution to the effort was the four-seat Corvette Impala hardtop coupe, which would lend its name and a few styling details to production cars a few years hence. As first envisioned, the show car would have had a more bubblelike windshield.

▲ Besides slick new styling, more power, and much improved handling, the fully redesigned 1956 Corvette was a more civilized sports car, thanks to new options like a power soft top. This Chevy PR photo sequence emphasized the convenience of the $100 extra. As on all earlier 'Vettes, the top was stowed in a well beneath a hard cover.

▶ Corvette was just in its fourth year in '56, but was making history faster than ever. GM documented progress to that point by posing stock and factory-experimental 'Vettes with various corporate and Chevy division executives. Taking center stage was the bestriped SR-2 derived from the late-1956 Daytona and Sebring racing 'Vettes, and, just above it, a slightly tamer street version built for GM president Harlow Curtice.

▲ Edward N. Cole was Chevy chief engineer by 1956. One of the perks was taking a spin in the racing-oriented SR-2 experimental built for Jerry Earl, son of GM styling supremo Harley Earl.

▲ Zora Arkus-Duntov kicked up some sand at Daytona with this test Corvette prior to '56 runs on the famed beach and at Sebring. Snow tires were tried here in a bid for maximum acceleration.

▲ Corvette offered a pair of 265 V-8s for 1956: a standard four-barrel 210-horsepower version, up 15 from '55, and a new 225-horse job with twin-four-barrel carbs and racier "Duntov" camshaft. The latter mill was made optional for '56 passenger Chevys at midyear.

▶ Previewed on a 1954 Motorama show car was the '56 Corvette's new lift-off hardtop. A $200 option, it provided better winter-weather comfort than the folding fabric roof, plus better top-on visibility. It was a tad bulky for one person, though, as this photo suggests.

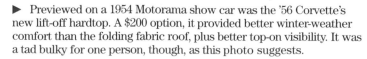

▲ ▶ Though GM almost killed the Corvette after 1955, design chief Harley Earl helped keep it alive with stunning new '56 styling that helped boost 'Vette sales nearly fivefold to 3467 for the model year. New concave bodyside "coves" were a natural for the two-toning option, which proved popular, while the overall design was recognizably 'Vette yet more coherent and dynamic. A close-ratio three-speed manual transmission and more V-8 power completed a great package for sports car enthusiasts.

◀ Pedal cars had been popular children's toys since the earliest days of motoring. This '56 Corvette was one of the more faithful kid-powered copies, surprisingly accurate in its details and proportions. Manufacturers often sold pedal-car versions of their "grownup" models through dealers. After all, what better way to engender "brand loyalty" than by appealing to customers before they're even old enough to drive?

137

▲ General Motors pioneered four-door hardtops in 1955 at Buick and Oldsmobile. For '56, Chevy joined in by adding a pillarless sport sedan to its top-line Bel Air and middle-range Two-Ten series. This is the snazzier Bel Air version, which got heavy advertising play in '56. Priced from $2230, it did healthy model-year sales of 103,682. The $2217 Two-Ten version sold 20,021 copies.

▶ Only tiny detail changes differentiated the '56 Bel Air dash design from that of '55.

▼ You'd pay a small fortune today for a '56 Bel Air convertible this nice, yet it sold new for $2344. Exactly 41,268 were built. This beauty, finished in India Ivory/ Sherwood Green, sports optional wire wheel covers. Chevy's 1956 facelift added two to three inches to overall length, and combined with new side trim for a longer, lower look.

▲ ▼ Though the Bel Air series had its share of flashy cars, sedans proved to be the bread-and-butter offerings at the top of the Chevrolet model range. Nearly 270,000 orders were placed for the four-door sedan (*above*) and almost 105,000 copies of the two-door sedan (*below*) were issued. Prices now topped $2000.

▲ The singular Nomad station wagon (*above*) entered its sophomore year looking a bit more "connected" to the Bel Air series to which it belonged. New styling features including elliptical instead of round rear wheel cutouts and side trim modeled after the brightwork used on other Bel Air body styles. Base price rose only $37 to $2608, but sales eased by 500 units to 7886.

▶ Many a gas station attendant was confounded by the '56 Chevys' newly hidden filler cap.

▲ The mid-Fifties "Classic" Chevys have been prized collectibles for years, none more than the rakish Bel Air sport coupe hardtop. This like-new Onyx Black/Crocus Yellow '56 was one of 128,382 built. List price was $2176 with Blue-Flame six, somewhat more with one of the V-8 options, which were now signified by a chrome "V" beneath the Chevrolet hood crest. This year's base two-barrel 265-cube V-8 again produced 162 horsepower with manual shift, 170 with available Powerglide automatic. The four-barrel carb version here made 205 horses.

◄ This Nassau Blue/India Ivory Two-Ten four-door sedan has the stalwart Blue-Flame six, though that engine was tweaked for '56 to 140 horsepower regardless of transmission. Prices began at $1955; with 283,125 built, it edged out the four-door Bel Air as most popular Chevy.

▲ As on other '56 Chevys, the interior of the Bel Air sport coupe was little changed from the year before except for the expected revisions to colors, trim, and fabrics.

▲ As before, Chevy Two-Tens had less elaborate side trim than counterpart Bel Airs. Midrange cars and low-line One-Fiftys lacked overt identification, getting by with Chevrolet fender script.

Model Breakdown

150

		Wght	Price	Prod
1502	sedan 2d	3,154	1,826	82,384
1503	sedan 4d	3,196	1,869	51,544
1512	utility sedan 2d	3,117	1,734	9,879
1529	Handyman wagon 2d	3,299	2,171	13,487

210

		Wght	Price	Prod
2102	sedan 2d	3,167	1,912	205,545
2103	sedan 4d	3,202	1,955	283,125
2109	Townsman wagon 4d	3,371	2,263	113,656
2113	sport hardtop sedan	3,252	2,117	20,021
2119	Beauville wgn 4d, 9P	3,490	2,348	17,988
2124	Delray coupe	3,172	1,971	56,382
2129	Handyman wagon 2d	3,334	2,215	22,038
2154	sport hardtop coupe	3,194	2,063	18,616

Bel Air

		Wght	Price	Prod
2402	sedan 2d	3,187	2,025	104,849
2403	sedan 4d	3,221	2,068	269,798
2413	sport hardtop sedan	3,270	2,230	103,602
2419	Beauville wgn 4d, 9P	3,506	2,482	13,279
2429	Nomad wagon 2d	3,352	2,608	7,886
2434	convertible coupe	3,330	2,344	41,268
2454	sport hardtop coupe	3,222	2,176	128,382

Corvette

		Wght	Price	Prod
2934	convertible roadster	2,764	3,149	3,467

▲ Chevy increased its market share to nearly 28 percent for '56 despite building fewer cars: some 1.57 million for the model year, though that was in line with the general industry dip after torrid '55.

▲ Chevy's factory "Continental kit" was still not too popular in '56, and seemed rather pretentious on practical models like this Two-Ten four-door sedan.

▲ A '56 Chevrolet One-Fifty four-door sedan sports the bodyside spear and bright window trim newly added to relieve some of the stark "fleet car" aura that had permeated the budget series.

▲ Chevy again catered to commercial users in 1956 with a bare-bones sedan delivery. As before, it was based on the One-Fifty Handyman wagon and used a top-hinged rear door first seen on '55s.

▼ Chevy's new-generation "Task-Force" light-duty truck line had its first full model year in 1956. Changes from 1955 models were confined mostly to badges and trim. A "cadet" windshield visor, custom-built wood bed rails, whitewalls, and passenger-car wheel covers (typically restyled for '56) dress up this V-8-equipped ½-ton 3100 model.

▲ Chevy styling became rather Cadillac-like for '56, but wealthy Detroit industrialist Ruben Allender decided to make it even more so by customizing Bel Air convertibles and sport coupes with Eldorado-style fins and various borrowed trim pieces. The handsome result, called El Morocco, cost half as much as a real Cadillac Eldorado but at least $1000 more than the parent Chevy. That may be why only about 18 ragtops and two hardtops were built as '56 models.

1957

- A bigger small-block V-8 and new "Ramjet" fuel injection boost available punch to one horsepower per cubic inch

- Standard Chevys get a handsome "baby Cadillac" facelift

- Futuristic Sebring SS Corvette enters the tough 12-hour Florida race, but it's the regular 'Vettes that finish

▲ Pioneer automotive journalist "Uncle Tom" McCahill of *Mechanix Illustrated* (*left*) gets a briefing on Chevy's new 1957 "Ramjet" fuel injection from Corvette chief engineer Zora Arkus-Duntov. As a "fuelie," Chevy's newly enlarged 283 V-8 offered 250 or 283 horsepower, the latter on a tighter 10.5:1 compression ratio instead of 9.5.

◄ ▼ Engineered by GM's Rochester carburetor division, Chevy's new Ramjet fuel injection was a mechanical setup that fed the cylinders via a high-pressure pump running off the distributor. The system made for a distinctive top-end look via a special two-piece intake manifold made of cast aluminum. The upper part contained air passages and fuel-metering system, the lower portion fuel "ram" tubes and cylinder-head cover. Fuel and air fed directly to each cylinder in a more precise way than a carburetor could manage. Unfortunately, Ramjet often caused rough idling because the fuel injectors tended to absorb engine heat, and the system was tricky to service. It was also expensive at around $500, so orders were few: just 240 Corvettes and a handful of standard Chevys. Still, "fuelie" power was a great talking point in '57.

Model Breakdown

150		Wght	Price	Prod
1502	sedan 2d	3,211	1,996	70,774
1503	sedan 4d	3,230	2,048	52,266
1512	utility sedan 2d	3,163	1,885	8,300
1529	Handyman wgn 2d	3,406	2,307	14,740
210				
2102	sedan 2d	3,225	2,122	160,090
2103	sedan 4d	3,270	2,174	260,401
2109	Townsman wgn 4d	3,461	2,456	127,803
2113	sport hardtop sdn	3,320	2,270	16,178
2119	Beauville wgn 4d	3,561	2,563	21,083
2124	Delray coupe	3,220	2,162	25,644
2129	Handyman wgn 2d	3,406	2,402	17,528
2154	sport hardtop cpe	3,260	2,204	22,631
Bel Air				
2402	sedan 2d	3,232	2,238	62,751
2403	sedan 4d	3,276	2,290	254,331
2409	Townsman wgn 4d	3,460	2,580	27,375
2413	sport hardtop sdn	3,340	2,364	137,672
2429	Nomad wagon 2d	3,465	2,757	6,103
2434	convertible coupe	3,409	2,511	47,562
2454	sport hardtop cpe	3,278	2,299	166,426
Corvette				
2934	convertible rdstr	2,730	3,465	6,339

Fuel Injection

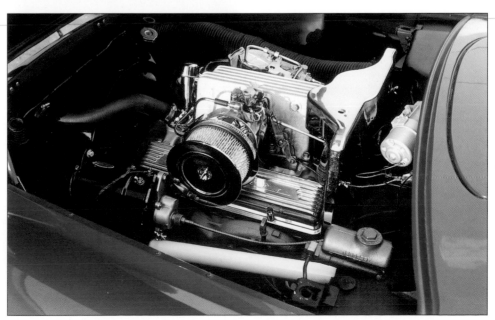

141

1957

▲ Corvette styling was unchanged, but performance lovers were quick to spot those '57s bearing the discreet "Fuel Injection" name script in the front-fender "coves." With one horsepower per cubic inch—just like the ads read—the 'Vette was a near race-ready flyer right off the showroom floor. That helped boost model-year production to 6339.

▶ Completing Corvette's transformation to pure sports car was a new four-speed manual gearbox option for 1957. Supplied by Borg-Warner but engineered by Chevy, it featured close-ratio gearing that combined with the 283-horsepower V-8 for 0-60 mph in a sizzling 5.7 seconds, 0-100 in just 16.8 seconds, and a top speed of 132 mph.

▲ Just so you'll know, here's what the '57 Corvette looks like without bodyside "cove" two-toning. The base price for this monochome silver metallic beauty was $3465, up a sizable $316 from the previous year. Period inflation at least partly explained the increase.

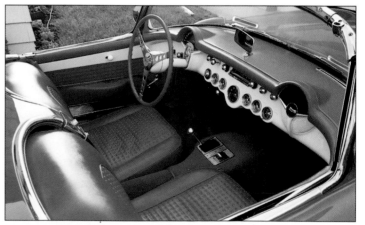

▲ Corvette's '56 redesign brought a more civilized interior that carried into 1957 with few changes. Gauges still marched across the dash—not the best for legibility—with the tachometer still dead-center. The floor shift here controls 1957's new four-speed gearbox.

◄ Conceived in July 1956 with an eye toward the '57 LeMans 24-hour race, the unique Corvette Sebring SS experimental had a super-light magnesium body, advanced tubular space frame, and high-power fuelie V-8. It should have been a world-beater, but it lasted only 23 laps in a warmup run at the April 1957 Sebring 12 Hours in Florida. That would be its only competition appearance, as Chevy was forced to abandoned the SS program in the wake of Detroit's self-imposed "racing ban," announced that same month.

▼ Closer to production Corvettes was the SR-2, built in summer 1956. Like the Sebring SS, it was as much GM show car as serious racing contender. Come '57, the SR-2 acquired headlight covers and other changes. It contested that year's Sebring 12 Hours, as did two near-stock Corvettes running with the factory-optional hardtop. The SR-2 finished a creditable 16th overall, driven by Paul O'Shea and Pete Lovely.

► The SR-2, here getting a pre-race pit check at Sebring '57, was quite dressy for a competition car even in those simpler times. It was, in fact, as much a rolling billboard for Chevrolet as engineering test bed—and a far cry in appearance from modern racers festooned with sponsor decals. Ironically, the SR-2 was upstaged in Florida by its two stock-based teammates, one of which finished 12th overall, the other 15th. The lead 'Vette was driven by Dr. Richard Thompson and ace Gaston Andrey. Thompson, known as the "flying dentist," was well on his way to becoming one of the winningest racers in Corvette history. Ed Cole, who became Chevy general manager in '56, was on hand to applaud Thompson and Andrey after the race.

◄ Chevy began using the "1 USA" logo in 1957 to extol its perennial number-one sales rank—ironic, as archrival Ford finished slightly ahead in model-year production. This ad from the January 19 *Saturday Evening Post* features a Bel Air sport coupe, with a Corvette just behind—a "dream garage" then and now. Though performance was emphasized here, other ads described the more powerful, restyled '57 Chevys as "Sweet, Smooth, and Sassy."

▼ Styling is a big reason why '57 Chevys have long been coveted collector's items, especially top-line models like this Bel Air sport coupe. Though the basic '55 body was facelifted a second time, Chevy designers somehow captured the spirit of the age without undue flash. A "baby Cadillac" look was part of the plan, though, highlighted by Chevy's first fins and a new combination bumper/grille. A switch from 15- to 14-inch wheels contributed to the "lower-longer-wider" look then in vogue. And indeed, overall length went up 2.5 inches, though width and height were little changed.

▲ ► Chevy also redesigned its dashboard for '57 (*above*), with most controls positioned nearer the driver. A 1.5-inch lower cowl improved forward visibility. Bel Airs retained a bright-metal trim panel above a new central glovebox. The four-door Bel Air sport sedan hardtop (*right*) returned with a base price of $2364, up $134 from debut '56. This model wears rubber-capped "bombs" outboard of the grille, as well as accessory inboard bumper guards.

144

▲ The Bel Air convertible started at $2511 in 1957 dollars. Today you'd pay at least 10 times as much for a restored beauty like this. Happily, a good many are still around, in part because Chevy convertible sales set a new record at 47,562 units. Still, that amounted to only 6.8 percent of the 702,220 total Bel Airs built for the model year.

◄ A broad "V" on the hood again identified V-8-powered '57 Chevys like this Bel Air convertible. That year's base V-8 was a lone 265 with 162 hp. The new 283 was available in six versions ranging from 185 to 283 horsepower via two-barrel, four-barrel, and twin-four-barrel carburetor setups, plus the new Ramet fuel injection. The veteran "Blue-Flame Six," rarely seen in ragtops, remained at 140 horsepower.

▲ Chevy built more than 254,000 of its '57 Bel Air four-door sedan, and many still survive despite the relatively low interest in sedans among collectors. Indeed, thousands of these cars have likely been "parted out" for sport coupe, convertible, and Nomad restorations. In its day, this Bel Air was quite a buy, delivering for less than $2400 even when equipped with one of the new, more-potent 283-cubic-inch V-8s.

▲ The Bel Air Nomad looked better than ever in '57, but this would be the last year for the distinctive two-door "hardtop" wagon, as sales fell to a three-year low of 6103. High price was factor: now $2747, up $149 from '56 and still well above the Bel Air convertible. Buyers also preferred the easier entry/exit of four-door wagons. Chevy has since used the Nomad name many times, but on nothing so glamorous as this.

◄ Far more popular with Chevy station wagon customers than the Nomad, the Townsman offered Bel Air ammenities with four-door convenience for six passengers—at a base-price savings of $177 no less. Townsman customers also got more load space in practically every direction as well. (For instance, with the rear seat folded down in a Townsman, the effective load floor to the tailgate was 10.1 inches longer than in a similarly configured Nomad and there were 16 more cubic feet of cargo space.) Regardless of the number of doors, Bel Air wagons featured vinyl coverings on cargo compartment sidewalls and wheelhouses, and chromed steel edging to protect the ribbed linoleum load-floor surface.

1957

▲ A four-door sport sedan hardtop returned for '57 in the midrange Two-Ten line, priced from $2270. Typical of the age, this Dusk Pearl/Imperial Ivory example was photographed with a special lens to make it appear longer, lower, and wider than actual.

▲ Here's the Two-Ten sport sedan you saw on the street (if you saw one at all; production was a fairly modest 16,178). Fan-style side trim was adopted for all Two-Tens soon after production began, replacing the single full-length molding originally shown.

▶ Dusk Pearl/Imperial Ivory two-toning also graces this Two-Ten sport coupe (with a few Bel Air trim touches). Chevy's lower 1957 hood carried twin inset "windsplits" instead of a centrally mounted ornament.

▶Though some rival wagons boasted rolldown tailgate windows for '57, Chevy stayed with its traditional separate liftgate. Buyers were probably confused by another change in wagon availability. This year, Chevy dropped the nine-seat Beauville four-door from the Bel Air line, leaving the Two-Ten Beauville as a companion for the six-passenger Townsman, shown here. The full wagon family included the Bel Air Townsman, Handyman two-doors in the Two-Ten and low-priced One-Fifty series, and the high-style Bel Air Nomad. The Two-Ten Townsman was by far the most popular of the lot, attracting almost 128,000 orders at a base price of $2456. After '57, Chevy grouped wagons into their own series.

▲ Even the cheaper 1957 Chevys weren't short on style, though One-Fiftys like this Handyman wagon certainly benefited from extra-cost dressing like two-toning and whitewall tires. This six-cylinder model appears to be pretty basic, and probably sold at or near its suggested $2307 base price. Exactly 14,740 were built.

◄ The rear fender emblems on this One-Fifty three-passenger utility sedan signify fuelie V-8 power. Though a rare option in this model's 8,300-unit run, it made for great performance in Chevy's lightest passenger car. Even the "mild" 270-horsepower engine would net 0-60 mph in under 10 seconds and a standing quarter-mile of about 17.5 at 80 mph—rapid for what looked like just a "mom and pop" car.

◄ ▲ Detroit industrialist Ruben Allender took advantage of Chevy's '57 facelift to make his El Morocco look even more the "poor man's Cadillac." Starting with a Two-Ten sport coupe, sport sedan, or Bel Air convertible, his follow-up borrowed styling elements from all three '57 Caddy Eldorados, including the Biarritz convertible/Seville hardtop "shark" fin shape and a rear bumper and side trim like those of the new flagship Eldorado Brougham. Again, Chevrolet badging was removed, but structure and mechanicals were left stock, though each car carried a non-Chevy serial number. Still, too few buyers were interested, so the El Morocco disappeared for good after Allender struggled to sell a mere 16 of his '57 models.

147

▲ A new grille and hood emblem marked Chevy's 1957 pickups, which offered their own version of the 265 V-8. This ½-ton 3100 has the optional custom cab trim and exterior chrome package.

▲ Base-trim pickups again came with painted bumpers, grille, and hubcaps, plus a smallish rear window behind the "Flight Ride" cab. A deep-dish "safety" steering wheel was new for the year.

▲ For its third season, the Cameo Carrier added chrome boxside trim defining a secondary color area. But competitors now had high-style trucks of their own, which helped depress Cameo sales to only 2572 for the model year.

▲ A Chevy truck staple since 1935, the roomy Suburban Carryall looked good in '57 trim. Entry/exit through the narrow side doors was a bit tough, but loading up was easy through the buyer's choice of either a liftgate/tailgate or dual center-opening cargo doors.

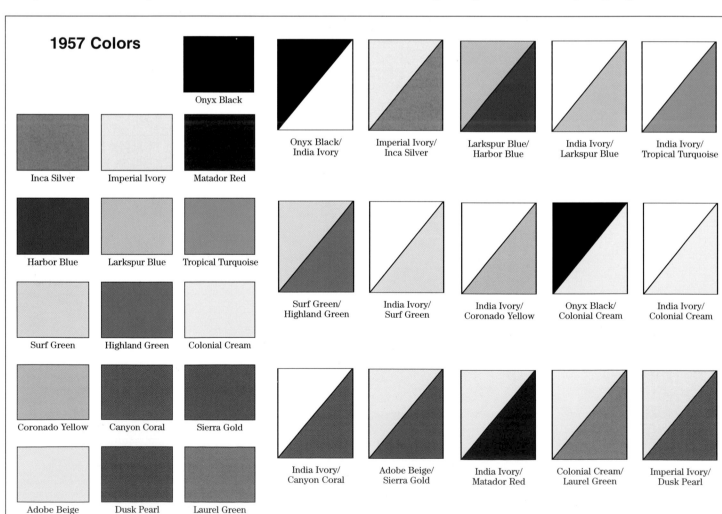

1957 Colors

Onyx Black

Inca Silver

Imperial Ivory

Matador Red

Harbor Blue

Larkspur Blue

Tropical Turquoise

Surf Green

Highland Green

Colonial Cream

Coronado Yellow

Canyon Coral

Sierra Gold

Adobe Beige

Dusk Pearl

Laurel Green

Onyx Black/ India Ivory

Imperial Ivory/ Inca Silver

Larkspur Blue/ Harbor Blue

India Ivory/ Larkspur Blue

India Ivory/ Tropical Turquoise

Surf Green/ Highland Green

India Ivory/ Surf Green

India Ivory/ Coronado Yellow

Onyx Black/ Colonial Cream

India Ivory/ Colonial Cream

India Ivory/ Canyon Coral

Adobe Beige/ Sierra Gold

India Ivory/ Matador Red

Colonial Cream/ Laurel Green

Imperial Ivory/ Dusk Pearl

1958

- Chevy unwraps an "eye opener" with larger, redesigned standard cars headlined by lush new Impala models

- Lower-line series get new names in place of numbers

- New "big-block" 348 V-8 ups passenger-car power choices

- Corvette gets more available power and a dazzling facelift

- Fleetside pickups replace costly Cameo

▲ Chevy moved toward the midprice field with its new 1958 Impala, here fronting that year's newly restyled Corvette. At the top is the Biscayne show car from the '55 GM Motorama; to the far right, the sleek '57 Corvette Sebring SS racer. The Impala's name and a few styling details were taken from a 1956 Motorama special. This "family portrait" graced *Motor Trend* magazine's December 1957 cover. It suggests that Chevy was reaching above its traditional market slot as one of the "Low-Priced Three"—as indeed it was.

◄ ▲ Though it didn't share in Chevy's new big-block V-8, the '58 Corvette did get more small-block power, as the top fuel-injected option went from 283 to 290 horsepower. The 250-horse version returned from '57, along with carbureted engines rated at 230 (standard), 245, and 270 ponies. Seemingly at odds with the 'Vette's recent metamorphosis to European-style sports car was bulky new styling that added 10 inches in length and two inches in width to the basic 1956-57 body. New elements included quad headlamps, then all the rage in Detroit, plus dummy front-fender air scoops, "washboard" hood contouring, and twin chrome strips on the decklid. For all the added glitz, weight was little changed.

▲ A recession hit the U.S. economy just as 1958 models hit showrooms, and Chevrolet suffered like most other Detroit makes. Model-year production slid to just over 1.1 million, down 363,450 units from '57. Even so, Chevy reclaimed its rank as "USA-1," besting archrival Ford by some 154,500 cars. Volume would go even higher for '59.

▲ GM celebrated its 50th anniversary in 1958, and PR types used the occasion to demonstrate pictorially what was then called "the high degree of technical skill that is typical of today's automobile production." That was then; this is now, but the point was made about "men being aided by tools and machines of utmost accuracy and precision."

▲ Chevy's '58 passenger-car styling exchanged the previous year's bumper/grille combination for a somewhat more conventional assembly, though the visual effect was similar. Note the paired parking lamps at the outboard ends of the grille, which neatly echoed the newly adopted quad headlights above.

▲ One of several new nameplates at Chevy in '58, the lush top-line Impala naturally got pride of place in most of that year's ads, including this "slice of life" illustration of a convertible by Austin Briggs. The Corvette taillight in the foreground contrasts with the new "gullwing" rear end used on all standard Chevys.

▲ Technically part of the 1958 Bel Air series but not badged as such, Impala arrived in sport coupe hardtop and convertible models. Prices ranged from $2586 for a six-cylinder coupe to $2841 for a V-8 convertible like this accessorized beauty. All '58 passenger Chevys were longer, lower, wider, and heavier, with a 117.5-inch wheelbase—up 2.5 inches from 1955-57—and a brand-new X-member frame with coil-spring suspension at the rear as well as the front. Ride was smoother, yet handling stability was little affected. "Level Air" suspension was optional, but pricey, trouble-prone, and thus rarely ordered.

◄ ▲ Impala interiors for 1958 boasted colorful all-vinyl upholstery and a racy steering wheel worthy of Corvette. Standard Chevys featured a new-design instrument panel with strip-style horizontal speedometer, which not everyone liked. Round ducts at the panel's far ends signal the installation of optional factory air conditioning; door switches activate power windows.

◄ ▲ A broad hood "V" again denoted a V-8 under '58 Chevy hoods, and most Impalas, like this sport coupe, were so equipped. Designed to meet the needs of larger, more accessory-laden cars, the new 348-cubic-inch option was a good match for the heavier '58 models. The regular four-barrel "Turbo-Thrust" made 250 horsepower, while the "Super Turbo-Thrust" delivered 280 horses with triple two-barrel carbs or 315 with high-compression heads and solid lifters. Impala's '58 sales were good, all things considered; about 125,000 hardtops and 56,000 convertibles.

▲ The Bel Air two-door sedan started at $2386 with six-cylinder engine, now up to 145 horsepower, or $2493 with the base two-barrel 283 V-8, rated at 185 horsepower.

▲ Respective Bel Air four-door hardtop six/V-8 prices were $2511 and $2618. The series also included a two door sport coupe hardtop that sold for just $64 less.

▲ The mainstay Bel Air four-door sedan listed at $2440/$2547 in base six/V-8 form for '58. Bel Air side trim was similar to, but not identical with, that of the new Impalas.

◄ Chevy's mid-priced Two-Ten series was renamed Biscayne for '58. This is the two-door sedan, priced at $2236 with six or $2343 with V-8.

▶ The the only other Biscayne was the four-door sedan, listed at $2290/$2397 with six/V-8. Besides the trio of big new 348s, Chevy's '58 V-8 options included 283 small-blocks with 230, 250, and 290 horsepower.

▲ The most affordable Chevys were also renamed for '58, as Delray replaced the One-Fifty moniker. The series included this regular two-door sedan, priced at $2101/$2208 with six/V-8, as well as a three-passenger utility version with extra cargo room for $2013/$2120.

▲ Comparing this Delray two-door sedan to the one to the left suggests why white-wall tires were so popular for so many years. They really dressed up a "plain Jane" car for relatively little money, though keeping them clean was a bit of a chore.

▲ Taking a tip from street-racing miscreants, some law-enforcement agencies in the Fifties paired a manufacturer's lightest two-door model with special high-power "police" V-8s. Here's how the formula was applied to a '58 Delray for highway patrol duty in Michigan.

▲ The high-style two-door Nomad was dropped for '58, but this conventional four-door Nomad led a new separate wagon line. Price was $2728/$2835 with six/V-8.

▲ A step below the Nomad were six- and nine-seat Brookwoods sporting Biscayne-level equipment and prices as low as $2571. Total '58 wagon output topped 187,000 cars.

▲ Chevy's lone two-door wagon for '58 went from being a Handyman to a Yeoman. It and a six-passenger four-door companion were equipped like Delrays.

▲ Chevy's 1958 sedan delivery was decked out like a member of the Delray series. It started at $2123 and drew 4003 orders.

▶ Chevy trucks also got new names for '58—Apache for light-duty models—and quad headlamps. The Cameo Carrier, seen here, was phased out early in the year.

Model Breakdown

Delray—178,000* built		Wght	Price	Prod
1121	utility sedan 2d, I-6	3,351	2,013	—
1141	sedan 2d, I-6	3,396	2,101	—
1149	sedan 4d, I-6	3,439	2,155	—
1221	utility sedan 2d, V-8	3,156	2,120	—
1241	sedan 2d, V-8	3,399	2,208	—
1249	sedan 4d, V-8	3,442	2,262	—
Biscayne—176,200* built				
1541	sedan 2d, I-6	3,404	2,236	—
1549	sedan 4d, I-6	3,447	2,290	—
1641	sedan 2d, V-8	3,407	2,343	—
1649	sedan 4d, V-8	3,450	2,397	—
Bel Air—592,000* built				
1731	sport hardtop cpe, I-6	3,455	2,447	—
1739	sport hardtop sdn, I-6	3,511	2,511	—
1741	sedan 2d, I-6	3,424	2,386	—
1747	Impala htp cpe, I-6	3,458	2,586	—
1749	sedan 4d, I-6	3,467	2,440	—
1767	Impala conv cpe, I-6	3,522	2,734	—
1831	sport hardtop cpe, V-8	3,458	2,554	—
1839	sport hardtop sdn, V-8	3,514	2,618	—
1841	sedan 2d, V-8	3,427	2,493	—
1847	Impala htp cpe, V-8	3,459	2,693	—
1849	sedan 4d, V-8	3,470	2,547	—
1867	Impala conv cpe, V-8	3,523	2,841	—
Station Wagon—187,063				
1191	Yeoman 2d, I-6	3,693	2,413	—
1193	Yeoman 4d, I-6	3,740	2,467	—
1291	Yeoman 2d, V-8	3,696	2,520	—
1293	Yeoman 4d, V-8	3,743	2,574	—
1593	Brookwood 4d, 6P, I-6	3,748	2,571	—
1594	Brookwood 4d, 9P, I-6	3,837	2,678	—
1693	Brookwood 4d, 6P, V-8	3,751	2,678	—
1694	Brookwood 4d, 9P, V-8	3,839	2,785	—
1793	Nomad 4d, I-6	3,768	2,728	—
1893	Nomad 4d, V-8	3,771	2,835	—
Corvette				
867	convertible roadster	2,793	3,631	9,168
*To nearest 100.				

▲ Chevy offered two cargo-box types for '58 pickups: traditional "Stepside," shown here, and new flush-fender "Fleetside" with a wider bed than that of the Cameo Carrier.

◀ Besides light-duty Apaches, Chevy's 1958 truck fleet included medium-duty Viking models and heavy-duty Spartans, the last represented here by a low-cab-forward (LCF) tractor. Chevy's 348 V-8 was designed as much for brutes like this as it was for use in the growing passenger cars.

1959

- Full-size Chevys are "All New, All Over Again!"

- Impala adds models, expands to full series

- Corvette cleans up its act and piles up more racing victories

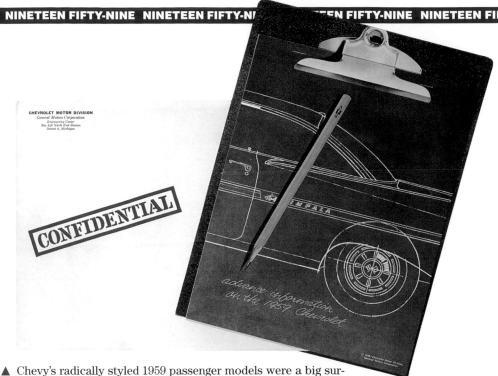

▲ Chevy's radically styled 1959 passenger models were a big surprise, rendering the all-new '58s completely obsolete. The "stealthy" theme of the 1959 press kit only hinted at the wild changes in store.

▲ Bill Mitchell (shown) replaced Harley Earl as GM design chief in 1958. The following year, he put a new body on a test chassis rescued from the aborted Sebring SS project. The resulting Stingray was later raced.

▶ Corvette got a welcome visual cleanup for '59, as the hood was smoothed out and rear-deck trim strips left off. There were a number of convenience and comfort modifications made to the interior as well.

▶ Mighty General Motors could afford to do most anything in the Fifties, even experiment with single-seat racing cars. This CERV I was built in 1959 with an eye to hillclimb and Indianapolis 500 competition the following year. The initials stood for "Chevrolet Engineering Research Vehicle." Corvette chief engineer Zora Arkus-Duntov supervised the project, which explored a number of ideas for possible use on future GM showroom models, including four-wheel independent suspension and a rear-engine/transaxle. A Corvette small-block V-8 modified to produce 353 horsepower sat behind the driver, a layout that would soon dominate Formula I and Indy-car design.

153

▲ Chevy's new 1959 passenger cars like this Impala sport coupe generated big controversy with their "batwing" fins, "cat's eye" taillights, and a rear deck "big enough to land a Piper Cub," as one journalist wrote.

▲ Created amid a "crash program" response to Chrysler Corporation's 1957 cars, the wild new '59 Chevys rode a 119-inch wheelbase and grew approximately two inches longer and wider, and 150 pounds heavier than the '58s. Here, the $2717 V-8 Impala sport coupe.

▲ Impala grew into a full series for 1959, including this four-door sport sedan hardtop. Engines were much the same as in '58, ranging from the stalwart 235.5-cubic-inch six to 283- and 348-cube V-8s. This model priced at $2664/$2782 with six/base V-8.

▲ Chevy trunks were bigger than ever for '59 at 32 cubic feet, but rather tough to reach.

▲ ▶ Not counting wagons, the ragtop Impala was Chevy's costliest '59 offering, beginning at $2967 with V-8 power. Production of all Impala convertibles came to 72,765. Chevy's bold new face dropped the headlights seven inches from '58 to the minimum height allowable. Interiors gained nearly five inches in width, plus a bulkier new-design dashboard. A four-speed transmission with floor shift was optional for any '59 V-8 Chevy.

Model Breakdown

		Wght	Price	Prod
Biscayne—311,800* built				
1111	sedan 2d, I-6	3,535	2,247	—
1119	sedan 4d, I-6	3,605	2,301	—
1121	utility sedan 2d, I-6	3,480	2,160	—
1211	sedan 2d, V-8	3,530	2,365	—
1219	sedan 4d, V-8	3,600	2,419	—
1221	utility sedan 2d, V-8	3,490	2,278	—
Bel Air—447,100* built				
1511	sedan 2d, I-6	3,515	2,386	—
1519	sedan 4d, I-6	3,600	2,440	—
1539	sport hardtop sdn, I-6	3,660	2,556	—
1611	sedan 2d, V-8	3,510	2,504	—
1619	sedan 4d, V-8	3,615	2,558	—
1639	sport hardtop sdn, V-8	3,630	2,674	—
Impala—473,000* built				
1719	sedan 4d, I-6	3,625	2,592	—
1737	sport hardtop cpe, I-6	3,570	2,599	—
1739	sport hardtop sdn, I-6	3,665	2,664	—
1767	convertible coupe, I-6	3,660	2,849	—
1819	sedan 4d, V-8	3,620	2,710	—
1837	sport hardtop cpe, V-8	3,580	2,717	—
1839	sport hardtop sdn, V-8	3,670	2,782	—
1867	convertible coupe, V-8	3,650	2,967	—
Station Wagon—209,400* built				
1115	Brookwood 2d, I-6	3,870	2,571	—
1135	Brookwood 4d, I-6	3,955	2,638	—
1215	Brookwood 2d, V-8	3,860	2,689	—
1235	Brookwood 4d, V-8	3,955	2,756	—
1535	Parkwood 4d, I-6	3,965	2,749	—
1545	Kingswood 4d, 9P, I-6	4,020	2,852	—
1635	Parkwood 4d, V-8	3,970	2,867	—
1645	Kingswood 4d, 9P, V-8	4,015	2,970	—
1735	Nomad 4d, I-6	3,980	2,891	—
1835	Nomad 4d, V-8	3,975	3,009	—
Corvette				
869	convertible roadster	2,840	3,875	9,670
To nearest 100.				

▲ With Impala ascending to Chevy's top rung, Bel Air became the midrange series for '59. Choices included a four-door sedan and hard-top sport sedan, plus this two-door sedan, but no sport coupe or convertible. Bel Air sales were about 447,100 for the model year.

▲ Chevrolet's 1959 series realignment left Biscayne to displace Delray as the bottom-end group. It offered this two-door sedan starting at $2247, a $2301 four-door, and a $2160 utility two-door with cargo space in place of a back seat. Series sales were around 311,000.

▲ This Biscayne four-door sedan shows how Chevy's much wider '59 bodies left wheels well inboard, creating a look that one stylist termed "a football player in ballet slippers." Sister division Pontiac avoided this with its new "Wide Track" chassis.

▲ As in 1957, Chevy and Ford completed the '59 production race in a photo finish. Chevy came out ahead in model-year output with 1.48 million versus 1.39 million, but Ford was victor in calendar-year volume at 1.53 million versus 1.43 million.

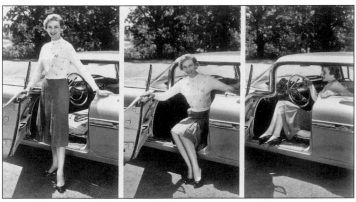

▲ All 1959 GM cars sported a lot more glass, but awkwardly angled windshield pillars still hindered graceful entry/exit. Answering the apparent problems some women were having with this, Chevy PR issued these photos illustrating a recommended technique.

▲ Chevy built some 209,400 of its '59 wagons. This midrange six-passenger Parkwood four-door started at $2749. A nine-seat version called Kingswood sold for $2852 and up.

▲ No, it's not a bowling alley, but the spacious cargo deck of Chevy's top-line 1959 Nomad wagon. Trimmed and equipped to Impala level, the six-seat four-door started at $2891.

▲ Brookwoods replaced Yeoman models as Chevy's most affordable wagons for '59. This two-door started at $2571, $67 below its four-door companion.

▲ This nine-passenger Kingswood wagon has been lightly modified as a fill-in fire chief's car or ambulance. It's certainly spacious enough for either task. This worm's-eye view emphasizes the newly "kinked" A-pillars framing Chevy's much larger 1959 windshield, as well as the sweep of the horizontal tailfins. All wagons adopted a one-piece tailgate.

155

▼ ▲ Chevy pickups saw little change for 1959, but flush-sided Fleetside models (*below*) got greater advertising emphasis to the benefit of sales. Even so, many buyers still resisted the new style, preferring the more "serious," tried-and-true Stepside (*above*).

▲ Answering Ford's 1957-58 Ranchero, Chevrolet's new '59 El Camino was basically a two-door wagon with a pickup box instead of an enclosed cargo deck. Billed as "combining ultra style with utility," it effectively replaced the slow-selling truck-based Cameo Carrier; 22,246 were built.

◄ A familiar sight all across America, Chevy's Step-Van employed the division's "forward control" truck chassis to provide maximum cargo room within 1959 wheelbases of 104, 125, and 137 inches. All had a nominal rated payload of ¾-ton.

- **Chevy thinks small with the import-fighting, rear-engine Corvair compact**

- **Standard Chevys go conservative with a "second-thoughts" facelift**

- **Corvette model-year production breaks the 10,000-unit barrier for the first time**

- **Chevy builds more than 1.6 million cars**

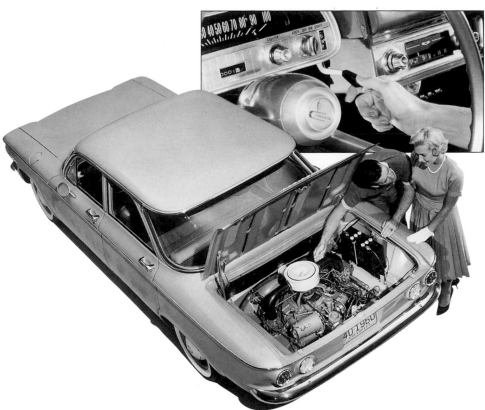

▲ Detroit's Big Three answered growing public interest in economy imports by introducing smaller, all-new "compact" cars for 1960. Chevy's Corvair was the most radical and "European" in engineering. The engine was a Volkswagen-like air-cooled unit with horizontally opposed cylinders mounted at the rear, but there were six cylinders, not four, giving 140 cubic inches, good for 80 horsepower standard or 95 optional. Transmissions were three-speed manual or a specialized two-speed Powerglide automatic, operated from a dash-mounted selector (*top*).

▲ ▶ Corvair bowed with coupe and four-door sedan body styles in plain 500 and slightly ritzier 700 trim. A full-perimeter chrome strip identified 700s like this sedan, which carried a starting price of $2103. All models rode a 108-inch wheelbase and measured 180 inches long. That was big by European standards, but Corvair sedans looked remarkably like certain small German NSUs. Also setting the car apart from its American rivals was its four-wheel independent suspension—later a point of controversy—with rear swing axles and torsion bars instead of coil springs. Ads said Corvair's engine was "in the rear where an engine belongs." Edward N. Cole masterminded the overall engineering effort.

157

▲ Chevy charged $2049 for this 1960 Corvair 700 club coupe, $1984 for the 500 version. Model-year sales totaled just over 250,000, which looked good except against Ford's conventional new Falcon, which scored a smashing 435,000 that same season.

▲ Another look at the 1960 Corvair 700 coupe, which became even sportier when Chevy added vinyl bucket seats and other custom trim to create the 900 Monza as a late-season addition. It attracted 11,926 sales to the 700 coupe's 36,562, but would do far better in later years.

▲ Chevy's largest 1960 cars—which writers began calling "standard" or "full-size"— were toned down outside from '59, but were no less roomy inside. No less flashy, either, as this Impala convertible shows.

▲ Though not immediately evident, Chevrolet changed most every body panel on its 1960 standard cars save the roof. It seemed a curious change of heart after the wild '59s, but General Motors designers later admitted that they knew they'd gone too far with those, hence the more conservative approach for 1960. The new look well suited the glamorous Impala convertible, which cost $2954 with base V-8 and garnered 79,903 total sales.

▲ Chevy's 1960 big-car styling softened the '59 rear-end look with reshaped and separated "bat wing" tailfins, plus orthodox round tail-lamps. Impalas like this sport coupe returned to 1958's triple-light motif, with a backup lamp splitting pairs of stop/taillights on each side. This Impala sold new for $2597 in six-cylinder form, $2704 with base V-8. Its rear window remained immense.

▲ Chevy began emphasizing "jet smooth-ness" with its 1960 standards, evident in the new aircraft-inspired side trim on Impalas like this four-door sport sedan hardtop. A unique roofline with a slight lip above a huge wraparound rear window was carried over from '59. Starting prices were $2597 with six, $2769 with V-8. Powerglide and Turboglide automatics remained optional.

▲ Full-size 1960 Chevy four-door sedans retained their clean "six-light" roofline from 1959; the triangular rear-quarter windows were fixed. Accessory fender skirts were a bit unusual for a sedan, but look just fine on this Impala, which priced at $2590/$2697 with six/V-8. Big Chevys dropped fuel injection for 1960, but seven carbureted V-8s were available with up to 335 horsepower.

▲ Presidential hopeful John F. Kennedy used this Impala convertible to make a 1960 campaign stop in Des Plaines, Illinois, near Chicago. The new Ford police car just behind seems to be giving him a push.

▲ Nomad remained Chevy's most luxurious wagon for 1960. It was again offered only as a six-passenger four-door with Impala-level trim and equipment. Base price was up to $2889/$2996 with six/V-8.

▲ Chevy's full-size two-door sedans again differed from pillarless sport coupes in having a smaller rear window, yet still looked sporty. Suggested price for this 1960 Bel Air was $2384 with six, $2491 with base 283-cube V-8.

▲ Not counting wagons, Bel Air was again overshadowed by Impala as Chevy's best-seller for 1960. Still, this Bel Air four-door sedan was quite popular starting at $2438. Two-tone paint, with the contrast color on the roof and rear cove, cost extra.

▲ After a year's hiatus, the two-door sport coupe hardtop returned to the midrange Bel Air lineup for 1960. Attractively priced at $2489 with six and $2596 with base V-8, it's shown in another of those special advertising photos shot to exaggerate lowness and length.

▲ Companion to the sport coupe was this '60 Bel Air sport sedan four-door hardtop, with the flat roof and wide rear window style used by all GM makes. It cost $2554 with six, $2661 with base V-8. Chevy continued its practice of listing sixes and V-8s as separate models.

▲ Even low-line 1960 Biscaynes got the "jet smooth" treatment, though the recontoured rear fenders bore a smaller chrome "plane." This six-cylinder two-door sedan sold for $2262 in six-passenger form, $2175 as a stripped three-seat utility model.

▲ Chevy again offered two- and four-door Brookwood wagons, trimmed to Biscayne level, but the two-door was making its last stand, thanks to decling demand. (Fewer than 15,000 were made for 1960.) A six-passenger car, it sold new for as little as $2586.

◄ General Motors recycled some of its Fifties and Sixties show cars to test new thinking in design and features. This wild-looking creation is XP-700 (XP for "experimental project") as the public saw it in 1960. It was originally built in 1958 as a roadster for GM styling chief Bill Mitchell. For its second incarnation, the red/silver paint scheme was changed to silver/white, the tail extended, and a clear "double-bubble" top applied. A year on, Mitchell used XP-700 as the starting point for his first experimental "Shark," a futuristic Corvette that accurately previewed later production models.

159

▲ The 1960 Corvette looked identical to the '59, but model-year volume set a record at 10,261, thus convincing GM brass to give the sports car a permanent place in the Chevy line. Engines were unchanged (though special aluminum heads were available for fuel-injected mills), but the suspension gained a rear sway bar and other revisions. A 'Vette finished eighth in this year's grueling LeMans 24 Hours. Base price actually declined—by three dollars.

Engine Availability

Engines	bore × stroke	bhp	availability
I-6, 235.5	3.56 × 3.94	135	S-six
V-8, 283.0	3.88 × 3.00	170	S-V-8
V-8, 283.0	3.88 × 3.00	230	O-all
V-8, 348.0	4.13 × 3.25	250-335	O-all
Corvair			
flat 6, 140.0	3.38 × 2.60	80	S-all
flat 6, 140.0	3.38 × 2.60	95	O-all
Corvette			
V-8, 283.0	3.88 × 3.00	230	S-all
V-8, 283.0	3.88 × 3.00	245/270	O-all
V-8, 283.0	3.88 × 3.00	275/315	O-all (FI)

▲ The end of the two-door Brookwood after 1960 also meant the end for the sedan delivery, priced at $2468 in this final year, when just 3034 were produced. However, Chevy would offer new products for the light-duty commercial user.

▲ One automotive journalist appraised the El Camino as "too handsome for hauling and too posh for pulling." Base-priced at $2355, the 14,163 '60s were the last full-size El Caminos, though Chevy's car/pickup would return as one of 1964's new intermediate Chevelles.

▲ Chevy's 1960 trucks were fully redesigned, with Fleetside pickups increasingly popular. Cabs were lower, roomier, more durable, and arguably more contemporary in appearance, though the double nostrils above the grille looked a throwback to '59 car styling.

▲ Americans wouldn't go mad for four-wheel-drive trucks until the Nineties, but those who needed one in 1960 found plenty to like in Chevy's K-Series line. It included this Fleetside pickup, Stepside models, and a two-door Suburban Carryall wagon.

▶ Medium-duty Chevy trucks were still called Viking for 1960, but shared in the new styling and improved cab comfort accorded light-duty Apache models. This brawny stake-body rig rides the Series 50 chassis with 157-inch wheelbase and stout gross vehicle weight ratings of up to 16,000 pounds. A "Low-Cab-Forward" style was available in addition to the conventional cab.

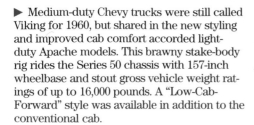

Model Breakdown

		Wght	Price	Prod
Biscayne—287,662 built				
1111	sedan 2d, I-6	3,485	2,262	—
1119	sedan 4d, I-6	3,555	2,316	—
1121	utility sedan 2d, I-6	3,455	2,175	—
1211	sedan 2d, V-8	3,500	2,369	—
1219	sedan 4d, V-8	3,570	2,423	—
1221	utility sedan 2d, V-8	3,470	2,282	—
Biscayne Fleetmaster—prod incl. with Biscayne				
1311	sedan 2d, I-6	3,480	2,230	—
1319	sedan 4d, I-6	3,545	2,284	—
1411	sedan 2d, V-8	3,495	2,337	—
1419	sedan 4d, V-8	3,560	2,391	—
Bel Air—381,517 built				
1511	sedan 2d, I-6	3,490	2,384	—
1519	sedan 4d, I-6	3,565	2,438	—
1537	sport hardtop cpe, I-6	3,515	2,489	—
1539	sport hardtop sdn, I-6	3,605	2,554	—
1611	sedan 2d, V-8	3,505	2,491	—
1619	sedan 4d, V-8	3,500	2,545	—
1637	sport hardtop cpe, V-8	3,530	2,596	—
1639	sport hardtop sdn, V-8	3,620	2,661	—
Impala—511,925 built				
1719	sedan 4d, I-6	3,575	2,590	—
1737	Sport hardtop cpe, I-6	3,530	2,597	—
1739	Sport hardtop sdn, I-6	3,625	2,662	—
1767	convertible cpe, I-6	3,625	2,847	—
1819	sedan 4d, V-8	3,580	2,697	—
1837	Sport hardtop cpe, V-8	3,540	2,704	—
1839	Sport hardtop sdn, V-8	3,625	2,769	—
1867	convertible cpe, V-8	3,635	2,954	—
Station Wagon—212,729 built				
1115	Brookwood 2d, I-6	3,845	2,586	—
1135	Brookwood 4d, I-6	3,935	2,653	—
1215	Brookwood 2d, V-8	3,855	2,693	—
1235	Brookwood 4d, V-8	3,935	2,760	—
1535	Parkwood 4d, I-6	3,945	2,747	—
1545	Kingswood 4d, 9P, I-6	3,990	2,850	—
1635	Parkwood 4d, V-8	3,950	2,854	—
1645	Kingswood 4d, 9P, V-8	4,000	2,957	—
1735	Nomad 4d, I-6	3,955	2,889	—
1835	Nomad 4d, V-8	3,960	2,996	—
Corvair 500				
0527	coupe	2,270	1,984	14,628
0569	sedan 4d	2,305	2,038	47,683
Corvair 700				
0727	coupe	2,290	2,049	36,562
0769	sedan 4d	2,315	2,103	139,208
Corvair 900 Monza				
0927	coupe	2,280	2,238	11,926
Corvette				
0867	convertible roadster	2,840	3,872	10,261

1961

- **Full-size cars totally redesigned**

- **Corvette receives a "tail lift"**

- **Super Sport option for Impalas bows at midyear**

- **"Real fine" 409-cubic-inch V-8 debuts**

- **Corvair adds wagon and truck models**

▲ Along with their corporate sisters, Chevy's 1961 "standards" were the first General Motors cars to bear the full imprint of corporate design chief Bill Mitchell. The result, as this Impala sport sedan shows, was a cleaner, more coherent big Chevy that was 1.5 inches shorter, yet looked much trimmer despite an unchanged 119-inch wheelbase. This model started at $2769 with base 283 V-8, or $107 more than when equipped with the veteran 235.5 six-cylinder engine.

▲ Standard Chevys were newly "finless" for '61. Top-line Impalas, like the convertible, retained a three-lamp motif at the rear; lesser models had two-light ensembles. "Gullwing" back-panel sculpturing faintly recalled 1959. The ragtop Impala saw production of some 64,624 for 1961, the vast majority equipped with one of eight available V-8s, ranging from the base 170-horsepower 283 small-block up to the thumping new 360-horse 409 big-block.

▲ Chevy's '61 big-car styling struck another blow for convenience in new sickle-shaped windshield A-pillars that didn't impede entry/exit like the old "dogleg" design. Glass was still plentiful, though, so visibility was great. This Bel Air two-door sedan listed at $2491 with base V-8.

▲ Another vestige of 1959-60 styling was seen on '61 pillared sedans, which took over the overhanging rear roof and big wrapped window from previous sport sedan hardtops. This four-door Bel Air listed at $2545 with base V-8. All big '61 Chevys featured a more convenient bumper-height trunk opening.

▲ Both full-size sport coupe hardtops got a new roofline with the '61 redesign. Racers were quick to note its good high-speed aerodynamics. With that and less weight than the Impala sport coupe, this Bel Air version became the preferred choice among Chevy-loyalist oval-track and drag racers in 1961.

▲ As in recent years, full-size Chevy wagons had their own names for 1961, though still outfitted in parallel with the three nonwagon series. The Impala-level four-door Nomad remained top of the line, but a nine-passenger version joined the six-seat model this year. Nomad prices started at $2996 with base V-8.

1961

▲ ▶ Arriving in January 1961, the "Turbo-Fire" 409-cubic-inch V-8 (*right*) was basically a larger, stronger 348 (*above*) intended to make Chevy a power in stock-car and drag racing, even though the division still didn't officially compete in '61. The street engine bowed with four-barrel carburetor and 360 horses, but was capable of much more. As Chevy was still aiding racers with "back-door" heavy-duty parts, the 409 became the overnight dragstrip king in '61, copping the year's NHRA Stock Eliminator crown. Only 142 409s were built for the model year, and most were race-tuned. As a regular option, the burly new mill cost a hefty $425.

◀ ▼ Appearing at about the same time as the 409 was the Super Sport package. Though available for any Impala in '61, it's not likely that it came on anything but a convertible or sport coupe (shown). The kit contained spinner wheel covers, narrow-band whitewall tires (which this car lacks), tachometer, a passenger "grab bar" on the padded dashboard, and "SS" badges. Metallic brake linings and heftier shocks were also included in the $54 price, as were power steering and brakes. Factory engine choices were the 409 and three hottest 348s. The SS found just 453 takers for '61.

◄ ▲ Corvette received a "taillift" for '61, its first major styling change since 1958. Also reflecting Bill Mitchell's influence, the new treatment was patterned on the "ducktail" of his experimental Stingray racer and incorporated four round taillights, destined to become a 'Vette hallmark. Up front, Mitchell had the familiar grille "teeth" replaced by simple mesh; he also shuffled emblems and other minor trim. Additional refinements included standard sunvisors for the first time, plus a narrower transmission tunnel and a wider choice of axle ratios. Engines were unchanged, but a 315-horsepower "fuelie" with four-speed manual shift could hit 60 mph in 5.5 seconds and top 130 mph. Base price went to $3934, which may explain why sales rose only fractionally to 10,939, though that was still a second consecutive Corvette record.

▲ Though introduced as an economy car, Chevy's compact Corvair increasingly sold as an affordable, practical sports car after the bucket-seat Monza debuted. Quick to spot the trend, GM Styling created this racy Sebring Spyder coupe for 1961 auto shows to further enhance the Corvair's growing reputation as a "driver's car."

▲ Among regular '61 Corvairs were two new Lakewood wagons, which had been planned as part of the original design effort. This is the fancier 700 version, which started at $2331, versus $2266 for the 500 Lakewood. Corvair wagon volume totaled 26,042 for the model year, with all but 5591 being 700s.

1961

▲ Showing marked Volkswagen influence were 1961's three new "Corvair 95" truck models: this "Ramp-Side" pickup, plus a "Corvan" panel and a passenger Greenbrier van.

▲ Chevy trucks saw little change for '61, but buyers were discovering the slicker looks and extra carrying capacity of Fleetside pickups like this long-wheelbase, ½-ton Apache 10.

▲ Despite the Fleetside's growing popularity, many Chevy pickup buyers in 1961 still preferred a Stepside like this Apache 10 on the shorter 115-inch wheelbase for "real work."

Engine Availability

Engines	bore × stroke	bhp	availability
I-6, 235.5	3.56 × 3.94	135	S-six
V-8, 283.0	3.88 × 3.00	170	S-V-8
V-8, 283.0	3.88 × 3.00	230	O-all
V-8, 348.0	4.13 × 3.25	250-350	O-all
V-8, 409.0	4.31 × 3.50	360	O-Impala SS
Corvair			
flat 6, 145.0	3.44 × 2.60	80	S-all
flat 6, 145.0	3.44 × 2.60	98	O-all
Corvette			
V-8, 283.0	3.88 × 3.00	230	S-all
V-8, 283.0	3.88 × 3.00	245/270	O-all
V-8, 283.0	3.88 × 3.00	275/315	O-all (FI)

Model Breakdown

		Wght	Price	Prod
Biscayne—201,000* built				
1111	sedan 2d, I-6	3,415	2,262	—
1121	utility sedan 2d, I-6	3,390	2,175	—
1169	sedan 4d, I-6	3,500	2,316	—
1211	sedan 2d, V-8	3,425	2,369	—
1221	utility sedan 2d, V-8	3,395	2,282	—
1269	sedan 4d, V-8	3,505	2,423	—
Biscayne Fleetmaster—3,000* built				
1311	sedan 2d, I-6	3,410	2,230	—
1369	sedan 4d, I-6	3,495	2,284	—
1411	sedan 2d, V-8	3,415	2,337	—
1469	sedan 4d, V-8	3,500	2,391	—
Bel Air—330,000* built				
1511	sedan 2d, I-6	3,430	2,384	—
1537	sport hardtop cpe, I-6	3,475	2,489	—
1539	sport hardtop sdn, I-6	3,550	2,554	—
1569	sedan 4d, I-6	3,515	2,438	—
1611	sedan 2d, V-8	3,435	2,491	—
1637	sport htp cpe, V-8	3,480	2,596	—
1639	sport htp sdn, V-8	3,555	2,661	—
1669	sedan 4d, V-8	3,520	2,545	—
Impala—491,000* built				
1711	sedan 2d, I-6	3,445	2,536	—
1737	sport hardtop cpe, I-6	3,485	2,597	—
1739	sport hardtop sdn, I-6	3,575	2,662	—
1767	convertible cpe, I-6	3,605	2,847	—
1769	sedan 4d, I-6	3,530	2,590	—
1811	sedan 2d, V-8	3,440	2,643	—
1837	sport htp cpe, V-8	3,480	2,704	—
1839	sport htp sdn, V-8	3,570	2,769	—
1867	convertible cpe, V-8	3,600	2,954	—
1869	sedan 4d, V-8	3,525	2,697	—
Station Wagon—168,900* built				
1135	Brookwood 4d, I-6	3,850	2,653	—
1145	Brookwd 4d, 9P, I-6	3,900	2,756	—
1235	Brookwood 4d, V-8	3,845	2,760	—
1245	Brookwd 4d, 9P, V-8	3,895	2,864	—
1535	Parkwood 4d, I-6	3,865	2,747	—
1545	Parkwood 4d, 9P, I-6	3,910	2,850	—
1635	Parkwood 4d, V-8	3,860	2,854	—
1645	Parkwood 4d, 9P, V-8	3,905	2,957	—
1735	Nomad 4d, I-6	3,885	2,889	—
1745	Nomad 4d, 9P, I-6	3,935	2,992	—
1835	Nomad 4d, V-8	3,880	2,996	—
1845	Nomad 4d, 9P, V-8	3,930	3,099	—
Corvair 500				
0527	coupe	2,320	1,920	16,857
0535	Lakewood wagon 4d	2,530	2,266	5,591
0569	sedan 4d	2,355	1,974	18,752
Corvair 700				
0707	coupe	2,350	1,985	24,786
0735	Lakewood wagon 4d	2,555	2,331	20,451
0769	sedan 4d	2,380	2,039	51,948
Corvair 900 Monza				
0927	coupe	2,395	2,201	109,945
0969	sedan 4d	2,420	2,201	33,745
Corvette				
0867	convertible roadster	2,905	3,934	10,939

*To nearest 100.

1962

- Full-size Chevys get refined styling

- Potent 327 V-8 bows; 348 engine dropped

- Compact Chevy II introduced

- New Corvair Spyder offers turbo power

▲ Taking over for Corvair as Chevy's mainstream compact, the 1962 Chevy II was as simple and conventional as its targeted rival, the successful Ford Falcon. Topping the new line was this snazzy Nova 400 convertible, which saw 23,741 copies.

Luxury and low price...beautifully blended

Chevy II Nova
CHEVROLET

▲ Unadorned bodysides marked Chevy II's most affordable 100-series models, which included this two-door sedan, plus a four-door sedan and wagon. All were available with a standard four-cylinder engine or a related 194-cubic-inch inline six with 120 horsepower.

▲ Another *Saturday Evening Post* ad promotes the new "... frisky, family-sized Chevy II" with a picture of the new compact line's only hardtop, the Nova 400 Sport Coupe, of which 59,586 were built for 1962.

▲ The Chevy II way outsold Corvair in debut '62, but even with 327,000 units, it couldn't beat Ford's still-popular Falcon. Here, the midline 300-series two-door sedan, priced from $2084.

▲ Standard for all Chevy IIs except Nova 400s was a simple but sturdy new inline four-cylinder engine, the first from Chevy since 1928. Efficient short-stroke design helped it deliver 90 horsepower and great fuel economy. Like the Chevy II six, it teamed with either "three-on-the-tree" manual shift or a new lightweight version of Chevy's veteran Powerglide automatic transmission.

▲ Chevy IIs were designed to sell on low price with their orthodox front-engine/rear-drive layout, simple leaf-spring rear suspension, and careful cost-cutting throughout. The basic 100-series models went even further with serviceable, but very plain, interior furnishing like this. Even so, Chevy II got off to a great start saleswise.

165

▲ New outer sheetmetal gave full-size '62 Chevys a more "important" look, one now much favored by collectors. Here, one of that year's Impala convertibles equipped with the SS package. Super Sport goodies could now be had with any engine, even the six.

▲ A literal new wrinkle showed up on the 1962 Impala sport coupe: a ribbed rear roofline and smaller back window to mimic the look of a cloth convertible top. This non-SS example started at $2776 with base V-8, which remained a 170-horsepower 283 job.

▲ This four-door sedan is one of the 365,500 Bel Airs built for '62. That compares with nearly 705,000 Impalas and some 166,000 low-line Biscaynes. Base price for this model was $2510 with standard 235.5-cube six, still hanging on with 135 horsepower. As part of its big-car facelift, Chevy shaved the rear roof lip from all pillared sedans.

▲ Big-Chevy wagons lost their separate model names for '62, but remained four-doors available with six- or nine-passenger seating. This Bel Air started at $2819 with standard six.

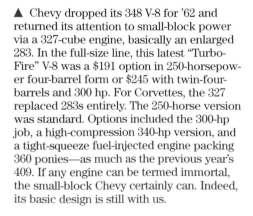

▲ Chevy dropped its 348 V-8 for '62 and returned its attention to small-block power via a 327-cube engine, basically an enlarged 283. In the full-size line, this latest "Turbo-Fire" V-8 was a $191 option in 250-horsepower four-barrel form or $245 with twin-four-barrels and 300 hp. For Corvettes, the 327 replaced 283s entirely. The 250-horse version was standard. Options included the 300-hp job, a high-compression 340-hp version, and a tight-squeeze fuel-injected engine packing 360 ponies—as much as the previous year's 409. If any engine can be termed immortal, the small-block Chevy certainly can. Indeed, its basic design is still with us.

▲ Many folks still regard Chevy's full-size '62s as some of the finest cars in Detroit history. Illinois's finest would likely agree, especially those who patrolled the state's highways in Biscayne sedans like this. Typical of the breed, Chevy's police package included a high-power V-8 and special "severe-use" components for cooling system, suspension, and brakes.

▲ Unlike its Impala sister, the 1962 Bel Air sport coupe retained the more aerodynamic "bubbletop" roofline from '61. This rare beauty started at $2668 with base V-8, but packs 1962's new 409-horsepower V-8, a $484 option with solid lifters and twin four-barrel carbs.

▲ With a stronger 409 and other special options at their disposal, drag racers again flocked to Chevy's lighter full-size cars in '62. Here, the legendary "Dyno" Don Nicholson launches his modified Bel Air sport coupe in NHRA competition. Chevy built 15,019 big-block '62s. Even a stock four-speed 380-hp 409 (with single carb) could run 0-60 in 7.5 seconds or less and top 140 mph.

▲ Champion Corvette racer John Fitch loved Chevy's Corvair. In 1962, he offered his first performance and cosmetic upgrades for the sporty Monza coupe under the name Fitch Sprint. His Connecticut-based company also sold complete cars. Fitch's bargain-priced $29 engine kit boosted horsepower to 155, good for 0-60 mph times of around 9.5 seconds.

▲ The interior of this 409 Bel Air sport coupe gives little hint of the car's ferocious performance, but note the tachometer on the steering column and the four-speed stick on the floor, two factory options that no self-respecting leadfoot would be without.

▲ The 409 was newly optional for any full-size '62 Chevy, but only 57 cars so equipped—including the pictured Bel Air sport coupe—were built with light aluminum front body panels that shaved 130 pounds off the nose.

▲ A close look at the "business end" of the '62 Fitch Sprint Corvair. Despite its chump-change price, the engine kit included four carbs among many power-boosting tweaks.

◄ Corvair's Lakewood wagons returned for '62, but would not be back the following year, thanks to sluggish sales. Rarest and most desirable of the lot was the new 1962 Monza Lakewood, offering all the sporty accoutrements of its coupe and sedan sisters starting at $2569. Just 2362 were built. Corvair's 145-cubic-inch "flat" six now came three ways: standard 80-horse, optional 102-hp (up from 95/98), and—as standard for the new Monza Spyder models—a 180-horsepower turbocharged edition.

1962

▲ Corvette won its first B-Production championship in Sports Car Club of America racing in 1962. Here, driver Don Yenko's Number 10 and Dr. Dick Thompson's Number 11 get ready for a three-hour contest at Daytona. To the left is builder Jim Hall's first racing Chaparral.

▲ First airing in 1960, TV's *Route 66* sent Martin Milner (*left*) and George Maharis on weekly adventures in a Corvette. They got a new car with each new season.

▲ Here's where Tod and Buzz, the main characters on *Route 66*, saw the USA in 1962. Except for details, Corvette's cockpit hadn't changed much since 1958.

▲ Corvette looked cleaner for '62 via less chrome and without the two-tone option, though bright rocker-panel trim was added. Sales jumped to another new record at 14,531.

▲ ▶ A more conventional hood did wonders for the appearance of 1962 Chevy trucks, though the new single-headlight grille with its oversized bezels was debatable. As before, both Fleetside (*above*) and separate-fender Stepside (*above right*) pickups offered a choice of standard or Custom cab trim, short and long wheelbases, two- or four-wheel drive, three payload ratings, and several powertrains, all to match competitors' similarly broad lineups.

168

Model Breakdown

Chevy II 100		Wght	Price	Prod
0111	sedan 2d, I-4	2,410	2,003	11,500*
0169	sedan 4d, I-4	2,445	2,041	
0135	wagon 4d, I-4	2,665	2,399	—
0211	sedan 2d, I-6	2,500	2,063	35,500*
0269	sedan 4d, I-6	2,535	2,101	
0235	wagon 4d, I-6	2,755	2,399	—
Chevy II 300				
0311	sedan 2d, I-4	2,425	2,084	10,400*
0369	sedan 4d, I-4	2,460	2,122	
0345	wagon 4d, 9P, I-4	2,765	2,517	—
0411	sedan 2d, I-6	2,515	2,144	92,800*
0469	sedan 4d, I-6	2,550	2,182	
0445	wagon 4d, 9P, I-6	2,855	2,577	—
Chevy II Nova 400—160,000* built				
0435	wagon 4d	2,775	2,497	—
0437	sport hardtop cpe	2,550	2,254	59,586
0441	sedan 2d	2,540	2,198	—
0449	sedan 4d	2,575	2,336	—
0467	convertible cpe	2,745	2,475	23,741
Biscayne—160,000* built				
1111	sedan 2d, I-6	3,405	2,324	—
1135	wagon 4d, I-6	3,845	2,725	—
1169	sedan 4d, I-6	3,480	2,378	—
1211	sedan 2d, V-8	3,400	2,431	—
1235	wagon 4d, V-8	3,840	2,832	—
1269	sedan 4d, V-8	3,475	2,485	—
Bel Air—365,500* built				
1511	sedan 2d, I-6	3,410	2,456	—
1535	wagon 4d, I-6	3,845	2,819	—
1537	sport htp cpe, I-6	3,445	2,561	—
1545	wagon 4d, 9P, I-6	3,895	2,922	—
1569	sedan 4d, I-6	3,480	2,510	—
1611	sedan 2d, V-8	3,405	2,563	—
1635	wagon 4d, V-8	3,840	2,926	—
1637	sport htp cpe, V-8	3,440	2,668	—
1645	wagon 4d, 9P, V-8	3,890	3,029	—
1669	sedan 4d, V-8	3,475	2,617	—
Impala—704,900* (inc SS models)				
1735	wagon 4d, I-6	3,870	2,961	—
1739	sport htp sdn, I-6	3,540	2,734	—
1745	wagon 4d, 9P, I-6	3,925	3,064	—
1747	sport htp cpe, I-6	3,455	2,669	—
1767	conv cpe, I-6	3,565	2,919	—
1769	sedan 4d, I-6	3,510	2,662	—
1835	wagon 4d, V-8	3,865	3,068	—
1839	sport htp sdn, V-8	3,535	2,841	—
1845	wagon 4d, 9P, V-8	3,920	3,171	—
1847	sport htp cpe, V-8	3,450	2,776	—
1867	conv cpe, V-8	3,560	3,026	—
1869	sedan 4d, V-8	3,505	2,769	—
Corvair 500				
0527	coupe	2,350	1,992	16,245
Corvair 700				
0727	coupe	2,390	2,057	18,474
0735	wagon 4d	2,590	2,407	3,716
0769	sedan 4d	2,410	2,111	35,368
Corvair 900 Monza				
0927	coupe	2,440	2,273	144,844
0927	Spyder coupe	2,465	2,636	6,894
0935	wagon 4d	2,590	2,569	2,362
0967	convertible cpe	2,625	2,483	13,995
0967	Spyder conv cpe	2,650	2,846	2,574
0969	sedan 4d	2,455	2,273	48,059
Corvette				
0867	convertible rdstr	2,925	4,038	14,531

*To nearest 100; does not include 59,900 Chevy II and 187,600 full-size wagons.

Engine Availability

Engines	bore × stroke	bhp	availability
I-4, 153.0	3.88 × 3.25	90	S-Chevy II 100, 300
I-6, 194.0	3.56 × 3.25	120	S-Chevy II all
I-6, 235.5	3.56 × 3.94	135	S-Chevrolet
V-8, 283.0	3.88 × 3.00	170	S-Chevrolet
V-8, 327.0	4.00 × 3.25	250/300	O-V8-all Chev
V-8, 409.0	4.31 × 3.50	380/409	O-V8-all Chev

Corvair			
flat 6, 145.0	3.44 × 2.60	80	S-all exc Spyder
flat 6, 145.0	3.44 × 2.60	102	O-all exc Spyder
flat 6, 145.0	3.44 × 2.60	150	S-Monza Spyder
Corvette			
V-8, 327.0	4.00 × 3.25	250	S-all
V-8, 327.0	4.00 × 3.25	300/340	O-all
V-8, 327.0	4.00 × 3.25	360	O-all (FI)

- **All-new Corvette Sting Ray stuns the sports-car world**

- **Full-size Chevys are restyled**

- **Chevy II Nova gets the SS treatment**

- **Chevy sets another production record with 2.15 million cars**

▲ Corvair Spyders were in short supply during 1962, but more readily available as '63 models. Priced at $317, the package was fitted to 11,627 Monza coupes like this and 7472 Monza convertibles. That compares with the previous year's 6894 and 2574 installations.

▼ New for '62, Corvair's convertible body style returned for '63 in Monza and Monza Spyder trim. This Spyder again packed 150 horsepower, other Corvairs 80 standard or 102 optional. Seen here are Kelsey-Hayes wire wheels with racing-style knock-off hubs, available on any '63 Corvair as a $404 factory option.

▲ Corvair's face wore a succession of trim treatments, starting with 1960's large, winged Chevy bow tie logo. After a slim full-width bright strip for '61 and pairs of dummy air vents for '62 came a broad chevron between the headlights, as on this ragtop Monza Spyder. Corvair production eased to near 254,600, excluding Greenbrier vans, after peaking at around 292,500 for model-year '62.

▲ Looking a bit like a metal snail, the Monza Spyder's power-boosting turbocharger sat at the forward end of the rear engine bay and close to the intake manifold. The "blown" engine also used a hardened crankshaft, chromed upper piston rings, special valves, three-barrel sidedraft carburetor, and 8.0:1 compression ratio.

▲ Save carryover engines, Corvette was all-new for 1963, gaining Sting Ray badges in a nod to its arresting styling patterned on GM design chief Bill Mitchell's recent Stingray show car. Joining the traditional 'Vette roadster was this sleek fastback coupe with a split rear window that hampered visibility but looked terrific. The coupe helped lift Corvette model-year volume by a smashing 48 percent to 21,513 units, accounting for 10,594 of the total. Still, the convertible would always be more popular during the Sting Ray generation's five-year run. All Sting Rays are highly prized today, but the '63 coupe most of all, because its split window would appear only that one year.

▲ New Sting Ray shape was wind tunnel tested, but its aerodynamics weren't the best.

◄ ▼ The '63 Sting Ray convertible started at $4037, versus $4252 for the new coupe. Bodies were still fiberglass, but on a lighter yet stiffer new ladder-type frame with a 98-inch wheelbase, trimmer by four inches. A European-style independent rear suspension replaced the old solid axle for much improved handling. A new structural steel "cage" enhanced safety and refinement in both body types. Hidden headlamps were new, and there was no exterior trunklid; cargo access was from inside the cockpit. Handsome multispoke cast-aluminum wheels with knock-off hubs were optional.

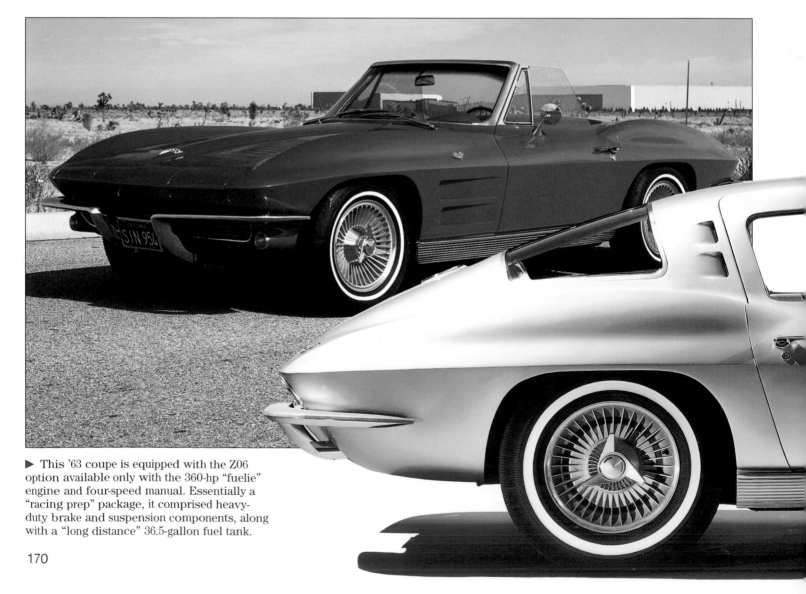

► This '63 coupe is equipped with the Z06 option available only with the 360-hp "fuelie" engine and four-speed manual. Essentially a "racing prep" package, it comprised heavy-duty brake and suspension components, along with a "long distance" 36.5-gallon fuel tank.

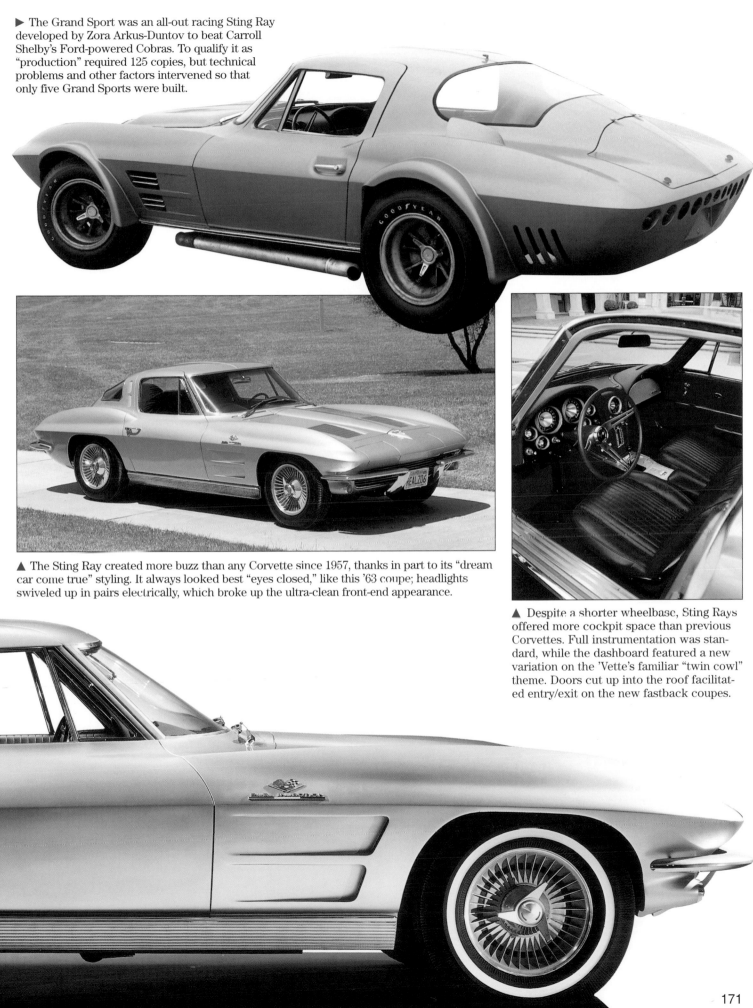

▶ The Grand Sport was an all-out racing Sting Ray developed by Zora Arkus-Duntov to beat Carroll Shelby's Ford-powered Cobras. To qualify it as "production" required 125 copies, but technical problems and other factors intervened so that only five Grand Sports were built.

▲ The Sting Ray created more buzz than any Corvette since 1957, thanks in part to its "dream car come true" styling. It always looked best "eyes closed," like this '63 coupe; headlights swiveled up in pairs electrically, which broke up the ultra-clean front-end appearance.

▲ Despite a shorter wheelbase, Sting Rays offered more cockpit space than previous Corvettes. Full instrumentation was standard, while the dashboard featured a new variation on the 'Vette's familiar "twin cowl" theme. Doors cut up into the roof facilitated entry/exit on the new fastback coupes.

171

▶ The Sting Ray was designed to be a much more civilized Corvette in the European *Gran Turismo* mold—so much so that Chevy briefly considered a long-wheelbase four-passenger coupe as a possible rival to Ford's posh Thunderbird. The idea went as far as this full-size mockup, photographed in the GM Design studios, but was finally rejected as inappropriate to Corvette's sports-car heritage. It was just as well, as those riding in back would likely have felt quite cramped, and the stretched body didn't have the same eye appeal as the two-seat coupe. If nothing else, this episode suggests Chevy's determination to keep Corvette a "pure" sports car.

▲▼ Brand-new body designs brought a crisp new look to full-size 1963 Chevrolets. Impala SS remained the most exciting of the bunch, and was far more numerous this year as production soared to 153,271 convertibles (*above*) and Sport Coupes, about 18 percent of total Impala output. The SS option now included a buckets-and-console interior (*below*), but all big '63 Chevys sported a more imposing dash and slightly more passenger space.

▲ Chevy advertising continued to portray a "See the USA" theme in 1963. Typical was this portrait of an Impala convertible and Sport Coupe out in the wilds of the West.

▲ Full-size cars were on the way out for stock-car racing in 1963, but Chevrolet matched Ford that year with a big new 427-cubic-inch competition V-8 that outran everything at Daytona early in the season. Johnny Rutherford's Impala used it to give Chevy one of its five season wins in NASCAR. Ford, Plymouth, and Pontiac split the rest.

▲ Chevy aided its cause in 1963 drag racing by offering dealer-installed aluminum front bumpers as well as lightweight front sheetmetal. This deceptively stock-looking Impala Sport Coupe is only one of 57 cars so equipped for '63.

▲ Still "real fine," the fabled 409 V-8 came three ways for '63: a more streetable new 340-hp four-barrel version, beefed-up 400 hp, and a new solid-lifter high-compression brute making 425. Chevy big-block installations this year rose to 16,902.

▲▶ With 195 hp, Chevy's base 283 V-8 was 25-hp stronger for '63. So equipped, an Impala Sport Coupe (above) listed at $2774. The 327 continued in 250-, 300-, and 340-hp versions. A crisp rear deck above a newly concave taillight panel (right) marked all full-size '63s such as this high-value Bel Air four-door sedan. Chevy's total production again broke the 2-million barrier for '62, tacking on some 70,000 to the prior year's total.

Model Breakdown

Chevy II 100—50,400* built	Wght	Price	Prod
0111 sdn 2d, I-4	2,430	2,003	—
0135 wgn 4d, I-4	2,725	2,338	—
0169 sdn 4d, I-4	2,455	2,040	—
0211 sdn 2d, I-6	2,520	2,062	—
0235 wgn 4d, I-6	2,810	2,397	—
0269 sdn 4d, I-6	2,545	2,099	—
Chevy II 300—78,800* built			
0311 sdn 2d, I-4	2,440	2,084	—
0345 wgn 4d, 9P, I-4	2,810	2,516	—
0369 sdn 4d, I-4	2,470	2,121	—
0411 sdn 2d, I-6	2,530	2,143	—
0445 wgn 4d, 9P, I-6	2,900	2,575	—
0469 sdn 4d, I-6	2,560	2,180	—
Chevy II Nova 400, I-6			
0435 wgn 4d	2,835	2,494	—
0437 Sport htp cpe	2,590	2,267	87,415
0449 sdn 4d	2,590	2,235	58,862
0467 conv cpe	2,760	2,472	24,823
Biscayne—186,500* built			
1111 sdn 2d, I-6	3,205	2,322	—
1135 wgn 4d, I-6	3,685	2,723	—
1169 sdn 4d, I-6	3,280	2,376	—
1211 sdn 2d, V-8	3,340	2,429	—
1235 wgn 4d, V-8	3,810	2,830	—
1269 sdn 4d, V-8	3,415	2,483	—
Bel Air—354,100* built			
1511 sdn 2d, I-6	3,215	2,454	—
1535 wgn 4d, I-6	3,685	2,818	—
1545 wgn 4d, 9P, I-6	3,720	2,921	—
1569 sdn 4d, I-6	3,280	2,508	—
1611 sdn 2d, V-8	3,345	2,561	—
1635 wgn 4d, V-8	3,810	2,925	—
1645 wgn 4d, 9P, V-8	3,850	3,028	—
1669 sdn 4d, V-8	3,415	2,615	—
Impala—832,600* built (inc 153,271 SS models)			
1735 wgn 4d, I-6	3,705	2,960	—
1739 Sport htp sdn, I-6	3,350	2,732	—
1745 wgn 4d, 9P, I-6	3,745	3,063	—
1747 Sport htp cpe, I-6	3,265	2,667	—
1767 conv cpe, I-6	3,400	2,917	—
1760 sdn 4d, I-6	3,310	2,661	—
1835 wgn 4d, V-8	3,835	3,067	—
1839 Sport htp sdn, V-8	3,475	2,839	—
1845 wgn 4d, 9P, V-8	3,870	3,170	—
1847 Sport htp cpe, V-8	3,390	2,774	—
1867 conv cpe, V-8	3,525	3,024	—
1869 sdn 4d, V-8	3,435	2,768	—
Corvair 500			
0527 cpe	2,330	1,992	16,680
Corvair 700			
0727 cpe	2,355	2,056	12,378
0769 sdn 4	2,385	2,110	20,684
Corvair 900 Monza			
0927 cpe	2,415	2,272	117,917
0927 Spyder cpe	2,440	2,589	11,627
0967 conv cpe	2,525	2,481	36,693
0967 Spyder conv cpe	2,550	2,798	7,472
0969 sdn 4d	2,450	2,326	31,120
Corvette Sting Ray			
0837 cpe	2,859	4,252	10,594
0867 conv rdstr	2,881	4,037	10,919

*To nearest 100; does not include wagons. Total wagons 198,542; Chevy II wagons 75,274.

▲ Though fundamentally unchanged for '63, the compact Chevy II offered its own SS package as a new option for Nova 400 Sport Coupes (*above*) and convertibles. The $161 option was strictly for show, delivering SS emblems, a bright molding atop the beltline, silver-look taillight panel and, with the $42 14-inch wheel option, spinner hubcaps.

▲ A new grille insert and other trim changes spruced-up all '63 Chevy IIs. This six-passenger Nova 400 carried a $2494 base price. Total Chevy II model-year sales rose to 375,626.

▲ A forerunner of the modern minivan, the Corvair Greenbrier Sport Wagon started at $2655 as a little-changed '63 sophomore. Sales were a modest 13,761.

▲ Far removed from Chevy's 1963 passenger cars was this burly tilt-cab Series T-60 cab-over tractor in the heavy-duty diesel truck line. This year's big rigs featured redesigned front suspension, a heavier-gauge steel frame, and I-beam axles. Engines made 140 or 165 hp. Conventional-cab models and gas V-8s were also available.

▲ Americans had long since discovered the great outdoors by 1963, and Chevy again encouraged them by offering heavy-duty Camper Packages for its mainline pickups. Here, a '63 Fleetside C-10 toting a slide-in aftermarket camper heads off with a boat in tow.

1963 Engine Availability

Engines	bore × stroke	bhp	availability
I-4, 153.0	3.88 × 3.25	90	S-Chevy II
I-6, 194.0	3.56 × 3.25	120	S-Chevy II
I-6, 230.0	3.87 × 3.25	140	S-Chevrolet
V-8, 283.0	3.88 × 3.00	195	S-Chevrolet
V-8, 327.0	4.00 × 3.25	250-340	O-Chevrolet
V-8, 409.0	4.31 × 3.50	340-425	O-Chevrolet
Corvair			
flat 6, 145.0	3.44 × 2.60	80	S-all exc Spyder
flat 6, 145.0	3.44 × 2.60	102	O-all exc Spyder
flat 6T, 145.0	3.44 × 2.60	150	S-Monza Spyder
Corvette			
V-8, 327.0	4.00 × 3.25	250	S-all
V-8, 327.0	4.00 × 3.25	300/340	O-all
V-8, 327.0	4.00 × 3.25	360	O-all (FI)

1964

- **Midsize Chevelle introduced, revives El Camino car/pickup**

- **Full-size line restyled; other Chevys receive mild styling changes**

- **Chevy builds over 2.3 million '64 cars, another new record**

- **Corvette hits a new sales high at 22,229**

- **Corvair volume falls**

▶ "For 1964, Chevrolet Motor Division will offer a total of 43 models in five separate car lines. Each line is distinguishable by its own styling and wheelbase." So said this ad from September 1963 showing the "fit" of a new Chevelle Malibu sedan versus the Impala Sport Sedan below it and, above, a Chevy II Nova sedan and Corvair Monza coupe.

'64 JET-SMOOTH LUXURY CHEVROLET

A CAR THAT'S NEVER BEEN SO LUXURIOUS BEFORE! More luxurious outside with that long clean new look. And much more luxurious inside. The new Impala Super Sport Series, for example, has a new kind of ultra-soft vinyl upholstery and door-to-door deep-twist carpeting that would cost you a small fortune to put in your home. And even the lowest priced Biscayne models are now fully carpeted and have arm rests and foam-cushioned seats both front and rear. Then these new Chevrolets have a Jet-smooth luxurious way of going. Quiet. Soft. Transmissions operate more smoothly and quietly. That sturdy Body by Fisher and generous coil spring at each wheel cushion you against every kind of road shock. Actually, the whole idea for '64 was to see how much luxury and comfort we could add to the car—but still keep it reasonably priced. And everything worked out just beautifully. Wait until you see it. SEE CHEVROLET'S GREATEST AT YOUR CHEVROLET SHOWROOM.

NEW Chevelle! by CHEVROLET

A KIND OF CAR YOU'VE NEVER SEEN BEFORE! Not a new model or just a new name, but a completely different kind of car from Chevrolet for 1964. Outside, it's a good foot shorter and a few inches narrower than the big cars. Parks in the tightest places. But the passenger space, leg room and trunk capacity are surprisingly generous. Eleven sedans, wagons, coupes and convertibles to choose from. Four engines: A 120-hp Six. A 195-hp Six. An extra-cost 155-hp Six. And an extra-cost 220-hp V8 with four-barrel carburetion. Body is by Fisher—and you know what that means in terms of quality and comfort. Brakes are self-adjusting. Service is seldom. Quality is by Chevrolet clear through. And so is the price, you'll be happy to know. SEE CHEVROLET'S LATEST AT YOUR CHEVROLET SHOWROOM.

THE '64 CHEVY II by CHEVROLET

NEW CHEVY II V8! An optional-at-extra-cost 195-hp V8, to be exact. Chevy II is now the only car made that gives you a choice of Four, Six or V8 power. Two Sixes, by the way. A 120-hp and a new extra-cost 155-hp. And all the new II's are trimmer outside and nicer inside. Each with Body by Fisher, of course. And rust-fighting rocker panels and long-life muffler. And self-adjusting brakes. And all those other Chevrolet engineering features that keep you from dipping into your savings to keep it going. Come dr-r-r-rive a Chevy II V8 at your Chevrolet dealer's showroom.

THE '64 CORVAIR and '64 CORVETTE

NEW CORVAIR POWER! Nearly 15% more horsepower in the standard engine. A full 110 horsepower in the extra-cost engine. And 150 hp in the Monza Spyder. You'll want to climb a hill just because it's there. Some nice new interior refinements, too—like softer, more deeply tufted seats in the Monza and sporty map pockets on the front doors. Out side of that, it's still very much the same easy-to-park, easy-to-handle, hard-to-keep-your-hands-off-of Corvair.

NEW CORVETTE RIDE! Smoother and quieter than it's ever been, but by no means any less of a sports car than it's always been. New extra-cost V8 engines up to 375 hp. And note the new one-piece rear window in the coupe, so you can see who's behind you better. You'll be surprised at what a beautiful boulevard car Corvette is. Yet it's one of the world's few great sports cars, too. . . . Chevrolet Division of General Motors, Detroit, Michigan.

THERE'S 5 IN 64 CHEVROLET

◀ Corvette was excluded from the ad above, but appeared with its linemates in this display bearing the tagline "There's 5 in '64." Though the midsize Chevelle was the big news that year, most Chevy ads continued featuring the full-size Impala.

▲ Chevy II again changed little for '64, but lost its midline 300 models, Nova convertible—and a lot of sales, which slumped to 191,700, probably due to "cannibalizing" from the larger, but little costlier, Chevelles. This Nova four-door sedan started at $2243 with six-cylinder engine, which was newly standard for all '64 Novas.

175

▲ "Suddenly, it's 1955!" was an apt description for the '64 Chevelle, as the new midsizer returned to a classic Chevy-size package with an identical 115-inch wheelbase. Chevelle's top-line Malibu series arrived with a snazzy SS option for the Sport Coupe (shown) and convertible. So equipped, the hardtop started at $2646 with base 195-horsepower 283 V-8.

▲ The hottest '64 Chevelles carried a 300-hp 327 V-8 option that arrived at midyear to supplement a 250-hp version. The base engine was the 120-hp 194.4-cubic-inch Chevy II six; the 230-cid 140-hp big-car six-cylinder was also available.

▲ Chevelle also harked to the "classic" mid-'50s Chevys in having a simple dashboard design, shown here within the Malibu convertible pictured below. The new midsize line had a smashing debut sales year, attracting some 330,000 buyers.

► This Malibu convertible shows off the clean, handsome lines that distinguished every new '64 Chevelle. GM design chief Bill Mitchell was starting to favor more flowing lines, evident here in the slight swell of the rear fenders, the so-called "Coke bottle" look that soon swept Detroit. Wire wheel covers with dummy knock-off hubs were one of many accessories sold through dealers. Chevelle bowed with six body styles divided among Malibu and entry-level "300" series. The convertible and Sport coupe were Malibu exclusives; a two-door wagon was reserved for the 300 group. Both offered four-door sedans and wagons. The ragtop started at $2695 with base V-8 and saw 23,158 copies, including SS-equipped models. Combined SS installations for the model year totaled 76,860.

▲ This '64 Chevelle wagon is actually a late prototype without the rear-fender series ID, but the small hubcaps suggest it's the less expensive 300-series model. Malibus most always wore full wheel covers. The 300 four-door wagon started at $2566 with base six.

▲ A styling echo of the 1955-57 "hardtop" Nomad, the '64 Chevelle 300 two-door wagon was a sporty yet practical package priced as low as $2528. Only a few thousand were built, however.

▶ After three years in limbo, Chevrolet's El Camino car/pick-up returned as part of the new '64 Chevelle line, though it was again derived from a two-door wagon. Base prices were $2271 for a lowly six-cylinder job, $2460 with base V-8. Ordering Custom trim delivered bucket seats, center console, and rocker and rear-fender moldings as on SS Malibu, but no SS emblems.

▲ Corvair's original 1960 design made a final bow for '64. All models, including this Monza Sport Coupe, offered improved handling via a "camber compensator" newly added to the rear suspension.

▲ The '64 Corvairs also got a larger 164-cid "flat" six with 95 hp standard, 110 optional; Spyder horsepower was unchanged. This ragtop Monza is one of 31,045; another 4761 were built as Spyders.

1964 Engine Availability

Engines	bore × stroke	bhp	availability
I-4, 153.0	3.88 × 3.25	90	S-Chevy II 100
I-6, 194.0	3.56 × 3.25	120	S-Chevy II 100/400, Chevelle
I-6, 230.0	3.87 × 3.25	140	S-Chevrolet; O-others
I-6, 230.0	3.87 × 3.25	155	O-all
V-8, 283.0	3.88 × 3.00	195	S-V-8 Chevelle, Chevrolet; O-Chevy II
V-8, 283.0	3.88 × 3.00	220	O-Chevelle
V-8, 327.0	4.00 × 3.25	250/300	O-Chevrolet, Chevelle
V-8, 409.0	4.31 × 3.50	340-425	O-Chevrolet
Corvair			
flat 6, 164.0	3.44 × 2.94	95	S-all exc 600
flat 6, 164.0	3.44 × 2.94	110	O-all exc 600
flat 6, 164.0	3.44 × 2.94	150	S-600
Corvette			
V-8, 327.0	4.00 × 3.25	250	S-all
V-8, 327.0	4.00 × 3.25	300-365	O-all
V-8, 327.0	4.00 × 3.25	375	O-all (FI)

▲The Chevy Van arrived late in the '64 model year. Its front-engine design provided a flat cargo floor, unlike the Corvair-based Greenbriers and Corvans with their rear-engine humps. The Chevyvans (both spellings were used) had nominal ½-ton payload ratings, though Chevrolet claimed actual capacity of 2225 pounds.

▲ The big "Jet Smooth" Chevys returned for '64 with a more rounded look on the new-for-'63 bodyshells. Impala SS sales rose to 185,325 Sport Coupes (shown) and rag-tops.

▶ Though still available with a six, most SS '64 Impalas were built with V-8s, which now involved two small-block 283s, three 327s, and burly 400- and 425-hp 409s. But big-block orders plunged to 8864 this year, as speed demons quickly saw the performance potential of the lighter midsize Chevelles.

▲ Impala SS was promoted for '64 from option package to subseries status. This Sport Coupe started at $2947, the companion convertible at $3196.

◀ Four-door sedans remained a mainstay of full-size Chevy sales in 1964, none more than this $2671 Impala. Chevy built over 536,000 big sedans for the model year, and the Impala line outsold the midrange Bel Air series by better than 2-to-1, with the low-end Biscaynes trailing way behind. Any big Chevy was a solid family-car choice.

▲ Many collectors seek out '64 full-size Chevys for the smooth, "correct" styling that still looks good some 40 years later. Here, the highly coveted Impala convertible, priced at $3025 with base V-8.

▲ It may look like blue-collar transport, but this '64 Biscayne two-door sedan is a veritable wolf in sheep's clothing. A discreet front-fender badge reveals the reason. It reads "409."

▲ A one-piece rear window was the Corvette coupe's big style change for 1964.

▲ New wheel covers and less brightwork also marked '64 Sting Rays, but the fast-back coupe kept its handsome, racy profile.

▲ The first Sting Rays earned a reputation as excellent handling and driving machines, though on irregular roads the ride could be a bit rough. For '64, Chevrolet smoothed the ride somewhat with redesigned shock absorbers and changes to the front and rear springs. More body insulation, along with revised transmission mounts and shift linkage, combined to quiet interior noise levels.

▲ Chevy's 1964 pickups, both Fleetsides like this and flare-fender Stepsides, again offered a 127-inch wheelbase for ¾-ton models and a 115-inch chassis for half-tonners (shown). This photo is typical of how Chevy promoted its pickups as "recreational vehicles" in the years before purpose-designed RVs and motorhomes appeared on the scene.

▲ Chevy's 1964 big-rig truck line again listed tilt-cab T-Series models (shown) and conventional-cab C-Series equivalents, plus cab/chassis platforms for special-use bodies.

Model Breakdown

Chevy II 100—53,100* built		Wght	Price	Prod
0111	sdn 2d, I-4	2,455	2,011	—
0169	sdn, I-4	2,495	2,408	—
0211	sdn 2d, I-6	2,540	2,070	—
0235	wgn 4d, I-6	2,840	2,406	—
0269	sdn 4d, I-6	2,580	2,108	—
Chevy II Nova 400, I-6—102,900* built (includes SS)				
0411	sdn 2d	2,560	2,206	—
0435	wgn 4d	2,860	2,503	—
0437	Sport htp cpe	2,660	2,271	—
0469	sdn 4d	2,595	2,243	—
Chevy II Nova SS, I-6				
0447	Sport htp cpe	2,675	2,433	10,576
Chevelle 300—68,300* built				
5311	sdn 2d, I-6	2,825	2,231	—
5315	wgn 2d, I-6	3,050	2,528	—
5335	wgn 4d, I-6	3,130	2,566	—
5369	sdn 4d, I-6	2,850	2,268	—
5411	sdn 2d, V 8	2,995	2,339	—
5415	wgn 2d, V-8	3,170	2,636	—
5435	wgn 4d, V-8	2,250	2,674	—
5469	sdn 4d, V-8	2,980	2,376	—
Chevelle Malibu—149,000* built				
5535	wgn 4d, I-6	3,140	2,647	—
5537	Sport htp cpe, I-6	2,850	2,376	—
5545	wgn 4d, 9P, I-6	3,240	2,744	—
5567	conv cpe, I-6	2,995	2,587	—
5569	sdn 4d, I-6	2,870	2,349	—
5635	wgn 4d, V-8	3,265	2,755	—
5637	Sport htp cpe, V-8	2,975	2,484	—
5645	wgn 4d, 9P, V-8	3,365	2,852	—
5667	conv cpe, V-8	3,120	2,695	—
5669	sdn 4d, V-8	2,996	2,457	—
Chevelle Malibu SS—76,860 built				
5737	Sport htp cpe, I-6	2,875	2,538	—
5767	conv cpe, I-6	3,020	2,749	—
5837	Sport htp cpe, V-8	3,000	2,646	—
5867	conv cpe, V-8	3,145	2,857	—
Biscayne—173,900* built				
1111	sdn 2d, I-6	3,230	2,363	—
1135	wgn 4d, I-6	3,700	2,763	—
1169	sdn 4d, I-6	3,300	2,417	—
1211	sdn 2d, V-8	3,365	2,471	—
1235	wgn 4d, V-8	3,820	2,871	—
1269	sdn 4d, V-8	3,430	2,524	—

Bel Air—318,100* built		Wght	Price	Prod
1511	sdn 2d, I-6	3,235	2,465	—
1535	wgn 4d, I-6	3,745	2,828	—
1545	wgn 4d, 9P, I-6	3,705	2,931	—
1569	sdn 4d, I-6	3,305	2,519	—
1611	sdn 2d, V-8	3,370	2,573	—
1635	wgn 4d, V-8	3,825	2,935	—
1645	wgn 4d, 9P, V-8	3,865	3,039	—
1669	sdn 4d, V-8	3,440	2,626	—
Impala—889,600* built (includes 185,523 SS)				
1735	wgn 4d, I-6	3,725	2,970	—
1739	Sport htp sdn, I-6	3,370	2,742	—
1745	wgn 4d, 9P, I-6	3,770	3,073	—
1767	conv cpe, I-6	3,400	2,927	—
1769	sdn 4d, I-6	3,340	2,671	—
1835	wgn 4d, V-8	3,850	3,077	—
1839	Sport htp sdn, V-8	3,490	2,850	—
1845	wgn 4d, 9P, V-8	3,895	3,181	—
1847	Sport htp cpe, V-8	3,415	2,786	—
1867	conv cpe, V-8	3,525	3,035	—
1869	sdn 4d, V-8	3,460	2,779	—
Impala SS				
1347	htp cpe, I-6	3,325	2,839	—
1367	conv cpe, I-6	3,435	3,088	—
1447	Sport htp cpe, V-8	3,450	2,947	—
1467	conv cpe, V-8	3,555	3,196	—
Corvair 500				
0527	cpe	2,365	2,000	22,968
Corvair 600 Monza Spyder				
0627	cpe	2,470	2,599	6,480
0667	conv cpe	2,580	2,811	4,761
Corvair 700				
0769	sdn 4d	2,415	2,119	16,295
Corvair 900 Monza				
0927	cpe	2,445	2,281	88,440
0967	conv cpe	2,555	2,492	31,045
0969	sdn 4d	2,470	2,335	21,926
Corvette Sting Ray				
0837	cpe	2,960	4,252	8,304
0867	conv rdstr	2,945	4,037	13,925

*To nearest 100; does not include wagons. Wagon production: Chevy II 35,700; Chevelle 44,000; others 192,800.

- Corvair, full-size Chevy are new from the ground up

- 396 V-8 begins new era in big-block power

- Chevy car sales hit a new record of nearly 2.4 million

▲ A preproduction '65 Impala Sport Sedan undergoes a windshield wiper test at the GM Proving Grounds in Milford, Michigan, north of Detroit.

Some cars pamper passengers.
Some cars pamper drivers.
Chevrolet pampers both.

Foam-cushioned seats and deep-twist carpeting underfoot—you passengers have it made. So do you drivers with new engines, transmissions and Wide-Stance handling. Now everybody's happy—have a great trip!

CHEVROLET

▲ Though still on a 119-inch wheelbase, Chevy's big '65s were longer, wider, and roomier overall, enhanced by a fulsome, flowing new shape. The Impala Sport Coupe started at $2785 with 283 V-8, which again checked in with 195 horsepower.

▲ This March 1965 ad in *Holiday* magazine extolled the fully redesigned Impala Sport Coupe for its "foam-cushioned seats and deep-twist carpeting, new engines, transmissions, and Wide-Stance handling." Other ads said the all-new full-size Chevys had a "beautiful shape." The Sport Coupe's semi-fastback roofline was certainly more rakish.

▶ Impala Super Sport production jumped to 243,114 units for '65, again split between a convertible and this Sport Coupe, which was far more numerous with estimated sales of 222,000. Full-size SS sales would never be so high again. Neither would V-8 options, which again included 283- and 327-cubic-inch small-blocks plus an all-new 396, which replaced the veteran 409 in February 1965. For the big-car line, the new big-block came with four-barrel carburetors to produce 325, 375, or 425 horsepower, the last mainly for racing. "Super Sport" name-script replaced SS badges for '65.

▲ Biscayne remained Chevy's cheapest big car for 1965, again offering two- and four-door sedans and this four-door wagon with six-passenger seating. Prices started at $2764 with standard six.

▲ Chevy's most popular big wagon again wore Impala nameplates for '65. Total Impala sales this model year eased to some 803,400. The wagon listed at $2970/$3078 with six/base V-8.

▲▶ All of General Motors' full-size '65 cars switched from '50s-style X-member frames to a so-called "full-perimeter" type that reinstated side rails, which better supported the larger new bodies, provided superior structural strength, and enhanced quietness and ride comfort. The change was perhaps most evident in convertibles like this handsome Impala Super Sport, one of 27,842 built that year. Prices started at $3212 with base V-8. The regular ragtop, listing at $2943 in six-cylinder form, saw some 45,800 copies as Chevy built slightly fewer big convertibles than it had in '64. Both Super Sport models reprised a standard buckets-and-console interior, and shared a somewhat more compact new dashboard design with other big Chevys. Full instrumentation, including tachometer, was a desirable Impala SS option. V-8 Impalas totaled some 746,800 against 56,600 six-cylinder models, no surprise in those days of cheap gas and affordable horsepower.

▲ Full-size Chevy engine choices for 1965 ran the full gamut, emphasized in this advertising photo fronted by the burly new-design 396 big-block.

▲▼ Again trying the "luxury Impala" idea, Chevy added a $200 Caprice option for the Impala Sport Sedan at mid '65. Included were a lush interior (*below*), special trim, and a heavy-duty frame.

1965 Engine Availability

Engines	bore × stroke	bhp	availability
I-4, 153.0	3.88 × 3.25	90	S-Chevy II 100
I-6, 194.0	3.56 × 3.25	120	S-Chevy II, Chevelle
I-6, 230.0	3.87 × 3.25	140	S-Chevrolet; O-others
I-6, 250.0	3.87 × 3.25	150	O-Chevrolet
V-8, 283.0	3.88 × 3.00	195	S-Chevrolet, Chevelle; O-Chevy II
V-8, 283.0	3.88 × 3.00	220	O-all
V-8, 327.0	4.00 × 3.25	250/300	O-all
V-8, 327.0	4.00 × 3.25	350	O-Chevelle
V-8, 396.0	4.09 × 3.75	325-425	O-Chevrolet, Chevelle
V-8, 409.0	4.31 × 3.50	340/400	O-Chevrolet
Corvair			
flat 6, 164.0	3.44 × 2.94	95	S-all exc Corsa
flat 6, 164.0	3.44 × 2.94	110	O-all exc Corsa
flat 6, 164.0	3.44 × 2.94	140	S-Corsa; O-others
flat 6T, 164.0	3.44 × 2.94	180	O-Corsa
Corvette			
V-8, 327.0	4.00 × 3.25	250	S-all
V-8, 327.0	4.00 × 3.25	300-365	O-all
V-8, 327.0	4.00 × 3.25	375	O-all (FI)
V-8, 396.0	4.09 × 3.75	425	O-all

▲ The sporty Corvair was redesigned for '65 to be a much safer car at any speed. A thoroughly redone suspension got much of this credit, as this photo strove to emphasize, just as Ralph Nader was beginning his attack on earlier Corvairs.

▲ Styled largely by Ron Hill, the '65 Corvair embodied GM design chief Bill Mitchell's fondness for graceful curves and swells. Both coupes and sedans became pillarless styles, and all models looked larger even though wheelbase and other dimensions weren't greatly changed. *Motor Trend* termed the new look "a fine blend of dignity with a little flair..." Sport Coupes came as a $2066 500 model, $2347 Monza (shown), and new $2519 Corsa, the last replacing the Spyder and available with up to 180 hp.

▲ John Fitch again offered his enhanced Corvair-based Sprints for 1965 as both a series of kits and as complete cars. Add-on "flying buttress" sail panels set his styling package apart from Chevy's.

▲ Chevelle got the usual second-year cosmetic changes and little else for '65—at first. This Malibu was one of 19,765 Chevelle ragtops built that model year. Price was $2696 with base V-8.

▲ This Malibu SS Sport Coupe is one of a handful of late-season '65s packing Chevy's new 396 big-block V-8. Total Malibu SS sales were 101,577, about a third of total Malibu production.

▲ A 160-mph speedometer and a dashtop 6000-rpm tachometer hinted at the big-inch power of the rare '65 Chevelle SS396, which was cataloged as Regular Production Option (RPO) Z16.

◀ *Motor Trend* timed a '65 SS 306 Chevelle at just 6.7 seconds 0-60 mph, with a quarter-mile of 15.3 at a blazing 96 mph. The option included lots of chrome engine dress-up to impress anyone looking under the hood.

▶ The El Camino car/pickup mostly marked time with other '65 Chevelles. Price was now $2270 with the 120-hp 194-cid six or $2355 with the base 195-hp 283 V-8.

183

▲ Standard side exhaust pipes marked '65 Corvettes with the new big-block 396 option.

▲ Corvette set another sales record for '65 at 23,572; 8186 were coupes (shown).

▲ A slick lift-off hardtop was again available for Corvette roadsters in 1965.

▶ Chevy II again saw only detail changes for '65, but a 195-hp 283 V-8 option returned from '64 along with new 250- and 300-hp 327s. Most went into Novas like this SS Sport Coupe, of which 9100 were built.

▲ Though no head-turner, the 1965 Chevy II 100 two-door sedan offered reliable, economical transport for as low as $2011. Total Chevy II sales fell this year to some 120,000.

▲ Chevy pickups continued to evolve through the '60s with minor trim and equipment changes each year, plus the occasional new mechanical or convenience feature. This ½-ton '65 Fleetside C-10 used the longer 127-inch-wheelbase chassis to accommodate an 8-foot cargo box. The 115-inch short chassis mounted a 6.5-foot bed.

▲ Not many folks bought pickups as "alternative cars" in 1965, and Chevy's standard-trim cabs reflected that with practical but spartan, work-oriented interior decor.

Model Breakdown

Chevy II 100	Wght	Price	Prod
11111 sdn 2d, I-4	2,505	2,011	1,300*
11169 sdn 4d, I-4	2,520	2,048	
11311 sdn 2d, I-6	2,605	2,077	
11335 wgn 4d, I-6	2,875	2,413	39,200*
11369 sdn 4d, I-6	2,620	2,115	

Chevy II Nova 400, I-6—51,700* built

	Wght	Price	Prod
11535 wgn 4d	2,880	2,510	—
11537 htp cpe	2,645	2,270	—
11569 sdn 4d	2,645	2,243	—

Chevy II Nova SS, I-6

	Wght	Price	Prod
11737 htp cpe	2,690	2,433	9,100

Chevelle 300—31,600* built (plus 41,600* DeLuxe)

	Wght	Price	Prod
13111 sdn 2d, I-6	2,870	2,156	—
13115 wgn 2d, I-6	3,140	2,453	—
13169 sdn 4d, I-6	2,900	2,193	—
13211 sdn 2d, V-8	3,010	2,262	—
13215 wgn 2d, V-8	3,275	2,561	—
13269 sdn 4d, V-8	3,035	2,301	—
13311 Del sdn 2d, I-6	2,870	2,231	—
13335 Del wgn 4d, I-6	3,185	2,567	—
13369 Del sdn 4d, I-6	2,910	2,269	—
13411 Del sdn 2d, V-8	3,010	2,339	—
13435 Del wgn 4d, V-8	3,320	2,674	—
13469 Del sdn 4d, V-8	3,050	2,377	—

Chevelle Malibu—152,200* built

	Wght	Price	Prod
13535 wgn 4d, I-6	3,225	2,647	—
13537 htp cpe, I-6	2,930	2,377	—
13567 conv cpe, I-6	3,025	2,588	—
13569 sdn 4d, I-6	2,945	2,250	—
13635 wgn 4d, V-8	3,355	2,755	—
13637 htp cpe, V-8	3,065	2,485	—
13667 conv cpe, V-8	3,160	2,696	—
13669 sdn 4d, V-8	3,080	2,458	—

Chevelle Malibu SS—101,577 built (201 SS 396)

	Wght	Price	Prod
13737 htp cpe, I-6	2,980	2,539	—
13767 conv cpe, I-6	3,075	2,750	—
13837 htp cpe, V-8	3,115	2,647	—
13867 conv cpe, V-8	3,210	2,858	—

Biscayne

	Wght	Price	Prod
15311 sdn 2d, I-6	3,305	2,363	107,700*
15335 wgn 4d, I-6	3,765	2,764	
15369 sdn 4d, I-6	3,365	2,417	
15411 sdn 2d, V-8	3,455	2,470	37,600*
15435 wgn 4d, V-8	3,900	2,871	
15469 sdn 4d, V-8	3,515	2,524	

Bel Air	Wght	Price	Prod
15511 sdn 2d, I-6	3,310	2,465	107,800*
15535 wgn 4d, I-6	3,765	2,828	
15545 wgn 4d, 9P, I-6	3,810	2,931	
15569 sdn 4d, I-6	3,380	2,519	
15611 sdn 2d, V-8	3,460	2,573	163,600*
15635 wgn 4d, V-8	3,905	2,936	
15645 wgn 4d, 9P, V-8	3,950	3,039	
15669 sdn 4d, V-8	3,530	2,626	

Impala—803,400* built (includes Caprice pkg)

	Wght	Price	Prod
16335 wgn 4d, I-6	3,825	2,970	56,600*
16337 htp cpe, I-6	3,385	2,678	
16339 htp sdn, I-6	3,490	2,742	
16345 wgn 4d, 9P, I-6	3,865	3,073	
16367 conv cpe, I-6	3,470	2,943	
16369 sdn 4d, I-6	3,460	2,672	
16435 wgn 4d, V-8	3,960	3,078	746,800*
16437 htp cpe, V-8	3,525	2,785	
16439 htp sdn, V-8	3,630	2,850	
16445 wgn 4d, 9P, V-8	4,005	3,181	
16467 conv cpe, V-8	3,605	3,051	
16469 sdn 4d, V-8	3,595	2,779	

Impala SS—243,114 built

	Wght	Price	Prod
16537 htp cpe, I-6	3,435	2,839	—
16567 conv cpe, I-6	3,505	3,104	—
16637 htp cpe, V-8	3,570	2,947	—
16667 conv cpe, V-8	3,655	3,212	—

Corvair 500

	Wght	Price	Prod
10137 htp cpe	2,385	2,066	36,747
10139 htp sdn	2,405	2,142	17,560

Corvair Monza

	Wght	Price	Prod
10537 htp cpe	2,440	2,347	88,954
10539 htp sdn	2,465	2,422	37,157
10567 conv cpe	2,675	2,493	26,466

Corvair Corsa

	Wght	Price	Prod
10737 htp cpe	2,475	2,519	20,291
10767 conv cpe	2,710	2,665	8,353

Corvette Sting Ray

	Wght	Price	Prod
19437 cpe	2,975	4,321	8,186
19467 conv rdstr	2,985	4,106	15,376

*To nearest 100; does not include wagons. Wagon production: Chevy II 21,500; Chevelle 37,600; others 184,400. Convertible production: Malibu 19,765; Impala SS 27,842.

1966

- **Stylish facelifts for Chevy II and Chevelle**

- **Caprice ousts Impala as Chevy's top-line full-size**

- **Corvair sales plunge as safety controversy mounts**

- **New 427 big-block option for Corvette and full-size Chevys**

▲ Unlike '65, the SS396 Chevelle was more readily available in handsomely restyled 1966 guise. This convertible started at $2984. The 396 was now the sole SS Chevelle powerplant.

▼ The '66 Chevelle SS396 Sport Coupe started at $2776, far less than the limited-run '65. SS production was far higher, with 72,300 convertibles and hardtops.

1966 Engine Availability

Engines	bore × stroke	bhp	availability
I-4, 153.0	3.88 × 3.25	90	S-Chevy II 100
I-6, 194.0	3.56 × 3.25	120	S-Chevy II, Chevelle
I-6, 230.0	3.87 × 3.25	140	O-Chevy II, Chevelle
I-6, 250.0	3.87 × 3.25	155	S-Chevrolet; O-Chevy II
V-8, 283.0	3.88 × 3.00	195	S-Chevelle, Chevrolet
V-8, 283.0	3.88 × 3.00	220	O-Chevrolet
V-8, 327.0	4.00 × 3.25	275/300	O-all
V-8, 327.0	4.00 × 3.25	350	O-Chevelle, Chevy II
V-8, 396.0	4.09 × 3.76	325	S-Chevelle 396; O-Chevrolet, Chevelle
V-8, 396.0	4.09 × 3.76	360/375	O-Chevelle
Corvair			
flat 6, 164.0	3.44 × 2.94	95	S-all exc Corsa
flat 6, 164.0	3.44 × 2.94	110	O-all exc Corsa
flat 6, 164.0	3.44 × 2.94	140	S-Corsa; O-others
flat 6, 164.0	3.44 × 2.94	180	O-Corsa
Corvette			
V-8, 327.0	4.00 × 3.25	300	S-all
V-8, 327.0	4.00 × 3.25	350	O-all
V-8, 427.0	4.25 × 3.76	390/425	O-all

▲ By 1966, the lighter midsize Chevelle had replaced the full-size Chevy as the bow tie brand's NASCAR warrior, though the division scored only two season wins. Shown here is Curtis Turner's '66 in 1967 Grand National action with an approved race-prepped 427 V-8. Street 1966 SS Chevelles had one of three 396 Turbo Jet engines: a base 325-horsepower version, a tuned 360-hp, and a rare 375-hp monster with mechanical lifters.

185

▲ Caprice expanded from posh trim option to a full three-model 1966 series above Impala. This wagon was the year's costliest passenger Chevy at $3234-$3347.

▲ Expanding Caprice models for '66 was this formal-roof two-door Custom Coupe hardtop priced at $3000 with the 283 V-8 that was also standard in wagons and the Custom Sedan four-door hardtop.

► Echoing prewar days—and perhaps with a nod to Lincoln's contemporary Continental convertible sedan—was the 1966 Caribe show car. Essentially, it was a ragtop Impala with four doors instead of two, plus Caprice-level trim. Seats were unique to this one-of-a-kind exercise. The front looks like a three-person bench here, but the center section could be converted to make bucketlike seating for two. Caribe and other mid '60s "concept cars" were far less special than GM's wild 1950s Motorama "dream cars," being built mainly to glamorize the regular models on which they were increasingly based. Ironically, Lincoln would drop its production four-door convertible after 1967.

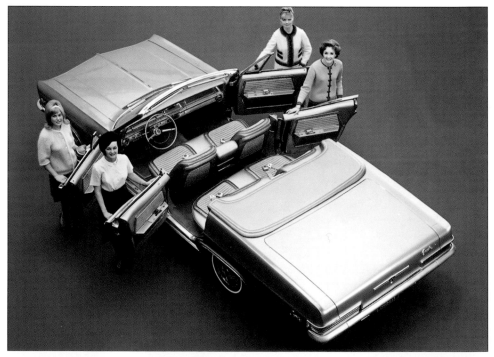

▼ Caprice was a quick response to the posh 1965 Ford LTD, but was a big success on its own, garnering 181,000 sales with three 1966 models. Here, a two-door Custom Coupe hardtop comes off the final assembly line. Early styling proposals envisioned a more radical roofline for this model.

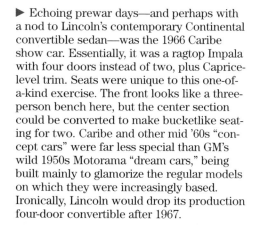

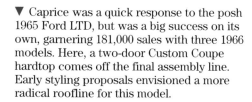

▲ Chevy's full-size convertible for 1966 was still an Impala, again offered in this regular-trim model and as a Super Sport. The latter saw 15,872 copies. Standard-model production is unknown.

◄ Chevrolet offered 14 wagon models for 1966, including three versions of the compact Sportvan, which were included in the separate wagon brochure but not this group portrait. Shown (*from left*) are the full-size Caprice, Impala, Bel Air, and Biscayne wagons, a Chevelle Malibu, and a Chevy II Nova.

▲ Bel Airs remained the "middle" full-size Chevys in both price and popularity. The two-door sedan started at $2479.

► Low-line Biscaynes weren't particularly popular with civilians, but the four-door sedans remained in demand for law enforcement, like this example in Chicago Police Department uniform.

◄▲▼ The '66 Chevy II Nova SS Sport Coupe saw some 23,000 copies, nearly three-quarters of which were V-8 powered. Fatter-than-stock tires suggests this beauty packs one of the 327 options, which again offered 275, 300, or a rousing 350 hp. New lower-body sheetmetal freshened the basic 1962 bodies; hardtops got a "faster" roofline as well. The new look was a likely factor in lifting total Chevy II sales to some 165,300 for the model year. With base V-8, the Nova SS started at an attractive $2535.

▲ Chevy II again offered two four-door six-passenger wagons for '66. The Nova (shown) remained the uplevel version, priced at $2518 with standard six-cylinder engine or $2623 with base V-8.

▲ The pretty second-generation Corvair saw little change in its second season except on the sales chart, where orders declined almost 50 percent. The Monza coupe (shown) was the best-selling model.

▲ Corvair's base-trim 500 four-door hardtop found only 8779 customers for 1966 despite its affordable $2157 starting price. By this point, Chevy had halted further Corvair development work.

▲ This '66 Corvair Monza convertible is one of 10,345 built; the turbocharged Corsa version saw a mere 3142 copies. Growing public concern over Ralph Nader's charges of unsafe handling was a major factor in Corvair's fast declining sales curve, even though the second-generation models were much more predictable "at the limit" than earlier 'Vairs. Monzas again offered 95 standard hp and 110- and 140-hp options, all from the same 164-cid six.

▲ Limited space in an awkwardly shaped trunk had always been a sales handicap of Corvair's rear-engine design versus conventional front-engine compacts. That continued into the second-generation models, though Chevy engineers provided as much room as they could by dropping the front floor area and mounting the spare tire above the engine in back. On the other hand, the rear-engine layout meant a relatively light front end that eliminated the need for power steering. It also made for a flat-floor interior offering better-than-average legroom for the exterior size. Interestingly, a 108-inch wheelbase would make a '66 Corvair a midsize car by today's standards, not a compact.

▲ Chevy's new 427 big-block V-8 replaced the 396 as Corvette's top 1966 power option, offering 390 or 425 hp. Model-year production set another record with 17,762 ragtops and 9958 coupes like this.

▲ Chevy Sportvans returned on a 90-inch wheelbase in base, Custom, and Deluxe models listing at $2390-$2745. All used a 230-cid six placed between driver and front passenger for maximum interior space utilization.

▶ Again showing little evident year-to-year change was the 1966 edition of Chevy's workhorse C-10 Stepside pickup, here in short-box 115-inch-wheelbase form.

Model Breakdown

Chevy II 100	Wght	Price	Prod
11111 sdn 2d, I-4	2,520	2,028	
11169 sdn 4d, I-4	2,535	2,065	
11311 sdn 2d, I-6	2,620	2,090	44,500*
11335 wgn 4d, I-6	2,855	2,430	
11369 sdn 4d, I-6	2,635	2,127	
11411 sdn 2d, V-8	2,775	2,197	
11435 wgn 4d, V-8	2,990	2,536	2,500*
11469 sdn 4d, V-8	2,790	2,234	
Chevy II Nova			
11535 wgn 4d, I-6	2,885	2,518	
11537 htp cpe, I-6	2,675	2,271	54,300*
11569 sdn 4d, I-6	2,640	2,245	
11635 wgn 4d, V-8	3,010	2,623	
11637 htp cpe, V-8	2,830	2,377	19,600*
11669 sdn 4d, V-8	2,800	2,351	
Chevy II Nova SS			
11737 htp cpe, I-6	2,740	2,430	6,700*
11837 htp cpe, V-8	2,870	2,535	16,300*
Chevelle 300			
13111 sdn 2d, I-6	2,895	2,156	23,300*
13169 sdn 4d, I-6	2,935	2,202	
13211 sdn 2d, V-8	3,040	2,271	5,300*
13269 sdn 4d, V-8	3,080	2,308	
13311 Del sdn 2d, I-6	2,910	2,239	
13335 Del wgn 4d, I-6	3,210	2,575	
13369 Del sdn 4d, I-6	2,945	2,276	
13411 Del sdn 2d, V-8	3,060	2,345	37,600*
13435 Del wgn 4d, V-8	3,350	2,681	
13469 Del sdn 4d, V-8	3,095	2,382	
Chevelle Malibu—241,600* built			
13517 htp cpe, I-6	2,935	2,378	—
13535 wgn 4d, I-6	3,235	2,651	—
13539 htp sdn, I-6	3,035	2,458	—

Chevelle Malibu (cont.)	Wght	Price	Prod
13567 conv cpe, I-6	3,030	2,588	—
13569 sdn 4d, I-6	2,960	2,352	—
13617 htp cpe, V-8	3,075	2,484	—
13635 wgn 4d, V-8	3,375	2,766	—
13639 htp sdn, V-8	3,180	2,564	—
13667 conv cpe, V-8	3,175	2,693	—
13669 sdn 4d, V-8	3,110	2,456	—
Chevelle Malibu SS, V-8—72,300* built			
13817 htp cpe	3,375	2,776	—
13867 conv cpe, V-8	3,470	2,984	—
Biscayne			
15311 sdn 2d, I-6	3,310	2,379	
15335 wgn 4d, I-6	3,770	2,772	83,200*
15369 sdn 4d, I-6	3,375	2,431	
15411 sdn 2d, V-8	3,445	2,484	
15435 wgn 4d, V-8	3,895	2,877	39,200*
15469 sdn 4d, V-8	3,519	2,537	
Bel Air			
15511 sdn 2d, I-6	3,315	2,479	
15535 wgn 4d, 2S, I-6	3,770	2,835	
15545 wgn 4d, 3S, I-6	3,815	2,948	72,100*
15569 sdn 4d, I-6	3,390	2,531	
15611 sdn 2d, V-8	3,445	2,584	
15635 wgn 4d, 2S, V-8	3,895	2,940	
15645 wgn 4d, 9P, V-8	3,940	3,053	164,500*
15669 sdn 4d, V-8	3,525	2,636	
Impala			
16335 wgn 4d, 2S, I-6	3,805	2,971	
16337 htp cpe, I-6	3,430	2,684	
16339 htp sdn, I-6	3,525	2,747	
16345 wgn 4d, 3S, I-6	3,860	3,083	33,100*
16367 conv cpe, I-6	3,484	2,935	
16369 sdn 4d, I-6	3,435	2,678	

Impala (continued)	Wght	Price	Prod
16435 wgn 4d, 2S, V-8	3,990	3,076	
16437 htp cpe, V-8	3,555	2,789	
16439 htp sdn, V-8	3,650	2,852	621,800*
16445 wgn 4d, 3S, V-8	4,005	3,189	
16467 conv cpe, V-8	3,610	3,041	
16469 sdn 4d, V-8	3,565	2,783	
Impala SS—119,314 built			
16737 htp cpe, I-6	3,460	2,842	—
16767 conv cpe, I-6	3,505	3,093	—
16837 htp cpe, V-8	3,585	2,947	—
16867 conv cpe, V-8	3,630	3,199	—
Caprice, V-8—181,000* built			
16635 wgn 4d, 2S	3,970	3,234	—
16639 htp sdn	3,675	3,063	—
16645 wgn 4d, 3S	4,020	3,347	—
16647 htp cpe	3,600	3,000	—
Corvair 500			
10137 htp cpe	2,400	2,083	24,045
10139 htp sdn	2,445	2,157	8,779
Corvair Monza			
10537 htp cpe	2,445	2,350	37,605
10539 htp sdn	2,495	2,424	12,497
10567 conv cpe	2,675	2,493	10,345
Corvair Corsa			
10737 htp cpe	2,485	2,519	7,330
10767 conv cpe	2,720	2,662	3,140
Corvette Sting Ray			
19437 cpe	2,985	4,295	9,958
19467 conv rdstr	3,005	4,084	17,762

*To nearest 100; does not include wagons. Wagon production: Chevy II 21,400; Chevelle 31,900; others 185,500. Impala SS convertible cpe 15,872.

1967

- **Mustang-fighting Camaro bows with new 350 small-block option, paces Indy 500**

- **Corvair drops Corsa models, turbo engine**

- **Rare 560-hp L88 option for Corvette**

- **Full-size cars get new, curvier bodies**

- **Impala SS offers big-block 427 option**

▲ The caption supplied with this 1967 announcement photo from Chevy PR describes members of the division's five existing car lines "standing at attention as the Camaro, newest member of the family, makes its introductory bow to the public." Interestingly enough, those existing lines all recorded lower model-year sales, while Camaro made its debut with a very impressive production total of 220,917 units.

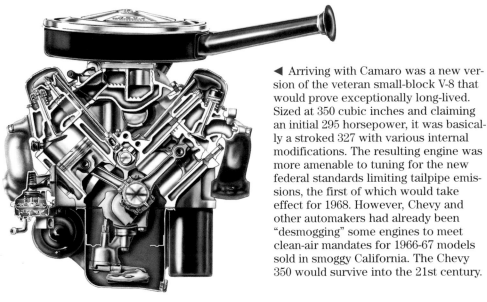

◄ Arriving with Camaro was a new version of the veteran small-block V-8 that would prove exceptionally long-lived. Sized at 350 cubic inches and claiming an initial 295 horsepower, it was basically a stroked 327 with various internal modifications. The resulting engine was more amenable to tuning for the new federal standards limiting tailpipe emissions, the first of which would take effect for 1968. However, Chevy and other automakers had already been "desmogging" some engines to meet clean-air mandates for 1966-67 models sold in smoggy California. The Chevy 350 would survive into the 21st century.

◄ The "Command performance" Camaro was extolled in this early ad as "Chevrolet's new driving machine with big-car stability and big-car power." Actually, it was the bow tie answer to Ford's phenomenally successful 1965-66 Mustang "ponycar."

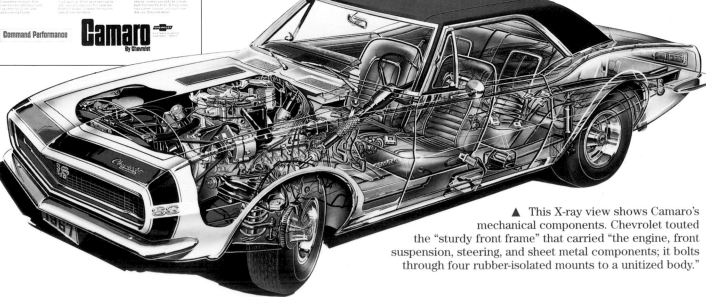

▲ This X-ray view shows Camaro's mechanical components. Chevrolet touted the "sturdy front frame" that carried "the engine, front suspension, steering, and sheet metal components; it bolts through four rubber-isolated mounts to a unitized body."

◄▲ Camaro didn't bother with a fastback like Mustang, but wore its own very clean styling in the curvy, contemporary GM mold. This convertible priced from $2704 with 230-cid six, $2809 with base 210-hp 327 V-8. The dashboard (*above*) was a reverse-slant design similar to Corvair's. A tachometer and full engine gauges were part of a mile-long options list.

▲ The heart of Camaro's Z-28 package was this special high-tune, high-winding 302 V-8, basically the 327 block running a 283 V-8 crankshaft. Horsepower was conservatively rated at 290, with as many pound-feet of torque, but was actually closer to 400. Z-28s won only three '67 Trans-Am races, but would soon dominate the series.

▲ Hidden headlamps identified Camaros equipped with the Rally Sport appearance package, which could be combined with the performance-oriented SS option. As this photo shows, grille sections at each end powered aside to uncover the lamps.

▲▼ Bowing in early 1967, the Camaro Z-28 package was created for the Sports Car Club of America's year-old Trans-American race series for compact "sedans." Broad dorsal stripes, "Rally" wheels, wide red-stripe tires, and uprated F41 suspension were included in the option, which was available only for the hardtop Sport Coupe at about $3800 delivered. Just 602 were built for '67 and have long been among the most prized of early Camaros.

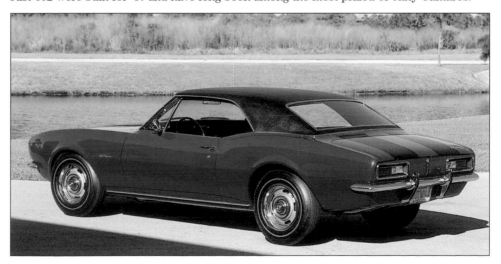

▲ Mark Donohue, driving for Camaro team owner Roger Penske, wheels his Z-28 in a 1967 Trans-Am race. The previous year, Donohue had driven…a Ford Mustang.

▲ Chevy wasted no time conjuring concept Camaros for 1967 auto shows. One was the Waikiki with simulated wood paneling and not-yet-legal square headlamps.

▲ Built in '67 for 1968 show duty, the Camaro-based Caribe concept was part "ponycar," part pickup. It would have made a dandy partner for the midsize El Camino.

▶ In another ploy to publicize its new Mustang-fighter, Chevrolet lobbied officials at Indianapolis Motor Speedway to choose Camaro as pace car for the 1967 Indy 500. The actual pacer was this convertible with the RS and SS396 packages, but about 100 replicas were built with 350 V-8s and Powerglide transmissions for official use during race week. All were later sold to the public. They're naturally prized collectibles today.

▼ Keeping to a two-year design cycle, full-size '67 Chevys got brand-new bodyshells with flowing lines that made the cars appear longer, though overall length and wheelbase were unchanged. A rounded "coke bottle" rear fenderline is evident in this profile view of the Impala Super Sport convertible, which started at $3254 with standard V-8 and saw 9545 copies. A 155-hp 230-cid six was still available for SS Impalas, but only 400 were built this year.

▲ A fastback roofline continued for '67 on the Impala Sport Coupe (left) and its SS sister, but it had a "faster" slope that faired more gently into the rear deck. Respective prices with base V-8 were $2845 and $3003. Taillamps faintly echoed 1958's "gullwing" look. Up front was a new "lattice-work grille playing peekaboo around the front fenders," or so said Chevy's PR staff.

◄ The Biscayne two-door sedan remained the most affordable big Chevy for 1967, starting at $2442 with standard 230-cid six. It was as plain as low-end cars got in those days, but delivered a lot of metal for the money.

▼ Still regarded by many as one of the best 'Vette's of all time, the '67 Sting Ray got five smaller front fender vents, new rocker panel trim, slotted Rally wheels, and slight interior changes, including a parking brake moved to the center console. Ironically, year-to-year sales eased for the first time in years, slipping to 22,940 units. The convertible again took the majority: 14,436. A large functional hood scoop again signaled the big-block 427 options.

▲ Corvette's top regular power option was a triple-two-barrel 427 with 435 hp. Just 20 '67s were built with a 530-hp L88 version.

▲ Corvair lost its turbo engine and sportiest Corsa models for '67, both due to flagging demand, leaving this Monza convertible to top the line at $2540. Just 2109 were built. Overall Corvair sales were now in a tailspin, and competition from the sporty new Camaro only hastened the downward spiral. As a result, total 'Vair production hit a new one-year low of 27,253 units.

▲ Like John Fitch, Pennsylvania-based Chevy racer and tuner Don Yenko built and sold small numbers of modified Corvairs for road and track. Here, the '67 version of his "Stinger," which was named for the sharp performance of its tail-mounted engine.

Engine Availability

Engines	bore × stroke	bhp	availability
I-4, 153.0	3.88 × 3.25	90	S-Chevy II 100 sdns
I-6, 194.0	3.56 × 3.25	120	S-Chevy II, Chevelle
I-6, 230.0	3.88 × 3.25	140	S-Camaro
I-6, 250.0	3.88 × 3.53	155	S-Chevrolet exc Caprice; O-others
V-8, 283.0	3.88 × 3.00	195	S-all exc Camaro
V-8, 302.0	4.00 × 3.00	290	O-Camaro (Z-28)
V-8, 327.0	4.00 × 3.25	210	O-Camaro
V-8, 327.0	4.00 × 3.25	275	O-all
V-8, 327.0	4.00 × 3.25	325	O-Chevelle
V-8, 350.0	4.00 × 3.48	295	O-Camaro
V-8, 396.0	4.09 × 3.76	325	S-Chevelle 396; O-Camaro, Chevrolet
V-8, 396.0	4.09 × 3.76	350	O-Chevelle 396
V-8, 427.0	4.25 × 3.76	385	O-Chevrolet
Corvair			
flat 6, 164.0	3.44 × 2.94	95	S-all
flat 6, 164.0	3.44 × 2.94	110/140	O-all
Corvette			
V-8, 327.0	4.00 × 3.25	300	S-all
V-8, 327.0	4.00 × 3.25	350	O-all
V-8, 427.0	4.25 × 3.76	390-425	O-all

▲ Restyled only the previous year, Chevelles sported just minor trim changes for '67. SS396s now offered a "base" 325-hp big-block and optional 350- and 375-hp versions. This $3033 ragtop was one of 63,000 SS Chevelles built for the model year.

▲ A "tunnelback" roofline carried over for '67 on Chevelle Sport Coupes, including the muscular SS396, which priced from $2825. Total Chevelle sales this model year slipped to 369,100, in part because of newly styled and muscled-up competition from Ford.

▲ Even in Super Sport trim, the Chevy II Nova Sport Coupe looked a bit conservative next to most of its '67 linemates. Sales declined for the model year to 10,100, of which 8200 were equipped with the base 327 V-8.

▲ Again the very model of high-value small-car utility, the '67 Chevy II Nova wagon listed at $2566 with six, $2583 with V-8. The latter was still seldom ordered in these compact haulers.

▲ Chevy pickups got a complete restyle for 1967. Fleetsides again had wider cargo boxes than the Stepside models. This ¾-ton Series 20 Fleetside looks pretty slick for a work truck with few visible options.

Model Breakdown

Chevy II 100	Wght	Price	Prod
11111 sdn 2d, I-4	2,555	2,090	
11169 sdn 4d, I-4	2,560	2,120	
11311 sdn 2d, I-6	2,640	2,152	34,200*
11335 wgn 4d, I-6	2,865	2,478	
11369 sdn 4d, I-6	2,650	2,182	
11411 sdn 2d, V-8	2,770	2,258	
11435 wgn 4d, V-8	2,985	2,583	1,700*
11469 sdn 4d, V-8	2,780	2,287	
Chevy II Nova			
11535 wgn 4d, I-6	2,890	2,566	
11537 htp cpe, I-6	2,660	2,330	34,400*
11569 sdn 4d, I-6	2,660	2,298	
11635 wgn 4d, V-8	3,015	2,671	
11637 htp cpe, V-8	2,790	2,435	13,200*
11669 sdn 4d, V-8	2,790	2,403	
Chevy II Nova SS			
11737 htp cpe, I-6	2,690	2,487	1,900*
11837 htp cpe, V-8	2,820	2,590	8,200*
Camaro (includes 602 Z-28s)			
12337 htp cpe, I-6	2,770	2,466	
12367 conv cpe, I-6	3,025	2,704	58,808
12437 htp cpe, V-8	2,920	2,572	
12467 conv cpe, V-8	3,180	2,809	162,109
Chevelle 300			
13111 sdn 2d, I-6	2,935	2,221	19,900*
13169 sdn 4d, I-6	2,955	2,250	
13211 sdn 2d, V-8	3,070	2,326	4,800*
13269 sdn 4d, V-8	3,090	2,356	
13311 Del sdn 2d, I-6	2,955	2,295	
13335 Del wgn 4d, I-6	3,230	2,619	19,300*
13369 Del sdn 4d, I-6	2,980	2,324	
13411 Del sdn 2d, V-8	3,090	2,400	
13435 Del wgn 4d, V-8	3,360	2,725	7,000*
13469 Del sdn 4d, V-8	3,110	2,430	

Chevelle Malibu	Wght	Price	Prod
13517 htp cpe, I-6	2,980	2,434	
13535 wgn 4d, I-6	3,260	2,695	
13539 htp sdn, I-6	3,065	2,506	40,600*
13567 conv cpe, I-6	3,050	2,637	
13569 sdn 4d, I-6	3,000	2,400	
13617 htp cpe, V-8	3,115	2,540	
13635 wgn 4d, V-8	3,390	2,801	
13639 htp sdn, V-8	3,200	2,611	187,200*
13667 conv cpe, V-8	3,185	2,743	
13669 sdn 4d, V-8	3,130	2,506	
Chevelle Concours			
13735 wgn 4d, I-6	3,270	2,827	5,900
13835 wgn 4d, V-8	3,405	2,933	21,400
Chevelle Super Sport—63,000* built			
13817 htp cpe	3,415	2,825	—
13867 conv cpe, V-8	3,485	3,033	—
Biscayne			
15311 sdn 2d, I-6	3,335	2,442	
15335 wgn 4d, I-6	3,765	2,817	54,200*
15369 sdn 4d, I-6	3,395	2,484	
15411 sdn 2d, V-8	3,465	2,547	
15435 wgn 4d, V-8	3,885	2,923	38,600*
15469 sdn 4d, V-8	3,525	2,589	
Bel Air			
15511 sdn 2d, I-6	3,340	2,542	
15535 wgn 4d, 2S, I-6	3,770	2,881	
15545 wgn 4d, 3S, I-6	3,825	2,993	41,500*
15569 sdn 4d, I-6	3,410	2,584	
15611 sdn 2d, V-8	3,470	2,647	
15635 wgn 4d, 2S, V-8	3,890	2,986	
15645 wgn 4d, 9P, V-8	3,940	3,098	138,200*
15669 sdn 4d, V-8	3,535	2,689	

Impala	Wght	Price	Prod
16335 wgn 4d, 2S, I-6	3,805	3,016	
16339 htp sdn, I-6	3,540	2,793	
16345 wgn 4d, 3S, I-6	3,868	3,129	18,800*
16367 conv cpe, I-6	3,515	2,991	
16369 sdn 4d, I-6	3,455	2,723	
16387 htp cpe, V-8	3,475	2,740	
16435 wgn 4d, 2S, V-8	3,920	3,122	
16439 htp sdn, V-8	3,660	2,899	
16445 wgn 4d, 3S, V-8	3,990	3,234	556,800*
16467 conv cpe, V-8	3,625	3,097	
16469 sdn 4d, V-8	3,575	2,828	
16487 htp cpe, V-8	3,590	2,845	
Impala SS—76,055 built (includes 2,124 SS427)			
16767 conv cpe, I-6	3,535	3,149	400*
16787 htp cpe, I-6	3,500	2,898	
16867 conv cpe, V-8	3,650	3,254	73,600*
16887 htp cpe, V-8	3,615	3,003	
Caprice, V-8—124,500* built			
16635 wgn 4d, 2S	3,935	3,301	—
16639 htp sdn	3,710	3,130	—
16645 wgn 4d, 3S	3,990	3,413	—
16647 htp cpe	3,605	3,078	—
Corvair 500			
10137 htp cpe	2,435	2,128	9,257
10139 htp sdn	2,470	2,194	2,959
Corvair Monza			
10537 htp cpe	2,465	2,398	9,771
10539 htp sdn	2,515	2,464	3,157
10567 conv cpe	2,695	2,540	2,109
Corvette Sting Ray			
19437 cpe	3,000	4,353	8,504
19467 conv rdstr	3,020	4,141	14,436

*To nearest 100; does not include wagons. Wagon production: Chevy II 12,900; Chevelle 27,300; others 155,100. Convertible production: Camaro 25,141; Impala SS 9,545.

1968

- **Radically restyled Corvette debuts**

- **New bodies, new styling rejuvenate Chevelle, Chevy II**

- **Camaro wins Trans-Am championship**

- **Impala SS reverts to option status**

- **Corvair hits a new sales low**

- **307 V-8 replaces 283**

▲ Like all 1968 General Motors intermediates, Chevelle was fully redesigned on a brand-new "A-body" platform designed around two wheelbases. The shorter, 112-inch span was exclusive to two-door models like this $2899 SS396 Sport Coupe. Big-block Chevelles again offered 325 standard horsepower, plus 350- and new 375-hp options.

▶ Another SS396 Sport Coupe shows off optional "bumblebee" nose striping, a treatment seen on several late-'60s Detroit "muscle cars," Chevys among them. Chevelle's new styling made all coupes and convertibles look rather more aggressive, abetted on SS models by a black-finish on the grille, lower body, and back-panel. Chevy built 60,499 SS Sport Coupes for '68 but only 2266 ragtops, plus an unknown number of SS-equipped El Camino car/pickups, which shared Chevelle's basic new design.

▲ Again answering the growing demand for midsize wagons with full-size luxury was the Chevelle Concours, back from '67 with a one-inch longer wheelbase and more simulated wood side paneling. Price was $3083 with base V-8, which was now a 200-hp 307, basically a stroked version of the veteran 283, which it replaced.

▲ Chevelle's only hardtop sedan for 1968 was again reserved for the Malibu series. Front and rear side marker lights were among numerous safety enhancement features that were added per federal mandate. This Malibu priced from $2629 with standard 230-cid six, $2735 with the new 307 base V-8.

▲ Originally planned for 1967 but delayed by development problems, the '68 Corvette wore a swoopy new body atop the 1963-67 chassis and dispensed with the Sting Ray name. It also dispensed with conventional door handles in favor of a pushbutton next to a hand grip covered by a spring-loaded metal flap. Front-fender slots reduced underhood air pressure and heat, but cooling problems still dogged the new design. Though the styling was controversial at the time, Corvette production rose to 28,566, a new all-time high. The convertible (shown) still outsold the coupe by far, accounting for 18,630 units. It priced from $4320.

▶ GM design chief Bill Mitchell poses with his 1965 Mako Shark II concept (*left*) and a red '68 'Vette convertible with optional hardtop. The intentional resemblance led to the nickname "shark" for the basic '68 design.

▶ Corvette's racing fortunes had long since passed from the factory to private teams by 1968. Writing a successful new chapter in the saga was ace driver Tony DeLorenzo, who began campaigning both open and closed 'Vettes starting in the summer of '68 with help from Owens-Corning Fiberglas— a natural sponsor for the "plastic" sports cars. DeLorenzo was 1968 A-production champ in SCCA's central division, then claimed the national crown in '69.

196

◀▲ Like the first Sting Ray, the '68 Corvette kept the previous year's engines, so the top option remained a 427 big-block (*above*) with 390, 400, or 435 hp. A special domed hood (*top*), necessary for clearance, identified cars so equipped. Big-block or small-block, all '68 'Vettes had a new, very space-age dash (*left*), but also less usable cockpit space, one of the new design's most often criticized aspects. A big right-side grab bar was still provided, but an in-dash glovebox was nowhere to be found.

◀ Replacing the Sting Ray fastback for '68 was a new notchback coupe with "tunnel" roofline, newly removable rear window, and a novel "T-bar" anchoring twin liftoff roof panels above the seats. There was still no trunklid, though, making the accessory luggage rack almost a necessity, and bumper protection remained minimal.

197

▲ Chevrolet's "ponycar" wasn't much altered for its sophomore year, but optional four-wheel disc brakes arrived at midyear and were especially welcome on high-power models like the Z-28. This one wears the separately available Rally Sport appearance package, hence the front-fender ID. Other Z-28 improvements included standard quick-ratio steering and more racing-oriented options.

▼ Camaro's Z-28 package was more readily available for '68, but still far from common with just 7199 installations. However, Z-28s were common in the Trans-Am winner's circle that season, claiming 10 of 13 races to win the SCCA series title. The achievement was owed to team owner/manager Roger Penske, lead driver Mark Donohue, and ample support from Chevy Engineering.

◄ This view of the '68 Camaro dash shows the outboard air registers that were part of the new flow-through "Astro Ventilation" system, which dispensed with door vent windows on all of that year's models.

► A revised grille freshened the appearance of all '68 Camaros without the hidden-headlamp RS package. "Bumblebee" nose stripes again identified cars like this with the optional SS350 or SS396 options.

▲ Reflecting the waning interest in sporty big cars, the Impala Super Sport returned to option status for '68. The $179 package saw 38,210 installations, as on this ragtop.

▲ Full-size '68s wore a nice update of their new '67 styling. Here, the Impala wagon, which continued in six- and nine-passenger versions and started at $3245. The standard V-8 for all big Chevys was now a more emissions-friendly 307 small-block with 200 hp. An accessory rear-roof air deflector helped to keep the tailgate window cleaner in mucky weather.

▲ The big-Chevy dash had become Cadillac grand by 1968. In '65, automatic transmissions were Powerglide or superior three-speed Hydra-Matic, both options.

▲ A hidden-headlamp grille was newly optional for '68 Caprices, but the hardtop coupe in this ad no longer had an exclusive formal roofline, as a similar-looking Impala Custom model was added, though few were apparently built this year. The Caprice was priced from $3219.

◀▲ Biscayne sedans again anchored the big-Chevy line for '68. Six-cylinder versions retained a 250-cid engine with 155 hp, as did counterpart Bel Air models, which were only a bit fancier.

199

Engine Availability

Engines	bore × stroke	bhp	availability
I-4, 153.0	3.88 × 3.25	90	S-Chevy II
I-6, 230.0	3.88 × 3.25	140	S-Chevy II, Camaro, Chevelle
I-6, 250.0	3.88 × 3.53	155	S-Chevrolet; O-Camaro, Chevelle
V-8, 302.0	4.00 × 3.00	290	O-Camaro (Z-28)
V-8, 307.0	3.88 × 3.25	200	S-Chevy II, Chevelle, Chevrolet
V-8, 327.0	4.00 × 3.25	210	S-Camaro
V-8, 327.0	4.00 × 3.25	250	O-Chevelle, Chevrolet
V-8, 327.0	4.00 × 3.25	275	O-all
V-8, 327.0	4.00 × 3.25	325	O-Chevelle
V-8, 350.0	4.00 × 3.48	295	O-Chevy II, Camaro
V-8, 396.0	4.09 × 3.76	325	S-Chevelle 396; O-Camaro, Chevrolet
V-8, 396.0	4.00 × 3.00	350/375	O-Camaro, Chevelle
V-8, 427.0	4.25 × 3.76	385/425	O-Chevrolet
Corvair			
flat 6, 164.0	3.44 × 2.94	95	S-all
flat 6, 164.0	3.44 × 2.94	110	O-all
Corvette			
V-8, 327.0	4.00 × 3.25	300	S-all
V-8, 327.0	4.00 × 3.25	350	O-all
V-8, 427.0	4.25 × 3.76	390-425	O-all

▲ Chevy II went to almost intermediate size for 1968 with a full redesign on a new 111-inch-wheelbase chassis that owed much to Chevelle. Models were cut to just two- and four-door Nova sedans. Available only for the two-door (shown) was an SS package delivering a 295-hp 350 V-8, wide tires, special hood, and black grille and rocker panel trim. Installations this year numbered 6571. Total Chevy II output came to 201,000 units.

▶ The Corvair lineup shrank for '68 to a "500" coupe and Monza coupe and convertible. Changes reflected federal mandates only, including side marker lights, additional interior padding, and standard shoulder belts. Powertrains were untouched, but not sales, which withered to 15,399 for the model year. Base price for this Monza coupe was up to $2507.

Model Breakdown

	Wght	Price	Prod
Chevy II Nova—201,000* built			
(includes 6,571 SS cpes)			
11127 cpe, I-4	2,760	2,222	—
11169 sdn 4d, I-4	2,790	2,252	—
11327 cpe, I-6	2,860	2,284	—
11369 sdn 4d, I-6	2,890	2,314	—
11427 cpe, V-8	2,995	2,390	—
11469 sdn 4d, V-8	3,025	2,419	—
Camaro (includes 7,199 Z-28s)			
12337 htp cpe, I-6	2,810	2,588	50,937
12367 conv cpe, I-6	3,110	2,802	
12437 htp cpe, V-8	2,955	2,694	184,178
12467 conv cpe, V-8	3,245	2,908	
Chevelle 300			
13127 cpe, I-6	3,020	2,341	2,900*
13135 Nmd wgn 4d, I-6	3,370	2,625	
13227 cpe, V-8	3,155	2,447	9,700*
13235 Nmd wgn 4d, V-8	3,500	2,731	
13327 Del cpe, I-6	3,035	2,415	
13335 Cus Nmd wgn 4d, I-6	3,415	2,736	25,500*
13337 Del htp cpe, I-6	3,050	2,479	
13369 Del sdn 4d, I-6	3,105	2,445	
13427 Del cpe, V-8	3,170	2,521	
13435 Cus Nmd wgn 4d, V-8	3,545	2,841	17,700*
13437 Del htp cpe, V8	3,185	2,584	
13469 Del sdn 4d, V-8	3,240	2,550	
Chevelle Malibu			
13535 wgn 4d, I-6	3,440	2,846	
13537 htp cpe, I-6	3,070	2,558	
13539 htp sdn, I-6	3,185	2,629	33,100*
13567 conv cpe, I-6	3,135	2,757	
13569 sdn 4d, I-6	3,125	2,524	

Chevelle Malibu (cont.)	Wght	Price	Prod
13635 wgn 4d, V-8	3,575	2,951	
13637 htp cpe, V-8	3,204	2,663	
13639 htp sdn, V-8	3,315	2,735	233,200*
13667 conv cpe, V-8	3,260	2,863	
13669 sdn 4d, V-8	3,255	2,629	
Chevelle Concours			
13735 wgn 4d, I-6	3,450	2,978	—
13835 wgn 4d, V-8	3,580	3,083	—
Chevelle SS 396			
13837 htp cpe	3,550	2,899	60,499
13867 conv cpe	3,570	3,102	2,286
Biscayne			
15311 sdn 2d, I-6	3,400	2,581	
15335 wgn 4d, I-6	3,790	2,957	44,500*
15369 sdn 4d, I-6	3,465	2,623	
15411 sdn 2d, V-8	3,520	2,686	
15435 wgn 4d, V-8	3,900	3,062	37,600*
15469 sdn 4d, V-8	3,585	2,728	
Bel Air			
15511 sdn 2d, I-6	3,405	2,681	
15535 wgn 4d, 2S, I-6	3,800	3,020	28,800*
15545 wgn 4d, 3S, I-6	3,845	3,133	
15569 sdn 4d, I-6	3,470	2,723	
15611 sdn 2d, V-8	3,525	2,786	
15635 wgn 4d, 2S, V-8	3,910	3,125	123,400*
15645 wgn 4d, 3S, V-8	3,955	3,238	
15669 sdn 4d, V-8	3,590	2,828	
Impala—38,210 SS built (includes 1,778 SS427)			
16339 htp sdn, I-6	3,605	2,917	
16369 sdn 4d, I-6	3,520	2,846	11,400*
16387 htp cpe, I-6	3,250	2,863	

Impala (continued)	Wght	Price	Prod
16435 wgn 4d, 2S, V8	3,940	3,245	
16439 htp sdn, V-8	3,715	3,022	
16445 wgn 4d, 3S, V-8	3,905	3,358	
16447 Cus htp cpe, V-8	3,645	3,021	699,500*
16467 conv cpe, V-8	3,680	3,197	
16469 sdn 4d, V-8	3,630	2,951	
16487 htp cpe, V-8	3,630	2,968	
Caprice—115,500* built			
16635 wgn 4d, 2S	3,950	3,458	—
16639 htp sdn	3,755	3,271	—
16645 wgn 4d, 3S	4,005	3,570	—
16647 htp cpe	3,660	3,219	—
Corvair 500			
10137 htp cpe	2,470	2,243	7,206
Corvair Monza			
10537 htp cpe	2,500	2,507	6,807
10567 conv cpe	2,725	2,626	1,386
Corvette			
19437 cpe	3,055	4,663	9,936
19467 conv rdstr	3,065	4,320	18,630

*To nearest 100; does not include wagons. Wagon production: Chevelle 45,500; others 175,600. Camaro convertible cpe 20,440.

1969

- **Corvair discontinued**

- **Camaro facelifted, repeats as Trans-Am champion, again paces Indy 500**

- **Corvette revives the Stingray name, sets another sales record**

▲ In a move that surprised no one, Chevy ended Corvair production on May 14, 1969, after five years of controversy and falling sales. Exactly 6000 of the '69s were built, again divided among "500" and Monza coupes and this $2641 Monza convertible, one of a final 521.

▶ Amber instead of clear side marker lights were one of the very few changes made to the last Corvairs. Here, the $2522 Monza coupe, one of 2717 built. Its $2528 "500" counterpart garnered 2762 orders. Though Ralph Nader and the safety advocates he encouraged loomed large in Corvair's demise, the rear-engine Chevy still has a legion of loyal fans today. To their undoubted delight, a government report released in 2001 at least partly exonerated the handling that Nader had condemned in the early '60s, confirming what 'Vair fans and many auto writers had said all along. The last Corvair buyers got a $150 credit toward the purchase of any new Chevy through 1974.

Engine Availability

Engines	bore × stroke	bhp	availability
I-4, 153.0	3.88 × 3.25	90	S-Chevy II
I-6, 230.0	3.88 × 3.25	140	S-Chevelle, Chevy II, Camaro
I-6, 250.0	3.88 × 3.53	155	S-Chevrolet; O-Chevelle, Chevy II, Camaro
V-8, 302.0	4.00 × 3.00	290	O-Camaro (Z-28)
V-8, 307.0	3.88 × 3.25	200	S-Chevy II, Chevelle
V-8, 327.0	4.00 × 3.25	210	S-Camaro
V-8, 327.0	4.00 × 3.25	235	S-Chevrolet
V-8, 350.0	4.00 × 3.48	255	O-all
V-8, 350.0	4.00 × 3.48	300	O-Chevrolet, Chevelle, II SS, Camaro SS
V-8, 396.0	4.09 × 3.76	265	S-Chevelle 396; O-Chevrolet
V-8, 396.0	4.09 × 3.76	325	O-Chevelle 396, Camaro SS
V-8, 396.0	4.09 × 3.76	350/375	O-Chevelle/Nova/Camaro SS
V-8, 427.0	4.25 × 3.76	335-425	O-Chevrolet
Corvair			
flat 6 164.0	3.44 × 2.94	95	S-all
flat 6 164.0	3.44 × 2.94	110	O-all
Corvette			
V-8, 350.0	4.00 × 3.48	300	S-all
V-8, 350.0	4.00 × 3.48	350	O-all
V-8, 427.0	4.25 × 3.76	390-435	O-all

▲ Though Corvair development was effectively stopped by 1966, designers continued to dream up ideas for a possible third-generation series. This scale model is one of several such proposals for a "next Corvair," though it arguably evolves, rather than improves upon, the near-timeless styling of 1965-69.

▲► New for '69 Camaros was a "Liquid Tire Chain" option (*above*)—a dashboard pushbutton controlling an aerosol can of traction "improver" in the rear fenderwell. Meanwhile, one '69 Camaro ad (*right*) played on Packard's famous "Ask the man who owns one" slogan and carried Chevy's new umbrella tagline, "Putting you first."

Ask the kid who owns one.

▲ The '69 Z-28 Camaro's 302 V-8 again carried dual four-barrel carbs and aluminum intake manifold, plus a new "cowl induction" air-cleaner assembly mating to a functional "reverse scoop" hood. Advertised horsepower was still grossly understated at 290. Z-28 sales rose to 19,014. The package was still restricted to the Sport Coupe.

▲ Recontoured below-the-belt sheetmetal with racy rear fender "speedlines" gave a huskier, "more performance" look to all '69 Camaros. This convertible is decked out with the SS350 package, which added about $300 to the $2940 base price. A power top cost another $53.

▲ Camaro again offered two six-cylinder engines for '69: base 140-hp 230 and optional 155-hp 250. Only some 65,000 buyers chose one this year, versus total V-8 sales of over 178,000.

▲ The '69 Camaro facelift was unusually extensive for a two-year Detroit design, but Chevy was responding to early criticism that the original styling didn't look "tough" enough for a performance machine. This convertible was one of 17,573 built for the model year. Camaro would then do without a ragtop for the next 17 years.

▲ Created by veteran tuner Don Yenko, the 1969 Yenko/SC was basically a Z-28 Camaro stuffed with a factory-installed 427 big-block making an alleged 450 hp. A mere 201 of these cars were reportedly built.

▲ This '69 Camaro Sport Coupe is about go, not show, signaled by its fat tires, menacingly muscular bulged hood, and few cosmetic frills. In stock form this model started at $2726 with base 200-hp 307 V-8.

▲ Besides a new look outside, '69 Camaros sported a revised instrument panel with soft or recessed switchgear per federal safety mandates. Note the four-on-the-floor stickshift, still a freestanding option.

▲ The mostly innocent-looking Camaro Sport Coupe at the far left carries the big-block 427 that many drag racers stuffed in their cars. Chevy considered but rejected a regular production model coded ZL-1.

▲ Camaro paced the '69 Indy 500. Chevy reeled off 3675 convertibles with a replica "Pacesetter Value Package."

▲ Among '69 Corvettes, the coupe outsold the ragtop for the first time, while combined sales jumped by 10,000 units to 38,762, a record that would stand for some time. Base power was now a 350 V-8, though with the same 300 hp as the old 327. A 350-hp version was optional, as were three variations of the 427, shown here with signature side exhaust.

▲ Corvette big-blocks again began with this "base" 400-hp unit. A 435-hp version was reprised, too. A new super-high-compression version packed a nominal 430 hp.

◄ As expected, Chevelle's year-old styling was just mildly tweaked for 1969. SS396 production hit a new one-year high at 86,307 units (including a few El Caminos), but the SS Chevelle was demoted from separate-model status to a $422 performance package for two-door Malibus (Sport Coupe shown) and the humble 300 Deluxe pillared coupe. Included were a 325-hp big-block V-8, power front disc brakes, new five-spoke road wheels, and special trim. A 350-hp engine cost $122 more; a 375-hp version added $252.

▲ Chevelle posted another healthy sales gain for '69, led by some 367,100 Malibus like this Sport Coupe. Wagons totaled 45,900, nonwagon 300 Deluxes 42,000.

▲ Chevelle interiors were attractive, but none too exciting. Round instrument pods were used in place of the linear design found in the full-size cars.

▲ Chevelle's optional vinyl roof still looked a bit awkward on the 1969 Malibu Sport Coupe, which priced from $2601 with base 230-cid six, $2690 with base 307 V-8.

◄ The two-year-old styling of full-size Chevys was handsomely updated for 1969, announced by a broad loop-style bumper/grille. The Impala Super Sport made one final stand as a $422 package for the two-door hardtop (shown) and convertible. Installations totaled just 2425.

▲ Chevy's 1969 big-car restyle also included a revised rear bumper echoing the new loop-type front-end ensemble. It's shown to good effect on this rare Impala SS ragtop, which delivered for about $3700. The only engines for the SS Impala's swan-song season were a new 390-hp version of the big-block 427 V-8 and a rare 425-horse job.

◄ Big-Chevy wagons again had separate model names for '69. Top of the line was the Brookwood Estate, trimmed to Caprice level and identified by woody-look side trim. This example carries the optional hidden-headlamp grille and, unusually for a wagon, the burly 427 V-8 available for any full-size Chevy. The roof rack seen here was available over the parts counter.

▲ The Chevy II name was retired for 1969 in favor of Nova. Three engines—four-cylinder, six, and V-8—and one trim level continued for the four-door sedan and its two-door sister (shown), which Chevy usually termed a coupe. Model-year sales rose to nearly 252,000. Nova's X-body platform remained exclusive to Chevrolet.

▲ The work-oriented Chevy Van and passenger Sportvan had seen only evolutionary changes in their first five seasons, and 1969 was another year of detail updates. Shown here is a long-wheelbase model with a "pop-top" camper conversion, one of several developed for this vehicle by "aftermarket" companies and Chevrolet itself.

▲ Chevy's Panel Delivery soldiered on for 1969 despite dwindling demand. Its basic body and 127-inch wheelbase were shared with the truck-based Suburban wagon, but blank rear side windows and center-opening rear cargo doors remained unique. Both the ½-ton C-10 and ¾-ton C-20 models offered an optional 255-hp 350 V-8.

▶ Continuing on the 116-inch Chevelle wagon chassis, El Camino offered truck utility and car style. The '69 started at $2550 with six, $2640 with base V-8.

Model Breakdown

	Wght	Price	Prod
Chevy II Nova (includes 17,564 SS coupes)			
11127 cpe, I-4	2,785	2,237	6,100*
11169 sdn 4d, I-4	2,810	2,267	
11327 cpe, I-6	2,895	2,315	157,400*
11369 sdn 4d, I-6	2,920	2,345	
11427 cpe, V-8	3,035	2,405	88,400*
11469 sdn 4d, V-8	3,065	2,434	
Camaro (includes 19,014 Z-28s)			
12337 htp cpe, I-6	3,040	2,638	65,008**
12367 conv cpe, I-6	3,160	2,852	
12437 htp cpe, V-8	3,050	2,726	178,087**
12467 conv cpe, V-8	3,295	2,940	

Note: wagon destination "CT" refers to conventional tailgate, opening from top. Most wagons had dual-action tailgates, opening from top or from side, from 1969 onward.

	Wght	Price	Prod
Chevelle Nomad			
13135 wgn 4d, CT, I-6	3,390	2,668	—
13136 wgn 4d, I-6	3,475	2,170	—
13235 wgn 4d, CT, V-8	3,515	2,758	—
13236 wgn 4d, V-8	3,600	2,800	—
Chevelle 300 Deluxe			
13327 cpe, I-6	3,035	2,458	
13337 htp cpe, I-6	3,075	2,521	11,000*
13369 sdn 4d, I-6	3,100	2,488	
13427 cpe, V-8	3,165	2,548	
13437 htp cpe, V-8	3,205	2,611	31,000*
13469 sdn 4d, V-8	3,230	2,577	
Chevelle Greenbrier			
13335 wgn 4d, CT, I-6	3,445	2,779	7,400*
13336 wgn 4d, I-6	3,530	2,821	

Chevelle Grnbr.(cont.)	Wght	Price	Prod
13435 wgn 4d, CT, V-8	3,585	2,869	
13436 wgn 4d, 2S, V-8	3,665	2,911	38,500*
13446 wgn 4d, 3S, V-8	3,740	3,020	
Chevelle Malibu			
13537 htp cpe, I-6	3,095	2,601	
13539 htp sdn, I-6	3,205	2,672	23,500*
13567 conv cpe, I-6	3,175	2,800	
13569 sdn 4d, I-6	3,130	2,567	
13637 htp cpe, V-8	3,230	2,690	
13639 htp sdn, V-8	3,334	2,762	343,600*
13667 conv cpe, V-8	3,300	2,889	
13669 sdn 4d, V-8	3,265	2,657	
Chevelle Concours			
13536 wgn 4d, I-6	3,545	2,931	—
13636 wgn 4d, 2S, V-8	3,685	3,021	—
13646 wgn 4d, 3S, V-8	3,755	3,141	—
13836 del wgn 4d, 2S, V-8	3,680	3,153	—
13846 del wgn 4d, 3S, V-8	3,730	3,266	—
Biscayne			
15311 sdn 2d, I-6	3,530	2,645	
15336 wgn 4d, I-6	4,045	3,064	27,400*
15369 sdn 4d, I-6	3,590	2,687	
15411 sdn 2d, V-8	3,670	2,751	
15436 wgn 4d, V-8	4,170	3,169	41,300*
15469 sdn 4d, V-8	3,725	2,793	
Bel Air			
15511 sdn 2d, I-6	3,540	2,745	
15536 wgn 4d, 2S, I-6	4,045	3,127	17,000*
15546 wgn 4d, 3S, I-6	4,100	3,240	
15569 sdn 4d, I-6	3,590	2,787	

Bel Air (continued)	Wght	Price	Prod
15611 sdn 2d, V-8	3,675	2,851	
15636 wgn 4d, 2S, V-8	4,175	3,232	139,700*
15646 wgn 4d, 3S, V-8	4,230	3,345	
15669 sdn 4d, V-8	3,725	2,893	
Impala—2,455 SS427 built			
16337 htp cpe, I-6	3,650	2,927	
16339 htp sdn, I-6	3,735	2,981	8,700*
16369 sdn 4d, I-6	3,640	2,911	
16436 wgn 4d, 2S, V-8	3,725	3,352	
16437 htp cpe, V-8	3,775	3,033	
16439 htp sdn, V-8	3,855	3,056	
16446 wgn 4d, 3S, V-8	4,285	3,465	768,300*
16447 Cus htp cpe, V-8	3,800	3,085	
16467 conv cpe, V-8	3,835	3,261	
16469 sdn 4d, V-8	3,760	3,061	
Caprice, V-8—166,900* built			
16636 wgn 4d, 2S	4,245	3,565	—
16639 htp sdn	3,895	3,346	—
16646 wgn 4d, 3S	4,300	3,678	—
16647 htp cpe	3,815	3,294	—
Corvair 500			
10137 htp cpe	2,515	2,528	2,762
Corvair Monza			
10537 htp cpe	2,545	2,522	2,717
10567 conv cpe	2,770	2,641	521
Corvette Stingray			
19437 cpe	3,140	4,781	22,154
19467 conv rdstr	3,145	4,438	16,608

*To nearest 100; does not include wagons.
**Includes 1970 extension of 1969 model. Wagon production: Chevelle 45,900; others 59,300. Camaro convertible cpe 17,573.

1970

- Second-generation Camaro debuts

- New Monte Carlo puts Chevy in the personal-luxury game

- Big-block V-8 swells to 454 cubic inches

- A 65-day strike hampers production, sales at Chevrolet and all of General Motors

▲ Camaro was totally redesigned for 1970, but didn't go on sale until February 26 of that year. Wheelbase was unchanged for an improved chassis that held a new and rather "European" body measuring two inches longer and an inch lower. The Rally Sport appearance option returned without hidden headlamps, but was easily spotted by the "driving lights"—actually parking lamps—inboard of the headlamps; it also featured hidden wipers.

▲ Camaro's "1970½" redesign brought a new but still cozy cockpit with a large instrument cluster that curved in toward the driver at its outboard ends. Climate controls lived below to the left, the radio to the right. The console's "stirrup" shifter engaged the optional automatic transmission.

▲ The Camaro Z28 looked terrific in "1970½" trim, sporting racy "mag-style" wheels, discreet rear "lip" spoiler, and its traditional dorsal stripes. Under the hood sat a solid-lifter 350 V-8, not a revvy 302, though it made a strong 360 horsepower. Automatic transmission was available for the first time. Z28 production for this short season totaled 8733 units.

▲ Because the second-generation Camaro was delayed six months, little changed '69 coupes were built for the first part of the new season as "early 1970" models. Production is unknown. Here, an SS350 equipped with the RS package and other options.

▶ Chevy's vintage-1967 full-size design made its last stand for 1970. This "phantom" drawing shows basic body and chassis architecture hadn't changed much in the intervening years.

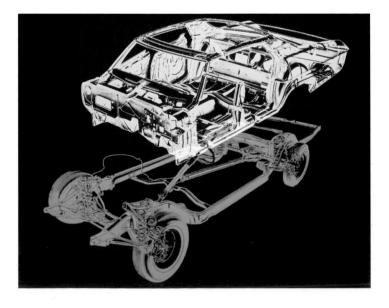

◄▲ Though this looks to be just an early second-generation Z28, this Camaro is a one-of-a-kind custom created by Hurst Performance, Inc. Originally ordered by funny-car drag racer Dick Jesse, it quickly ended up at Hurst, which used it to prototype two products the company was planning: a sliding fabric sunroof with plexiglas wind deflector and a "slap stick" shifter for GM's Turbo-Hydra-Matic transmission. The shifter soon found its way onto the aftermarket, while the sunroof was adopted by GM as an option for some of its early-'70s compact models. Hurst named this Camaro the "Sunshine Special." Today it's in the hands of a private collector. Note the Hurst badge added next to the Z28 logo.

▼ Chevy introduced two important V-8s for 1970: a big-block punched out to 454 cid and this new 400, an enlarged small-block 350. Increasing displacement was one of the easiest ways for automakers to meet the ever-stricter emissions limits decreed for the 1970s while maintaining horsepower. The 400 arrived as an option for full-size Chevys, midsize Chevelles, and the new Monte Carlo in 265- and 330-hp versions.

A group picture of all the cars in Monte Carlo's field.

▲ Responding to Pontiac's personal-luxury Grand Prix, the new 1970 Monte Carlo was billed as "a fine car at a Chevrolet price."

207

◄▲ Basically a Chevelle hardtop with a six-foot-long hood to fit the 116-inch mid-size wheelbase, the new Monte Carlo was Chevy's entry into the "personal-luxury" market dominated by Pontiac's Grand Prix and Ford's Thunderbird. This example is one of 3823 with the SS454 package, which delivered a 360-hp version of Chevy's newly enlarged big-block V-8, plus uprated suspension and buckets-and-console interior (*above*). Delivered price? About $3500.

◄▲ Corvette sales fell by over half to 17,316, the result of a two-month strike that paralyzed General Motors just as 1970 production was getting underway. A "cheese-grater" grille insert and front-fender vents provided visual ID, but the big news was the burly 454 V-8, replacing the 427 in 390- and thumping 460-hp versions. Also new—actually postponed from '69—was the LT-1, a solid-lifter 350 small-block conservatively rated at 370 hp. Base prices rose to $5192 for the coupe (*left*) and $4849 for the ragtop.

◄▲ Chevelle got a handsome facelift for 1970, plus new engines that were mostly featured in hot Super Sport models like this Malibu-based Sport Coupe. Besides the new 454, the list now included a "402" (a slightly enlarged 396, and still badged as such), that made 350, 375, or, in high-output form, 415 hp. The basic 396 package cost $445. The brawnier mills added another $200-$300.

▲► Chevelle's 1970 SS454 package added $840 to the $2809 starting price of a Malibu hardtop coupe. This beauty is one of 3733 such installations. A new dashboard (*right*), with curved "cockpit" gauge cluster *a la* Camaro and Monte Carlo, graced all 1970 Chevelle interiors.

► This 1970 Chevelle SS454 boasts the year's new reverse-facing "Cowl Induction" hood, a $148 must-have for speed demons. Chevelle SS production totaled 53,599 units for all engines, including the rare 360- and 450-hp 454s.

Engine Availability

Engines	bore × stroke	bhp	availability
I-4, 153.0	3.88 × 3.25	90	S-Nova
I-6, 230.0	3.88 × 3.25	140	S-Camaro; O-Nova
I-6, 250.0	3.88 × 3.53	155	S-Chevrolet exc Caprice & Impala cpe, Chevelle; O-Nova, Camaro
V-8, 307.0	3.88 × 3.25	200	S-Nova, Camaro; O-Chevelle
V-8, 350.0	4.00 × 3.48	250	S-Chevr, MC; O-Others
V-8, 350.0	4.00 × 3.48	300	O-Chevr, MC, Chevl, Cam, Nova SS
V-8, 350.0	4.00 × 3.48	360	O-Camaro (Z28)
V-8, 402.0*	4.13 × 3.76	375	O-Camaro, Chevelle
V-8, 402.0*	4.13 × 3.76	350	O-Camaro, Chevelle
V-8, 400.0	4.12 × 3.75	265	O-Chevrolet, Monte Carlo
V-8, 400.0	4.12 × 3.25	330	O-Monte Carlo, Chevelle
V-8, 454.0	4.25 × 4.00	345	O-Chevrolet
V-8, 454.0	4.25 × 4.00	360	O-Monte Carlo
V-8, 454.0	4.25 × 4.00	390	O-Chevrolet
Corvette			
V-8, 350.0	4.00 × 3.48	270	S-all
V-8, 350.0	4.00 × 3.48	350/370	O-all
V-8, 454.0	4.25 × 4.00	365/425	O-all

*Commonly known as "396", actual displacement was 402 cid.

▲ Malibu remained Chevy's mainstay midsize line for 1970, pulling in very healthy sales of some 375,800. It's represented here by the four-door Sport Sedan hardtop, priced at $2881 with base 350 V-8. Among new features for all this year's Malibus were standard fiberglass-belted tires, variable-ratio steering, and steel side-guard safety beams in the doors.

Model Breakdown

		Wght	Price	Prod
Nova—254,242 built (including 19,558 SS models)				
11127	htp cpe, I-4	2,820	2,335	—
11169	sdn 4d, I-4	2,843	2,365	—
11327	cpe, I-6	2,919	2,414	—
11369	sdn 4d, I-6	2,942	2,443	—
11427	cpe, V-8	3,048	2,503	—
11469	sdn 4d, V-8	3,071	2,533	—
Camaro (includes 8,733 Z28s)				
12387	spt cpe, I-6	3,076	2,749	12,566
12487	spt cpe, V-8	3,190	2,839	112,323
Chevelle—354,855 built (including Malibu)				
13337	htp cpe, I-6	3,142	2,620	—
13369	sdn 4d, I-6	3,196	2,585	—
13437	htp cpe, V-8	3,260	2,710	—
13469	sdn 4d, V-8	3,312	2,679	—
Chev Malibu (53,599 SS; 3,733 w/454 V-8)				
13537	htp cpe, I-6	3,197	2,719	—
13539	htp sdn, I-6	3,302	2,790	—
13567	conv cpe, I-6	3,243	2,919	—
13569	sdn 4d, I-6	3,221	2,685	—
13637	htp cpe, V-8	3,307	2,809	—
13639	htp sdn, V-8	3,409	2,881	—
13667	conv cpe, V-8	3,352	3,009	—
13669	sdn 4d, V-8	3,330	3,775	—
Chevelle Wagon				
13136	Nmd 4d, 2S, I-6	3,615	2,835	—
13236	Nmd 4d, 2S, V-8	3,718	2,925	—
13336	Grnbr 4d, 2S, I-6	3,644	2,946	—
13436	Grnbr 4d, 2S, V-8	3,748	3,100	—
13446	Grnbr 4d, 3S, V-8	3,794	3,213	—
13536	Cncrs 4d, 2S, I-6	3,687	3,056	—
13636	Cncrs 4d, 2S, V-8	3,794	3,210	—
13646	Cncrs 4d, 3S, V-8	3,836	3,323	—
13836	Cncrs del wgn 4d, 2S, V-8	3,821	3,342	—
13846	Cncrs del wgn 4d, 3S, V-8	3,880	3,455	—
Biscayne				
15369	sdn 4d, I-6	3,600	2,787	12,300*
15469	sdn 4d, V-8	3,759	2,898	23,100*
Bel Air				
15569	sdn 4d, I-6	3,604	2,887	9,000*
15669	sdn 4d, V-8	3,763	2,998	66,800*
Impala—495,909 built exc 16467				
16337	htp cpe, I-6	3,641	3,038	—
16369	sdn 4d, I-6	3,655	3,021	—
16437	htp cpe, V-8	3,788	3,149	—
16439	htp sdn, V-8	3,871	3,203	—
16447	Cus htp cpe, V-8	3,801	3,266	—
16467	conv cpe, V-8	3,843	3,377	9,562
16469	sdn 4d, V-8	3,802	3,132	—
Caprice				
16639	htp sdn	3,905	3,527	92,000*
16647	htp cpe	3,821	3,474	
Monte Carlo (inc. 3,823 w/SS454 pkg.)				
13857	htp cpe	3,460	3,123	130,657
Chevrolet Station Wagon				
15436	Brkwd 4d, 2S	4,204	3,294	—
15636	Twnsmn 4d, 2S	4,208	3,357	—
15646	Twnsmn 4d, 3S	4,263	3,469	—
16436	Kingswd 4d, 2S	4,269	3,477	—
16446	Kingswd 4d, 3S	4,329	3,589	—
16636	Kngwd del 4d, 2S	2,495	3,753	—
16646	Kngwd del 4d, 3S	4,361	3,886	—
Corvette Stingray				
19437	cpe	3,184	5,192	10,668
19467	conv rdstr	3,196	4,849	6,648

*Rounded off to closest 100.

▲ This late prototype for the 1970 Caprice hardtop coupe differs from showroom actuality in a few trim details, but rear-fender skirts were again on the options list.

▲ Here's the showroom-ready Caprice hardtop coupe, which priced from $3474. A similar Impala Custom model offered a bit less luxury for around $200 less.

▲ The 1970 Nova was little changed from '69. Though the 300-horsepower 350 was the top engine "officially" offered, a few Chevelle 396s (nee 402s) were dropped into a handful of the two-door compacts.

▲ An answer to the Jeep CJ and Ford Bronco, the Chevy Blazer arrived for 1969 with four-wheel drive only. It continued for '70 with few changes, plus a new two-wheel-drive version. Here, the 4×4.

▲ This 1970 Fleetside rides Chevy's longer 127-inch pickup wheelbase. As such, it could be optioned with an extra stowage locker, auxiliary fuel tank, and one of the new 400 V-8s.

▲ Chevy's truck fleet still encompassed a broad array of big rigs in 1970, including this heavy-duty conventional-cab tractor and numerous special-purpose models.

▲ Basic Stepside pickups like this didn't show up in many 1970 Chevrolet truck ads, though Fleetside models and those with Custom Sport Trim (CST) did.

1971

- **Chevy gets small with subcompact Vega**

- **Full-size cars get big in complete redesign**

- **Engines detuned to run on low-lead gas**

- **GM is hit by another two-month strike**

- **Chevy bows to Ford for the second straight year as Detroit's number-one in production**

▲ Big Chevys became as big as they'd ever be with a 1971 redesign introducing round-sided "fuselage" styling on a new 121.5-inch wheelbase. Caprice again topped the line, offering this $4081 hardtop coupe, an equally posh $4134 hardtop sedan, and parallel Kingswood Estate wagons at $4400-$4500.

◀ Chevy again fielded three full-size four-door sedans for '71: low-end Biscayne, this step-up Bel Air, and the volume-selling Impala. Total Impala sales this year were over 475,000, not counting wagons.

▲▶ Full-size '71 Chevys shared a new General Motors "B-body," imparting a close visual kinship with GM's more expensive big cars. All body styles had rear louvers for venting cabin air, but the system proved ineffective, so the louvers were dropped after one year.

◀ Like GM sister models, Chevrolet's big 1971 wagons featured a new "Glide-Away" liftgate/tailgate resembling a cross between a clamshell and a roll-top desk. As shown on this Brookwood Estate, the push of a button retracted the rear window into the roof and the tailgate under the cargo floor. Novel it was, but the sections were prone to binding and water often dripped onto the floor when opening them.

CHEVY NAMES IT VEGA 2300!

▲ Ending a long "teaser" campaign, Chevrolet flew this banner over downtown Detroit in early summer 1970 to announce that the name of its all-new subcompact import-fighter would be Vega 2300.

CAR OF THE YEAR.

Motor Trend magazine has named the Chevy Vega its 1971 Car of the Year.

Naturally, we're pretty happy about it. Because this is obviously the year of the little car in the big automotive world. And while there are lots of little cars that could have been Car of the Year, only one is. Ours.

Here's another reason we're happy. We've been saying for months now that Vega is the little car that does everything well. Lucky for us, lots of you took our word for it and bought a Vega. Our thanks.

As for the rest of you, you not only have our word for it, you have Motor Trend's: "For the money, no other American car can deliver more." Vega. It's a lot of little car.

☐ I'm interested. Please send me some literature on the Vega.
☐ I'm very interested. Please send me literature and contact me for a Vega test-drive.
☐ I'm so interested that I already bought a Vega. Please send me a Car of the Year sticker for my car window.

Name_____
Address_____
City_____
State_____ Zip_____
Send to: Chevrolet Motor Division, Dept. 25, Box W, Detroit, Mi. 48202 (Licensed drivers only, please.)

GM MARK OF EXCELLENCE

VEGA CHEVROLET

▲▶ Designed for good interior space on a very trim 97-inch wheelbase, the Vega won *Motor Trend* magazine "Car of the Year" honors in its debut season, mainly due to uncommonly good small-car handling. A brand-new aluminum-block 4-cylinder engine delivered 90 standard horsepower or 110 optional from 2300cc—just 140 cubic inches.

▶ Vega made its debut the same year as Ford's subcompact Pinto, but was sportier in appearance and on the road. It also offered three body styles instead of one: this nifty "Kammback" wagon, a notchback sedan, and a slick-looking hatchback coupe, all two-doors. There was also a Panel Express wagon *sans* rear side windows. Despite a two-month plant strike, Vega got off to a strong start with some 269,905 total sales, but Pinto scored over 352,000.

▶ The Vega arrived with a Camaro-like face, which enhanced its appeal for many buyers. Besides manual and automatic transmissions, Vega offered a semi-automatic called Torque Drive. Also available for base six-cylinder 1971 Novas, it used a torque converter instead of a clutch, but otherwise operated like a manual. Orders amounted to just 7835 Vegas and 2992 Novas, prompting Chevy to drop Torque Drive after one year.

▲ Some critics found the Vega too spartan even for an economy car —"built down to a price," they said. At least the prices were low— just $2090 for this sedan, the least expensive model in the new line.

◀ Vega's 140-cid four used a cast-iron cylinder head with single overhead camshaft atop a block made of a special silicon-impregnated aluminum alloy. Unhappily for Chevy buyers, the engine soon proved prone to chronic oil leaks and other problems.

▲ The license plate identifies this '71 Corvette as one of just 12 built with the ZR2 package featuring a 425-hp 454 V-8—aka production option LS6—with aluminum cylinder heads. A milder 365-hp all-iron big-block was also available and rather more numerous.

▼ Even rarer than the ZR2 was the ZR1 package built around the solid-lifter 350 LT1 V-8 with a nominal 330 hp. Just eight '71s were so equipped. Though power was down across the board with GM's decision to detune all its engines to run on low-lead fuel, the 'Vette was still an E-ticket ride. Total Corvette sales recovered to 21,801 units, with the coupe extending its lead over the convertible to more than two-to-one. The "shark" had become more hospitable inside since its 1968 debut, as Chevy had found a little more passenger space and cleaned up a few details (*below*).

Engine Availability

Engines	bore × stroke	bhp	availability
I-4, 140.0	3.50 × 3.63	90	S-Vega
I-4, 140.0	3.50 × 3.63	110	O-Vega
I-6, 250.0	3.88 × 3.53	145	S-Nova, Chevl, Cam, Chevr*
V-8, 307.0	3.88 × 3.25	200	S-Nova, Chevl, Cam
V-8, 350.0	4.00 × 3.48	245	S-MC, Chevr* exc K/Est & Cap; O-Nova, Chevl, Cam
V-8, 350.0	4.00 × 3.48	270	O-Chevl, Cam, MC, Chevr*
V-8, 350.0	4.00 × 3.48	330	O-Camaro (Z28)
V-8, 400.0	4.12 × 3.75	255	S-Chevr K/Est & Cap; O-Chevr*
V-8, 402.0**	4.13 × 3.76	300	O-Chevl, Cam, MC, Chevr*
V-8, 454.0	4.25 × 4.00	365	O-Chevl, MC, Chevr*
V-8, 454.0	4.25 × 4.00	425	O-Chevl, MC
Corvette			
V-8, 350.0	4.00 × 3.48	270	S-all
V-8, 350.0	4.00 × 3.48	330	O-all
V-8, 454.0	4.25 × 4.00	365/425	O-all

* "Chevr" for 1971-80 means full-size Chevrolets. In above context, this includes Biscayne, Bel Air, Impala, Caprice, and Chevrolet station wagons.
**Commonly known as "396," actual displacement was 402 cid.

▲▶ Demand for muscle cars like the Chevelle SS was flagging by 1971, thanks to rising gas prices and soaring insurance premiums. Chevy responded at midseason by offering a low-cost SS-style trim option for the standard Chevelle hardtop coupe. Called "Heavy Chevy" in the argot of those times, it was available with any V-8 save the 454 big-block and even used the same hood and grille as the SS, though it did *not* include its heavy-duty suspension or standard front disc brakes.

▲ "Heavy Chevy" installations are unknown, but this beauty must be among the best of the survivors. Bold front-fender name decals and bodyside stripes were included in the package, along with upsized performance tires on "Rally" styled steel wheels. Vinyl roof covering here was, as ever, a freestanding option.

▲ The 307 small-block remained Chevelle's base V-8 for 1971. Rated horsepower remained at 200 despite a half-point cut in compression-ratio per corporate decree.

▲ A quartet of round taillamps replaced the 1970 models' dual rectangular units on '71 Chevelles. This SS454 convertible is rare, as Chevy built only 19,292 SS454s this year, including hardtops, and just 5089 ragtop Malibus of all kinds. With the industry scaling back on high-power engines, the '71 Chevelle SS was the first since '65 to be available with any passenger-Chevy V-8 (except the base 307). A six was still prohibited, though.

▲ Dual "Power Beam" headlights ousted the 1970's quads to give all '71 Chevelles a bolder face, accompanied by a modified grille. The changes were most striking on Super Sports like this SS454 hardtop. Total Chevelle SS orders for the model year throttled back to an estimated 80,000. Overall Chevelle sales fell too, partly due to another protracted strike that curbed production to 335,566, including wagons.

◀▲ As expected, Monte Carlo returned for its second year with relatively few changes, though a new fine-bar grille insert was evident. This example carries the SS454 package, which remained quite understated visually. Discreet badges and fat tires on 15×7-inch Rally rims were the only give-aways. This year's Monte SS option included a 365-hp big-block and added $485 to the base model's $3416 price tag. Just 1919 cars were so equipped in a slightly lower total model run of 128,600 units.

▲▶ The '71 El Camino naturally got most of the styling and mechanical changes made to that year's Chevelles, but the car/pickup was still technically part of Chevy's truck line, which partly explains why production figures are spotty and hard to get. This beauty is done up in SS trim, which now meant a 350 V-8 with 245 or 270 hp or a 454 with 365 or 425 hp. Base package prices were also the same as for the cars at $357 and $485, respectively.

Model Breakdown

Vega		Wght	Price	Prod
14111	sdn 2d	2,146	2,090	58,804
14177	hatchback cpe 3d	2,190	2,196	168,308
14115	Kammbk wgn 3d	2,230	2,328	42,793
Nova				
11327	cpe 2d, I-6	2,952	2,376	65,891
11369	sdn 4d, I-6	2,976	2,405	29,037
11427	cpe 2d, V-8	3,084	2,471	77,344
11469	sdn 4d, V-8	3,108	2,501	22,606
Camaro (inc 4,862 Z28s)				
12387	spt cpe, I-6	3,094	2,921	11,178
12487	spt cpe, V-8	3,218	3,016	103,452
Chevelle				
13337	htp cpe, I-6	3,166	2,712	6,660
13369	sdn 4d, I-6	3,210	2,677	6,621
13437	htp cpe, V-8	3,296	2,807	17,117
13469	sdn 4d, V-8	3,338	2,773	9,042
13537	Malibu htp cpe, I-6	3,212	2,885	6,220
13539	Malibu sdn, I-6	3,250	2,851	4,241
13637	Malibu htp cpe, V-8	3,342	2,980	180,117
13639	Malibu htp sdn, V-8	3,450	3,052	20,775
13667	Malibu conv, V-8	3,390	3,260	5,089

Chevelle *(continued)*		Wght	Price	Prod
13669	Malibu sdn 4d, V-8	3,380	2,947	37,385
Chevelle Wagon				
13136	Nomad 4d, 2S, I-6	3,632	2,997	2,801
13236	Nomad 4d, 2S, V-8	3,746	3,097	6,528
13436	Greenbrier 4d, 2S, V-8	3,820	3,228	6,128
13446	Greenbrier 4d, 3S, V-8	3,882	3,340	2,129
13636	Concours 4d, 2S, V-8	3,864	3,337	12,716
13646	Concours 4d, 3S, V-8	3,908	3,450	4,276
13836	Cncrs Est, 4d 2S, V-8	3,892	3,514	4,502
13846	Cncrs Est, 4d 3S, V-8	3,944	3,626	3,219
Biscayne				
15369	sdn 4d, I-6	3,732	3,096	5,846
15469	sdn 4d, V-8	3,888	3,448	16,463
Bel Air				
15569	sdn 4d, I-6	3,732	3,233	3,452
15669	sdn 4d, V-8	3,888	3,585	38,534
Impala				
16357	htp cpe, I-6	3,742	3,408	939
16369	sdn 4d, I-6	3,760	3,391	1,606
16439	htp sdn, V-8	3,978	3,813	140,300

Impala *(continued)*		Wght	Price	Prod
16447	Cstm htp cpe, V-8	3,912	3,826	139,437
16457	htp cpe, V-8	3,896	3,759	52,952
16467	conv, V-8	3,960	4,021	4,576
16469	sdn 4d, V-8	3,914	3,742	135,334
Caprice				
16639	htp sdn 4d	4,040	4,134	64,093
16647	htp cpe	3,964	4,081	46,404
Monte Carlo				
13857	htp cpe	3,488	3,416	128,600
Chevrolet Wagon				
15435	Brookwood 4d, 2S	4,542	3,929	5,314
15635	Townsman 4d, 2S	4,544	4,020	12,951
15645	Townsman 4d, 3S	4,598	4,135	6,870
16435	Kingswood 4d, 2S	4,588	4,112	26,638
16445	Kingswood 4d, 3S	4,648	4,227	32,311
16635	Kingswd Est 4d, 2S	4,678	4,384	11,913
16645	Kingswd Est 4d, 3S	4,738	4,498	19,010
Corvette Stingray				
19437	cpe	3,202	5,533	14,680
19467	conv rdstr	3,216	5,296	7,121

1972

NINETEEN SEVENTY-TWO NINETEEN SEVENTY-TWO NINETEEN SEVENTY-TWO NINETEE

- **Engines shift from gross to net ratings, power slides again**

- **Camaro comes close to extinction**

- **Despite yet more strikes, Chevy returns to being "USA-1"**

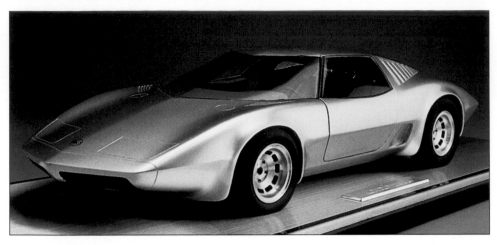

▲ Chevrolet wowed auto show crowds in 1972 with this Corvette-like concept featuring a midmounted four-rotor Wankel rotary engine engineered by General Motors. Known internally as XP-882, the car was later given a V-8 and called "AeroVette." Many thought it a preview of the next showroom 'Vette, and it did come close to reaching production for 1980.

▲ The 1972 Corvette convertible started at $5246, the companion coupe at $5472. Engines now comprised a standard 200-horsepower 350 V-8, a high-output LT1 version with 255, and a lone 454 big-block with 270, which lurks beneath this car's hood. The industry-wide shift from SAE gross to net ratings for '72 made the power losses seem even greater than they actually were. A standard burglar alarm was one of Corvette's few changes this season.

▲ Corvette tacked on nearly 5200 sales to finish model-year '72 at 27,004 units. The margin of coupe to convertible sales was now well over three-to-one. Appearance was virtually unchanged from 1970 to '71.

▲ The "shark" lost a formerly standard fiber-optic light monitoring system for '72, which cleaned up the center console. Note the dash map pockets at right.

▲ Detroit was fast downplaying all-out performance by 1972, emphasizing lower emissions and greater safety instead. Corvette was not immune. Even big-block models like this coupe were no longer offered with side exhaust pipes—a sign of the times.

▲ Performance fans were dismayed by Corvette's continuing power losses, but at least Chevy kept faith by making the big 454 available for '72. And there was a positive aspect to the emissions-prompted detuning: better low-speed tractability.

▲ Full-size 1972 Chevys returned from their '71 makeover with a half-inch longer wheelbase and minor styling changes that added 2-3 inches to overall length.

▲ Here's a peek inside the 1972 Impala four-door sedan, shown left. Like their Detroit contemporaries, the big Chevys offered vast room for six passengers on wide bench seats front and rear.

▲ A more formal, squared-up roofline and standard V-8 again distinguished the Impala Custom Coupe from the sister Sport Coupe. Respective base prices: $3787 and $3720.

▲ The Brookwood Estate again offered Caprice-level equipment as Chevy's top-line 1972 full-size wagon. A new grille and front bumper graced all full-size '72 Chevys.

▲ Fronting the Detroit skyline in a view used many times through the years by automaker photographers is the 1972 Caprice hardtop coupe, priced from $4026.

◄ Some lawmakers in 1972 wondered aloud about the rollover safety of pillarless body styles. As if in reply, Chevy added a "post" four-door to the Caprice line. Priced from $4009, the new model attracted 34,174 sales out of 178,455 total Caprices.

1972

▲ All-new midsize Chevrolets had been planned for 1972, but last-minute problems forced a one-year postponement. As a result, '72 Chevelles received only hasty minor changes. Hidden windshield wipers were newly standard for all Malibu models, including this $2991 hardtop sedan. Total Malibu sales numbered 290,008.

▶ Though there would be SS Chevelles after 1972, most enthusiasts regard this as the last year for "true" Detroit muscle cars in the original 1960s mold. This Sport Coupe is one of 24,946 SS Chevelles built for '72. Of those, a mere 300 left the factory with a 454 big-block, which was now rated at 270 *net* hp and was no longer available in smoggy California. Remaining production was strictly SS350, even though the package could be ordered with a 307 or 400 V-8 instead.

▲ As had been the case since 1969 and like the big Chevys, Chevelle wagons had distinct model names and were grouped in a separate series. The Concours Estate, with its woody-look, remained the best of this bunch for 1972. Also continued was a dual-action tailgate that could be dropped down or opened from the right.

▲▶ Though less visually macho than a Chevelle SS, the 1972 Malibu Sport Coupe offered the same qualities—performance included—at a friendlier price. This example carries one of Chevelle's available 350 V-8s, as proclaimed by the front fender badge.

▲ Nova sales got a big boost in 1972 from renewed buyer interest in less costly, more economical transportation. Indeed, demand for Chevy's compact jumped 79.5 percent to nearly 350,000 units. Here, the two-door "Sport Coupe" sedan with base V-8 and available vinyl roof covering.

◄ This base-trim '72 Nova two-door looks pretty plain compared to the model above, but it offered a fine blend of value, space, and comfort for as little as $2351. Other GM divisions, perhaps jealous of Nova's consistent high popularity, lobbied successfully for their own versions, the first of which was Pontiac's new-for-'71 Ventura. Olds and Buick would join in for '73. Even so, Nova always outsold its intramural clones, usually running a strong third in the compact market.

◄ ► A new large-check grille marked 1972 Camaros without the Rally Sport package, but high-back front bucket seats were newly standard across the board. The Camaro at right carries both the SS350 package, priced at $306, and the Rally Sport group, listing for $118. Respective total installations were 6562 and 11,364. Z28s numbered just 2575 this year.

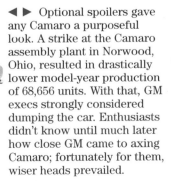

◄ ► Optional spoilers gave any Camaro a purposeful look. A strike at the Camaro assembly plant in Norwood, Ohio, resulted in drastically lower model-year production of 68,656 units. With that, GM execs strongly considered dumping the car. Enthusiasts didn't know until much later how close GM came to axing Camaro; fortunately for them, wiser heads prevailed.

▲ Severe early body rust-out was a major problem with subcompact Vegas, so it's rare to see an early model now in such good condition as this '72 Kammback wagon. As a new car, this model priced from $2285 and attracted 71,957 orders.

▲ The hatchback coupe remained by far the most popular Vega in 1972, with 262,682 sales out of a line total of 390,478. All Vegas were virtually unchanged for the subcompact Chevy's second year.

▲ Like parent Chevelle, El Camino mostly marked time for '72, pending a redesign postponed to 1973. Base price with V-8 was up to $2960. A specific SS package was still available.

Engine Availability

Engines	bore × stroke	bhp	availability
I-4, 140.0	3.50 × 3.63	80	S-Vega
I-4, 140.0	3.50 × 3.63	90	O-Vega
I-6, 250.0	3.88 × 3.53	110	S-Nova, Chevl, Cam, Chevr exc Cap & K/Est
V-8, 307.0	3.88 × 3.25	130	S-Nova, Chevl, Cam exc Cal
V-8, 350.0	4.00 × 3.48	165	S-Chevl & Cam in Cal. O-Nova, Chevl, Chevr
V-8, 350.0	4.00 × 3.48	175	O-Chevl, MC
V-8, 350.0	4.00 × 3.48	200	O-Cam, Chevr
V-8, 350.0	4.00 × 3.48	255	O-Camaro (Z28)
V-8, 400.0	4.12 × 3.75	170	S-Chevr Cap & K/Est; O-Chevr
V-8, 402.0	4.13 × 3.76	210	O-Chevr
V-8, 402.0	4.13 × 3.76	240	O-Chevl, Cam, MC
V-8, 454.0	4.25 × 4.00	270	O-Chevl, MC, Chevr
Corvette			
V-8, 350.0	4.00 × 3.48	200	S-all
V-8, 350.0	4.00 × 3.48	255	O-all
V-8, 454.0	4.25 × 4.00	270	O-all

▶ Monte Carlo lost its SS package for 1972, but was otherwise much as before. Sales jumped nearly 41 percent.

▲ This dealer-installed "Flame by Chevy" decal package was briefly offered for El Caminos, but found few takers. A like-named ensemble proved more popular on regular Chevy pickups.

Model Breakdown

Vega		Wght	Price	Prod
1V11	sdn 2d	2,158	2,060	55,839
1V15	wgn 3d	2,333	2,285	71,957
1V77	htchbk cpe 3d	2,294	2,160	262,682
Nova				
1X27	cpe 2d, I-6	2,949	2,351	96,740
1X27	cpe 2d, V-8	3,083	2,441	163,475
1X69	sdn 4d, I-6	2,982	2,379	43,029
1X69	sdn 4d, V-8	3,116	2,469	46,489
Camaro (inc 2,575 Z28s)				
1Q87	spt cpe, I-6	3,121	2,730	4,824
1Q87	spt cpe, V-8	3,248	2,820	63,832
Chevelle				
1C37	htp cpe, I-6	3,172	2,669	6,993
1C37	htp cpe, V-8	3,300	2,759	22,714
1C69	sdn 4d, I-6	3,204	2,636	6,764
1C69	sdn 4d, V-8	3,332	2,726	12,881
1D37	Mlbu htp cpe, I-6	3,194	2,833	4,790
1D37	Mlbu htp cpe, V-8	3,327	2,923	207,598
1D39	Mlbu htp sdn, V-8	3,438	2,991	24,192

Chevelle (continued)		Wght	Price	Prod
1D67	Mlbu conv, V-8	3,379	3,187	4,853
1D69	Mlbu sdn 4d, I-6	3,240	2,801	3,562
1D69	Mlbu sdn 4d, V-8	3,371	2,891	45,013
Chevelle Wagon				
1B36	Nmd 4d, 2S, I-6	3,605	2,926	2,956
1B36	Nmd 4d, 2S, V-8	3,732	3,016	7,768
1C36	Grnbr 4d, 2S, V-8	3,814	3,140	6,975
1C46	Grnbr 4d, 3S, V-8	3,870	3,247	2,370
1D36	Cncrs 4d, 2S, V-8	3,857	3,244	17,968
1D46	Cncrs 4d, 3S, V-8	3,909	3,351	6,560
1H36	Cncrs Est 4d, 2S, V-8	3,887	3,431	5,331
1H46	Cncrs Est 4d, 3S, V-8	3,943	3,538	4,407
Chevrolet				
1K69	Bscyn sdn 4d, I-6	3,857	3,074	1,504
1K59	Bscyn sdn 4d, V-8	4,045	3,408	19,034
1I-69	Bel Air sdn 4d, I-6	3,854	3,204	868
1I-69	Bel Air sdn 4d, V-8	4,042	3,538	41,020
1M39	Imp htp sdn, V-8	4,150	3,771	170,304
1M47	Imp Cst htp cpe, V-8	4,053	3,787	183,493
1M57	Imp htp cpe, I-6	3,864	3,385	289

Chevrolet (continued)		Wght	Price	Prod
1M57	Imp htp cpe, V-8	4,049	3,720	52,403
1M67	Imp conv, V-8	4,125	3,979	6,456
1M69	Imp sdn 4d, I-6	3,928	3,369	1,235
1M69	Imp sdn 4d, V-8	4,113	3,708	183,361
1N39	Cap htp sdn, V-8	4,203	4,076	78,768
1N47	Cap htp cpe, V-8	4,102	4,026	65,513
1N69	Caprice sdn 4d	4,166	4,009	34,174
Chevrolet Station Wagon				
1K35	Brkwd 4d, 2S	4,686	3,882	8,150
1L35	Twnsmn 4d, 2S	4,687	3,969	16,482
1L45	Twnsmn 4d, 3S	4,769	4,078	8,667
1M35	Kingwd 4d, 2S	4,734	4,056	43,152
1M45	Kingwd 4d, 3S	4,817	4,165	40,248
1N35	Kingwd Est 4d, 2S	4,798	4,314	20,281
1N45	Kingwd Est 4d, 3S	4,883	4,423	34,723
Monte Carlo				
1H57	htp cpe, V-8	3,506	3,362	180,819
Corvette Stingray				
1Z37	cpe	3,215	5,472	20,496
1Z67	conv rdstr	3,216	5,246	6,508

1973

- **Redesigned Chevelle drops hardtops and convertibles**

- **Second-generation Monte Carlo debuts**

- **Corvette deftly facelifted to meet the government's new "5-mph" bumper rule**

▲ Another showcase for General Motors' experimental Wankel-type rotary engine was XP-987GT, a hint that a midengine Corvette might be on the way. It was more commonly known as the "Two-Rotor" car for its two-rotor GM Rotary Combustion Engine (GMRCE).

▲ While midengine concepts played 1973 auto shows, the production "shark" got its first major styling change since introduction: a reshaped nose with a stronger bumper covered in body-color plastic. The new ensemble shrugged off minor dings and was capable of meeting the government's new standard that front bumpers absorb impacts up to 5 mph with no damage to the bumper or surrounding area.

▲ The Stingray coupe retained its trademark T-bar roof with removable panels, demonstrated in this Chevy PR photo. Restyled wheels and a fixed coupe rear window were among other changes for '73.

▶ Nose emblems weren't stuck on in time for this '73 Corvette press picture, but the facelift was an artful piece of work anyway. Engines were down to 350s with 190 or 250 *net* horsepower, plus one 275-hp 454, but at least the 'Vette itself was still around. And despite inflation-fueled price hikes, sales improved to 30,465, of which 6093 were convertibles.

▲▼► Chevelle joined other 1973 GM intermediates in a full redesign that eliminated convertibles and pillarless hardtops, partly due to fears of a government standard for rollover crash protection that, ironically, never materialized. Shown here is a Malibu coupe with the $243 Super Sport package, a mostly cosmetic reminder of hotter days that was also available for the Malibu wagon. Total installations were 28,647, of which some 2500 were equipped with a 245-hp (net) big-block 454, a separate $235 option. Others left with either a 145- or 160-hp 350 V-8.

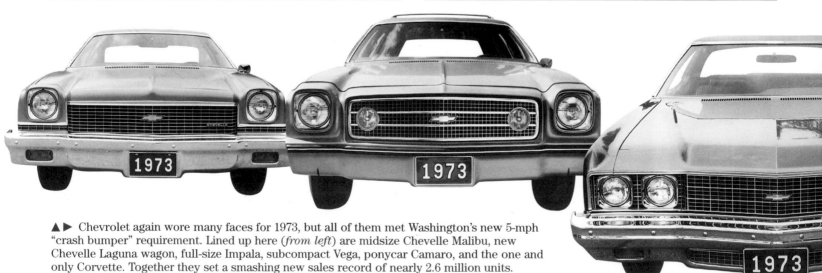

▲► Chevrolet again wore many faces for 1973, but all of them met Washington's new 5-mph "crash bumper" requirement. Lined up here (*from left*) are midsize Chevelle Malibu, new Chevelle Laguna wagon, full-size Impala, subcompact Vega, ponycar Camaro, and the one and only Corvette. Together they set a smashing new sales record of nearly 2.6 million units.

▲ All '73 Chevelle coupes wore large tri-angular rear side windows. This Malibu version started at $3010 with base V-8.

▲ The '73 Malibu four-door sedan featured Chevelle's new "Colonnade" styling, in which several pillars ran to the roof.

▲ Chevelle's top-line '73 wagon was this new Laguna Estate, with the usual simulated wood side trim. Prices started at $3662.

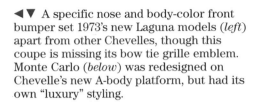

◄▼ A specific nose and body-color front bumper set 1973's new Laguna models (*left*) apart from other Chevelles, though this coupe is missing its bow tie grille emblem. Monte Carlo (*below*) was redesigned on Chevelle's new A-body platform, but had its own "luxury" styling.

Engine Availability

Engines	bore × stroke	bhp	availability
I-4, 140.0	3.50 × 3.63	72	S-Vega
I-4, 140.0	3.50 × 3.63	85	O-Vega
I-6, 250.0	3.88 × 3.53	100	S-Nova, Chevl, Cam, exc LT Chevr
V 8, 307.0	3.88 × 3.25	115	S-Nova, Chevl, exc Lag, Cam exc LT
V-8, 350.0	4.00 × 3.48	145	S-Lag, Cam LT, MC, Chevr exc Cap; O-Nova, Chevl exc Lag, Cam exc LT, Chevr exc Cap
V-8, 350.0	4.00 × 3.48	175	O-Nova, Chevelle, Camaro, MC
V-8, 350.0	4.00 × 3.48	245	O-Camaro (Z28)
V-8, 400.0	4.12 × 3.75	150	O-Chevrolet
V-8, 454.0	4.25 × 4.00	215	O-Caprice
V-8, 454.0	4.25 × 4.00	245	O-Chevelle, Monte Carlo, Caprice
Corvette Stingray			
V-8, 350.0	4.00 × 3.48	190	S-all
V-8, 350.0	4.00 × 3.48	250	O-all
V-8, 454.0	4.25 × 4.00	275	O-all

▲ Though wheelbase was still 116 inches, Monte Carlo's 1973 redesign ushered in florid fenderlines, a marked midbody beltline dip, small rear-quarter "opera" windows, and a slightly vee'd hood and rear window. Sales were better than ever at 290,693.

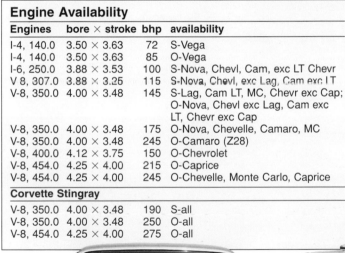

▲ The top-line full-size Caprice became Caprice Classic for 1973 and added a convertible, which shifted up from the Impala series. Two- and four-door hardtops continued along with this four-door sedan. Standard for all was Chevy's 400-cubic-inch V-8, this year rating just 150 net hp. Caprice sales totaled a strong 212,754.

▲ Cadillac-style rear fender skirts were also standard for all '73 Caprice Classics, but the vinyl roof covering on this sedan was a $106 extra. All big Chevys this year boasted slightly tighter suspension tuning as well as a larger 22-gallon fuel tank—timely for the unprecedented national "energy crisis" that began in October.

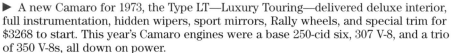

▶ A new Camaro for 1973, the Type LT—Luxury Touring—delivered deluxe interior, full instrumentation, hidden wipers, sport mirrors, Rally wheels, and special trim for $3268 to start. This year's Camaro engines were a base 250-cid six, 307 V-8, and a trio of 350 V-8s, all down on power.

▲ The compact Nova for '73 offered a fresh face, heftier "5-mph" front bumper, plus more rounded lines, a new hatchback body style, and better-furnished Custom models.

▲ Another look at Nova's practical new 1973 hatchback coupe. This Custom model priced from $2701, about $200 above the base-trim version. Nova notched higher total sales this year of 369,509 units.

▲ Nova hatchbacks maximized cargo room with a "space-saver" spare tire, still rather novel in 1973. Despite its greater versatility, the hatch was outsold by the regular two-door sedan with separate enclosed trunk.

▲ Looking like another future Corvette, the XP-898 was really a testbed for a new "sandwich" type of fiberglass body construction. It was built with a modified Vega powertrain on a 90-inch wheelbase. The body comprised just four lightweight sections, resulting in a curb weight of only 2285 pounds. Despite its promise, the project ultimately proved a dead-end.

◄▲ El Camino got its own "Colonnade" styling for '73 on an unchanged wheelbase. The rear bumper was shared with Chevelle wagons. An SS option continued, still visually much like the car package except for bodyside tape stripes. The $280 El Camino group included a 115-hp 307 V-8, but 350s and the big 454 were available separately. El Camino was still technically a truck, so its high-power engines were likely less emissions-strangled and a bit stronger than they were in passenger-car tune.

▲ Chevy also redesigned its light-duty trucks for 1973, marked by big, square grilles and more sculpted lines. This is the popular ½-ton C-10 Fleetside pickup with new Cheyenne appearance package.

▲ Still basically a short-chassis pickup, the Blazer sport-utility naturally shared in 1973's light-truck redesign. A "Sports Cap" roof was a $313 extra for this two-wheel-drive C-10 model and its 4×4 K-10 sibling.

▲ It took at least two people to do it, but Blazer's optional "Sports Cap" roof could be removed for sunny day backwoods exploring. As before, the cargo box was integral with and open to the four/five-seater cab.

Model Breakdown

Vega		Wght	Price	Prod
V11	sdn 2d	2,219	2,087	58,425
V15	wgn 3d	2,317	2,323	102,751
V77	htchbk cpe 3d	2,313	2,192	266,124
Nova				
X17	htchbk cpe 3d, I-6	3,145	2,528	11,005
X17	htchbk cpe 3d, V-8	3,274	2,618	33,949
X27	cpe, I-6	3,033	2,377	54,140
X27	cpe, V-8	3,162	2,467	81,679
X69	sdn 4d, I-6	3,065	2,407	27,440
X69	sdn 4d, V-8	3,194	2,497	32,843
Y17	Cstm htchbk cpe 3d, I-6	3,152	2,701	3,172
Y17	Cstm htchbk cpe 3d, V-8	3,281	2,792	42,886
Y27	Custom cpe, I-6	3,073	2,551	6,336
Y27	Custom cpe, V-8	3,202	2,741	52,042
Y69	Custom sdn 4d, I-6	3,105	2,580	4,344
Y69	Custom sdn 4d, V-8	3,234	2,671	19,673
Camaro (inc 11,574 Z28s)				
Q87	spt cpe, I-6	3,119	2,781	3,614
Q87	spt cpe, V-8	3,238	2,872	60,810
S87	LT spt cpe, V-8	3,349	3,268	32,327
Chevelle				
C29	Dlx Colnnde sdn 4d, I-6	3,435	2,719	5,253
C29	Dlx Colnnde sdn 4d, V-8	3,585	2,835	15,502

Chevelle (continued)		Wght	Price	Prod
C37	Dlx Colnnde cpe, I-6	3,423	2,743	6,332
C37	Dlx Colnnde cpe, V-8	3,580	2,860	15,045
D29	Mlbu Colnnde sdn 4d, I-6	3,477	2,871	2,536
D29	Mlbu Colnnde sdn 4d, V-8	3,627	2,987	58,143
D37	Mlbu Colnnde cpe, I-6	3,430	2,894	3,157
D37	Mlbu Colnnde cpe, V-8	3,580	3,010	165,627
E39	Lgna Colnnde sdn 4d, V-8	3,627	3,179	13,095
E37	Lgna Colnnde cpe, V-8	3,687	3,203	42,941
Chevelle Wagon				
C35	Deluxe 5d, 2S, I-6	3,849	3,106	1,870
C35	Deluxe 5d, 3S, V-8	4,054	3,331	1,316
C37	Deluxe 5d, 2S, V-8	4,006	3,198	7,754
D37	Malibu 5d, 3S, V-8	4,075	3,423	5,961
D35	Malibu 5d, 2S, V-8	4,027	3,290	18,592
G35	Mlbu Est 5d, 3S, V-8	4,808	3,608	4,099
G35	Mlbu Est 5d, 2S, V-8	4,032	3,475	5,527
E35	Lgna 5d, 3S, V-8	4,158	3,616	2,200
E35	Lgna 5d, 2S, V-8	4,110	3,483	4,419
H35	Lgna Est 5d, 3S, V-8	4,189	3,795	3,709
H35	Lgna Est 5d, 2S, V-8	4,141	3,662	3,661
Chevrolet				
K69	Bel Air sdn 4d, I-6	3,895	3,247	1,394
K69	Bel Air sdn 4d, V-8	4,087	3,595	40,438
L39	Imp htp sdn, V-8	4,162	3,822	139,143

Chevrolet (continued)		Wght	Price	Prod
L47	Imp Cstm cpe, V-8	4,110	3,836	176,824
L57	Impala cpe, V-8	4,096	3,769	42,979
L69	Impala sdn 4d	4,138	3,752	190,536
N39	Cap Clsc htp sdn, V-8	4,208	4,134	70,155
N47	Cap Clsc htp cpe, V-8	4,103	4,082	77,134
N67	Cap Clsc conv cpe, V-8	4,191	4,345	7,339
N69	Cap Clsc sdn 4d, V-8	4,176	4,064	58,126
Chevrolet Station Wagon				
K47	Bel Air 4d, 3S	4,770	4,136	6,321
K35	Bel Air 4d, 2S	4,717	4,022	14,549
L35	Impala 4d, 2S	4,742	4,119	46,940
L45	Impala 4d, 3S	4,807	4,233	43,664
N35	Cap Est 4d, 2S	4,779	4,382	22,969
N45	Cap Est 4d, 3S	4,858	4,496	39,535
Monte Carlo				
H57	spt cpe	3,713	3,415	4,960
H57	S spt cpe	3,720	3,562	177,963
H57	Landau spt cpe	3,722	3,806	107,770
Corvette Stingray—30,465 built				
Z37	cpe	3,326	5,635	24,372*
Z67	conv rdstr	3,333	5,399	6,093*
Z67	above, two tops	3,387	5,676	

*Estimates; proportioned from total.

1974

- **Vega and Camaro restyled; Corvette gets new-look rear end**

- **Other models modified for required 5-mph rear bumpers**

- **"Energy crisis" shakes up car buyers**

SPECS.

EXTERIOR COLORS

Corvette Dark Green Metallic - New
Corvette Gray Metallic - New
Corvette Brown Metallic - New
Corvette Bright Yellow - New
Corvette Medium Red Metallic - New
Corvette Silver Mist
Corvette Medium Blue Metallic
Mille Miglia Red
Corvette Orange Metallic
Classic White

INTERIOR TRIM COLORS

All Vinyl - Standard
- Silver - New • Light Neutral - New
- Medium Saddle • Dark Blue
- Dark Red • Black
Custom Interior - Available
- Silver - New • Medium Saddle - New
- Black

SAFETY AND SECURITY FEATURES

POWER TEAMS

(spec table, illegible)

Chevrolet GM
September 1973

▲ Corvette always had huge appeal for hardcore car enthusiasts. This 1974 ad was created for "buff" publications around a no-nonsense "just the facts" theme, though it didn't have many new facts to report and was preaching to believers anyway.

▲ The 'Vette had been evolving from hairy-chested screamer to sophisticated *gran turismo*, a trend evident inside and on the sales chart. For example, 67 percent of '74 models were ordered with automatic transmission, 78.4 percent with air conditioning.

▲ The government required that all 1974 cars provide 5-mph "crash" protection at the rear as well as the front. Corvette designers came through with a new tail carrying a suitable bumper sheathed in body-color plastic, a neat match for the similarly revamped nose of 1973. This Mille Miglia Red convertible shows the handsome overall result. Despite few changes elsewhere, Corvette again scored higher model-year production of 37,502 units.

◄ Corvette's 1974 "taillift" looked equally great on the coupe, which recorded 32,028 sales versus a mere 5474 convertibles. Functional front-fender "gills" continued from '73. So did engines, again comprising 195- and 250-hp 350 V-8s, plus a 454 with 270 net hp, down five. This paint color was titled "Bright Corvette Yellow."

▲▶ Perhaps the most interesting 1974 Chevelle was the Laguna Type S-3 coupe, which replaced the previous three-model Laguna series and the SS option package. Chevy kept the Laguna grille but added lower-body two-toning, Rally wheels, radial tires, uprated shock absorbers, variable-ratio steering and—shades of late-'50s Chrysler products—swivel front bucket seats (*right*). The price was right at $3723, but only 15,792 S-3s were called for.

▶ Chevy sales materials still relied on the time-honored practice of exaggerating interior space by means of special artwork or photography. As a result, the 1974 Chevelle four-door sedan wasn't quite as spacious as this brochure illustration implies, though it was certainly adequate for six medium-size adults with standard front bench seat. A fold-down front center armrest was included on this year's new top-trim Malibu Classic coupe, sedan, and wagon.

▲▶ Convertibles had always been relatively weak sellers due to their high prices, rattle-prone bodies, and frequent woes with the folding tops. Still, ragtop demand was really plunging by 1974. Chevy's full-size Caprice Classic was no exception, sales tumbling from 7339 units to just 4670. A $400 price hike, to $4745, didn't help. All big Chevys this year got a more squarish grille and a rear end reprofiled to accept a newly required 5-mph bumper. Despite a buyer rush to smaller, thriftier cars during this year's energy crisis, big-Chevy sales held up quite well at nearly 630,000 units, including 91,407 wagons.

◀ A crisp new pillared roofline with large fixed rear side windows enhanced the "more formal" look of the 1974 Impala Custom coupe and this $4483 Caprice Classic version.

▶ The rise of pillared coupes left Impala with a pair of true hardtops for 1974, this $4162 sport coupe and its four-door sport sedan cousin, priced from $4215.

▲▶ Federal "crash bumper" rules prompted an adept facelift for 1974 Camaros, the first for the basic second-generation line. A newly sloped, vee'd grille was featured on all models, including the posh Type-LT (*above*), which scored higher sales of 48,963 units. The sporty Z28 (*right*) moved up to 13,802, but was now a $600 option package with a bold hood graphic and a solid-lifter 245-horsepower 350 V-8 as its only engine. Overall Camaro sales rose to 151,008 from the previous year's 96,751.

▲ Vega followed Camaro for 1974 with new front- and rear-end styling, again in deference to federal requirements. This hatch coupe wears its original price sticker listing a new "Spirit of America" package that included white paint and wheels, red and blue contrast striping, and white vinyl interior.

▲ Chevy worked hard to spruce up Vega interiors without adding to price, but inflation kept pushing stickers up anyway. A right-side passenger grab bar was again included in Vega's GT package, fitted to this hatch coupe.

◄ Anticipating America's Bicentennial, Vega's 1974 "Spirit of America" package was eye-catching. So was the subcompact's new sloped, slotted grille. The much larger new front and rear bumpers were more dubious. Caprice and Nova offered their own "Spirit" packages, also starting at midseason.

▲ Vega's engine and rust problems were well known by 1974, but the Middle East oil embargo and gasoline shortages helped boost the small Chevy's sales to 456,085 units, though that would be the peak. The hatch coupe accounted for over half of the total. A newcomer was this Estate wagon with deluxe interior and woody-look side paneling. It started at $2976, a $228 premium over the plain-sided Kammback model. Respective production figures were 27,089 and 88,248 units.

▲ Announced in 1974 but not made available until '75, the Cosworth-Vega was an extra sporty hatch coupe powered by this new 2.0-liter version of the 2.3 Vega four-cylinder with an aluminum cylinder head and twin overhead camshafts. Created with help from England's Cosworth Engineering, the engine made 111 net hp and boasted electronic fuel injection, a first for a production General Motors car.

Engine Availability

Engines	bore × stroke	bhp	availability
I-4, 140.0	3.50 × 3.63	75	S-Vega
I-4, 140.0	3.50 × 3.63	85	O-Vega
I-6, 250.0	3.88 × 3.53	100	S-Nova, Chevl, Cam
V-8, 350.0	4.00 × 3.48	145	S-Nova, Chevl, Cam, MC, Chevr exc Cap
V-8, 350.0	4.00 × 3.48	160	O-as above
V-8, 350.0	4.00 × 3.48	185	O-Nova, Camaro
V-8, 350.0	4.00 × 3.48	245	O-Camaro (Z28)
V-8, 400.0	4.12 × 3.75	150	O-Caprice exc wgns
V-8, 400.0	4.12 × 3.75	180	S-wgns; O-Chevl, MC
V-8, 454.0	4.25 × 4.00	235	O-Chevl, MC, Cap
Corvette Stingray			
V-8, 350.0	4.00 × 3.48	195	S-all
V-8, 350.0	4.00 × 3.48	250	O-all
V-8, 454.0	4.25 × 4.00	270	O-all

▲ Monte Carlo got its own "battering rams" for '74 to grow three inches longer overall, plus standard radial tires. As in '73, buyers could choose from a base "S" model and this fancier Landau, which priced from $4129. Total Monte sales improved to 312,217.

▲ Four-wheel drive was an $820 option for '74 Chevy pickups. So ordered, this long-bed ½-ton wore K-10 badges.

▲ Larger parking lights, a bow tie grille emblem, and a bigger back bumper identified 1974 Nova coupes, as well as the sedans, regular and Custom. National fuel jitters helped lift sales to 390,537, a new Nova record, yet most buyers ordered a V-8, now a 350 exclusively. Coupes still offered an SS appearance package, priced at $140; 21,419 were so equipped.

▲ Chevy's big 454 V-8 remained a regular light-truck option for '74, though most Blazer sport-utilities like this carried a 350, often in concert with four-wheel drive.

Model Breakdown

Vega		Wght	Price	Prod
V11	sdn 2d	2,369	2,505	58,724
V11	LX sdn 2d	—	2,833	5,996
V15	wgn 3d, 2S	2,514	2,748	88,248
V15	Estate wgn 3d,2S	—	2,976	27,089
V77	htchbk cpe 3d	—	—	276,028
Nova				
X17	htchbk cpe 3d, I-6	3,260	2,935	13,722
X17	htchbk cpe 3d, V-8	3,398	3,034	20,627
X27	cpe, I-6	3,150	2,811	87,399
X27	cpe, V-8	3,288	2,919	72,558
X69	sdn 4d, I-6	3,192	2,841	42,105
X69	sdn 4d, V-8	3,330	2,949	32,017
Y17	Cstm htchbk cpe 3d, I-6	3,299	3,108	9,631
Y17	Cstm htchbk cpe 3d, V-8	3,437	3,217	36,653
Y27	Custom cpe, I-6	3,206	2,985	11,115
Y27	Custom cpe, V-8	3,344	3,093	39,912
Y69	cstm sdn 4d, I-6	3,233	3,014	7,458
Y69	Cstm sdn 4d, V-8	3,371	3,123	17,340
Camaro (inc 13,802 Z28s)				
Q87	spt cpe, I-6	3,309	3,162	22,210
Q87	spt cpe, V-8	3,450	3,366	79,835
S87	Type LT spt cpe, V-8	3,566	3,713	48,963

Chevelle *(continued)*		Wght	Price	Prod
C29	Mlbu Colnnde sdn 4d, I-6	3,638	3,049	11,399
C29	Mlbu Colnnde sdn 4d, V-8	3,788	3,340	26,841
C37	Mlbu Colnnde cpe, I-6	3,573	3,054	15,790
C37	Mlbu Colnnde cpe, V-8	3,723	3,345	37,583
D29	Mlbu Clsc sdn 4d, I-6	3,695	3,304	4,457
D29	Mlbu Cl Col sdn 4d, V-8	3,845	3,595	51,468
D37	Mlbu Cl Col cpe, I-6	3,609	3,307	4,132
D37	Mlbu Cl Col cpe, V-8	3,759	3,598	116,962
D37	Mlbu Cl Col Lnd cpe, I-6	—	3,518	351
D37	Mlbu Cl Col Lnd cpe, V-8	—	3,800	27,490
E37	Lgna S3 Col cpe, V-8	3,951	3,723	15,792
Chevelle Wagon				
C35	Malibu 5d, 3S	4,223	3,834	2,583
C37	Malibu 5d, 2S	4,191	3,701	12,408
D35	Mlbu Clsc 5d, 3S	4,315	4,251	4,909
D35	Mlbu Clsc 5d, 2S	4,283	4,118	13,986
G35	Mlbu Clsc Est 5d, 3S	4,338	4,424	4,742
G35	Mlbu Clsc Est 5d, 2S	4,306	4,291	5,480
Chevrolet				
K69	Bel Air sdn 4d	4,148	3,960	24,778
L39	Imp spt sdn 4d	4,256	4,215	76,492

Chevrolet *(continued)*		Wght	Price	Prod
L47	Imp Cstm cpe	4,169	4,229	98,062
L57	Impala spt cpe	4,167	4,162	50,036
L69	Impala sdn 4d	4,205	4,135	133,164
N39	Cap Clsc spt sdn 4d	4,344	4,534	48,387
N47	Cap Clsc Cstm cpe	4,245	4,483	59,484
N67	Cap Clsc conv cpe	4,308	4,745	4,670
N69	Cap Clsc sdn 4d	4,294	4,465	43,367
Chevrolet Wagon				
K35	Bel Air 4d, 2S	4,829	4,464	6,437
K45	Bel Air 4d, 3S	4,884	4,578	2,913
L35	Impala 4d, 2S	4,891	4,561	23,455
L45	Impala 4d, 3S	4,936	4,675	23,259
N35	Cap Est 4d, 2S	4,960	4,800	12,280
N45	Cap Est 4d, 3S	5,004	4,914	23,063
Monte Carlo				
H57	S spt cpe	3,926	3,885	184,873
H57	Landau spt cpe	3,928	4,129	127,344
Corvette Stingray				
Z37	cpe	3,309	6,082	32,028
Z67	conv rdstr	3,315	5,846	5,474

1975

- **Sporty Vega-based Monza introduced**

- **Cosworth-Vega bows**

- **Nova fully restyled**

- **Camaro Z28 dropped**

- **Flip-tops furloughed at season's end**

- **Car sales plunge to 1.76 million**

▲ Though planned well before the 1973-74 "energy crisis," the Vega-based Monza was a timely arrival for the economy-car sales boom that continued into '75. This notchback Towne Coupe, as Chevy spelled it, was added at midmodel year as a companion to the inaugural "fasthatch" coupe. Priced from $3570, it garnered 69,238 debut-year sales.

▲ Like the new Monza Towne Coupe, the 2+2 hatchback shared the Vega's 97-inch-wheel-base chassis and base four-cylinder engine, but offered nicer appointments, sportier looks, and two V-8 options: a new 262-cubic-incher making 110 net horsepower or a 125-hp 350. The "fasthatch" priced from around $3953 and found 57,170 buyers.

◄▼ Corvette ad text for 1975 (*left*) glossed over the fact that the big-block 454 was no longer available. It also stressed the coupe almost exclusively, as the convertible would be phased out at year's end after a mere 4629 sales. The romantic 'Vette roadster would be back, but not until 1986. Total Corvette sales this year inched up to 38,465.

▲ Though most Detroit convertibles were gone with the wind by 1975, Chevrolet and other General Motors makes persisted with full-size ragtops for one last year—save Cadillac, which would make hay with a "last convertible" '76 Eldorado. This '75 Caprice Classic started at $5113, but speculators and nostalgia buffs drove actual transaction prices much higher.

▶ Because the expected demise of Chevy's big ragtop was widely reported in 1975, the model actually sold better than in '74, jumping 79 percent to 8349. However, Chevy expected extra-strong demand and upped output accordingly. Today this Caprice Classic has become a minor collector's item, even though it wouldn't be Chevy's last factory-built convertible.

▼ All big '75 Chevys wore a mildly revised nose and grille inserts, but a new roofline with fixed rear quarter windows was featured on this Caprice Classic hardtop sedan, now priced from $4891. Also new was a fancier $5075 Landau version of the Caprice Classic coupe, which started at $4837.

◄▲ The 1975 Impala four-door Sport Sedan hardtop got the same new roofline as its Caprice counterpart, but had a different grille insert, no rear fender skirts, and a somewhat less opulent interior (*above*). It remained more affordable, though, at $4631 to start. Total Impala sales this year were 249,151, including wagons, versus 150,244 for Caprice.

▲ The revised roofline on big 1975 hardtop sedans was partly designed to look, if not be, sturdier. Still, buyers were tiring of pillarless body styles, so this Impala was much less popular than in prior years, with relatively modest sales of 47,125.

▲ By contrast, Impala's pillared four-door scored almost twice as many 1975 sales as its pillarless cousin, a healthy 91,330. Oddly, the situation was reversed among Caprice Classics, where the respective numbers were 33,715 and 40,482.

◄ Camaro lost its Z28 package for 1975, but gained a wraparound rear window and a revived Rally Sport trim option. Like many '75 Detroit cars, Camaro engines adopted catalytic converters that permitted cleaner exhaust and improved drivability. Camaro sales slipped to 145,770 units.

233

▲ A standard rear-quarter vinyl roof covering again set the upmarket Monte Carlo Landau apart from its lower-priced S-model sibling. Their 1975 price spread was $270.

▲ The '75 Monte Carlo Landau listed at $4519 with base two-barrel 350 V-8. Power options were a four-barrel 350, a 400, or a 454, the last making 235 net horsepower.

▲ Like the '75 Monte, Chevelles sported mild styling changes and better-running engines via the catalytic converter. Here, the low-end Malibu "Colonnade" coupe.

▲ Full instrumentation surrounded by a gold-color appliqué was featured inside the sporty new '75 Cosworth-Vega, Chevy's take on the Euro-style performance small car.

▲ The Cosworth-Vega's 2.0-liter twincam four rated 111 net bhp—helped by a free-flow exhaust—but many owners think it was stronger. It was far from refined, though.

▲▼ The new 1975 Cosworth-Vega was available only as a hatchback coupe with black paint set off by gold-color body striping and wheels. The latter looked like expensive British Minilite magnesium rims, but were actually American-made steel wheels. Wider tires, front/rear stabilizer bars, a new torque-arm rear suspension and quicker steering improved the already good Vega handling. But at $5916—only $621 less than a new Corvette—the "CosVeg" was a tough sell despite its sophisticated engine. Worse, it was viewed by many as just another trouble-prone Vega. As a result, debut-year sales were only 2061 units. Chevrolet had projected some 5000 cars to leave the showroom floors.

Engine Availability

Engines	bore × stroke	bhp	availability
I-4, 122.0	3.50 × 3.16	111	S-Cosworth-Vega
I-4, 140.0	3.50 × 3.63	78	S-Vega, Monza exc 2+2
I-4, 140.0	3.50 × 3.63	87	O-Monza 2+2; O-Vega
I-6, 250.0	3.88 × 3.53	105	S-Nova, Chevl, Cam
V-8, 262.0	3.67 × 3.10	110	O-Nova, Monza
V-8, 350.0	4.00 × 3.48	125	O-Monza
V-8, 350.0	4.00 × 3.48	145	S-Nova, Chevl, Cam, MC, Chevr exc wgns
V-8, 350.0	4.00 × 3.48	155	O-Nova, Chevl, Cam, MC, Chev
V-8, 400.0	4.12 × 3.75	175	S-Chevr wgns; O-Chevl, MC, Chevr
V-8, 454.0	4.25 × 4.00	235	O-Chevl, MC, Chevr
Corvette Stingray			
V-8, 350.0	4.00 × 3.48	165	S-all
V-8, 350.0	4.00 × 3.48	205	O-all

▲▶ A newly styled GM X-body rejuvenated Nova for 1975, when roadability improved by borrowing some Camaro suspension components. Chevy also pushed its compact upmarket by adding posh LN—Luxury Nova—coupes (*above*) and sedans (*right*). All this should have benefited sales, yet Nova model-year volume actually dropped a steep 30 percent to 272,982 units.

▲ Six-cylinder engines had made Chevrolet an automotive juggernaut, and still loomed large in '75. However, this 250 was now in its fifth year as the only six in Chevy's stable, delivering 105 net hp as the standard engine for Nova, Camaro, and Chevelle.

▶ Chevy's 1975 Blazer, Suburban, and light-duty pickups introduced a bold cross-hatch grille that soon became a styling hallmark for the truck line. Here, the ever-popular C-10 Fleetside pickup in top-shelf Cheyenne trim, which included two-tone paint, deluxe wheel covers, even a stand-up hood ornament befitting a luxury car. Big "Western" mirrors were a separate option.

Model Breakdown

Vega		Wght	Price	Prod
V11	sdn 2d	2,415	2,786	33,878
V11	LX sdn 2d	—	3,119	1,255
V15	wgn 3d, 2S	2,531	3,016	47,474
V15	Est wgn 3d, 2S	—	3,244	8,659
V77	htchbk cpe 3d	2,478	2,899	112,912
V77	Cswrth htchbk cpe 3d	—	5,916	2,061

Monza				
M27	Towne cpe	2,675	3,570	69,238
R07	S htchbk cpe 3d	—	3,648	9,795
R07	2+2 htchbk cpe 3d	2,753	3,953	57,170

Nova				
X17	htchbk cpe 3d, I-6	3,391	3,347	7,952
X17	htchbk cpe 3d, V-8	3,493	3,422	8,421
X27	cpe, I-6	3,276	3,205	48,103
X27	S cpe, I-6	—	3,099	16,655
X27	cpe, V-8	3,378	3,280	33,921
X27	S cpe, V-8	—	3,174	5,070
X69	sdn 4d, I-6	3,306	3,209	43,760
X69	sdn 4d, V-8	3,408	3,284	22,587
Y17	Cstm htchbk cpe 3d, I-6	3,421	3,541	3,812
Y17	Cstm htchbk cpe 3d, V-8	3,523	3,616	11,438
Y27	Cstm cpe, I-6	3,335	3,402	7,214
Y27	LN cpe, I-6	—	3,782	1,138
Y27	Cstm cpe, V-8	3,437	3,477	19,074
Y27	LN cpe, V-8	—	3,857	11,395
Y69	Cstm sdn 4d, I-6	3,367	3,415	8,959

Nova (continued)		Wght	Price	Prod
Y69	LN sdn 4d, I-6	—	3,795	1,286
Y69	Cstm sdn 4d, V-8	3,469	3,490	13,221
Y69	LN sdn 4d, V-8	—	3,870	8,976

Camaro				
Q87	spt cpe, I-6	3,421	3,540	29,749
Q87	spt cpe, V-8	3,532	3,685	76,178
S87	Type LT spt cpe, V8	3,616	4,057	39,843

Chevelle				
C29	Mlbu sdn 4d, I-6	3,713	3,402	12,873
C29	Mlbu sdn 4d, V-8	3,833	3,652	24,989
C37	Mlbu cpe, I-6	3,642	3,407	13,292
C37	Mlbu cpe, V8	3,762	3,657	23,708
D29	Mlbu Clsc sdn 4d, I-6	3,778	3,695	1
D29	Mlbu Clsc sdn 4d, V-8	3,898	3,945	51,070
D37	Mlbu Clsc cpe, I-6	3,681	3,698	4,330
D37	Mlbu Clsc cpe, V-8	3,801	3,948	76,607
D37	Mlbu Clsc Lnd cpe, I-6	—	3,930	378
D37	Mlbu Clsc Lnd cpe, V-8	—	4,180	22,691
E37	Lgna S3 cpe, V-8	3,908	4,113	—

Chevelle Malibu Wagon				
C35	5d, 3S	4,237	4,463	2,377
C35	5d, 2S	4,207	4,318	11,600
D36	Classic 5d, 3S	4,305	4,701	6,394
D36	Classic 5d, 2S	4,275	4,556	15,974
G35	Clsc Est 5d, 3S	4,331	4,893	4,600
G35	Clsc Est 5d, 2S	4,301	4,748	4,637

Chevrolet		Wght	Price	Prod
K69	Bel Air sdn 4d	4,179	4,345	15,871
L39	Impl spt sdn 4d	4,265	4,631	47,125
L47	Impl Cstm cpe	4,190	4,626	49,455
L47	Impl Lndu cpe	—	4,901	2,465
L57	Impl spt cpe	4,207	4,575	21,333
L69	Impl sdn 4d	4,218	4,548	91,330
N39	Cap Clsc spt sdn 4d	4,360	4,891	40,482
N47	Cap Clsc cpe	4,275	4,837	36,041
N47	Cap Clsc Lnd cpe	—	5,075	3,752
N67	Cap Clsc conv cpe	4,343	5,113	8,349
N69	Cap Clsc sdn 4d	4,311	4,819	33,715

Chevrolet Wagon				
K35	Bel Air 4d, 2S	4,856	4,878	4,032
K45	Bel Air 4d, 3S	4,913	4,998	2,386
L35	Impala 4d, 2S	4,910	5,001	17,998
L45	Impala 4d, 3S	4,959	5,121	19,445
N35	Cap Est 4d, 2S	4,978	5,231	9,047
N45	Cap Est 4d, 3S	5,036	5,351	18,858

Monte Carlo				
H57	S spt cpe	3,927	4,249	148,529
H57	Landau spt cpe	3,930	4,519	110,380

Corvette Stingray				
Z37	cpe	3,433	6,797	33,836
Z67	conv rdstr	3,446	6,537	4,629

1976

- Chevette "minicar" bows as a second import-fighter and the smallest Chevy ever

- Coupe-only Corvette tallies record sales

- Chevy's total car output goes back above the 2-million mark

▶ Special "cutaway" exhibits at 1976 auto shows helped introduce Chevette, the smallest Chevy in history. Essentially an Americanized version of the Opel Kadett T-car from General Motors' German subsidiary, Chevrolet's latest import-fighter arrived as a two-door hatchback sedan with a petite 94.3-inch wheelbase, feathery sub-2000-pound curb weight, and a thrifty 1.6-liter/85 cubic-inch four-cylinder engine.

▲ Woody-look side trim, roof rack, and deluxe wheel covers were among numerous dress-up items available for the '76 Chevette, which priced from $3098 in regular trim with standard back seat. This version accounted for the vast majority of the new pint-size Chevy's strong debut-year sales of 187,817.

▲ Though it wore no bow tie emblem up front, the Chevette was clearly part of the Chevrolet family. Horsepower was just 85, but acceleration was decent and fuel economy excellent.

▶ Recalling the business coupes of old was the Chevette Scooter, which lacked a back seat and was very spartan inside and out. The upside was a miserly $2899 base price. Even with that, however, only 9810 buyers were persuaded. Chevette was at least partly prompted by the rush to economy cars during the 1973-74 gas crunch, but also aimed to stem the rising sales tide of high-quality Japanese small cars that continued once the energy crisis had passed.

◄ Taking advantage of a recent change in government regulations, Caprice Classic models switched from round to oblong sealed-beam headlamps for '76, something designers had anticipated for years. Aside from that, and a few adjustments to appearance and engine tuning, the big Chevys were much as before. There were fewer options, however, as the Caprice Classic convertible and Bel Air sedan were dropped. The latter had been the cheapest big Chevy since the last "fleet special" Biscayne sedans of 1972. This $5078 hardtop sedan attracted 55,308 buyers out of 184,639 Caprice Classics built for the model year, an improvement over the series' '75 showing.

▲ The Chevelle Laguna Type S-3 continued with the sloped nose adopted for '75, but its standard 350 V-8 was now an option, replaced by a new 305 small-block with 145 horsepower.

▲ Larger standard tires and louvered rear quarter windows were retained for the '76 Laguna Type S-3. The model attracted only 9100 sales and would not return for '77.

◄ Malibu Classics gained visual flair for '76 by wearing the newly allowed square headlamps in stacked pairs astride a mesh-type grille insert. Regular Malibus retained dual round lamps, plus a checked grille pattern. A rear-quarter vinyl roof covering again distinguished the top-line Landau from this regular Classic coupe. A non-Classic Malibu version was also still available.

▼ Though big-car sales had recovered throughout the industry by '76, the energy crisis had shifted the market's "center of gravity" to the midsize ranks. Chevelle reflected this by posting a near 21 percent model-year sales increase to 333,243 units. Among the most popular individual models was this Malibu Classic four-door sedan, priced from $4490 with base 305 V-8.

237

▼► Corvette advertising was still oriented toward "gearheads" in 1976, evidenced by the double-exposure photo of the hideaway headlamps (*below*) and the "phantom" illustration highlighting the chassis (*right*). More heartening news this year was provided by small power gains for the two 350 V-8s, reversing a trend. The base engine went from 165 to 180 hp and the optional high-tune version from 205 to 210. Less noticed, but appreciated, was a newly standard maintenance-free battery.

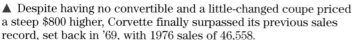

▲ Despite having no convertible and a little-changed coupe priced a steep $800 higher, Corvette finally surpassed its previous sales record, set back in '69, with 1976 sales of 46,558.

▲ Corvette's option list for 1976 again included the practical rear-deck luggage rack, but also the factory's first aluminum wheels in years. The latter added $299 to the delivered price.

◄ Monte Carlo's high popularity had spawned a good many competitors by 1976, including the Ford Gran Torino Elite, Chrysler Cordoba, and in-house rival Olds Cutlass Supreme. Even so, Monte Carlo sales this year jumped an impressive 36.4 percent to 353,272 in a market gone mad for midsize "personal luxury" coupes. A new vee'd hood and grille combined with stacked pairs of square headlamps to freshen the Monte's face. Here, the volume-selling standard S-model, priced from $4673 with its new 140-hp 305 base V-8.

► Though never intended as an all-out muscle machine, the Monte Carlo started showing its muscle in stock-car racing during 1976, thanks to private teams likely inspired by Cale Yarborough's efforts two years before. Though the NASCAR Montes only faintly resembled this production '76, they had surprisingly good high-speed aerodynamics, plus iron reliability to go the distance. As a result, Chevrolet won at least a dozen Winston Cup races each season from 1976 through 1980.

▲ Monzas were visual reruns for 1976 with shuffled engines. A new two-barrel four-cylinder with 84 hp arrived to supplement the base unit, which dropped to just 70 hp, and a 140-hp 305 V-8 replaced the 350 option. Shown here, the Towne Coupe, priced from $3359.

▲ The 1976 Monza 2+2 offered a new Spyder cosmetic option with front and rear spoilers, black body accents, and bold striping. It was little help to overall Monza sales, however, which plunged 40.6 percent for the model year to 80,905 units.

▲ A new grille with slim horizontal bars spruced up all '76 Vegas, as shown on this rare surviving Cosworth. Headlining mechanical improvements were larger rear drum brakes and a front crossmember for improved structural strength. Vega was billed this year as "Built to Take It," but was still dogged by its early, well-publicized engine and rust woes.

▲ The Cosworth-Vega's 111-hp 2.0-liter fuel-injected engine was unchanged for '76, but bolted to a standard five-speed close-ratio gearbox instead of the previous four-speed. This, and continuing strong period inflation, contributed to a higher $6066 base price, which depressed sales to only 1477.

▼ White was a new color choice for the '76 Cosworth-Vega, but scant demand meant the model's second year would be its last. As a whole, Vega sales dropped 22.2 percent this year to 160,524 units, this despite a booming small-car market. The regular hatch coupe remained the most popular single model at $3099 and up.

Engine Availability

Engines	bore × stroke	bhp	availability
I-4, 85.0	3.23 × 2.61	52	S-Chevt
I-4, 97.6	3.23 × 2.98	60	O-Chevt
I-4, 122.0	3.50 × 3.15	111	S-Cosworth-Vega
I-4, 140.0	3.50 × 3.63	70	S-Vega, Monza
I-4, 140.0	3.50 × 3.63	84	O-Vega, Monza
I-6, 250.0	3.88 × 3.53	105	S-Nova, Chevl, Cam
V-8, 262.0	3.67 × 3.10	110	O-Monza
V-8, 305.0	3.74 × 3.48	140	S-Nova, Chevl, Cam, MC; O-Monza
V-8, 305.0	3.74 × 3.48	145	S-Chevl wgn, Chevr; O-MC
V-8, 350.0	4.00 × 3.48	165	O-Nova, Chevl, Cam, MC, Chevr
V-8, 400.0	4.12 × 3.75	175	S-Chevr wgn; O-Chevl, MC, Chevr
V-8, 454.0	4.25 × 4.00	225	O-Chevr
Corvette Stingray			
V-8, 350.0	4.00 × 3.48	180	S-all
V-8, 350.0	4.00 × 3.48	210	O-all

1976 CHEVROLET POLICE VEHICLES

▲ Nova coupes still offered an SS option for 1976, but it was a pale echo of Super Sport glory days, comprising just Rally wheels, contrasting lower-body striping, and fender badges. LN models were retitled Concours and sold somewhat better. Indeed, total Nova sales improved by 22.6 percent for the model year to 334,728 units.

▲ Chevy chose a compact Nova for the cover of its 1976 Police Vehicles brochure, but most officers still preferred big cars.

▲ The Nova lineup consolidated for '76 to the usual three body styles in two trim levels, standard and upmarket Concours. This is the Concours four-door sedan, which carried a base sticker price of $3995 with V-8.

▲ Among Chevy's 1976 big-rig trucks was this aptly named Titan cab-over-engine tractor, one of many variations on the maximum-duty Series 90 chassis. Most were built with diesel engines supplied by Cummins, Caterpillar, and Detroit-Allison.

▲ As a full-line truckmaker, Chevrolet continued offering a choice of conventional and COE cabs on its medium- and heavy-duty chassis. "Cab-overs" like this van were designated T-Series and were available with a bewildering array of job-specific options.

Model Breakdown

Chevette		Wght	Price	Prod
B08	htchbk sdn 3d	1,927	3,098	178,007
J08	Scooter htchbk sdn 3d	1,870	2,899	9,810
Vega				
V11	sdn 2d	2,443	2,984	27,619
V15	wgn 3d, 2S	2,578	3,227	46,114
V15	Est wgn 3d, 2S	—	3,450	7,935
V77	htchbk cpe 3d	2,534	3,099	77,409
V77	Cswrth htchbk cpe 3d	—	6,066	1,447
Monza				
M27	Towne cpe	2,625	3,359	46,735
R07	2+2 htchbk cpe 3d	2,668	3,727	34,170
Nova				
X17	htchbk cpe 3d, I-6	3,391	3,417	10,853
X17	htchbk cpe 3d, V-8	3,475	3,579	7,866
X27	cpe, I-6	3,188	3,248	87,438
X27	cpe, V-8	3,272	3,413	44,421
X69	sdn 4d, I-6	3,221	3,283	86,600
X69	sdn 4d, V-8	3,305	3,448	37,167
Y17	Cncrs htchbk cpe 3d, I-6	3,401	3,972	2,088
Y17	Cncrs htchbk cpe 3d, V-8	3,485	4,134	5,486
Y27	Cncrs cpe, I-6	3,324	3,795	6,568
Y27	Cncrs cpe, V-8	3,408	3,960	15,730

Nova (continued)		Wght	Price	Prod
Y69	Cncrs sdn 4d, I-6	3,367	3,830	10,151
Y69	Cncrs sdn 4d, V-8	3,451	3,995	20,360
Camaro				
Q87	spt cpe, I-6	3,421	3,762	38,047
Q87	spt cpe, V-8	3,511	3,927	92,491
S87	Type LT spt cpe, V-8	3,576	4,320	52,421
Chevelle				
C29	Mlbu sdn 4d, I-6	3,729	3,671	13,116
C29	Mlbu sdn 4d, V-8	3,834	4,201	25,353
C37	Malibu cpe, I-6	3,650	3,636	12,616
C37	Malibu cpe, V-8	3,755	4,166	17,976
D29	Mlbu Clsc sdn 4d, I-6	3,827	4,196	4,253
D29	Mlbu Clsc sdn 4d, V-8	3,932	4,490	73,307
D37	Mlbu Clsc cpe, I-6	3,688	3,926	5,791
D37	Mlbu Clsc cpe, V-8	3,793	4,455	76,843
D37	Mlbu Clsc Lnd cpe, I-6	—	4,124	672
D37	Mlbu Clsc Lnd cpe, V-8	—	4,640	29,495
E37	Lgna S3 cpe, V-8	3,978	4,621	9,100
Chevelle Malibu Wagon				
C35	5d, 3S	4,268	4,686	2,984
C35	5d, 2S	4,238	4,543	13,581
D35	Classic 5d, 3S	4,330	4,919	11,617
D35	Classic 5d, 2S	4,300	4,776	24,635

Chevl Mlbu Wgn (continued)		Wght	Price	Prod
G35	Clsc Est 5d, 3S	4,356	5,114	6,386
G35	Clsc Est 5d, 2S	4,326	4,971	5,518
Chevrolet				
L39	Imp spt sdn 4d	4,245	4,798	39,849
L47	Imp Cstm cpe	4,175	4,763	43,219
L47	Imp Lnd cpe	—	5,058	10,841
L69	Imp S spt sdn 4d	—	4,507	18,265
L69	Impala sdn 4d	4,222	4,706	86,057
N39	Cap Clsc spt sdn 4d	4,314	5,078	55,308
N47	Cap Clsc cpe	4,244	5,043	28,161
N47	Cap Clsc Lnd cpe	—	5,248	21,926
N69	Cap Clsc sdn 4d	4,285	5,013	47,411
Chevrolet Wagon				
L35	Impala 4d, 2S	4,912	5,166	19,657
L45	Impala 4d, 3S	4,972	5,283	21,329
N35	Cap Est 4d, 2S	4,948	5,429	10,029
N45	Cap Est 4d, 3S	5,007	5,546	21,804
Monte Carlo				
H57	S spt cpe	3,907	4,673	191,370
H57	Landau spt cpe	—	4,966	161,902
Corvette Stingray				
Z37	cpe	3,445	7,605	46,558

- **Full-size line "down-sized" in complete redesign**

- **Vega discontinued at end of year**

- **Z28 returns to Camaro lineup**

- **Corvette drops Stingray name**

▲ Downsizing its popular full-size line was a risky gamble for Chevrolet. Period ads reassured buyers they would find all the space they'd need; claiming more head room, more rear leg room, and more trunk room. Wheelbase was cut by 5½ inches; curb weight by more than 500 pounds. Engines were downsized, too. A 250-cid inline six was now standard, with 305- and 350-cid V-8s optional. The 454 big block was history.

▲ Impalas in coupe, sedan, and wagon body styles anchored the line. Prices rose an average of about $200, and that with a six-cylinder engine rather than the previously standard V 8. Impalas featured a prominent eggcrate grille and rectangular taillights.

▲ Caprices in the same three body styles again topped the line, boasting noticeable styling tweaks to differentiate them from their Impala linemates. Grilles, bumpers, and taillights were altered; and only Caprices wore that icon of luxury, the hood ornament.

◄ Sales of the new down-sized Chevys soared, and the excellent press reviews included "Car of the Year" honors from *Motor Trend* magazine. The least-expensive Impala, the Custom coupe, started at $4876. These "B-body" Impalas would continue in use, with a minor 1980 facelift, through 1990.

▲ Full-size Chevrolet wagons were dramatically reduced in size for '77; wheelbase was cut from 125 inches to 116, overall length by more than a foot. Weight dropped by about 900 pounds, with base models tipping the scale at just over two tons.

▲ At 87.3 cubic feet, the wagon's cargo volume was down nearly 20 percent, but lockable storage bins were added in the cargo-area sidewalls. As before, wagons came in six- and nine-passenger versions. The "Glide-Away" tailgate gave way to a three-way tailgate.

▲ In mid 1977, the legendary Camaro Z28 returned from a three-year hiatus to do battle with Pontiac's Firebird Trans Am. With stiffer suspension and wider tires, the emphasis was on handling, not straight-line performance, although Z28 got a special 185-hp (vs. 170 in other Chevys), four-barrel, 350 V-8.

▲ Not to be outdone by the flashy Trans Am, the Z28 boasted the requisite sporty trim. Front and rear spoilers, body-colored bumpers, and an array of stripes and badges set it apart from garden-variety Camaros, which themselves proved quite popular in 1977; sales were up nearly 20 percent to close to 219,000.

◄► The classy Concours, available in both coupe and sedan body styles, continued to top the Nova line for 1977. With bench front seat, Nova was a six-passenger car priced about $1400 less than the new downsized Impala. Chevy's powerful 170-horsepower 350 V-8 was optional, which was likely one factor that led the Los Angeles Sheriff's Department to order 222 specially-equipped '76 sedans, encouraging other departments to order Novas as well.

◄▲ The difference between full-size and midsize became blurred when General Motors downsized its big cars for '77. In fact, the midsize Malibu wagon was almost identical in specification to the new full-size Impala wagon, and also came in six- and nine-passenger versions. Prices for the top-line Malibu Classic wagon started at $5065.

▲ While Malibu sedans and wagons rode the same 116-inch wheelbase as the new downsized Impalas, coupes sat on a 112-inch span. Base and Classic versions were offered, the latter shown here.

▲ Base Malibus traded stacked quad headlights for round dual units and didn't get a hood ornament. Least expensive of the bunch was the $3885 two-door coupe.

◀▲ Little changed outside for 1977, Corvette sales jumped by five percent despite a hefty $1043 boost in base price. Some of that, however, was owed to the fact that leather upholstery was now included in the base price of $8648. A 180-horsepower 350 V-8 remained standard, with a 210-hp L82 version optional; oddly, only 6148 of the more than 49,000 Corvettes produced got the L82. Just as telling, a mere 7103 carried a manual transmission. Also for '77, the Stingray name disappeared from bodies, and crossed-flag emblems were new.

▲ Though no convertible Corvette had been offered since 1975, T-tops were standard. New for '77 was an available decklid luggage carrier that could be used to conveniently store the roof panels.

▲ A slightly different interior included a redesigned center console that allowed the use of regular Delco radios (previous editions used a unique radio design), which could include a cassette player.

◄▲ The ill-fated Vega was in its final year, as sales plummeted to just 78,402—less than half the '76 total. Coupe (*above*), hatchback coupe (*left*), and wagon remained in the line, the most popular being the hatchback. The high-performance Cosworth-Vega was gone, leaving only GT option packages for the hatchback and wagon. An Estate wagon included "wood" siding. Prices started at $3249 for a base coupe.

▲ Monzas continued in coupe and hatchback form, and looked much the same as in '76—and '75. Sporty new Spyder packages included mechanical and cosmetic upgrades.

▲ Sportier still was the limited-edition Mirage package, which included bolt-on "aero" Fiberglass body panels, nifty striping, and sport suspension. It came only in white.

▲ Chevette appeared unchanged for its second model year, but both the 1.4- and 1.6-liter engines got a slight power boost, and Scooters got a standard rear seat.

▲ In 1977, Chevrolet found itself in the curious position of selling the "midsize" Malibu and Monte Carlo that were both as large as its downsized "full-size" models. In its last year before being downsized itself, the Monte Carlo remained tremendously popular.

▲ El Camino shared its exterior styling, interior trim, and engine choices with the midsize Malibu, and likewise was in its final year in this form. Shown is an El Camino Classic with unusual two-tone paint scheme.

▲ El Camino's 1973-77 generation has always been popular with enthusiasts, especially the rare SS version.

Engine Availability

Engines	bore × stroke	bhp	availability
I-4, 85.0	3.23 × 2.61	57	S-Chevt
I-4, 97.6	3.23 × 2.98	63	O-Chevt
I-4, 140.0	3.50 × 3.15	84	S-Vega, Monza
I-6, 250.0	3.88 × 3.53	110	S-Nova, Chevl, Cam, Chevr
V-8, 305.0	3.74 × 3.48	145	S-Nova, Chevl exc Clsc wgn, Cam, MC, Chevr; O-Monza
V-8, 350.0	4.00 × 3.48	170	S-Chevl Clsc wgn; O-Nova, Chevl, Cam, MC, Chevr

Corvette Stingray

V-8, 350.0	4.00 × 3.48	180	S-all
V-8, 350.0	4.00 × 3.48	210	O-all

◄ Despite its hefty appetite for fuel, the Blazer sport-utility vehicle was becoming increasingly popular, as 1977 sales topped those of 1976 by nearly a third.

▲ Still available with the big 454-cid V-8, the Suburban remained popular with the trailer-towing crowd.

▲ Huge Crew Cab pickups could carry six people and a full load of cargo, making them perfect for construction crews.

▲ The LUV (Light Utility Vehicle), built for Chevrolet by Isuzu of Japan, came in two- and four-wheel-drive versions with a 6- or 7½-foot bed. It was offered from 1971 to '81.

▲ This short-wheelbase, ½-ton panel van wears a badge on its front fender marking it as the "Caravan"—years before Dodge used the name on a very different kind of van.

▲ Chevy's Step Van was a popular local delivery vehicle. The boxy shape maximized interior space—and wind resistance.

▲ Here, a Chevrolet C65 medium-duty truck with tanker body makes a home delivery.

▲ Chevrolet's medium-duty tractors included the gasoline-powered Series 70 (left) and diesel-engined Series 90 (right).

▲ For heavy-duty over-the-road use, Chevy offered the Bison, shown here with a tanker in tow.

Model Breakdown

Chevette		Wght	Price	Prod
B08	htchbk sdn 3d	1,958	3,225	120,278
J08	Scootr htchbk sdn 3d	1,898	2,999	13,191
Vega				
V11	sdn 2d	2,459	3,249	12,365
V15	wgn 3d, 2S	2,571	3,522	25,181
V15	Estate wgn 3d, 2S	—	3,745	3,461
V77	htchbk cpe 3d	2,522	3,359	37,395
Monza				
M27	Towne cpe	2,580	3,560	34,133
R07	2+2 htchbk cpe 3d	2,671	3,840	39,215
Nova				
X17	htchbk cpe 3d, I-6	3,217	3,646	18,048
X17	htchbk cpe 3d, V-8	3,335	3,766	
X27	cpe, I-6	3,139	3,482	132,833
X27	cpe, V-8	3,257	3,602	
X69	sdn 4d, I-6	3,174	3,532	141,028
X69	sdn 4d, V-8	3,292	3,652	
Y17	Cncrs htchbk cpe 3d, I-6	3,378	4,154	5,481
Y17	Cncrs htchbk cpe 3d, V-8	3,486	4,274	
Y27	Cncrs cpe, I-6	3,383	3,991	28,602
Y27	Cncrs cpe, V-8	3,391	4,111	
Y69	Cncrs sdn 4d, I-6	3,329	4,066	39,272
Y69	Cncrs sdn 4d, V-8	3,437	4,186	
Camaro				
Q87	spt cpe, I-6	3,369	4,113	131,717
S87	Type LT spt cpe	3,422	4,478	72,787
Q87	Z28 spt cpe, V-8	—	5,170	14,349
Chevelle Malibu				
C29	sdn 4d, I-6	3,628	3,935	39,064
C29	sdn 4d, V-8	3,727	4,055	
C37	cpe, I-6	3,551	3,885	28,793
C37	cpe, V-8	3,650	4,005	
D29	Clsc sdn 4d, I-6	3,725	4,475	76,776
D29	Clsc sdn 4d, V-8	3,824	4,595	
D37	Clsc cpe, I-6	3,599	4,125	73,739
D37	Clsc cpe, V-8	3,698	4,245	
D37	Clsc Lnd cpe, I-6	—	4,353	37,215
D37	Clsc Lnd cpe, V-8	—	4,473	
Chevelle Malibu Wagon				
C35	5d, 3S	4,169	4,877	4,014
C35	5d, 2S	4,139	4,734	18,023
D35	Classic 5d, 3S	4,263	5,208	19,053
D35	Classic 5d, 2S	4,233	5,065	31,539
Chevrolet				
L35	Imp wgn 4d, 3S, V-8	4,072	5,406	28,255
L35	Imp wgn 4d, 2S, V-8	4,042	5,289	37,108
L47	Imp Cstm cpe, I-6	3,533	4,876	55,347
L47	Imp Cstm cpe, V-8	3,628	4,996	
L47	Imp Lnd cpe	—	—	2,745
L69	Imp sdn 4d, I-6	3,564	4,901	196,824
L69	Imp sdn 4d, V-8	3,659	5,021	
N35	Cap Clsc wgn 4d, 3S, V-8	4,118	5,734	33,639
N35	Cap Clsc wgn 4d, 2S, V-8	4,088	5,617	22,930
N47	Cap Clsc cpe, I-6	3,571	5,187	62,366
N47	Cap Clsc cpe, V-8	3,666	5,307	
N69	Cap Clsc sdn 4d, I-6	3,606	5,237	212,840
N69	Cap Clsc sdn 4d, V-8	3,701	5,357	
N69	Cap Lnd cpe	—	—	9,607
Monte Carlo				
H57	S spt cpe	3,852	4,968	224,327
H57	Landau spt cpe	—	5,298	186,711
Corvette Stingray				
Z37	cpe	3,448	8,648	49,213

1978

- **Smaller Malibu replaces Chevelle**

- **Monte Carlo also downsized**

- **Indy Pace Car and 25th Anniversary Corvettes offered**

- **Camaro's bumpers replaced by "soft" fascias**

▲ Chevy negotiated with the Indianapolis Motor Speedway to have a modified Corvette used as pace car for the '78 Indianapolis 500 race. Pace car replicas were among the most sought after new cars of 1978, and most sold for considerably more than the $13,653 sticker.

▲ Posing with a Corvette Pace Car are (*clockwise from left*) Corvette chief engineer David R. McLellan, Chevy engineers Paul J. King and Robert Stempl (later GM chairman), and Chevy general manager Robert Lund. Pace car editions included a unique silver-leather interior and a full complement of otherwise optional equipment. This was also Corvette's 25th Anniversary, commemorated by a two-tone Silver Anniversary Edition.

▼ All Corvettes for 1978 got a large compound-curved back window that added visibility and easier-loading luggage space.

▲ Camaro Z28's standard 350-cid V-8 for 1978 gained 15-base horsepower to 185. Also added to Z28 were nonfunctional front-fender vents and hood scoop.

▲ All Camaros for '78 got a facelift, in which soft front and rear fascias replaced the previous metal bumpers. The base Camaro was by far the most popular in the line, with 134,491 sold.

▶ Rally Sport models differed from regular Camaros primarily in their trim, most notably the two-tone exterior paint. The Rally Sport could also be combined with the Type LT, and that's the way most buyers bought them. Type LT Rally Sport production totaled 65,635 units for '78, versus 11,902 non-LT Rally Sport models.

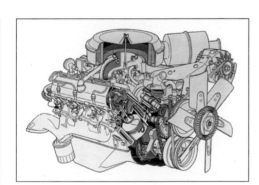

▲ The Impala Coupe (*top and left*) was a rather rare version of America's best-selling car line. Just 33,990 Impala coupes and an additional 4,652 Impala Landau coupes were built. Although these Impalas were nicely styled cars, most coupe buyers preferred the top-of-the-line Caprice Classic. A new grille and slightly restyled taillights identified the '78 Caprice Classic (*right*).

▲ A 5.7-liter, GM-built diesel engine (*top*) was a new option for the C10 pickup. Also making their debut for '78 were new V-6s. Shown here (*bottom*) is Malibu's standard 200-cid unit that made 95 bhp. A 231-cid, 105-bhp V-6 was optional on Malibus and Monzas, standard on Monte Carlos. Monzas could also get a 196-cid, 90-bhp V-6.

▲ In the quest for greater fuel economy and in response to the public's growing distaste for massive cars, Monte Carlo was downsized for '78. The third-generation Monte Carlo was a foot shorter and 800 pounds lighter than the '77. Standard power was provided by a 231-cid V-6, the first six-cylinder engine in Monte Carlo history. A 305 V-8 was optional.

◄ Monte Carlo shared Malibu's 108.1-inch wheelbase chassis, but had different styling that included a more formal roofline. Options included T-tops, wire wheels, and bucket seats. Shown here is the Landau Coupe, which tallied sales of 141,461 for '78. The Sport Coupe was the more popular Monte that year, selling 216,730 units.

▲ An all-new Malibu made its debut for 1978, and the Chevelle nameplate was discontinued. Two series, Malibu and Malibu Classic, were available.

▲ Malibu was offered in coupe form, shown here in Classic trim, along with sedans and station wagons.

◄ Standard power for the new Malibu series was a 200-cid V-6. Optional were a 231-cid V-6 or 305-cid V-8. The downsized Malibus were a foot shorter and about 500 to 1000 pounds lighter than the corresponding '77 models.

▲ The Monza line got a restyled front and a "new" wagon model—the old Vega wagon with a Monza grille—but other Monza/Vega hybrids were considered. Also new to all '78 Monzas was the Pontiac "Iron Duke" four-cylinder.

▲ A less costly Nova Custom replaced the Nova Concours for '78. Nova production dipped to about 288,100 cars, making it the only Chevy series to post a sales decline. Base and Custom Novas shared the same restyled grille with horizontal bars.

◄ Chevettes were the first to use Chevy's new automatic shoulder belt system, developed in anticipation of coming passive-restraint requirements. A traditional "active" lap belt and a knee bolster built into the lower part of the instrument panel were also incorporated into the system for additional protection.

◄▲ El Camino was once again based on the intermediate car line, so it carried the styling of the new, downsized Malibu. Engine choices ranged from a 3.3-liter V-6 to the 350-cid V-8. Shown here is the uplevel Conquista trim. A Super Sport version continued to be offered. Starting prices ranged from $3807 for a base V-6 model, to $5022 for a V-8 SS.

► El Camino's similarity with Malibus also carried over into the interior. Chevy said the new intermediate design provided greater room and comfort despite downsized exterior dimensions.

Engine Availability

Engines	bore × stroke	bhp	availability
I-4, 97.6	3.23 × 2.98	63	O-Chevt
I-4, 97.6	3.23 × 2.98	68	O-Chevt
I-4, 151.0	4.00 × 3.00	85	S-Monza
V-6, 196.0	3.50 × 3.40	90	O-Monza
V-6, 200.0	3.50 × 3.48	95	S-Malibu
V-6, 231.0	3.80 × 3.40	105	S-MC; O-Malibu, Monza
I-6, 250.0	3.88 × 3.53	110	S-Nova, Cam exc Z28, Chevr
V-8, 305.0	3.74 × 3.48	145	S-Nova, Mal, Cam exc Z28, MC Chevr; O-Monza
V-8, 350.0	4.00 × 3.48	170	O-Nova, Mal wgns, Cam, Chevr
V-8, 350.0	4.00 × 3.48	185	S-Camaro Z28
Corvette			
V-8, 350.0	4.00 × 3.48	185	S-all
V-8, 350.0	4.00 × 3.48	220	O-all

▶ New for 1978 was the Bruin line of big trucks *(left)*, which had a contemporary-styled Fiberglas tilt hood and offered Detroit Diesel or Cummins diesel engines. Meanwhile, 70-Series tractors *(right)* soldiered on with the old styling.

▲ Suburban continued in ½-ton C10, shown here in two-wheel-drive form, or in C20 ¾-ton versions. A tailgate was standard, but double swing-out rear doors were available. C10 prices started at $5810; C20s at $6381.

▲ Pickups continued basically unchanged for '78. Shown is a C10 ½-ton in Scottsdale trim. With base 305-cid V-8, C10 prices started at $4418 for the short bed, or $4493 with long bed. Both were available with stepside cargo box at no extra charge.

▲ The LUV pickup got this long-wheelbase model for '78, along with a restyled grille carrying single headlights.

▲ Vans were available in ½-ton G10 or ¾-ton G20 (shown). Available wheelbases for both versions were 110 and 125 inches.

▲ Blazer interiors got a restyled instrument panel for '78, along with a soft vinyl steering wheel.

Model Breakdown

Chevette		Wght	Price	Prod
B08	htchbk sdn 3d	1,965	3,644	118,375
B68	htchbk sdn 5d	2,035	3,764	167,769
J08	Scootr htchbk sdn 3d	1,932	3,149	12,829
Monza				
M07	2+2 htchbk cpe 3d	2,732	3,779	36,227
M15	wgn 3d	2,723	3,868	24,255
M15	Estate wgn 3d	—	4,102	2,478
M27	cpe	2,688	3,622	37,878
M77	S htchbk cpe 3d	2,643	3,697	2,326
R07	Sprt 2+2 htchbk cpe 3d	2,777	4,247	28,845
R27	spt cpe	2,730	4,100	6,823
Nova				
X17	htchbk cpe 3d, I-6	3,258	3,866	12,665
X17	htchbk cpe 3d, V-8	3,403	4,051	
X27	cpe, I-6	3,132	3,702	101,858
X27	cpe, V-8	3,277	3,877	
X69	sdn 4d, I-6	3,173	3,777	123,158
X69	sdn 4d, V-8	3,318	3,962	
Y27	Cstm cpe, I-6	3,261	3,960	23,953
Y27	Cstm cpe, V-8	3,396	4,145	
Y69	Cstm sdn 4d, I-6	3,298	4,035	26,475
Y69	Cstm sdn 4d, V-8	3,443	4,220	
Camaro				
Q87	spt cpe	3,300	4,414	134,491

Camaro *(continued)*		Wght	Price	Prod
Q87	Rally sport cpe	—	4,784	11,902
S87	Type LT spt cpe	3,352	4,814	65,635
S87	Typ LT Rally sprt cpe	—	5,065	5,696
Q87	Z28 spt cpe, V-8	—	5,604	54,907
Malibu				
T19	sdn 4d, V-6	3,006	4,276	44,426
T19	sdn 4d, V-8	3,143	4,469	
T27	cpe, V-6	3,001	4,204	27,089
T27	cpe, V-8	3,138	4,394	
T35	wgn 4d, 2S, V-6	3,169	4,516	30,850
T35	wgn 4d, 2S, V-8	3,550	4,706	
W19	Clsc sdn 4d, V-6	3,039	4,561	102,967
W19	Clsc sdn 4d, V-8	3,175	4,751	
W27	Clsc spt cpe, V-6	3,031	4,461	60,992
W27	Clsc spt cpe, V-8	3,167	4,651	
W27	Clsc Lnd cpe, V-6	—	4,684	29,160
W27	Clsc Lnd cpe, V-8	—	4,874	
W35	Clsc wgn 4d, 2S, V-6	3,196	4,714	63,152
W35	Clsc wgn 4d, 2S, V-8	3,377	4,904	
Chevrolet				
L35	Imp wgn 4d, 3S, V-8	4,071	5,904	25,518
L35	Imp wgn 4d, 2S, V-8	4,037	5,777	40,423
L47	Impala cpe, I-6	3,511	5,208	33,990
L47	Impala cpe, V-8	3,619	5,393	

Chevrolet *(continued)*		Wght	Price	Prod
L47	Imp Lnd cpe, I-6	—	5,598	4,652
L47	Imp Lnd cpe, V-8	—	5,783	
L69	Imp sdn 4d, I-6	3,530	5,283	183,161
L69	Imp sdn 4d, V-8	3,638	5,468	
N35	Cap Clsc wgn 4d, 3S, V-8	4,109	6,151	32,952
N35	Cap Clsc wgn 4d, 2S, V-8	4,079	6,012	24,792
N47	Cap Clsc cpe I-6	3,548	5,562	37,301
N47	Cap Clsc cpe V-8	3,656	5,511	
N47	Cap Lnd cpe I-6	—	5,830	22,771
N47	Cap Lnd cpe V-8	—	6,015	
N69	Cap Clsc sdn 4d, I-6	3,578	5,628	203,837
N69	Cap Clsc sdn 4d, V-8	3,686	5,811	
Monte Carlo				
Z37	spt cpe, V-6	3,040	4,785	216,730
Z37	spt cpe, V-8	3,175	4,935	
Z37	Lnd spt cpe, V-6	—	5,678	141,461
Z37	Lnd spt cpe, V-8	—	5,828	
Corvette				
Z87	cpe	3,401	9,645	41,467*
Z87/Z78 Pace Car Replica cpe		3,450	13,653	6,200*

*Includes 2,500 Silver Anniversary editions.

MECUM
COLLECTOR CAR AUCTIONEERS

950 Greenlee, Marengo, Illinois 60152

Very Hot Rods For Sale
To be offered at auction at the
Fall K.C. Dream Classic

**********************AUTO**3-DIGIT 640
T8 P1

LLOYD E POTTER
1280 HAPPY HOLLOW RD
NAPOLEON MO 64074-9114

DuPont Dominator
1940 Ford Coupe
Award winning DuPont US Tour Car
Drastically Modified by Dominator
Motor: 1992 Ford 4.6 Modular V8
Trans: AODE Rear: 9" w/3.25
Vintage A/C Power Everything
Killer CD Sound System

Erodica
1935 Ford
1999 Street Rod of t
Motor: 468 ci BBC
Trans: 700R4 Rear: 9" Ford
Killer CD Sound System
NSRA, Goodguys,
Street Rodder Top 10

MECUM *Sign Up Today!*
iNFONET
Auction news, results & more!
www.mecumauction.com

Intercity Lines, Inc.
Official Transport Company
of Mecum Auctions

GOODGUYS ROD AND CUSTOM ASSOCIATION

THE GRANDDADDY OF CORVETTE SHOWS
bloomington GOLD
Corvettes USA
A Mecum Affiliate

Make owning that dream
car a reality! It's easy when
you apply for and get
MBNA instant credit
at a Mecum Auction.
Or just call 800-533-9911
to prearrange financing;
mention Source Code DTKE.

MBNA AMERICA®

DECEMBER 6-7-8, 2002

Fall KC Dream Classic
MECUM IN KANSAS CITY
★★★ 2002 GRAND FINALE AUCTION ★★★
Mecum America Coast to Coast Auction Tour Final Event for 2002

MECUM
COLLECTOR CAR AUCTIONEERS

3 Big Days 500 Cars!

1950 Mercury Custom

1936 Ford Coupe

1970 Plymouth AAR Cuda

1957 Chevrolet Bel Air

1979 Dodge
"LIL" Red Express

1955 Buick Special-Custom
454-A/C, Lots of custom tricks

1963 Corvette Split Window
327-340 Hp

1965 Mustang Convertible

1970 Chevelle SS
Big Block

1977 Buick Regal S/R
Hurst T-Top

1966 Impala
"NO RESERVE"

Midget Race Car
"All New"

1934 Ford 5 Window Coupe

1957 Mercury Turnpike Cruiser
Indy Pace Car Convertible

1923 Packard Roadster

1972 Chevrolet Pickup
4x4 – 3/4 Ton

1982 Buick Regal

1969 GMC Truck
427 – 1/2 Ton, Short Box

1970 Chevelle SS
454

1973 Mustang Convertible
A/C, 302, Low Miles

1968 Buick LeSabre
"NO RESERVE"

1967 Cadillac Coupe Deville

1965 Mustang GT

1973 Buick Centurian
455, A/C, <u>LOADED</u>

1968 Plymouth Road Runner
383 4 spd.

1968 Camaro SS-Clone
355 Small Block

Chevrolet Truck

1972 Volkswagen
Karmann Ghia Convertible

1963 Ford 300
427 R-Code

1965 Pontiac GTO
389 Tripower 4 spd.

1979 Ferrari 308 GTS

1962 Impala SS

1965 Ford Thunderbird

1971 Chevrolet El Camino

1969 Camaro SS
4 spd.

1962 Impala Convertible
Factory A/C

1969 Plymouth GTX
440 4 spd.

1966 Impala SS Convertible

1929 Ford Roadster

1965 Plymouth Satellite
383–330 Hp. Hi Po

1988 Mustang Convertible
ASC McLaren/Limited Production, Low miles

1955 Chevrolet Bel Air
Nostalgic Cruiser

1949 Chrysler Windsor
California car – Restored

1966 Plymouth Belvidere

1967 Dodge 440 Hemi
1 of 1 produced

1976 GMC Jimmy
4x4

1937 GMC Truck

1971 VW Karmann Ghia

1990 Corvette Convertible

1982 Corvette
Collectors Edition

NEWS FLASH!
BANKRUPTCY COURT ORDER SALE!
27 cars from 1 collection to be sold
11:30 a.m. on Sunday, December 8th.

1937 Chevrolet Coupe
Cream color

1938 Chevrolet Coupe
Blue

1938 Chevrolet Truck
Black

1939 Chevrolet
Bright Blue

1940 Chevrolet
Black

1941 Chevrolet
Black

1941 Chevrolet
Maroon

1941 Chevrolet Truck
Red/Black

1942 Chevrolet
Maroon

1946 Chevrolet
Black/White

1947 Chevrolet
Black

1947 Chevrolet Truck
Light Blue

1948 Chevrolet
Light Blue

1950 Chevrolet Bel Air
Mint Green

1952 Chevrolet Bel Air
Peach

1953 Chevrolet Bel Air
White

1953 Chevrolet Truck
Blue

1957 Chevrolet Bel Air
Cream

1960 Chevrolet Truck
Turquoise/White

1960 Impala Convertible
Red

1972 Chevrolet Caprice
Red

1974 Cadillac Eldorado
Convertible, Yellow

1976 Cadillac Eldorado
Convertible, White

1976 Cadillac Eldorado
White

1977 Cadillac Eldorado
Black

1979 Cadillac Eldorado
"Biarrittz", Cream

1979

- **Nova is discontinued**

- **Citation bows in spring as an early 1980 model**

- **Camaro's new Berlinetta model replaces Type LT**

- **Corvette's best sales year ever**

▲ This was Corvette's best sales year ever, with production topping 50,000 for the first time. For '79, the base 350 V-8 got a less-restrictive air cleaner, which helped boost power by 10-bhp, to 195. The optional L82 V-8 gained 5 bhp to 225. Interior revisions included a standard AM/FM radio and seats similar to those used in the '78 Indy pace car replica.

THE 1979 CHEVROLETS
CAPRICE CLASSIC · IMPALA · MONTE CARLO · MALIBU · CAMARO · NOVA · MONZA · CHEVETTE · CORVETTE · WAGONS · RECREATIONAL VEHICLES

▲ A recession and a fuel crisis rocked the industry in '79, but Chevy held strong, selling some 170,000 more vehicles than in '78.

▲ Monte Carlo interior featured standard cloth bench seat. Bucket seats and console were optional.

▲ Standard Monte Carlo engine for '79 was a 94-bhp, 200-cid V-6 shared with Malibu. Optional were a 115-bhp, 231-cid V-6, or this 125-bhp, 267-cid V-8. Malibu's 350 V-8 wasn't available in Monte Carlos.

▲ After its drastic restyle a year earlier, Monte Carlo was virtually unchanged for '79. Wraparound taillights, a new fine-mesh grille, and different color and trim selections were among the few revisions. Vinyl roof treatment on Landau models such as this one were reversed for '79. Sales of the sporty personal coupe were nearly identical to those of the previous year, totaling an impressive 316,923 for '79.

▲ Chevy's sharply creased, full-size design entered its third season with few changes. Refinements to the top-line Caprice Classic included a new grille with bold vertical accents, and on coupes and sedans, an update of the traditional tri-segmented taillights. Caprices were available in all of the full-size body styles.

▲ The standard engine on big Chevy coupes and sedans was the 250-cid inline six that made 115 bhp. The wagons had a standard 305-cid V-8 that was optional on the other body styles. All were available with an optional 170-bhp 350-cid V-8. Two-tone paint, such as on this Caprice, was optional on all full-size Chevys.

▶ The full-size line continued to offer two-door coupes, but they weren't nearly as popular as sedans, even in Caprice Classic trim, shown here. The four-door sedan racked up sales of 375,734 units between the Impala and Caprice series, compared to 88,289 coupes.

▲ Monza's exterior appearance remained unchanged from '78, but functional improvements included a slightly more powerful standard 151-cid four-cylinder engine and enhanced corrosion protection.

▲ The Monza coupe was the line's most popular body style with 61,110 built in 1979. Coupes could be dressed up with this optional vinyl top with opera-style rear side windows.

▲ The base 2+2 hatchback coupe trailed close behind the coupe in popularity, selling 56,871 units for the year. Newly standard were full wheel covers, whitewall tires, and an AM radio.

▶ The top-line Monza 2+2 Sport hatchback had an exclusive sloping nose and could be equipped with the "Spyder" appearance package shown here. Helping back up the looks was an optional 130-bhp 305-cid V-8. Monza was popular with first-time new-car buyers in the late '70s. Lower prices and increased standard content sent Monza sales even higher in '79, and total production topped 160,000 cars.

▲ The 1979 Camaro Z28 got larger front fender flares along with revised graphics, which consisted of two-tone stripes that wrapped around the front air dam, terminating in a large "Z28" logo at the rear edge of each door.

▲ The 350 V-8 continued as standard in Z28, optional on other Camaros. The hottest Camaro gained popularity in '79, with Z28 production jumping to over 80,000 that year, an increase of over 30,000 from '78.

▲ A new and very popular addition to the Camaro line for '79 was the luxury-level Berlinetta. This high-style Camaro replaced the Type LT, and included aluminum wheels and dual pinstripes. Berlinettas were well received by the public, with 67,236 built for '79. However that was outdone by the base Camaro's 111,357 total that year.

▲ Standard on Camaro Berlinetta was the Custom Cloth interior. All '79 Camaros got a redesigned instrument cluster—tooling for the 1970-design panel had worn out.

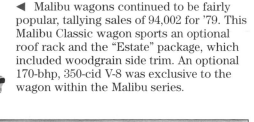

◀ Malibu wagons continued to be fairly popular, tallying sales of 94,002 for '79. This Malibu Classic wagon sports an optional roof rack and the "Estate" package, which included woodgrain side trim. An optional 170-bhp, 350-cid V-8 was exclusive to the wagon within the Malibu series.

▲ Changes to the popular Malibu series were minor this year, as only new grille and taillight designs served to identify the '79 models. A 267-cid V-8 was a new option.

▲ Chevy offered this Malibu police unit in two- and four-door versions. It was created to replace the previous compact police package, based on the soon-to-be-discontinued Nova.

253

▲ The 1979 model year was a very short one for Nova, with production actually ending in November 1978. In the spring of '79, it was replaced by the new front-wheel-drive Citation, introduced as an early 1980 model.

▲ A new grille design marked the 1979 Chevette. Standard on all models except the Scooter hatchback coupe were AM radio, sport steering wheel, center console, and bodyside moldings.

▲ Chevy introduced this "Royal Knight" cosmetic package for the '79 El Camino. Included was a "winged dragon" hood decal, along with a front spoiler and sport mirrors shared with the SS version.

Engine Availability

Engines	bore × stroke	bhp	availability
I-4, 97.6	3.23 × 2.98	70	S-Chevt
I-4, 97.6	3.23 × 2.98	74	O-Chevt
I-4, 151.0	4.00 × 3.00	90	S-Monza 4s
V-6, 196.0	3.50 × 3.40	105	S-Monza 6s
V-6, 200.0	3.50 × 3.48	94	S-Malibu, MC
V-6, 231.0	3.80 × 3.40	115	O-Mal, Monza, MC
I-6, 250.0	3.88 × 3.53	115	S-Nova, Cam exc Z28, Chevr exc wgns
V-8, 267.0	3.50 × 3.48	125	S-Malibu, MC
V-8, 305.0	3.74 × 3.48	130	S-Nova, Cam exc Z28, Chevr; O-Monza
V-8, 305.0	3.74 × 3.48	160	O-Monte Carlo, Chevelle
V-8, 350.0	4.00 × 3.48	170	O-Nova, Mal, Chevrolet
V-8, 350.0	4.00 × 3.48	175	S-Camaro Z28; O-Camaro
Corvette			
V-8, 350.0	4.00 × 3.48	195	S-all
V-8, 350.0	4.00 × 3.48	225	O-all

▲▼ Pickups now shared their grille with Blazers and Suburbans. The Beauville passenger van (below) sported a new grille for '79, and underneath, a catalytic converter was added.

254

◄▲ The big Blazer sport-utility vehicle was still popular in 1979 and Chevy apparently saw little reason to change it. A slightly revised grille and hood were noticeable, and a catalytic converter was added, but that was about all. Chevy touted the virtues of its Blazer police unit *(above)*, listing among its uses the towing of law-enforcement boat, horse, or command-post trailers—along with the obvious snow-rescue duty.

▲ This 108-inch version of Chevy's 6×4 Bison truck was intended mainly for construction or off-road work. Also available was a 116-inch version aimed at highway use. Bison cabs were constructed of aluminum and Fiberglas. Detroit Diesel and Cummins diesel engines were offered.

▲ Chevy's heavyweight Titan series was offered in this single-axle version, along with tandem-axle models. A wide choice of engines included naturally aspirated and turbocharged six- and eight-cylinder diesels from Caterpillar, Detroit Diesel, and Cummins.

▲ The LUV pickup continued virtually unchanged for '79. Four-wheel-drive models had a six-foot cargo box, while two-wheel-drive buyers had a choice of six- or 7½-foot boxes. LUV was also offered in a chassis and cab unit, to which a variety of custom bodies could be fitted.

Model Breakdown

Chevette		Wght	Price	Prod
B08	htchbk sdn 3d	1,978	3,948	136,145
B68	htchbk sdn 5d	2,057	4,072	208,865
J08	Scootr htchbk sdn 3d	1,929	3,437	24,099
Monza				
M07	2+2 htchbk cpe 3d	2,630	4,161	56,871
M15	wgn 3d	2,631	4,167	15,190
M27	cpe	2,577	3,850	61,110
R07	Sprt 2+2 htchbk cpe 3d	2,676	4,624	30,662
Nova				
X17	htchbk cpe 3d, I-6	3,264	4,118	4,819
X17	htchbk cpe 3d, V-8	3,394	4,353	
X27	cpe, I-6	3,135	3,955	36,800
X27	cpe, V-8	3,265	4,190	
X69	sdn 4d, I-6	3,179	4,055	40,883
X69	sdn 4d, V-8	3,309	4,290	
Y27	Cstm cpe, I-6	3,194	4,164	7,529
Y27	Cstm cpe, V-8	3,324	4,399	
Y69	Cstm sdn 4d, I-6	3,228	4,264	7,690
Y69	Cstm sdn 4d, V-8	3,358	4,499	
Camaro				
Q87	spt cpe	3,305	5,163	111,357
Q87	Rally sport cpe	—	5,572	19,101

Camaro *(continued)*		Wght	Price	Prod
S87	Berlinetta cpe	3,358	5,906	67,236
Q87	Z28 spt cpe, V-8	—	6,748	84,877
Malibu				
T19	sdn 4d, I-6	2,988	4,915	59,674
T19	sdn 4d, V-8	3,116	5,180	
T27	cpe, V-6	2,983	4,812	41,848
T27	cpe, V-8	3,111	5,077	
T35	wgn 4d, 2S, V-6	3,155	5,078	50,344
T35	wgn 4d, 2S, V-8	3,297	5,343	
W19	Clsc sdn 4d, V-6	3,024	5,215	104,222
W19	Clsc sdn 4d, V-8	3,152	5,480	
W27	Clsc cpe, V-6	3,017	5,087	60,751
W27	Clsc cpe, V-8	3,145	5,352	
W27	Clsc Lnd cpe, V-6	—	5,335	25,213
W27	Clsc Lnd cpe, V-8	—	5,600	
W35	Clsc wgn 4d, V-6	3,183	5,300	70,095
W35	Clsc wgn 4d, V-8	3,325	5,565	
Chevrolet				
L35	Imp wgn 4d, 3S, V-8	4,045	6,636	28,710
L35	Imp wgn 4d, 2S, V-8	4,013	6,497	39,644
L47	Impala cpe, I-6	3,495	5,828	26,589
L47	Impala cpe, V-8	3,606	6,138	

Chevrolet *(continued)*		Wght	Price	Prod
L47	Imp Lnd cpe, I-6	—	6,314	3,247
L47	Imp Lnd cpe, V-8	—	6,624	
L69	Imp sdn 4d, I-6	3,513	5,928	172,717
L69	Imp sdn 4d, V-8	3,624	6,238	
N35	Cap Clsc wgn 4d, 3S, V-8	4,088	6,960	32,693
N35	Cap Clsc wgn 4d, 2S, V-8	4,056	6,800	23,568
N37	Cap Clsc cpe I-6	3,538	6,198	36,629
N37	Cap Clsc cpe V-8	3,649	6,508	
N47	Cap Clsc Lnd cpe, I-6	—	6,617	21,824
N47	Cap Clsc Lnd cpe, V-8	—	6,927	
N69	Cap Clsc sdn 4d, I-6	3,564	6,323	203,017
N69	Cap Clsc sdn 4d, V-8	3,675	6,633	
Monte Carlo				
Z37	spt cpe, V-6	3,039	5,333	225,073
Z37	spt cpe, V-8	3,169	5,598	
Z37	Lnd spt cpe, V-6	—	6,183	91,850
Z37	Lnd spt cpe, V-8	—	6,448	
Corvette				
Z87	cpe	3,372	12,313	53,807

1980

- **All-new compact Citation debuts**

- **Monte Carlo adds turbo V-6 power**

- **Corvette spruces up, slims down**

- **Big Chevys get "aero" facelift**

▲ Ousting Nova as Chevy's 1980 compact, Citation was one of four new GM X-body models with a smaller front-wheel-drive package but similar interior space and superior fuel economy. Body styles consisted of this two-door hatchback, a four-door version, and a slant-roof coupe.

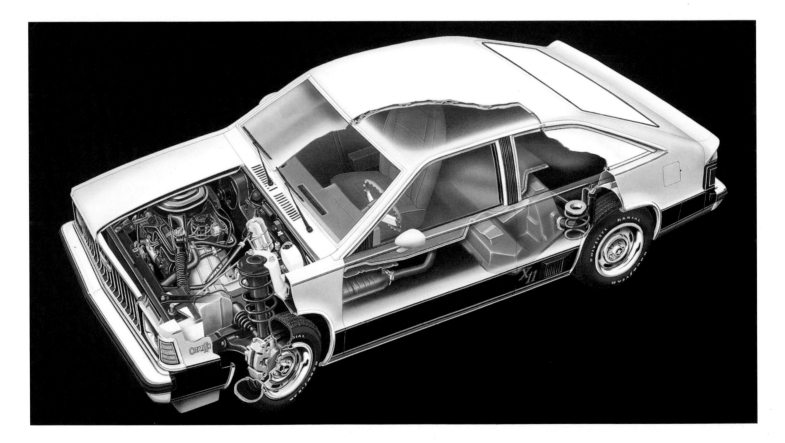

▲ ▶ Helped by an early launch in April 1979, Citation sold like gangbusters in its debut model year, attracting no fewer than 811,540 buyers. A cutaway drawing (*above*) shows the space-efficient transverse-engine/front-drive layout of a two-door hatchback equipped with the optional X-11 package, which included firmer steering and damping, Rally wheels, a rear spoiler, and other sporty exterior cosmetics. Base price was $5422 with 2.5-liter inline-4 or $5547 with a new 2.8-liter 60-degree V-6. Priced $130 higher, the four-door hatch (*right*) was Citation's most popular body style by far with 458,033 sales, over half the 1980-model total. The two-door hatch was runner-up at 210,258. All Citations rode a trim, new 104.9-inch wheelbase.

256

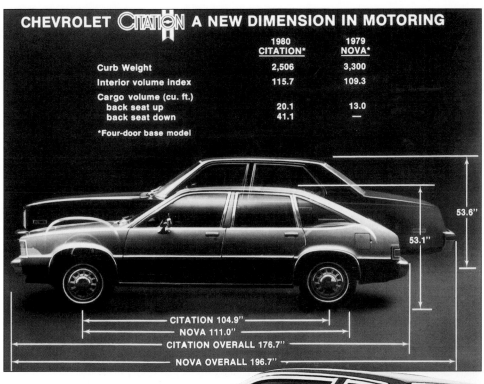

CHEVROLET CITATION A NEW DIMENSION IN MOTORING

	1980 CITATION*	1979 NOVA*
Curb Weight	2,506	3,300
Interior volume index	115.7	109.3
Cargo volume (cu. ft.)		
back seat up	20.1	13.0
back seat down	41.1	—

*Four-door base model

CITATION 104.9"
NOVA 111.0"
CITATION OVERALL 176.7"
NOVA OVERALL 196.7"

53.6"
53.1"

◀ As the first front-wheel-drive Chevy, Citation followed contemporary European small cars in having a compact powertrain situated "east-west" instead of the traditional "north-south." The result was a smaller exterior package with similar interior space versus the superseded Nova.

▲ ▼ Priced at $501, Citation's X-11 package was optional for both the two-door hatchback (*above*) and the "notchback" coupe (*below*). The option didn't add horsepower, but made an already good-handling car even more fun to drive. Available separately was Custom interior trim with cloth or vinyl front bucket seats.

▲ ▶ Monza sales improved by some 5600 units for 1980 to 169,418, but the six-year-old Vega-based sportsters had never caught fire as Chevy had hoped, so this would be their last year. The V-8 option was dropped, leaving a base 2.5-liter four and optional 3.8 V-6. The bestriped and bespoilered Spyder option was still available for the 2+2 hatchback coupe, adding $521 to the $5186 base price.

▲ Though little changed for 1980, Chevy's humble Chevette, like the new Citation, cashed in on renewed public interest in high-mileage cars that began in mid 1979 with the advent of a second energy crisis, touched off by the ouster of the Shah of Iran. Total Chevette sales rose 22 percent to just over 451,000. As usual, the four-door (shown) led the way, accounting for over half of 1980-model volume.

257

▲ ▼ ► Corvette got a cleaner, more contemporary look for 1980 with newly integrated front and rear spoilers that improved high-speed aerodynamics and thus stability. Corvette also went on a diet, shedding some 150 pounds via lighter body panels and greater use of aluminum components. Also improving fuel economy was adoption of a lock-up torque converter for the automatic transmission. The cockpit (*below*) was also tidied up. Despite all this, model-year volume dropped nearly 25 percent from record '79 to 40,614 units.

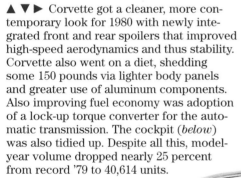

▲ ▲ ▶ Chevrolet teased the public with several experimental turbocharged Corvettes. The first one, called Turbo 'Vette (*left*) was based on the 1979 model, the later Turbo 'Vette 3 (*center*) on the restyled 1980 version. Both packed 350 V-8s (*right*) with around 300 net hp. In 1982, Chevy would achieve that same output by bolting dual turbos to a modified version of its everyday 229-cubic-inch V6 for the one-off Corvette Twin Turbo V-6 90.

▲ Camaro suffered along with other performance cars in the suddenly downbeat market of 1980, sales plunging 46.2 percent from the strong 1979 pace to 152,005 units. Here, the hot-rod Z28.

▲ Still keeping faith with performance fans against all odds, the Z28 was the only 1980 Camaro with a standard 350 V-8, good for 0-60 mph in about 9.5 seconds. Other models offered an efficient base 229 V-6, replacing the old inline 250, and economy-tune 267- and 305-cid V-8s. Z28 sales this model year totaled 45,137, about half the '79 tally.

◀ The Camaro Rally Sport remained a distinct model for 1980, but had as few changes as its linemates. Priced from $6086, it was the year's least popular Camaro with 12,015 sales.

▲ Like other full-size 1980 Chevys, this Caprice Classic Landau coupe got a smoother, lower nose and rear-end revisions that slightly reduced aerodynamic drag as an aid to fuel economy. Toward the same end, a thriftier 229 V-6 replaced the old 250 inline unit as base power for all but wagons, and smaller V-8s were emphasized.

◀ The 1980 full-size Chevys sported revised rooflines for a slightly more formal look. The Caprice Classic 4-door sedan, shown here with optional sport wheel covers and vinyl top, was the most popular full-size Chevrolet with 91,208 units sold.

▲ Monte Carlo got a boost in performance for 1980 with a standard 3.8-liter V-6, and the options list now included a 170-hp Buick-built 3.8-liter turbocharged V-6, fitted to this T-top model.

▲ A Chevy-built 3.8-liter (229-cid) V-6 was standard for all 1980 midsize Malibus, including this top-line Classic Estate wagon. Malibu sales sank to 278,350 in a much more difficult market.

▶ Market changes dictated that big trucks also had to use less fuel in 1980. That's why Chevy's C70 mediums offered this 8.2-liter/500-cid diesel V-8 as a new option. It was supplied by Detroit Diesel Allison.

1980 Engine Availability

Engines	bore × stroke	bhp	availability
I-4, 97.6	3.23 × 2.98	70	S-Chevt
I-4, 97.6	3.23 × 2.98	74	O-Chevt
I-4, 151.0	4.00 × 3.00	86	S-Monza
I-4, 151.0	4.00 × 3.00	90	S-Citation
V-6, 173.0	3.50 × 3.00	115	S-Citation
V-6, 229.0	3.74 × 3.48	115	S-Mal, Cam, MC, Chevr exc wgn
V-6, 231.0	3.80 × 3.40	110	O-Cam, Monza, MC, Chevr exc wgn
V-6T, 231.0	3.80 × 3.40	170	O-MC
V-8, 267.0	3.50 × 3.48	120	S-Mal, Cam, MC, Chevr
V-8, 305.0	3.74 × 3.48	155	O-Mal, Cam, MC, Chevr
V-8, 350.0	4.00 × 3.48	190	S-Camaro Z28; O-other Cam
V-8D, 350.0	4.06 × 3.39	105	O-Chevr wgn
Corvette			
V-8, 350.0	4.00 × 3.48	190	S-all
V-8, 350.0	4.00 × 3.48	230	O-all
V-8, 305.0	3.74 × 3.48	180	O-all

▲ Another round of trim changes, including a new grille, identified Chevy's 1980 light-duty trucks. Here, the popular 4-wheel-drive K-5 Blazer sport-utility in fancy Silverado trim.

Model Breakdown

Chevette	Wght	Price	Prod
B08 htchbk sdn 3d	1,989	4,601	148,686
B68 htchbk sdn 5d	2,048	4,736	261,477
J08 Scooter htchbk	1,935	4,057	40,998
Monza			
M07 2+2 htchbk cpe 3d	2,672	4,746	53,415
M27 cpe	2,617	4,433	95,469
R07 Sport 2+2 htchbk cpe 3d	2,729	5,186	20,534
Citation			
H11 cpe, I-4	2,391	4,800	42,909
H11 cpe, V-6	2,428	4,925	
X08 htchbk sdn 3d, I-4	2,417	5,422	210,258
X08 htchbk sdn 3d, V-6	2,454	5,547	
X11 club cpe, I-4	2,397	5,214	100,340
X11 club cpe, V-6	2,434	5,339	
X68 htchbk sdn 5d, I-4	2,437	5,552	458,033
X68 htchbk sdn 5d, V-6	2,474	5,677	
Camaro			
P87 spt cpe	3,218	5,843	68,174
P87/Z85RS cpe	—	6,068	12,015
S87 Berlinetta cpe	3,253	6,606	26,679
P87 Z28 spt cpe, V-8	—	7,363	45,137
Malibu			
T19 sdn 4d, V-6	3,001	5,617	67,696
T19 sdn 4d, V-8	3,122	5,697	

Malibu (continued)	Wght	Price	Prod
T27 spt cpe, V-6	2,996	5,502	28,425
T27 spt cpe, V-8	3,117	5,582	
T35 wgn 4d, 2S, V-6	3,141	5,778	30,794
T35 wgn 4d, 2S, V-8	3,261	5,858	
W19 Classic sdn 4d, V-6	3,031	5,951	77,938
W19 Classic sdn 4d, V-8	3,152	6,031	
W27 Classic spt cpe, V-6	3,027	5,816	28,425
W27 Classic spt cpe, V-8	3,148	5,896	
W27/Classic Landau cpe, Z03 V-6	—	6,009	9,342
W27/Classic Landau cpe, Z03 V-8	—	6,149	
W35 Classic wgn 4d, 2S, V-6	3,167	6,035	35,730
W35 Classic wgn 4d, 2S, V-8	3,307	6,115	
Full-Size Chevrolet			
L35 Impala wgn 4d, 3S, V-8	3,924	7,186	6,767
L35 Impala wgn 4d, 2S, V-8	3,892	7,041	11,203
L47 Impala spt cpe, V-6	3,344	6,535	10,756
L47 Impala spt cpe, V-8	3,452	6,615	

Full-Size Chevrolet (cont.)	Wght	Price	Prod
L69 Impala sdn 4d, V-6	3,360	6,650	70,801
L69 Impala sdn 4d, V-8	3,468	6,730	
N35 Caprice Classic wgn 4d, 3S, V-8	3,962	7,536	13,431
N35 Caprice Classic wgn 4d, 2S, V-8	3,930	7,369	9,873
N47 Caprice Classic cpe V-6	3,376	6,946	13,919
N47 Caprice Classic cpe V-8	3,484	7,026	
N47/Caprice Classic Z03 Landau cpe, V-6	—	7,400	8,857
N47/Caprice Classic Z03 Landau cpe, V-8	—	7,480	
N69 Caprice Classic sdn 4d, V-6/V-8	—	—	91,208
Monte Carlo			
Z37 spt cpe, V-6	3,104	6,524	116,850
Z37 spt cpe, V-8	3,219	6,604	
Z37/ Z03 Landau cpe, V-6	—	6,772	32,262
Z37/ Z03 Landau cpe, V-8	—	6,852	
Corvette			
Z87 cpe	3,206	13,965	40,614

1981

NINETEEN EIGHTY-ONE NINETEEN EIGHTY-ONE NINETEEN EIGHTY-ONE NINETEEN EIGHT

- **All engines adopt Computer Command Control electronics**

- **Monte Carlo gets "aero" facelift**

- **Corvette sheds more weight**

- **Chevy car sales dive to below 1.68 million**

▲ Like full-size Chevys the year before, 1981 Monte Carlos sported a lower-profile nose, flush rear quarter windows, and other subtle styling changes that reduced air drag for better highway fuel economy. Here, the $7349 standard Sport Coupe with full-metal roof.

▶ A reshaped rear end with crisper contours also improved "aero" on '81 Montes. The base V-8 remained a 4.4-liter/267-cubic-incher, Chevy's smallest small-block.

▲ Like other '81 Chevys, even the humble Chevette adopted General Motors' new Computer Command Control electronic engine management system. The aim was to further cut emissions without exchanging carburetors for costlier fuel injection. Chevette's 1.6-liter gasoline four-cylinder remained at 70 net hp. Chevette model-year sales eased to 433,600 units.

▲ The Camaro Rally Sport was gone again for '81, leaving the luxury Berlinetta as the midprice model at $7576. Total Camaro sales for the model year fell 17 percent to 126,139. Just 20,253 were Berlinettas.

▲ Bright grille and body accents and standard wire wheel covers again identified the Camaro Berlinetta for 1981. The model still included upscale interior trim and a special "Quiet/Sound" insulation package.

▲ The main visual changes for Chevy's 1981 midsize Malibu were a new grille insert and, as seen here, a more formally upright rear roofline for four-door sedans. Total Malibu sales slipped nearly 13 percent for the model year to 242,447.

▲ The second-generation Camaro put in its 12th and final appearance for 1981. The Z28 was demoted to a standard 165-hp 305 V-8, the only engine available with four-speed manual shift. An optional 350 delivered 10 hp more. Though the Z28 hadn't been a real fire-breather in many a year, 1981 sales were just fractionally lower at 43,272 units.

▲ Cancellation of the "notchback" coupe left the two-door hatchback as the only '81 Citation available with the X-11 option.

▲ This widely circulated Chevy PR photo shows the components of the 1981 X-11 package for the compact Citation. The big news was a more potent 2.8-liter V-6 with 135 hp, up 20 from the standard engine. Not many cars were so equipped, however.

▲ This 660 Turbo Citation show car helped publicize 1981's fortified X-11 package, but sporty styling add-ons remained unique.

◄ Corvette lost another 100 pounds for '81 via thinner door glass and a monoleaf rear spring made of plastic instead of steel.

▲ An "exploded" view of Corvette's 1981 front bumper highlights its plastic cover and twin energy-absorbing metal members.

1981 Engine Availability

Engines	bore × stroke	bhp	availability
I-4, 97.6	3.23 × 2.98	70	S-Chevette
I-4D, 111.0	3.31 × 3.23	51	O-late Chevette
I-4, 151.0	4.00 × 3.00	84	S-Citation
V-6, 173.0	3.50 × 2.99	110	O-Citation
V-6, 173.0	3.50 × 2.99	135	O-Citation
V-6, 229.0	3.74 × 3.48	110	S-Cam, Mal, MC, Chevr cpe/sdn
V-6, 231.0	3.80 × 3.40	110	O-Calif. Cam, Mal, MC, Chevr cpe/sdn
V-6T, 231.0	3.80 × 3.40	170	O-Monte Carlo
V-8, 267.0	3.50 × 3.48	115	O-Cam, Mal, MC, Chevr
V-8, 305.0	3.74 × 3.48	150	S-Chevr wgn; O-Cam, Mal, MC, Chevrolet
V-8, 305.0	3.74 × 3.48	165	S-Camaro Z28
V-8, 350.0	4.00 × 3.48	175	O-Camaro Z28
V-8D, 350.0	4.06 × 3.39	105	O-Chevrolet
Corvette			
V-8, 350.0	4.00 × 3.48	190	S-all

▲ Despite few changes, a higher $15,248 base price and a lone 190-hp 350 V-8, Corvette's 1981 sales held steady at around 40,600.

▲ A 350 diesel V-8 option was extended to 1981 full-size coupes and sedans like this four-door Caprice Classic.

▲ Mileage-boosting mechanical changes were the main news for Chevy's '81 full-sizers like this Impala Sport Coupe.

▲ Chevy still successfully courted law-enforcement agencies in 1981 with a special Police Package for the big Impala sedan.

◄ Reflecting growing buyer preference for long-bed pickups, Chevy offered its short-bed Fleetside only in ½-ton guise for 1981, though there was still the choice of rear-wheel-drive C-10 and 4-wheel-drive K-10 versions. Reflecting the growing buyer interest in fancy-pants pickups, this example wears the color-ful Sport Appearance Package first offered for 1979. This featured two-tone paint in several combinations, plus contrast bodyside striping in a complementary third color. Chevy built nearly 404,000 light-duty pickups of all kinds for 1981, but was outsold by that year's redesigned F-Series from archrival Ford.

▲ Chevy's '81 G-van line again listed a conversion model (*fore-ground*) and a plush passenger Nomad, here in "Van Sport" trim.

▲ A Chevy truck staple since 1975, the compact LUV (Light Utility Vehicle) pickup, built by Isuzu in Japan, was redesigned for '81.

Model Breakdown

Chevette		Wght	Price	Prod
B08	htchbk sdn 3d	2,000	5,225	114,621
B68	htchbk sdn 5d	2,063	5,394	250,616
J08	Scooter htchbk 3d	1,945	4,695	55,211
B08	Diesel htchbk sdn 3d	—	—	4,252
B68	Diesel htchbk sdn 5d	—	—	8,900
Citation				
X08	htchbk sdn 3d, I-4	2,404	6,270	113,983
X08	htchbk sdn 3d, V-6	2,459	6,395	
X68	htchbk sdn 5d, I-4	2,432	6,404	299,396
X68	htchbk sdn 5d, V-6	2,487	6,529	
Camaro				
P87	spt cpe, V-6	3,222	6,780	62,614
P87	spt cpe, V-8	3,392	6,830	
S87	Berlinetta cpe, V-6	3,275	7,576	20,253
S87	Berlinetta cpe, V-8	3,445	7,626	
P87	Z28 spt cpe, V-8	—	8,263	43,272
Malibu				
T69	sdn 4d, V-6	3,028	6,614	60,643
T69	sdn 4d, V-8	3,194	6,664	
T27	spt cpe, V-6	3,037	6,498	15,834
T27	spt cpe, V-8	3,199	6,548	

Malibu *(continued)*		Wght	Price	Prod
T35	wgn 4d, 2S, V-6	3,201	6,792	29,387
T35	wgn 4d, 2S, V-8	3,369	6,842	
W69	Classic sdn 4d, V-6	3,059	6,961	80,908
W69	Classic sdn 4d, V-8	3,225	7,011	
W27	Classic spt cpe, V-6	3,065	6,828	14,255
W27	Classic spt cpe, V-8	3,227	6,878	
W27/ Z03	Classic Landau cpe, V-6	—	7,092	4,622
W27/ Z03	Classic Landau cpe, V-8	—	7,142	
W35	Classic wgn 4d, 2S, V-6	3,222	7,069	36,798
W35	Classic wgn 4d, 2S, V-8	3,390	7,119	
Full-Size Chevrolet				
L35/ AQ	Impala wgn 4d, 3S, V-8	—	7,765	8,462
L35	Impala wgn 4d, 2S, V-8	3,897	7,624	11,345
L47	Impala spt cpe, V-6	3,326	7,129	6,067
L47	Impala spt cpe, V-8	3,458	7,179	
L69	Impala sdn 4d, V-6	3,354	7,241	60,090
L69	Impala sdn 4d, V-8	3,486	7,291	
N35/ AQ	Caprice Classic wgn 4d, 3S, V-8	—	8,112	16,348

Full-Size Chevrolet *(cont.)*		Wght	Price	Prod
N35	Caprice Classic wgn 4d, 2S, V-8	3,940	7,948	11,184
N47	Caprice Classic cpe, V-6	3,363	7,534	9,741
N47	Caprice Classic cpe, V-8	3,495	7,584	
N47/ Z03	Caprice Classic Landau cpe, V-6	—	7,990	6,615
N47/ Z03	Caprice Classic Landau cpe, V-8	—	8,040	
N69	Caprice Classic sdn 4d, V-6	3,400	7,667	89,573
N69	Caprice Classic sdn 4d, V-8	3,532	7,717	
Monte Carlo				
Z37	spt cpe, V-6	3,102	7,299	149,659
Z37	spt cpe, V-8	3,228	7,349	
Z37/Z03	Landau cpe, V-6	—	8,006	38,191
Z37/Z03	Landau cpe, V-8	—	8,056	
Corvette				
Y87	cpe	3,179	15,248	40,606

1982

- **Camaro completely redesigned**

- **Subcompact Cavalier introduced**

- **New midsize Celebrity debuts**

▶ Camaro was finally downsized for 1982, becoming 7 inches shorter, 3 inches slimmer, and fractionally lower on a new 101-inch wheelbase. Curb weight reductions of up to 400 pounds allowed using smaller engines: 90-horsepower 2.5-liter "Iron Duke" four for the base Sport Coupe, 112-hp 2.8-liter V-6 as standard for the midline Berlinetta, a carbureted 150-hp 5.0-liter V-8 option for both, and a new fuel-injected 165-hp V-8 for Z28. Here, the '82 Z fronts its 1981 predecessor in a view that gives little hint of Camaro's more rational new size.

▶ Designers aimed to give the '82 Camaro a crisp new look while continuing certain identifying styling cues such as single side window, wide rear roof pillar, and broad tri-color tailights. *Motor Trend* thought enough of the entire package to give Camaro its 1982 Car of the Year award. Buyers thought enough of Chevy's new ponycar to place orders for 182,068 of them, a healthy 44.3 percent gain on 1981. An improving national economy helped. Here, the racy Z28, priced from $9700; it tallied 63,563 sales.

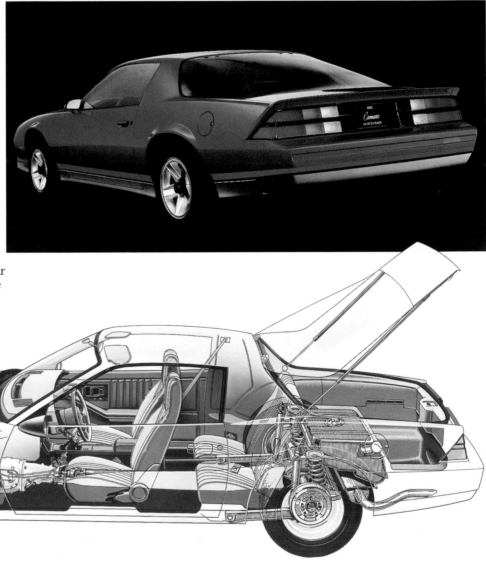

▼ The '82 Camaros rode a much-improved chassis with front MacPherson struts and lower control arms replacing dual A-arms, rear coil springs instead of leafs, and a torque tube to better locate the live rear axle. Four-wheel disc brakes were optional across the board. This "phantom" view also highlights the new hatch rear window that lifted up for access to greatly increased luggage space.

▲ Camaro was chosen pace car for the 1982 Indy 500, its third such honor. Chevy celebrated by building 6360 replicas. All were specially trimmed T-top Z28s, minus the roof light bar on the actual pacer (*shown*).

▲ The Berlinetta, priced from $9266 with base V-6, was arguably the best all-around '82 Camaro, but proved the least popular model, drawing a fairly modest 39,744 sales.

◀▲ Replacing all the Vega-based Monzas as Chevy's 1982 subcompact was the front-wheel-drive Cavalier, one of five General Motors "J-car" lines that were soon criticized for being too much alike. Power came from a new low-cost four-cylinder engine (*left*), initially a 1.8-liter with just 88 hp. Here, the mainstay four-door sedan in uplevel CL trim, priced from $8137. Cavalier made an impressive debut with total sales of just over 195,000.

▲ Cavalier arrived on a trim 101.2-inch wheelbase. This neat four-door wagon followed sedans in offering top-line CL trim (shown), as well as standard and price-leader Cadet models.

▲ The same trim options applied to Cavalier's two-door sedan body style, which Chevy called a coupe. The Cadet version was the most affordable '82 Cavalier, starting at just $6278.

▶ Cavalier's sportiest body style was this hatchback coupe, which preserved much of the design flavor of the superseded Monza fastback. It was also the only Cavalier with a sloped nose. Standard and better-equipped CL versions were offered.

▲ Rounding out a busy Chevrolet year, the 1982 Celebrity was a new front-wheel-drive intermediate built on a GM A-body platform based on the X-body Citation. Celebrity did not replace the rear-drive Malibu, which continued as a G-body car, but added a welcome 92,330 sales to Chevy's 1982 total. This two-door sedan wears optional CS (Custom Sport) trim.

▲ Celebrity shared Citation's wheelbase, suspension, and 4-cyl and V-6 power-trains, but had its own, more formal notchback styling, which made it both longer and wider. It also listed a 4.3-liter diesel V-6 not available in Citation. This Celebrity four-door sedan also carries uplevel CS trim.

▲ Chevette added a low-priced Scooter four-door and a 1.8-liter 4-cyl diesel option for 1981. But the smallest Chevy was looking quite dated by now, which may explain why sales plunged 46.3 percent to 232,808.

▲ GM was rapidly discarding carburetors throughout its corporate line in favor of throttle-body fuel injection, and Citation followed suit for '82. As result, the 2.5-liter four went to 90 hp, the 2.8 V-6 to 112. Chevy's compact received a number of other technical changes including a larger gas tank; automatic-transmission torque-converter lock-up; low-rolling-resistance tires; and revised mountings for engine, steering, and exhaust. Despite all this, mounting X-body recalls and publicity helped depress sales by nearly 60 percent to 165,647. Again, the vast majority were the hatchback four-door (shown).

▲ Citation's sporty X-11 package returned for '82 with a new domed hood above the included high-output 135-hp V-6, plus revised colors and graphics. Other features were much as before, but the option now cost a steep $1744, which likely limited demand (Chevy didn't keep separate records on X-11 installations).

▲ Malibu offered a 350-cid Olds-built diesel V-8 option for '82, but with the new Celebrity around, models were cut to this Classic sedan and a companion wagon. Total sales plunged to 116,125.

▲ Chevy's full-size line was also thinner for '82, losing Impala and Caprice Landau coupes and the two-seat Caprice wagon. Still, total sales remained fairly healthy at 188,189, led by this Classic sedan.

▲ ▶ Corvette sales sank to 25,407 for '82. Included were 6759 copies of this special Collector Edition with liftup rear glass and other unique features, a telltale farewell to the long-lived "shark."

1982 Engine Availability

Engines	bore × stroke	bhp	availability
I-4, 97.6	3.23 × 2.98	65	S-Chevette
I-4D, 111.0	3.36 × 3.28	51	O-Chevette
I-4, 112.0	3.50 × 2.91	88	S-Cavalier
I-4, 151.0	4.00 × 3.00	90	S-Cit, Camaro, Celebrity
V-6, 173.0	3.50 × 2.99	102	S-Cam, Berlinetta; O-Camaro
V-6, 173.0	3.50 × 2.99	112	O-Citation, Celebrity
V-6, 173.0	3.50 × 2.99	135	O-Citation
V-6, 229.0	3.74 × 3.48	110	S-Mal, MC, Chevr cpe/sdn
V-6, 231.0	3.80 × 3.40	110	O-Calif. Chevrolet
V-6D, 262.0	4.06 × 3.39	85	O-Malibu, Monte Carlo
V-8, 267.0	3.50 × 3.48	115	S-Chevr wag; O-Mal, MC, Chevrolet
V-8, 305.0	3.74 × 3.48	145	S-Cam Z28; O-Cam, Mal, MC, Chevrolet
V-8, 305.0	3.74 × 3.48	165	O-Camaro Z28
V-8D, 350.0	4.06 × 3.39	105	O-Chevr, Malibu, MC
Corvette			
V-8, 350.0	4.00 × 3.48	200	S-all

▲ Taking note of the growing demand for small imported pickups, Chevy introduced its all-new S-10 for '82 with 4-cyl and V-6 power and a slightly larger package. It was a hit from day one.

▲ S-10 bowed with just one choice of cab and pickup box, but offered rear-drive, 4WD, and numerous trim options. Styling was unique, but related to that of full-size Chevy pickups.

▲ Chevy's popular Suburban was fast moving toward greater luxury, but remained a true work truck. It still came with rear- or 4WD (shown) in ½-ton C-10 and ¾-ton C-20 models.

◀ More Americans in 1982 were discovering the off-road fun of sport-utility vehicles like Chevy's Blazer This K5 4×4 model is spruced up with the $931 Silverado trim package and styled steel wheels.

▲ A burly new 6.2-liter turbodiesel V-8 option boosted fuel economy and towing capacity of Chevy's 1982 full-size light-duty trucks.

Model Breakdown

Chevette		Wght	Price	Prod
B08	htchbk sdn 3d	2,004	5,513	51,431
B68	htchbk sdn 5d	2,064	5,660	111,661
J08	Scooter htchbk 3d	1,959	4,997	31,281
J68	Scooter htchbk 5d	2,006	5,238	21,742
B08/Z90	Diesel sdn 3d	—	6,579	4,874
B68/Z90	Diesel sdn 5d	—	6,727	11,819
Cavalier				
D27	cpe	2,318	6,996	30,245
E77	htchbk cpe 3d	2,389	7,199	22,114
D69	sdn 4d	2,372	7,137	52,941
D35	wgn 5d	2,432	7,354	30,853
D27/Z11	Cadet cpe	—	6,278	2,281
D69/Z11	Cadet sdn 4d	—	6,433	9,511
D35/Z11	Cadet wgn 5d	—	6,704	4,754
D27/Z12	CL cpe	2,315	7,944	6,063
E77/Z12	CL htchbk cpe 3d	2,381	8,281	12,792
D69/Z12	CL sdn 4d	2,362	8,137	15,916
Cavalier				
D35/Z12	CL wgn 5d	2,422	8,452	7,587
Citation				
H11	cpe, I-4	—	6,297	9,102
H11	cpe, V-6	—	6,515	—

Citation *(continued)*		Wght	Price	Prod
X08	htchbk sdn 3d, I-4	2,442	6,754	29,613
X08	htchbk sdn 3d, V-6	—	6,972	
X68	htchbk sdn 5d, I-4	2,409	6,899	126,932
X68	htchbk sdn 5d, V-6	—	7,024	
Camaro				
P87	spt cpe, I-4	—	7,631	78,761
P87	spt cpe, V-6	—	7,755	
P87	spt cpe, V-8	—	7,925	
S87	Berlinetta cpe, V-6	2,940	9,266	39,744
S87	Berlinetta cpe, V-8	—	9,436	
P87	Z28 spt cpe, V-8	2,870	9,700	63,563
Celebrity				
W27	cpe, I-4	2,691	8,313	19,629
W27	cpe, V-6	2,751	8,438	
W19	sdn 4d, I-4	2,734	8,463	72,701
W19	sdn 4d, V-6	2,794	8,588	
Malibu				
W69	Classic sdn 4d, V-6	3,091	8,137	70,793
W69	Classic sdn 4d, V-8	—	8,207	
Malibu				
W35	Classic wgn 4d, 2S,V-6	3,240	8,265	45,332
W35	Classic wgn 4d, 2S, V-8	—	8,335	

Full-Size Chevrolet		Wght	Price	Prod
L35/				
AQ4	Impala wgn 4d, 3S, V-8	4,050	8,670	6,245
L35	Impala wgn 4d, 2S, V-8	3,930	8,516	10,654
L69	Impala sdn 4d, V-6	3,361	7,918	47,780
L69	Impala sdn 4d, V-8	—	7,988	
N35/Caprice Classic wgn				
AQ4	4d, 3S, V-8	4,010	9,051	25,385
N47	Caprice Classic cpe, V-6	3,373	8,221	11,999
N47	Caprice Classic cpe, V-8	—	8,291	
N69	Caprice Classic sdn 4d, V-6	63,410	8,367	86,126
N69	Caprice Classic sdn 4d, V-8	—	8,437	
Monte Carlo				
Z37	spt cpe, V-6	3,190	8,177	92,392
Z37	spt cpe, V-8	—	8,247	
Corvette				
Y87	cpe	3,232	18,290	18,648
Y07	Collector Ed htchbk cpe	3,233	22,537	6,759

1983

- **Compact S-10 Blazer SUV debuts**

- **Cavalier adds larger engine, convertible**

- **No 1983 Corvette!**

- **Monte Carlo SS returns**

- **Chevy car sales fall to 1.18 million**

▲ A logical spinoff of the S-10 pickup, the new 1983 S-10 Blazer sport-utility vehicle used the same powertrains, chassis, front sheetmetal, and dashboard, but substituted an enclosed cargo area behind the doors. Sales were strong, as buyers were quick to appreciate the "baby Blazer's" superior mileage and handling versus the full-size C/K Blazer.

▲ S-10 Blazers normally stowed their spare tire inside, which ate into cargo space, but external carriers were available. Frameless glass liftgate was a novel truck design feature at the time.

▲ The traditional C/K Blazer poses with its new little brother. Size difference is readily apparent here, yet the 100.5-inch-wheelbase S-10 Blazer didn't sacrifice that much people and cargo room to achieve its trimmer size. Both models here have optional 4-wheel drive.

◄ You could spot a 1983 Chevette by a revived cross-hatch grille and higher-set front-fender nameplates. Also new, and shown on this two-door, was an S (for Sport) exterior package that exchanged chrome moldings for black-finish trim, set off by red name decals and accent stripes. But Chevette was mostly a rerun otherwise, and that (plus tougher-than-ever small-car competition) conspired for another sales loss, this time a 27 percent fall to 169,565.

▼ Citation entered its fourth model year with a revised dashboard, new low-back front seats, and a revived club coupe model (from mid-1982) as a $6333 price-leader. The X-11 package for the two-door hatch (shown) was downpriced to $998, as its high-output V-6 was made a separate option available for any model. Otherwise, Citation was a repeat of '82.

▲ The Citation four-door hatchback again drew the bulk of Chevy compact sales for 1983, but continued adverse publicity over brake problems dented total line sales to the tune of 44.3 percent and 92,184 units. The four-door accounted for 77 percent.

▲ Consumer Guide® lauded the '83 Citation for its "traction and packaging...good road-holding, easy handling, and ample interior room." Ride and fuel economy also earned kudos, "but assembly quality is neither consistent nor consistently high....As GM's first fling with front drive, Citation and its siblings have taught the company a lot. Too bad it had to learn at the expense of thousands of disgruntled owners."

► Typical of "sophomore" cars, Celebrity was a virtual carryover for '83. Even so, it proved a welcome bright spot in a troubled Chevy sales picture, as orders jumped 51 percent to 139,239. All but 19,221 were four-door sedans, which priced from $8209. This two-door "coupe" sedan started at $8059.

▲ Though Chevy had lately debated the need for full-size cars, an improving national economy helped boost 1983 sales by 17 percent to 220,795, which earned the line a stay of execution. The unpopular 4.4-liter/267-cubic-inch V-8 departed along with the Caprice coupe and Impala wagon. Changes were otherwise minimal. This Caprice Classic sedan again used a standard V-6.

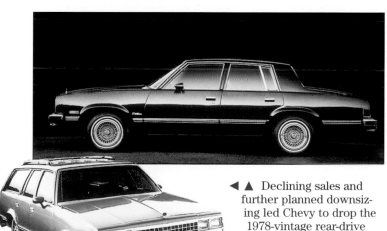

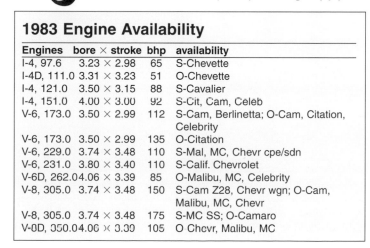

◄ ▲ Declining sales and further planned downsizing led Chevy to drop the 1978-vintage rear-drive Malibu after '83. Sales of 117,426 again split between a Classic sedan (*above*) and wagon (*left*).

▲ Cavalier's big 1983 news was a standard, longer-stroke, 2.0-liter, overhead-valve four with throttle-body fuel injection and more torque. This two-door sedan now priced from $5888.

▲ This wagon and other '83 Cavaliers had lower base prices, as some standard features became optional, and a five-speed manual gearbox was newly available. Total sales improved to 218,587.

1983 Engine Availability

Engines	bore × stroke	bhp	availability
I-4, 97.6	3.23 × 2.98	65	S-Chevette
I-4D, 111.0	3.31 × 3.23	51	O-Chevette
I-4, 121.0	3.50 × 3.15	88	S-Cavalier
I-4, 151.0	4.00 × 3.00	92	S-Cit, Cam, Celeb
V-6, 173.0	3.50 × 2.99	112	S-Cam, Berlinetta; O-Cam, Citation, Celebrity
V-6, 173.0	3.50 × 2.99	135	O-Citation
V-6, 229.0	3.74 × 3.48	110	S-Mal, MC, Chevr cpe/sdn
V-6, 231.0	3.80 × 3.40	110	S-Calif. Chevrolet
V-6D, 262.04.06 × 3.39		85	O-Malibu, MC, Celebrity
V-8, 305.0	3.74 × 3.48	150	S-Cam Z28, Chevr wgn; O-Cam, Malibu, MC, Chevr
V-8, 305.0	3.74 × 3.48	175	S-MC SS; O-Camaro
V-0D, 350.04.06 × 3.39		105	O Chevr, Malibu, MC

▲ Monte Carlo had lately put Chevy back in stock-car racing—unoffically. To better compete against the dominant Buick Regals, Chevy issued a new Monte SS in 1983 with a wind-cheating "droop snoot," heavy-duty suspension, and a 305 small-block V-8 tuned for 175 healthy horsepower. Sales were a modest 4714 this year, but would go higher.

▶ After long years and oft-changed plans, a new Corvette was finally ready by 1983—only it bowed early in the calendar year as an '84 model, which made satisfying certain federal standards more economical for Chevy. It was the first time the 'Vette had skipped a season, and enthusiasts didn't like being denied on the occasion of their favorite's 30th anniversary, but Chevy's newest sports car would prove well worth the wait. Here, a full-size prototype from late in the lengthy development program. Its shape is close to final except for the roofline, which ended up quite different.

▲ Camaro returned from its 1982 redesign with two new transmissions: a four-speed automatic with lockup torque converter and—good news for enthusiasts—a first-ever five-speed manual as standard for the Z28. Either was controlled from the console in a snug but comfortable cabin dominated by a "high tech" dashboard design. The brightly colored upholstery shown here was also newly standard for the Z28. Unhappily for Chevy, total Camaro sales fell 15.5 percent for the model year to 153,831.

▲ It didn't look any more muscular, but the '83 was a stronger Z28, as engineers extracted another 10 horsepower from the fuel-injected "Cross-Fire" 305 V-8, bringing it up to 175. This silver example was snapped by the editors during their original road test, which revealed plenty of muscle at most any speed, plus great handling and even a fairly comfortable performance-car ride. Z28 sales eased this year, though not much, totaling 62,100 units.

▲ El Camino was America's only car/pickup by 1983 (excluding GMC's Caballero clone), and would outlast parent Malibu despite modest sales. This standard model priced from $8191. Amazingly, an SS package was still available, complete with a solid 160 hp.

▲ Answering buyer pleas for more in-cab room and storage, Chevy's S-10 compact pickup added extended-cab models for '83, as well as a 7½-foot long-bed alternative to the regular 6-foot box. This one has both. Price was $6496 before options.

▲ Chevy van sales soared 44 percent in calendar '83 to 142,555. Here, a ½-ton G10 Chevy Van commercial with 110-inch-wheelbase. Sport Van, Bonaventure, and Beauville passenger models continued. All offered 125-inch G20/G30 versions as well.

▲ The '83 Chevy pickup line spanned three payload ranges, two box lengths, regular and four-door crew cabs, and Stepside or flush-fender Fleetside styling. This long-bed Fleetside base-priced at $6707, but was usually optioned up to suit buyer needs and taste.

Model Breakdown

Chevette		Wght	Price	Prod
B08	htchbk sdn 3d	2,088	5,469	37,537
B68	htchbk sdn 5d	2,148	5,616	81,297
J08	Scooter htchbk 3d	2,029	4,997	33,488
J68	Scooter htchbk 5d	2,098	5,333	15,303
B08/ Z90	Diesel sdn 3d	—	6,535	439
B68/ Z90	Diesel sdn 5d	—	6,683	1,501
Cavalier				
C27	cpe	2,384	5,888	23,028
C69	sdn 4d	2,403	5,999	33,333
C35	wgn 5d	2,464	6,141	27,992
D27	CS cpe	2,374	6,363	22,172
E77	CS htchbk cpe 3d	2,440	6,549	25,869
D69	CS sdn 4d	2,425	6,484	52,802
D35	CS wgn 5d	2,486	6,633	32,834
D27/ Z08	CS conv cpe	—	10,990	627
Citation				
H11	cpe, I-4	2,471	6,333	⎫ 6,456
H11	cpe, V-6	2,526	6,483	⎭

Citation *(continued)*		Wght	Price	Prod
X08	htchbk sdn 3d, I-4	2,463	6,788	⎫ 14,323
X08	htchbk sdn 3d, V-6	2,518	6,938	⎭
X68	htchbk sdn 5d, I-4	2,511	6,934	⎫ 71,405
X68	htchbk sdn 5d, V-6	2,566	7,084	⎭
Camaro				
P87	spt cpe, I-4	—	8,036	⎫
P87	spt cpe, V-6	2,959	8,186	⎬ 63,806
P87	spt cpe, V-8	3,116	8,386	⎭
S87	Berlinetta cpe, V-6	2,944	9,881	⎫ 27,925
S87	Berlinetta cpe, V-8	3,136	10,106	⎭
P87	Z28 spt cpe, V-8	3,061	10,336	62,100
Celebrity				
W27	cpe, I-4	2,710	8,059	⎫ 19,221
W27	cpe, V-6	2,770	8,209	⎭
W19	sdn 4d, I-4	2,730	8,209	⎫ 120,608
W19	sdn 4d, V-6	2,790	8,359	⎭
Malibu				
W69	Classic sdn 4d, V-6	3,199	8,084	⎫ 61,534
W69	Classic sdn 4d, V-8	3,307	8,309	⎭

Malibu *(continued)*		Wght	Price	Prod
W35	Classic wgn 4d, 2S, V-6	3,343	8,217	55,892
W35	Classic wgn 4d, V-8, 2S	3,470	—	8,442
Full-Size Chevrolet				
L69	Impala sdn 4d, V-6	3,490	8,331	⎫ 45,154
L69	Impala sdn 4d, V-8	3,594	8,556	⎭
N35	Caprice Classic wgn 4d, 3S, V-8	4,092	9,518	53,028
N69	Caprice Classic sdn 4d, V-6	3,537	8,802	⎫ 122,613
N69	Caprice Classic sdn 4d, V-8	3,641	9,027	⎭
Monte Carlo				
Z37	spt cpe, V-6	3,220	8,552	⎫ 91,605
Z37	spt cpe, V-8	3,328	8,777	⎭
Z37/ Z65	SS spt cpe, V-8	—	10,474	4,714
Corvette				
No Corvette model was produced.				

1984

- **First all-new Corvette in 15 years**

- **Wagons expand the Celebrity lineup**

- **Monte Carlo SS, Cavalier convertible more readily available**

- **Citation II debuts**

- **Chevy car sales recover to near 1.66 million units**

▶ The first fully redesigned Corvette since the original 1968 "shark" arrived in the spring of 1983 as an early '84 model. Styling was naturally all-new, though still recognizably Corvette. Among the car's many new features was a "clamshell" hood/front fender assembly that tilted up from the rear to provide almost unlimited service access to the powertrain. The big panel lifted easily on gas-filled support struts.

▲ Corvette's veteran 350-cubic-inch V-8 had been updated for the last "sharks" with fuel injection—the first since '65—and numerous internal modifications. Internally designated L83, this engine was one of the few components retained for the redesigned '84 'Vette, though horsepower was bumped up by 5 to 205. A four-speed overdrive automatic was the only transmission at first, but a novel "4+3" manual was offered from August '83, though it didn't prove very popular.

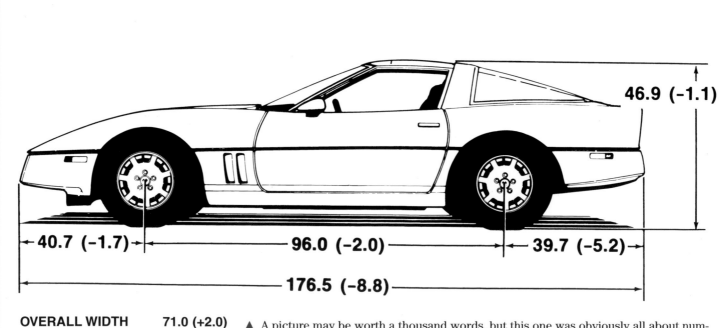

46.9 (−1.1)

40.7 (−1.7)   96.0 (−2.0)   39.7 (−5.2)

176.5 (−8.8)

OVERALL WIDTH	71.0 (+2.0)
TREAD — FRONT	59.4 (+0.7)
— REAR	60.4 (+0.9)

▲ A picture may be worth a thousand words, but this one was obviously all about numbers. Chevy PR issued it to highlight dimensional differences between the 1984 Corvette and the predecessor "shark." The new model was trimmer in every dimension save tracks and overall width. It was also lighter by a fairly substantial 145 pounds.

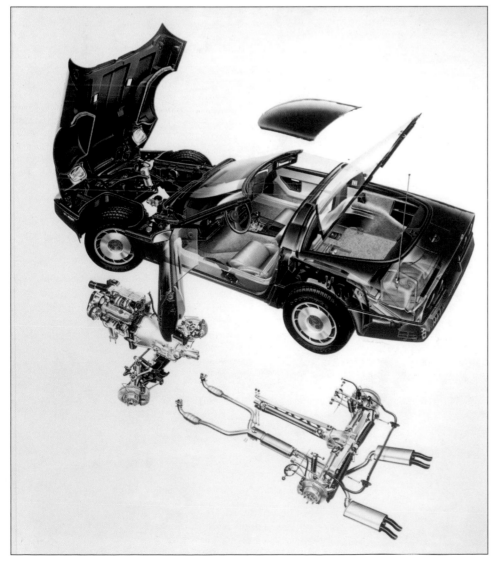

▲ Though some experts insist the '84 Corvette introduced a sixth design generation, Chevy counted it as number four and issued a stream of "heritage" photos like this to settle the matter. Most journalists and historians have since adopted Chevy's informal "C4" designation. Using that nomenclature, then, what we have here (*clockwise from bottom left*) are an '84, C2 Sting Ray and C3 "shark" coupes, and a 1953 or '54 solid-axle C1 roadster.

◄ ▲ Corvette made a big leap in technical sophistication with its 1984 redesign. Styling, executed under designer Jerry Palmer, was eye-catching yet tasteful—and 23.7 percent more aerodynamic, thanks to exhaustive wind-tunnel tests (*above*). Underneath, a much more rigid "uniframe" replaced the traditional body-on-chassis. Literally reinforcing it was a metal inner-body "birdcage," which also allowed closer dimensional tolerances around the doors and the new liftup glass hatch (previewed on the '82 Collector Edition "shark"). T-tops gave way to a single liftoff roof panel (*left*). Suspension was unchanged in concept, but extensive use of aluminum reduced unsprung weight for more precise handling.

▲ At $23,360 to start, the '84 was the costliest Corvette ever, yet sales bounced back to near record 1979 level with 51,547 units. Consumer Guide® neatly summed up the reason for this success, calling the newest 'Vette a "world-class sports car with few rivals in performance." The liftoff roof panel, here removed, was a $595 item on a short options list.

▲ A new interpretation of Corvette's hallmark four-lamp tail maintained design continuity on the '84, even though the new car shared nary a line with its predecessor. Full perimeter rub strip helped tie everything together.

▲ Looking like a natural-born track star, the '84 Corvette prompted renewed interest in "showroom stock" racing, where only minimum modifications were allowed. It quickly came to dominate that class in Sports Car Club of America competition.

► Yes, this wild thing really is a Chevrolet, a Corvette, actually. Corvettes have seldom been used as the basis for Italian design exercises—perhaps because they're pretty wild already—but the famed Carozzeria Bertone started with the new '84 'Vette chassis in creating the unique Ramarro for the 1985 European auto-show season. This profile view highlights a turretlike canopy atop a pronounced wedge-shape body, as well as sharp, "geometric" graphics (as on the wheel openings). Partly a packaging exercise, Ramarro claimed slightly more interior room than the production '84 'Vette despite being 1.3 inches shorter and much lower.

▲ Though not greatly changed for 1984, Camaro enjoyed a healthy model-year sales gain of nearly 70 percent with 261,108 units. The Berlinetta (shown) remained the least popular version, drawing a relatively modest 33,400 orders. Price this year was $10,895 with base V-6, $11,270 with four-barrel, 150-horsepower 305 V-8.

◄ By rights, the Camaro Berlinetta should have been more popular than it was, if only because of its tasteful interior with cord-cloth upholstery. A new '84 exclusive for this model was a very "Star Trek" instrument cluster with electronic instead of mechanical gauges, plus oft-used minor switches grouped on dual pods either side of the steering wheel. Though the digital-graphic display was judged as dubious as the new Corvette's similarly jazzy panel, the switch pods were adjustable to enhance driver accessibility and comfort.

▲ The Camaro Z28 returned for '84 with 190 hp, as its 305 V-8 reverted from fuel injection to a tried-and-true four-barrel carburetor. Injection would be back soon enough, however.

▲ Gasoline was again cheap and plentiful by 1984, so hot cars were back in style. Z28 sales reflected the trend, rising nearly 62 percent to just over 100,000. Base price was up to $10,620.

▲ The national economic recovery also boosted sales of Chevrolet's full-size cars like this woody-look Caprice Classic Estate. Orders jumped 25 percent to 276,495, not bad for a line that Chevrolet had considered killing just a few years before. A heavy-duty suspension was a new option for the luxury wagon.

▲ Also reflecting revived demand for full-size cars in 1984 was the return of the Caprice Classic coupe, with a slightly crisper roofline to boot. However, it attracted only 19,541 sales, as the vast majority of big-Chevy buyers continued to prefer sedans, either Caprice or, to a lesser extent, the line's sole surviving Impala model.

▲ Smart new six- and eight-passenger wagons helped Celebrity more than double its sales for 1984. The midsize Chevy also added four-speed manual and automatic transmission options this year.

▲ Any '84 Celebrity was more fun to drive when ordered with the new Eurosport option, as on this sedan. A firmer "handling" suspension and high-output 130-hp V-6 were included for about $200.

◄▲ Production constraints and not low demand had limited sales of the reborn Monte Carlo SS, but Chevy upped production six-fold for '84, reeling off 24,050 copies. Options also expanded to include front bucket seats and console, four-speed automatic transmission and a shorter 3.73:1 alternative to the normal 3.42 final drive. Colors were still limited to monochrome white or this dark blue. Base price rose $226 to $10,700. The SS V-8 featured a high-lift camshaft and free-flow dual-outlet exhaust system with Corvette-type catalytic converters, and horsepower was rated at 180, up 5 from last year. Tires were hefty P215/65R Goodyear Eagles on bold steel wheels. Performance was strong, with 0-60 mph available in well under 8 seconds.

▲ Chevy's 1984 compacts were little changed from the previous year's models, but their new Citation II badges suggested otherwise. The X-11 package again included a tuned V-6 with 135 hp, and was available for this two-door hatchback and the two-door club coupe.

▲ Though it hasn't been an "Iron Duke" in some time, General Motors' 2.5-liter four received detail changes most every year to become even thriftier and more dependable. By 1984 it was base power for Chevrolet's compact Citation II, midsize Celebrity, and even the most affordable Camaro, as well as the compact S-10 pickup and Blazer. If not as sophisticated in design as many European or Japanese fours, the 2.5 undoubtedly pleased a lot of Chevy owners.

▲ The first Citation II found 97,205 buyers, 5.4 percent more than the '83s. The four-door hatchback again accounted for most sales.

▲ Billed as a "Chevrolet Technology Showcase," the experimental Citation IV boasted a sensationally low drag factor of 0.14.

▲ The Citation IV was GM's 1984 vision of the future family car, a demonstration of how the interior space of the familiar showroom Citation could be preserved within a much sleeker envelope to reduce both fuel consumption and wind noise. Designers used every "aero" trick they could to achieve minimum air drag, including the gently tapered tail seen here. A normal front-drive V-6 Citation powertrain mounted snugly within a smaller, more radically sloped nose. Curb weight was 2600 pounds, about the same as contemporary Citation.

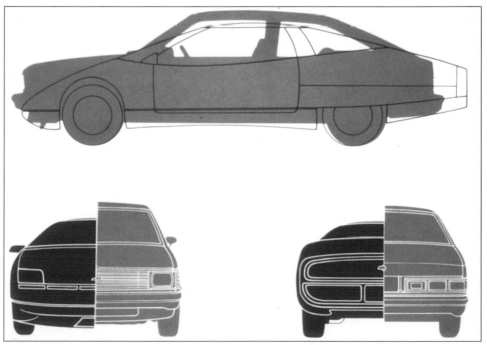

▲ Despite its extreme teardrop shape, the Citation IV claimed equal or better interior space versus a normal 1984 Citation II. As this comparison shows, the concept's main dimensional differences were being 6.4 inches longer overall and a startling 5.4 inches lower.

▲ Chevette changed little for '84, but sales jumped 43.8 percent to near 244,000 units.

▲ Chevy's S-10 compact pickups also drew higher '84 sales despite little change.

▲ Cavaliers were freshened up for '84 with quad rectangular headlights and a tidy eggcrate grille. The convertible was now in full production, tallying 5486 sales versus a mere 627 for inaugural '83. As before, it came only with Cavalier's sportiest Type 10 trim.

1984 Engine Availability

Engines	bore × stroke	bhp	availability
I-4, 97.6	3.23 × 2.98	65	S-Chevette
I-4D, 111.0	3.31 × 3.23	51	O-Chevette
I-4, 121.0	3.50 × 3.15	88	S-Cavalier
I-4, 151.0	4.00 × 3.00	92	S-Citation, Camaro, Celeb
V-6, 173.0	3.50 × 2.99	107	S-Cam, Berlinetta; O-Cam
V-6, 173.0	3.50 × 2.99	112	O-Citation, Celeb
V-6, 173.0	3.50 × 2.99	130/135	O-Citation, Celeb
V-6, 229.0	3.74 × 3.48	110	S-MC, Chevr cpe/sdn
V-6, 231.0	3.80 × 3.40	110	S-Calif. Chevr
V-6D, 262.0	4.06 × 3.39	85	O-Celebrity
V-8, 305.0	3.74 × 3.48	150	S-Cam Z28, Chevr wgn; O-Cam, Monte Carlo, Chevrolet
V-8, 305.0	3.74 × 3.48	180	S-Monte Carlo SS
V-8, 305.0	3.74 × 3.48	190	O-Camaro Z28
V-8D, 350.0	4.06 × 3.39	105	O-Chevr, MC
Corvette			
V-8, 350.0	4.00 × 3.48	205	S-all

▲ A few new trim and equipment options were the main news for the sophomore edition of Chevy's popular S-10 Blazer compact sport-utility. This 4×4 started at $9685.

Model Breakdown

Chevette		Wght	Price	Prod
J08	htchbk sdn 3d	1,999	4,997	66,446
J68	htchbk sdn 5d	2,051	5,333	28,466
B08	CS htchbk 3d	2,038	5,489	47,032
B68	CS htchbk 5d	2,102	5,636	94,897
J08/Z90	Diesel sdn 3d	—	5,550	1,495
J68/Z90	Diesel sdn 5d	—	5,851	1,180
B08/Z90	CS diesel sdn 3d	2,261	5,999	1,000
B68/Z90	CS diesel sdn 5d	2,320	6,161	3,384
Cavalier				
C69	sdn 4d	2,386	6,222	90,023
C35	wgn 5d	2,455	6,375	50,718
D69	CS sdn 4d	2,398	6,666	110,295
D35	CS wgn 5d	2,468	6,821	58,739
E27	Type 10 cpe	2,367	6,477	103,204
E77	Type 10 htchbk cpe 3d	2,418	6,654	44,146
E27/Z08	Type 10 conv cpe	2,583	11,299	5,486

Citation II		Wght	Price	Prod
H11	cpe, I-4	2,454	6,445	4,936
H11	cpe, V-6	2,529	6,695	
X08	htchbk sdn 3d, I-4	2,494	6,900	8,783
X08	htchbk sdn 3d, V-6	2,569	7,150	
X68	htchbk sdn 5d, I-4	2,506	7,046	83,486
X68	htchbk sdn 5d, V-6	2,581	7,296	
Camaro				
P87	spt cpe, I-4	2,899	7,995	127,292
P87	spt cpe, V-6	2,932	8,245	
P87	spt cpe, V-8	3,112	8,545	
S87	Berlinetta cpe, V-6	2,944	10,895	33,400
S87	Berlinetta cpe, V-8	3,126	11,270	
P87	Z28 spt cpe, V-8	3,135	10,620	100,416
Celebrity				
W27	cpe, I-4	2,663	7,711	29,191
W27	cpe, V-6	2,781	7,961	
W19	sdn 4d, I-4	2,703	7,890	200,259
W19	wgn 4d, V-6	2,816	8,140	
W35	wgn 5d, 2S, I-4	2,857	8,214	48,295
W35	wgn 5d, 2S, V-6	2,964	8,464	
W35/AQ4	wgn 5d, 3S, I-4	—	8,429	31,543
W35/AQ4	wgn 5d, 3S, V-6	—	8,679	

Full-Size Chevrolet		Wght	Price	Prod
L69	Impala sdn 4d, V-6	3,489	8,895	55,296
L69	Impala sdn 4d, V-8	3,628	9,270	
N35	Caprice Classic wgn 4d, 3S, V-8	4,053	10,210	65,688
N47	Caprice Classic spt cpe, V-6	3,633	9,253	19,541
N47	Caprice Classic spt cpe, V-8	3,834	9,628	
N69	Caprice Classic sdn 4d, V-6	3,532	9,400	135,970
N69	Caprice Classic sdn 4d, V-8	3,662	9,775	
Monte Carlo				
Z37	spt cpe, V-6	3,176	8,936	112,730
Z37	spt cpe, V-8	3,292	9,311	
Z37/Z65	SS spt cpe, V-8	3,434	10,700	24,050
Corvette				
Y07	cpe	3,087	21,800	51,547

1985

- **Chevy begins selling three Japanese-designed subcompacts**

- **Camaro adds hot IROC-Z model**

- **Midsize Astro van debuts**

- **Car production eases again, this time to 1.4 million units**

▲ The result of a recent General Motors alliance with Toyota bowed in June 1985 as a new Chevy Nova, based on the Japanese company's popular subcompact Corolla. Built at a joint-venture California plant called New United Motor Manufacturing, Inc. (NUMMI), this Nova offered front-wheel drive, a 74-horsepower 1.6-liter 4-cylinder engine, and a single sedan body style on a 95.7-inch wheelbase. Price was around $7300. Initial demand was strong.

▲ A second weapon in Chevy's expanded 1985 small-car arsenal was Spectrum, bowing at midyear as a retrimmed version of the front-drive I-Mark marketed by GM affiliate Isuzu of Japan. This hatchback priced from $6295. Its 1.5-liter 4-cyl engine made 70 hp.

▲ Spectrum was also available as this four-door notchback sedan priced from $6575. Both models were built by Isuzu and imported from Japan. Lack of factory capacity limited calendar-1985 sales to about 42,000, confined to 16 eastern U.S. states.

◄ Besides investing in Isuzu, General Motors had also bought a stake in Japan's Suzuki Motors Corporation, which sent over a retrimmed version of its front-drive Cultus minicar for sale through Chevrolet dealers. Called Sprint, the newcomer bowed in mid-1984 as an early '85 entry. The sole body style at first was this two-door hatchback on a petite 88.4-inch wheelbase. An inline 3-cylinder engine made just 70 hp, but only manual transmission was offered and curb weight was a feathery 1500 pounds, so performance was quite acceptable. Intended as Chevy's new economy leader, the Sprint priced from just $4949, about $400 less than the larger Chevette. As with Spectrum, lack of production capacity in Japan limited sales; Sprint managed some 20,400 for its first 12 months, all in nine western states. With Sprint, Spectrum, and Nova, Chevy aimed to steal small-car sales from import brands by offering similar products.

▲ Corvette production shifted in the 1980s from St. Louis to a new purpose-built plant in Bowling Green, Kentucky. GM was scurrying to automate all its factories, so this one made heavy use of computer-controlled robots for welding and other tasks.

▲ Robots don't get sick, so they were a natural for hazardous jobs like painting. Here, the automated workers do their work on an '85 Corvette in the Bowling Green paint shop. Another benefit: paint finish noticeably improved from prerobot days.

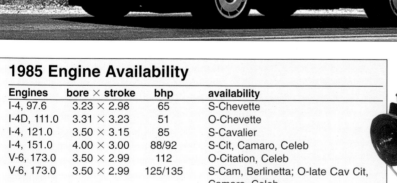

◄ Though only a year old, the new-generation Corvette got an unusual number of improvements for 1985, including revised damping for less ride harshness. The firmer Z51 handling option was smoother, too, and provided more cornering stick by adopting inch-wider 9.5-inch rear wheels and tires, plus new gas-charged shock absorbers. Unhappily for Chevy, 'Vette sales retreated to 39,729, down 23 percent from the extra-long 1984 model year.

◄ The '85 Corvette base-priced about $1500 higher than the '84, but the extra money bought 25 extra horsepower, thanks to a switch from throttle-body fuel injection to the more efficient multiport type. Chevy called its system "Tuned Port Injection," which appeared on discreet front-fender badges to signal the change.

▼ TPI was adopted for the '85 edition of Chevy's 5.0-liter/305-cubic-inch passenger-car V-8 (below) as well as the Corvette 350 (bottom). Unlike single or dual throttle-body systems, Tuned Port Injection squirted fuel directly into each cylinder, contributing to more efficient combustion that helped to improve fuel economy and reduce emissions.

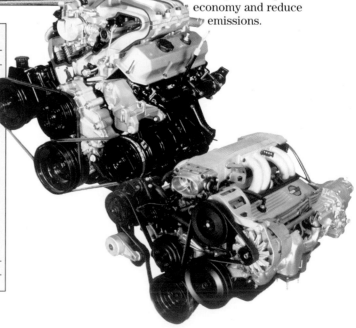

1985 Engine Availability

Engines	bore × stroke	bhp	availability
I-4, 97.6	3.23 × 2.98	65	S-Chevette
I-4D, 111.0	3.31 × 3.23	51	O-Chevette
I-4, 121.0	3.50 × 3.15	85	S-Cavalier
I-4, 151.0	4.00 × 3.00	88/92	S-Cit, Camaro, Celeb
V-6, 173.0	3.50 × 2.99	112	O-Citation, Celeb
V-6, 173.0	3.50 × 2.99	125/135	S-Cam, Berlinetta; O-late Cav Cit, Camaro, Celeb
V-6, 262.0	4.00 × 3.48	140	S-MC, Chevrolet
V-6D, 262.0	4.06 × 3.39	85	O-Celeb
V-8, 305.0	3.74 × 3.48	150/165	S-Cam Z28, Capr wgn; O-Cam, MC, Chevrolet
V-8, 305.0	3.74 × 3.48	180	S-Monte Carlo SS
V-8, 305.0	3.74 × 3.48	190	O-Camaro IROC-Z
V-8, 305.0	3.74 × 3.48	215	O-Camaro Z28/IROC-Z
V-8D, 350.0	4.06 × 3.39	105	O-Chevr
Corvette			
V-8, 350.0	4.00 × 3.48	230	S-all

▲ The big news for Monte Carlo in '85 was a new 140-hp 4.3-liter V-6 replacing the standard 3.8 liter as standard equipment. The 5.0-liter V-8 was still available as an option. Except for the new standard engine, new cloth interior trim, 5 new interior colors, and new standard wheel covers, Monte Carlo went virtually unchanged from '85, and sales dropped to 83,573.

◄ The notchback Monte SS offered more color choices for '85: the usual white, maroon, silver, and black. Interiors sported better-quality grey or maroon cloth upholstery, and exterior graphics were revised, but there were few other changes. Base price rose $680 to $11,380, but buyers snapped up 35,484 copies, up 47.5 percent. Chevy could probably have sold more had it been able to build them.

◄ Built to explore design ideas for future Camaros, the wild GTZ concept toured various auto shows in 1985. At the time it was widely thought to forecast a new-generation Camaro being readied for 1988, but that timing would prove five years premature. A special 4.3-liter V-6 with near V-8 power output sat within a lower, smoother new nose.

▼ With the arrival of the IROC-Z, the "ordinary" Z28 was no longer top dog of the Camaro lineup. However, it could still be had with the top-of-the-line Camaro engine: a new port-injected 5.7 V-8 making a strong 215 hp. Z28s also received a host of detail changes for '85, including grille and parking lamps, hood louvers, chin spoiler, ground effects cladding, and new body nameplates.

▲ The International Race of Champions drivers competition inspired the new IROC-Z. It featured a special front fascia, "ground effects" body skirts, and distinctive 16-inch cast aluminum wheels.

▲ Celebrity's optional high-output 130-hp V-6 benefited from port fuel injection for '85. It made a good match for the $199 Eurosport option, as shown on this sedan.

▲ Type 10 (coupe shown) was no longer the sportiest Cavalier for '85, as a new V-6 Z24 package option with 125 hp arrived for two-door models.

▲ Though again little changed, Chevette started '85 a little late so Chevy could meet government fuel economy numbers. Sales thus dropped by half this season to 123,499.

▲ Citation lost its notchback for '85, but the sporty X-11 package got a standard port-injected V-6. Sales still declined, however, so Citation would not be back for 1986.

▲ All full-size '85s, like this Caprice sedan, switched from a base 3.8-liter V-6 to a stronger 130-hp 4.3. V-8 options again comprised a gasoline 5.0 and a diesel 5.7. Sales slipped 4.2 percent to 264,793.

▲ ► Chevy's truck line again offered two tempting light-duty choices for '85: the trim S-10 pickup, shown above as a short-bed 4×4, and the car-based El Camino, which came as an $8933 standard model, shown right, and as a $9198 Super Sport. The S-10 attracted more sales by a country mile.

▲ Full-size '85 trucks like this long-bed C-10 Fleetside also got the 4.3-liter V-6 as base power, as the long-serving 250-cubic-inch inline six was finally retired.

▲ Chevy's big pickups remained big sellers despite only minor year-to-year changes. This 4×4 C-10 carries the short Stepside box, lately regaining popularity.

▲ A folding soft top was still technically available for the big Blazer, but the vast majority of buyers still chose the hardtop model. This 4×4 priced from $8856.

◄ ▼ Chrysler Corporation's new 1984-model minivans were proving a huge sales success, but Chevrolet felt their front-wheel drive wasn't the way to go for heavier loads and towing. Chevy thus replied with the rear-drive 1985 Astro, a somewhat larger, heavier minivan. Built on a modified version of the S-10 truck platform, Astro offered base, CS, and top-line CL models with a 155-hp 4.3 V-6 and five-speed manual or four-speed automatic transmissions. It got a warm reception, but didn't sell nearly as well as the more carlike Chrysler vans.

▼ Base-priced in the $9000-$10,200 range, Astro appealed to buyers who valued truck ruggedness and hauling capacity over the carlike handling of other small vans. Available seating for seven or eight was another attraction. Dual swing-out rear cargo doors were standard.

▲ Astro was also available as a metal-sided Cargo Van with a 2.5-liter 4-cyl engine for light commercial users like delivery services.

Model Breakdown

Chevette	Wght	Price	Prod	Camaro	Wght	Price	Prod	Full-Size Chevrolet	Wght	Price	Prod
B08 CS htchbk 3d	2,085	5,340	57,706	P87 spt cpe, I-4	2,881	8,363 ⌉		L69 Impala sdn 4d, V-6	3,508	9,519 ⌉	
B68 CS htchbk 5d	2,145	5,690	65,128	P87 spt cpe, V-6	2,977	8,698	97,966	L69 Impala sdn 4d, V-8	3,634	9,759 ⌋	53,438
B08/				P87 spt cpe, V-8	3,177	8,998 ⌋		N35 Caprice Classic			
Z90 CS diesel sdn 3d	2,261	5,850	203	S87 Berlinetta cpe, V-6	3,056	11,060 ⌉		wgn 4d, 3S, V-8	4,083	10,714	55,886
B68/				S87 Berlinetta cpe, V-8	3,221	11,360 ⌋	13,649	N47 Caprice Classic			
Z90 CS diesel sdn 5d	2,320	6,215	462	P87/				cpe V-6	3,525	9,888 ⌉	
Cavalier				Z28 Z28 spt cpe, V-8	3,251	11,060	47,022	N47 Caprice Classic			16,229
C69 sdn 4d	2,339	6,477	86,597	P87/				cpe V-8	3,651	10,128 ⌋	
C35 wgn 5d	2,409	6,633	34,581	B4Z IROC-Z spt cpe, V-8	3,319	11,739	21,177	N69 Caprice Classic			
D69 CS sdn 4d	2,352	6,900	93,386	**Celebrity**				sdn 4d, V-6	3,549	10,038 ⌉	
D35 CS wgn 5d	2,420	7,066	33,551	W27 cpe, I-4	2,689	8,102 ⌉		N69 Caprice Classic			139,240
E27 Type 10 cpe	2,320	6,737	106,021	W27 cpe, V-6	2,790	8,362 ⌋	29,010	sdn 4d, V-8	3,674	10,278 ⌋	
E77 Type 10 htchbk				W19 sdn 4d, I-4	2,722	8,288 ⌉		**Monte Carlo**			
cpe 3d	2,382	6,919	25,508	W19 wgn 4d, V-6	2,827	8,548 ⌋	239,763	Z37 spt cpe, V-6	3,139	9,540 ⌉	
E27/				W35 wgn 5d, 2S, I-4	2,857	8,479 ⌉		Z37 spt cpe, V-8	3,245	9,780 ⌋	83,573
Z08 Type 10 conv cpe	2,458	11,693	4,108	W35 wgn 5d, 2S, V-6	2,953	8,739 ⌋	45,602	Z37/			
Citation II				W35/				Z65 SS spt cpe, V-8	3,385	11,380	35,484
X08 htchbk sdn 3d, I-4	2,499	6,940 ⌉		AQ4 wgn 5d, 3S, I-4	—	8,699 ⌉		**Corvette**			
X08 htchbk sdn 3d, V-6	2,568	7,200 ⌋	7,443	W35/			40,547	Y07 cpe 3d	3,191	24,873	39,729
X68 htchbk sdn 5d, I-4	2,535	7,090 ⌉		AQ4 wgn 5d, 3S, V-6	—	8,959 ⌋					
X68 htchbk sdn 5d, V-6	2,603	7,350 ⌋	55,279								

1986

- Corvette convertible reborn, paces Indy 500

- Chevy fields Indy car racing team

- Impala dropped; more models for Nova and Sprint

- Domestic car sales slide to 1.37 million

▲ Chevy showed this ragtop version of the little Sprint at its 1986 press preview, but decided against production. Chevy would, however, sell something like it a few years later.

▲ Spectrum was little changed for 1986, but continued to take sales from Chevette.

▲ Nova's big 1986 news was adding this four-door hatchback. Base price was $7669.

▲ Spint offerings did expand for '86 with this four-door hatchback Plus on a 92.3-inch wheelbase. Also new was the ER two-door, which topped the year's EPA fuel-economy ratings at 55 mpg city, 60 highway.

▶ Cavalier kept its basic J-body design with few changes, but the Type 10 option was replaced by a quintet of even sportier RS models, including this line-topping $12,530 convertible. All came with wider tires, sport suspension, red and black exterior accents, and special interior. The RS was Cavalier's only 1986 ragtop, and fairly scarce with just 5765 sold.

▲ Again all but unchanged, Chevette continued its sales slide in 1986, dropping to 103,244. All models were now called CS. This four-door hatch priced from $5959.

▲ All '86 Cavaliers offered a choice of base 2.0-liter four or a new port-injected 2.8 V-6 with 120 horsepower. This RS wagon was one of just 6252 built for the model year.

▲ Cavalier sales rose 12.6 percent for '86 to 432,101, about 30,000 down from record 1984. Here, the new RS in four-door sedan guise. It priced from $7811.

▲ The Impala name disappeared after nearly 30 years, as Chevy's lower-priced full-size sedan became a non-Classic Caprice for '86. The unpopular diesel V-8 option disappeared, and all models got minor trim and equipment updates. Here, the Classic coupe.

▲ Joining the regular Caprice Classic sedan for 1986 was this plush Brougham version, apparently aimed at those who didn't like this year's smaller new front-drive Olds 88 and Buick LeSabre. It was a fair success, grabbing 28.3 percent of total Caprice sales.

◄ Chevy still catered well to the "John Law" market in 1986. Engineers always seemed to be tinkering with the full-size Caprice sedan's Police Package to make it stronger, faster, and more comfortable. No wonder so many law-enforcement agencies kept coming back for more year after year.

▼ The Chevrolet Design Staff used ground effects body cladding, a special front fascia, 16-inch Enkei wheels on Goodyear VR50 radials, and other tweaks to create the flashy '86 Celebrity Eurosport VR wagon concept car. The Eurosport VR concept would see limited production in 1987-88.

▲ The midsize Celebrity continued its winning ways for '86, ringing up nearly 405,000 sales, up 14 percent from '85. Changes included a mild facelift, as seen on this two-door sedan, and a newly optional split bench front seat.

▲ A new 1986 Celebrity option was a Classic package with formal-look roof treatment, ID badges and, missing on this prototype sedan, wire wheel covers. The obvious aim was giving a smaller new-wave car traditional "big car" Detroit style.

▲ A convertible had been on Chevy's agenda during the C4 Corvette design effort, and it made a big splash on reaching dealers in April 1986. Though not inexpensive at $32,032 to start, the reborn roadster made 7315 buyers very, very happy this year.

◄ America's fastest production car also got standard four-wheel antilock brakes for '86, thus matching much costlier European sports cars with stopping power equal to its go-power. Also new was an improved anti-theft system that prevented engine starting without a special electronically coded key. Added per government decree was a central high-mount stoplamp, which was roof-mounted on the popular coupe (shown).

► The Corvette convertible returned in grand style by being chosen pace car for the 1986 Indianapolis 500 race. Chevy stoked the publicity fire even higher by enticing famed aviator Chuck Yeager, the first human to break the sound barrier, to "pilot" the pacer on the opening lap. Unlike many pace cars, this yellow 'Vette was mechanically stock, yet had more than enough performance for leading the racers around the famous Brickyard track. All '86 Corvette convertibles were marketed as Pace Car Replicas. As with 1978's Pace Car Replica coupe, each came with regalia decals for owners to apply if desired. Many '86s were delivered in Indy Yellow (shown), though other colors were available.

288

▲ A smoother nose with flush "composite" headlamps identified a luxurious new 1986 Monte Carlo, the LS. It priced $180-$210 above the standard model, which retained the usual upright front end.

▲ Premium gas-charged shock absorbers and standard aluminum wheels were among the few changes for the 1986 Monte Carlo SS. Sales totaled 41,364, including just 200 "glassback" Aerocoupes.

▲ Camaro sales inched up 6.8 percent to 192,128. The luxury-oriented Berlinetta (*above*) was again the least popular model at 4479 units despite a $300 lighter base price. But the hot IROC-Z (*below*) more than doubled its volume to 49,585.

▲ Like Berlinetta, the Z28 was little changed for '86, but it, too, found fewer sales despite a $300 base-price cut, falling 18 percent to 38,547 units.

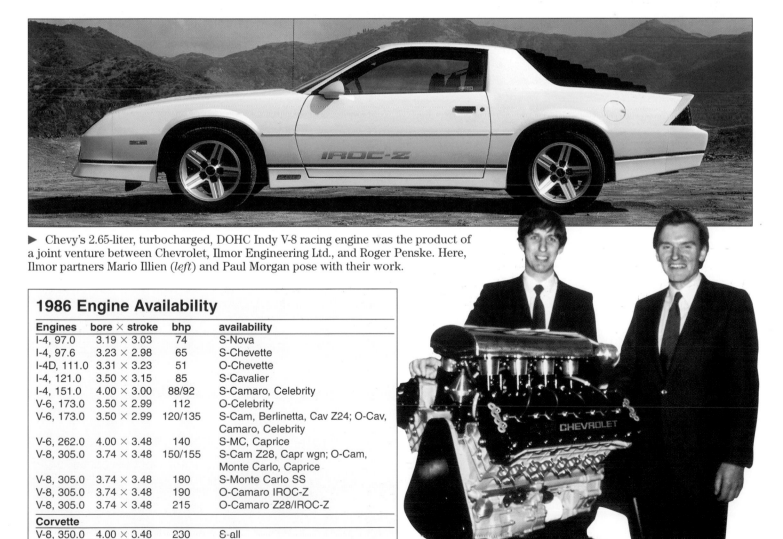

▶ Chevy's 2.65-liter, turbocharged, DOHC Indy V-8 racing engine was the product of a joint venture between Chevrolet, Ilmor Engineering Ltd., and Roger Penske. Here, Ilmor partners Mario Illien (*left*) and Paul Morgan pose with their work.

1986 Engine Availability

Engines	bore × stroke	bhp	availability
I-4, 97.0	3.19 × 3.03	74	S-Nova
I-4, 97.6	3.23 × 2.98	65	S-Chevette
I-4D, 111.0	3.31 × 3.23	51	O-Chevette
I-4, 121.0	3.50 × 3.15	85	S-Cavalier
I-4, 151.0	4.00 × 3.00	88/92	S-Camaro, Celebrity
V-6, 173.0	3.50 × 2.99	112	O-Celebrity
V-6, 173.0	3.50 × 2.99	120/135	S-Cam, Berlinetta, Cav Z24; O-Cav, Camaro, Celebrity
V-6, 262.0	4.00 × 3.48	140	S-MC, Caprice
V-8, 305.0	3.74 × 3.48	150/155	S-Cam Z28, Capr wgn; O-Cam, Monte Carlo, Caprice
V-8, 305.0	3.74 × 3.48	180	S-Monte Carlo SS
V-8, 305.0	3.74 × 3.48	190	O-Camaro IROC-Z
V-8, 305.0	3.74 × 3.48	215	O-Camaro Z28/IROC-Z
Corvette			
V-8, 350.0	4.00 × 3.48	230	S-all

▲ The Monte Carlo SS "droop snoot" was always an easy fit on the structurally related El Camino, and Chevy finally obliged for 1986. The result was one of the raciest looking pickups ever, but Chevy can't have built very many, as total El Camino sales remained modest.

▲ Beauville remained Chevy's top-line full-size van for '86. It now priced from $13,383.

▲ The year-old Astro minivan saw few changes. This one is carries fancy CL trim.

▲ "High Country" trim was a new option for Chevy's '86 S-10 Blazer compact SUV.

Model Breakdown

Chevette		Wght	Price	Prod
B08	CS htchbk 3d	2,080	5,645	48,756
B68	CS htchbk 5d	2,140	5,959	54,164
B08/Z90	CS diesel sdn 3d	2,261	6,152	124
B68/Z90	CS diesel sdn 5d	2,320	6,487	200

Nova		Wght	Price	Prod
K19	sdn 4d	2,163	7,435	124,961*
K68	htchbk sdn 5d	2,205	7,699	42,788*

Cavalier		Wght	Price	Prod
C27	cpe 2d, I-4	2,299	6,706	57,370
C27	cpe 2d, V-6	—	7,316	
C69	sdn 4d, I-4	2,342	6,888	86,492
C69	sdn 4d, V-6	—	7,498	
C35	wgn 5d, I-4	2,412	7,047	30,490
C35	wgn 5d, V-6	—	7,657	
D77	CS htchbk cpe, I-4	2,375	7,373	8,046
D77	CS htchbk cpe, V-6	—	7,983	
D69	CS sdn 4d, I-4	2,355	7,350	89,168
D69	CS sdn 4d, V-6	—	7,960	
D35	CS wgn 5d, I-4	2,423	7,525	23,101
D35	CS wgn 5d, V-6	—	8,135	
E27	RS cpe, I-4	2,325	7,640	53,941
E27	RS cpe, V-6	—	8,250	
E77	RS htchbk cpe 3d,I-4	2,387	7,830	7,504
E77	RS htchbk cpe 3d,V-6	—	8,440	
E69	RS sdn 4d, I-4	2,367	7,811	17,361
E69	RS sdn 4d, V-6	—	8,451	
E35	RS wgn 5d, I-4	2,440	7,979	6,252
E35	RS wgn 5d, V-6	—	8,589	

Cavalier (continued)		Wght	Price	Prod
E67	RS conv cpe, I-4	2,444	12,530	5,785
E67	RS conv cpe, V-6	2,642	13,140	
F27	Z24 spt cpe, V-6	2,519	8,878	36,365
F77	Z24 htchbk cpe 3d, V-6	2,581	9,068	10,266

Camaro		Wght	Price	Prod
P87	spt cpe, I-4	2,900	8,935	99,517
P87	spt cpe, V-6	2,994	9,285	
P87	spt cpe, V-8	3,116	9,685	
S87	Berlinetta cpe, V-6	3,063	11,902	4,479
S87	Berlinetta cpe, V-8	3,116	12,302	
P87/Z28	Z28 spt cpe, V-8	3,201	11,902	38,547
P87/B4Z	IROC-Z spt cpe, V-8	3,278	12,561	49,585

Celebrity		Wght	Price	Prod
W27	cpe, I-4	2,689	8,735	29,223
W27	cpe, V-6	2,794	9,170	
W19	sdn 4d, I-4	2,719	8,931	291,760
W19	wgn 4d, V-6	2,824	9,366	
W35	wgn 5d, 2S, I-4	2,847	9,081	36,655
W35	wgn 5d, 2S, V-6	2,912	9,516	
W35/AQ4	wgn 5d, 3S, I-4	2,850	9,313	47,245
W35/AQ4	wgn 5d, 3S, V-6	—	9,748	

Caprice		Wght	Price	Prod
L69	sdn 4d, V-6	3,535	10,243	50,751
L69	sdn 4d, V-8	3,628	10,633	
N35	Classic wgn 4d, 3S, V-8	4,095	11,511	45,183

Caprice (continued)		Wght	Price	Prod
N47	Classic spt cpe, V-6	3,546	10,635	9,869
N47	Classic spt cpe, V-8	3,638	11,025	
N69	Classic sdn 4d, V-6	3,564	10,795	67,772
N69	Classic sdn 4d, V-8	3,656	11,185	
N69/Classic Brgm sdn B45	4d, V-6	3,574	11,429	69,320
N69/Classic Brgm B45	sdn 4d, V-8	3,667	11,819	
N69/Classic LS Brgm B45	sdn 4d, V-6	—	—	2,117
N69/Classic LS Brgm B45	sdn 4d, V-8	—	—	

Monte Carlo		Wght	Price	Prod
Z37	spt cpe, V-6	3,138	10,241	50,418
Z37	spt cpe, V-8	3,244	10,631	
Z37/Z09	LS cpe, V-6	3,138	10,451	27,428
Z37/Z09	LS cpe, V-8	—	10,841	
Z37/Z65	SS spt cpe, V-8	3,387	12,466	41,164
Z37/Z65	SS aerocoupe, V-8	3,440	14,191	200

Corvette		Wght	Price	Prod
Y07	cpe 3d	3,239	27,027	27,794
Y67	conv cpe 2d	—	32,032	7,315

*27,945 additional Novas were built late in the 1985 model year.

1987

- **Camaro turns 20, revives convertible**

- **Sprint, Spectrum add turbocharged models**

- **Chevette dropped at midyear**

- **Domestic car production inches up to 1.38 million units**

▲ Camaro turned 20 in 1987, and Chevy celebrated with the first Camaro convertible in 18 years. Available in any trim level, the revived ragtop was a factory-approved conversion by Automobile Specialty Company, a division of ASC, Inc., which built only 1007 this season. Here, Livonia, Michigan, dealer Kit Tennyson (*at wheel*) takes delivery of the very first one, a hot IROC-Z version, from ASC executives John Hart (*standing*) and Michael Alexander.

► The IROC-Z became even faster for '87, as its available port-injected 5.7-liter/350-cubic-inch V-8 added 10 horsepower to 225, helped by new low-friction roller valve lifters. Performance was blistering: 0-60 mph in under 6.5 seconds, the standing quarter-mile in less than 14.5 seconds at around 95 mph. Unhappily for Chevy, total Camaro sales dropped 28.3 percent to 137,760.

▼ Seeking to boost Camaro sales in the ultra-competitive California market, employees at the Van Nuys Camaro plant near Los Angeles came up with what amounted to a V-6 Z28 coupe. Reviving the RS badge, it was sold only in Southern California, with production capped at around 2000. Price was $12,411 basic, $12,976 with an optional comfort/convenience package.

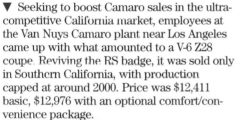

▲ Consumer Guide® editors snapped this '87 Camaro RS during an original road test. It wasn't that fast, but had the grippy handling and head-turning looks of a Z28.

291

▲ ► Caprice sales slipped 6.7 percent for '87, but were still hardly chicken feed at 228,500 units. Though sister General Motors divisions persisted with big rear-drive wagons like the Caprice (*above*), only Chevrolet still offered traditional full-size coupes and sedans, correctly concluding that many buyers still wanted such cars. Chevy gave them more choices this year by adding a base-trim Caprice wagon and an even more luxurious Brougham LS sedan above the already posh Caprice Classic Brougham (*right*). All Caprice engines adopted roller valve lifters this year for smoother running and better mileage, and flush composite headlamps were now standard across the board.

▲ Lighter, reengineered "Generation II" 4-cyl and V-6 engines appeared in several 1987 Chevy lines including the midsize Celebrity, where a five-speed manual transmission was newly optional for V-6 models.

▲ Unveiled at the February 1987 Chicago Auto Show was the Eurosport VR, a new cosmetic package for the Celebrity sedan (shown) and wagon. Included were a bold monochrome exterior with perimeter lower-body "aero" skirts, grille-less nose, decklid spoiler, and special interior. Price was a stiff $3550, but only 5000 installations were planned and all found buyers. Total Celebrity sales dipped 10.5 percent this model year to 362,524.

▲ Racy styling add-ons marked 1987's new Sprint Turbo two-door, whose 1.0-liter 3-cyl engine was puffed up from 48 to 70 hp.

292

▲ Corvette added 10 hp for '87 via low-friction roller-type valve lifters and a revised exhaust system. An optional tire-pressure monitor was announced, then temporarily withdrawn. The convertible (shown) improved sales to 10,625, but the coupe fell to 20,007.

▲ ▶ Limited to just 200 units in the '86 model year, the Monte Carlo SS Aerocoupe gained regular-production status for '87. But sales were modest at 6052, which apparently wasn't enough for Chevrolet, as the Aerocoupe's second year would also be its last. The car itself was basically a rerun, as was its notchback cousin, but the NASCAR-inspired Aerocoupe has already stirred interest among collectors as one of the rarest, quickest, and most interesting of 1980s Chevys. The notchback SS would live on for one year more.

1987 Engine Availability

Engines	bore × stroke	bhp	availability
I-4, 97.0	3.19 × 3.03	74	S-Nova
I-4, 97.6	3.23 × 2.98	65	S-Chevette
I-4, 121.0	3.50 × 3.15	90	S-Cav, Corsica, Beretta
I-4, 151.0	4.00 × 3.00	98	S-Celeb
V-6, 173.0	3.50 × 2.99	120/135	S-Camaro, Cav Z24; O-Cav, Celebrity, Cors, Beretta
V-6, 262.0	4.00 × 3.48	140/145	S-MC, Caprice cpe/sdn
V-8, 305.0	3.74 × 3.48	150/170	S-Cam Z28; O-Cam, MC, Caprice
V-8, 305.0	3.74 × 3.48	180	S-Monte Carlo SS
V-8, 305.0	3.74 × 3.48	215	S-Camaro IROC-Z; O-Camaro Z28
V-8, 307.0	3.80 × 3.38	140	S-Capr wgn
V-8, 350.0	4.00 × 3.48	225	O-Camaro IROC-Z
Corvette			
V-8, 350.0	4.00 × 3.48	240	S-all

▲ Monte Carlo lost its base model for '87, leaving the SS twins and the smooth-nose luxury LS, shown here. Total Monte sales took a beating, plunging 33.7 percent to 79,045. Higher base prices—by nearly $1100 for the LS—didn't help.

▲ The Cavalier RS convertible remained pretty rare in '87 with just 5826 sales, though the RS wagon and hatch coupe scored even lower. A new "Generation II" 2.0-liter four upped base horsepower to 90, and a similarly updated Gen II V-6 delivered 125 at extra cost.

▲ Total Cavalier sales dropped 19.9 percent for '87 to 346,254. Four-door sedans like this uplevel CS were the best-sellers.

▲ The racy Cavalier Z24 again offered V-6 power, uprated chassis, and special trim in a hatch coupe or this notchback two-door.

▲ Ragtop and Z24s aside, all Cavalier body styles still offered a choice of base, uplevel CS, and sporty RS trim. Here, the RS wagon.

Model Breakdown

Chevette

		Wght	Price	Prod
B08	CS htchbk 3d	2,078	4,995	26,135
B68	CS htchbk 5d	2,137	5,495	20,073

Nova

		Wght	Price	Prod
K19	sdn 4d	2,206	8,258	123,782
K68	htchbk sdn 5d	2,253	8,510	26,224

Cavalier

		Wght	Price	Prod
C27	cpe 2d, I-4	2,300	7,255	53,678
C27	cpe 2d, V-6	—	7,915	
E27	RS cpe, I-4	2,360	8,318	36,353
E27	RS cpe, V-6	—	8,978	
F27	Z24 spt cpe, V-6	2,511	9,913	42,890
D77	CS htchbk cpe, I-4	2,359	7,978	3,408
D77	CS htchbk cpe, V-6	—	8,638	
E77	RS htchbk cpe 3d, I-4	2,408	8,520	2,818
E77	RS htchbk cpe 3d, V-6	—	9,180	
F77	Z24 htchbk cpe 3d, V-6	2,560	10,115	4,517
C69	sdn 4d, I-4	2,345	7,449	84,445
C69	sdn 4d, V-6	—	8,109	
D69	CS sdn 4d, I-4	2,355	7,953	50,625
D69	CS sdn 4d, V-6	—	8,613	
E69	RS sdn 4d, I-4	2,397	8,499	15,482
E69	RS sdn 4d, V-6	—	9,159	
C35	wgn 5d, I-4	2,401	7,615	25,542
C35	wgn 5d, V-6	—	8,275	
D35	CS wgn 5d, I-4	2,411	8,140	15,023
D35	CS wgn 5d, V-6	—	8,800	
E35	RS wgn 5d, I-4	2,460	8,677	5,575
E35	RS wgn 5d, V-6	—	9,337	
E67	RS conv cpe, I-4	2,519	13,446	5,826
E67	RS conv cpe, V-6	—	14,106	

Camaro

		Wght	Price	Prod
P87	spt cpe, V-6	3,062	9,995	83,890
P87	spt cpe, V-8	3,181	10,395	
P87	LT cpe, V-6	—	11,517	—
P87	LT cpe, V-8	—	11,917	—
P87/				
Z28	Z28 spt cpe, V-8	3,228	12,819	52,863
P87/				
Z28	IROC-Z spt cpe, V-8	—	13,488	
P67	conv cpe, V-8	—	14,794	263
P67/				
Z28	Z28 conv cpe, V-8	—	17,218	744
P67/				
Z28	IROC-Z conv cpe, V-8	—	17,917	

Corsica

		Wght	Price	Prod
T69	sdn 4d, I-4	2,491	8,995	8,973
T69	sdn 4d, V-6	2,609	9,655	

Beretta

		Wght	Price	Prod
V37	cpe, I-4	2,550	9,555	8,072
V37	cpe, V-6	2,648	10,215	

Celebrity

		Wght	Price	Prod
W27	cpe, I-4	2,685	9,995	18,198
W27	cpe, V-6	2,769	10,605	
W19	sdn 4d, I-4	2,715	10,265	273,864
W19	sdn 4d, V-6	2,799	10,875	
W35	wgn 5d, 2S, I-4	2,847	10,425	33,894
W35	wgn 5d, 2S, V-6	2,931	11,035	
W35/				
AQ4	wgn 5d, 3S, I-4	—	10,672	36,568
W35/				
AQ4	wgn 5d, 3S, V-6	—	11,382	

Caprice

		Wght	Price	Prod
L35	wgn 4d, 3S, V-8	4,114	11,995	11,953
N35	Classic wgn 4d, 3S, V-8	4,125	12,586	28,387
N47	Classic cpe, V-6	3,512	11,392	3,110
N47	Classic cpe, V-8	3,605	11,802	
L69	sdn 4d, V-6	3,510	10,995	56,266
L69	sdn 4d, V-8	3,603	11,435	
N69	Classic sdn 4d, V-6	3,527	11,560	53,802
N69	Classic sdn 4d, V-8	3,620	12,000	
U69	Classic Brgm sdn 4d, V-6	3,576	12,549	51,341
U69	Classic Brgm sdn 4d, V-8	3,669	12,989	
U69/ B6N	Classic LS Brgm sdn 4d, V-6	—	13,805	23,641
U69/ B6N	Classic LS Brgm sdn 4d, V-8	—	14,245	

Monte Carlo

		Wght	Price	Prod
Z37	LS cpe, V-6	3,283	11,306	72,993
Z37	LS cpe, V-8	3,389	11,746	
Z37/ Z65	SS spt cpe, V-8	3,473	13,463	
Z37/ Z16	SS aerocoupe, V-8	3,526	14,838	6,052

Corvette

		Wght	Price	Prod
Y07	htchbk cpe 3d	3,216	27,999	20,007
Y67	conv cpe 2d	3,279	33,172	10,625

Note: Corsica and Beretta were actually early 1988 models, introduced during the 1987 model year.

▲ Like the related Monte Carlo, the El Camino was increasingly at odds with changing buyer tastes and Chevy product plans. And in fact, 1987 would prove to be the last full production year for both.

▲ Whitewall tires and ritzy Silverado trim dress up this 1987 K-10 Stepside 4×4 pickup. The white mirrors in this early-season press shot were changed before sales got underway.

◄ ▲ As ever, Chevy's full-size 1987 trucks had the power and stamina for most every need. The king-size Suburban (*top*) was a popular tow vehicle—especially in Texas, where it now outsold many cars. Outdoor types still liked the K-5 Blazer (*left*) for its roomy comfort and go-anywhere 4×4. Big Chevy pickups lent themselves to all manner of tasks, everything from fire fighting (*above*) to reliable daily transportation in town and country alike.

- **Compact Beretta and Corsica debut**

- **Monte Carlo departs at midyear**

- **Corvette gets "35th Anniversary" edition**

- **New-generation full-size pickups debut**

- **Domestic car sales climb to 1.2 million, but Ford is "USA-1"**

▲ Beretta bowed in March 1987 as an early '88 entry. After a few months, Chevy offered its new coupe with a sporty GTU option package, honoring the Berettas that won the Grand Touring/Under 3-Liter national championship in the International Motor Sports Association. Available only with Beretta's GT options, the GTU included a 2.8-liter V-6, prominent "duck-tail" spoiler, perimeter lower-body skirts, and 60-series performance tires on 16-inch aluminum wheels. Delivered price was around $13,000.

▲ The '88 Beretta GT priced from $11,851. Helped by a long debut model year, the new coupe line scored a healthy 283,170 sales.

▲ Effectively replacing two-door Citations, the Beretta was an underskin twin to Chevy's new 1988 Corsica compact sedan, but measured four inches longer by dint of smoother, well-formed styling. Here, a GT opens up to reveal a spacious, nicely appointed front cabin.

▲ Beretta also offered good rear-seat room for a sporty coupe. Its standard engine was the Cavalier's 90-horsepower 2.0-liter four.

▶ Corsica reached showrooms at the same time as Beretta. Both employed a new front-wheel-drive "L-body" platform that borrowed engineering concepts and many components from the departed X-cars, Cavalier, and GM's three-year-old N-body compacts like Pontiac Grand Am. Shared with Beretta were a 2.0-liter four and optional 2.8 V-6 with five-speed manual or available three-speed automatic transmissions. At $9555 to start, the lone sedan model cost $580 less than a base Beretta, but listed more individual options including heavy-duty and sport suspension packages and sporty LT trim and equipment groups. Corsica did strong business in its extended debut season, drawing a very healthy 300,136 total sales.

◄ Chevy found more ways to improve the C4 Corvette for 1987. New-design 16-inch wheels were evident outside, 17-inch rims were now optional, and both sizes wore Z-rated tires capable of up to 149 mph. Horsepower rose by five, to 245, via a reprofiled camshaft and modifications to the 5.7 V-8's aluminum cylinder heads. Chevy also tweaked the suspension for less dive in hard braking, and fitted thicker brake rotors with stronger twin-piston front calipers. Prices inevitably went up. The convertible (shown) jumped $1648 to $34,820. Just 7407 were built this season.

▲ The Corvette coupe cost $1481 more for '87 at $29,480 to start. Despite this year's worthy improvements, Corvette sales dropped again, this time by 24.7 percent to 22,789, the lowest since 1970.

▲ Like the rest of the C4 Corvette, the cockpit was also being refined as time passed, but the feel was always low-slung and surprisingly cozy despite considerable interior width.

▲ ► Chevy marked another milestone Corvette birthday with a special 35th Anniversary package for 1988 coupes. Listed as RPO Z01 and limited to 2050 installations, the option was easily spotted by its black roof with dark-tinted glass panel and white lower body, wheels, even nameplates. The color-keyed interior featured leather upholstery, power sports seats, automatic climate control, heated rear window and door mirrors, and a premium GM-Delco/Bose sound system—all pretty plush. Interestingly, Corvette production was now approaching a grand total of 900,000 units.

▲ ► After a dozen years, the Camaro Z28 was suddenly gone again. So was the slow-selling LT option that replaced the Berlinetta for '87. The upside was that base models inherited Z28 appearance and several features. IROCs (*convertible above, coupe right*) were now separate models. Both had a standard 5.0-liter/305-cubic-inch V-8 with throttle-body injection and 170 horsepower, up five. Options comprised a 220-hp version and a 230-hp 5.7 V-8, both port-injected. The last was also up five hp and again limited to four-speed automatic; other engines teamed with standard five-speed manual. Camaro sales remained sluggish at 96,275 for the model year, including just 5620 ragtops.

▲ Chevy again dropped full-size coupes for '88, leaving the line with this Caprice Classic wagon and three sedans. Only detail changes occurred. Total sales fell 17.2 percent to 189,208.

▲ A formal-look "landau" roof remained a hallmark of the top-line Caprice Classic Brougham LS sedan. All full-size '88s now included automatic on/off headlamps among several added features.

◄ ► Cavalier lost its hatch coupe for '88, but other models (*left*) gained new lower-body sheetmetal; notchback coupes got a sleeker roofline, too. The sporty Z24 was now available as a convertible (*right*) as well as a coupe, and its V-6 was newly optional for the wagon. Other offerings were trimmed to standard coupe, sedan, and wagon; RS two- and four-doors; and a new VL "Value Leader" coupe priced from just $6995. Mechanical changes were few. Cavalier's sales total dipped another 11 percent to 322,939.

▲ Sportside was the new name for 1988 flared-fender full-size Chevy pickups. Here, a nicely optioned C1500 with 2WD.

▲ Pickup buyers were demanding more interior room and storage, and Chevy obliged for '88 with two-door extended cabs in most configurations. This C1500 model carries the standard Fleetside cargo box.

▲ Full-size Chevy trucks began a new design generation with the 1988 rollout of fully revised light-duty pickups. This illustration highlights stronger frames and safer bodies that could better absorb crash forces. Rust resistance was also improved.

▲ Though most big Chevy trucks still sold with rear-wheel drive in 1988, demand for 4×4s was fast increasing. This photo pairs two of the several available choices, K1500s in Fleetside (*left*) and new Sportside trim.

▲ The Suburban did not move to the new full-size pickup platform for '88, but that didn't dim its appeal. Rear cargo doors (shown) remained a no-cost option to a conventional tailgate.

1988 Engine Availability

Engines	bore × stroke	bhp	availability
I-4, 97.0	3.19 × 3.03	74	S-Nova
I-4, 97.0	3.19 × 3.03	110	O-Nova (twin-cam)
I-4, 121.0	3.50 × 3.15	90	S-Cav, Corsica, Beretta
I-4, 151.0	4.00 × 3.00	98	S-Celeb
V-6, 173.0	3.50 × 2.99	120/135	S-Camaro, Cav Z24; O-Cav wgn, Celeb, Cors, Beretta
V-6, 262.0	4.00 × 3.48	140/145	S-MC, Caprice cpe/sdn
V-8, 305.0	3.74 × 3.48	150/170	S-Cam IROC-Z; O-Cam, MC, Caprice
V-8, 305.0	3.74 × 3.48	180	S-MC SS
V-8, 305.0	3.74 × 3.48	220	O-Camaro IROC-Z
V-8, 307.0	3.80 × 3.38	140	S-Caprice wgn
V-8, 350.0	4.00 × 3.48	230	O-Camaro IROC-Z
Corvette			
V-8, 350.0	4.00 × 3.48	245	S-all

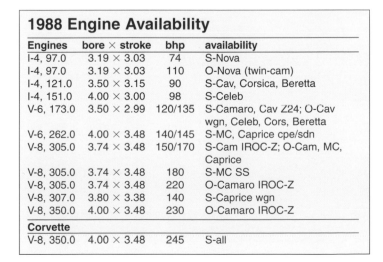

▲ Likewise, the full-size Blazer stayed with its existing design for 1988. Spiffy Silverado trim, shown on this 4×4 model, remained highly popular in all of Chevy's big light-duty truck lines.

◀ ▲ A five-position glass moonroof was a new 1988 option for Chevy's compact S-10 Blazers (*left*), which saw few other changes. S-10 pickups also stayed basically the same, but were now available with functional and appearance options inspired by the fast-growing sport of off-road racing (*above*), where modified S-10s were frequent winners.

▲ Nova added this sporty Twin-Cam sedan for '88 with a 110-hp Toyota DOHC four, firm chassis, bigger tires, and all-disc brakes.

▲ The Isuzu-built Spectrum entered 1988 with detail cosmetic changes and, as on this hatchback, a new Sport dressup option.

▲ Spectrum's Turbo sedan returned from its '87 debut with 110 hp, sporty styling, and a fortified chassis. It sold from $10,665.

▲ Chevy's little Sprints were little changed for '88. This Turbo hatchback remained the quickest, most entertaining model.

▲ The 1988 Celebrity boasted minor internal revisions to both engines. Suspension was retuned on Eurosports like this wagon.

▲ Celebrity sales dropped 28.7 percent for '88 to 258,456. Only 11,909 were coupes like this Eurosport-equipped model.

Model Breakdown

Cavalier		Wght	Price	Prod
C37	cpe 2d, I-4	2,359	8,120	34,470
C69	sdn 4d, I-4	2,363	8,159	107,438
C35	wgn 5d, I-4	2,413	8,490	29,806
C35	wgn 5d, V-6	—	9,150	
C37/				
WV9	VL cpe	—	6,995	43,611
E37	RS cpe, I-4	2,371	9,175	24,359
E69	RS sdn 4d, I-4	2,414	9,385	18,852
F37	Z24 cpe, V-6	2,558	10,725	55,658
F67	Z24 conv cpe, V-8	2,665	15,990	8,745
Camaro				
P87	spt cpe, V-6	3,054	10,995	66,605
P87	spt cpe, V-8	3,228	11,395	
P87/				
Z28	IROC-Z spt cpe, V-8	3,229	13,490	24,050
P87/				
Z08	conv cpe, V-8	3,350	16,225	1,859
P87/				
Z08	IROC-Z conv cpe, V-8	3,352	18,015	3,761
Corsica				
T69	sdn 4d, I-4	2,589	9,555	291,163
T69	sdn 4d, V-6	2,688	10,215	

Beretta		Wght	Price	Prod
V37	cpe, I-4	2,608	10,135	275,098
V37	cpe, V-6	2,707	10,795	
Celebrity				
W27	cpe, I-4	2,727	10,585	11,909
W27	cpe, V-6	2,793	11,195	
W19	sdn 4d, I-4	2,765	11,025	195,205
W19	wgn 4d, V-6	2,833	11,025	
W35/				
B5E	wgn 5d, 2S, I-4	2,903	11,350	23,759
W35/				
B5E	wgn 5d, 2S, V-6	2,970	11,960	
W35/				
AQ4	wgn 5d, 3S, I-4	—	11,590	27,583
W35/				
AQ4	wgn 5d, 3S, V-6	—	12,200	
Caprice				
L69	sdn 4d, V-6	3,540	12,030	60,900
L69	sdn 4d, V-8	3,633	12,470	
N69	Classic sdn 4d, V-6	3,556	12,575	42,292
Caprice				
N69	Classic sdn 4d, V-8	3,649	13,015	42,292

Caprice (continued)		Wght	Price	Prod
U69	Classic Brgm sdn			
	4d, V-6	3,607	13,645	33,685
U69	Classic Brgm sdn			
	4d, V-8	3,700	14,085	
U69/B6N	Classic LS Brgm sdn			
	4d, V-6	—	14,820	21,586
U69/				
B6N	Classic LS Brgm sdn			
	4d, V-8	—	15,260	
N35	Classic wgn			
	4d, 3S, V-8	4,158	14,340	30,645
Monte Carlo				
Z37	LS cpe, V-6	3,212	12,330	13,970
Z37	LS cpe, V-8	3,267	12,770	
Z37/Z65	SS cpe, V-8	3,239	14,320	16,204
Nova				
K19	sdn 4d	2,211	8,795	87,263
K68	htchbk sdn 5d	2,257	9,050	18,570
L19	Twin-cam sdn 4d	—	11,395	3,300
Corvette				
Y07	htchbk cpe 3d	3,229	29,480	15,382
Y67	conv cpe 2d	3,299	34,820	7,407

- **New Geo models replace Nova, Sprint, and Spectrum**

- **High-power Corvette ZR-1 breaks cover**

- **Corsica adds four-door hatchback**

- **Chevy returns to "USA-1" in car sales**

▲ Reversing several years of decline, Camaro sales jumped 15 percent for 1989 to 110,739 units. Base models were renamed RS, but still looked much like the hot IROC-Z (coupe shown). An antitheft system was newly standard across the board.

◄ Camaros were formidable competitors in the IMSA Firestone Firehawk Series, a "showroom stock" class of racing where relatively few modifications were allowed. Rockford, Illinois-based Mecum Racing's entries were race-prepared 1LE-optioned Camaros. Savvy performance-minded Camaro buyers could obtain a 1LE Camaro straight from their Chevrolet dealer by ordering a specific combination of options, which included the G92 axle ratio and air conditioner delete. The package included heavy-duty 1LE disc brakes, engine oil cooler, aluminum driveshaft, special fuel tank baffles, and fog lamp delete. Because the option package was virtually unknown at the time, only 111 1LE-equipped Camaros were ordered in 1989.

▲ The International Race of Champions still pitted the top drivers from all areas of motorsport in identically prepared Camaros—IROC-Zs, of course. Pictured from left to right are Geoff Brabham, Scott Pruett, Terry Labonte, Al Unser Jr., Bill Elliott, Rusty Wallace, A J Foyt, Rick Mears, Dale Earnhardt, Danny Sullivan, Hurley Haywood, and Richard Petty. Terry Labonte was the 1989 IROC Champion.

1989

▲ A "King of the Hill" Corvette was rumored for at least two years before Chevy released details in 1989. A good many changes were made before the ZR-1 went on sale as a 1990 model, shown here in a "cutaway" by famed illustrator Dave Kimble. But the basic concept remained: a sophisticated new high-power V-8 with tremendous performance potential, backed by a suitably upgraded chassis.

▶ The heart of the ZR-1 was its new 5.7-liter LT5 V-8, a racing-inspired all-aluminum engine with dual overhead camshafts, 32 valves, distributor-less coil ignition, forged crankshaft and conrods, sequential port fuel injection and tight 11.25:1 compression. Rated horsepower was a thumping 380.

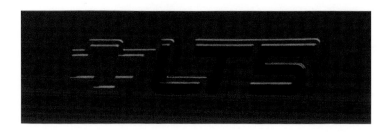

1989 Engine Availability

Engines	bore × stroke	bhp	availability
I-4, 121.0	3.50 × 3.15	90	S-Cav, Corsica, Beretta
I-4, 151.0	4.00 × 3.00	98	S-Celebrity
V-6, 173.0	3.50 × 2.99	125/135	S-Cam RS, Cav Z24; O-Cav wgn, Celeb, Cors, Beretta
V-8, 305.0	3.74 × 3.48	170	S-Cam RS conv, IROC-Z, Caprice; O-Camaro RS
V-8, 305.0	3.74 × 3.48	220/230	O-Camaro IROC-Z
V-8, 307.0	3.80 × 3.38	140	S-Caprice wgn
V-8, 350.0	4.00 × 3.48	230/240	O-Camaro IROC-Z
Corvette			
V-8, 350.0	4.00 × 3.48	240/245	S

◀ ▲ Though all but identical with other Corvettes in front (*above*), the ZR-1 was not only much broader in back (*left*) but sported different taillamps in a convex instead of concave panel. Its only transmission was a new six-speed manual that replaced the never-liked "4+3" unit as a no-charge option for 1989 Corvettes. ZR-1 also came with a new Selective Ride Control system that automatically varied shock-absorber damping and was newly optional for '89 models.

▲ This" family portrait" was taken at Mercury Marine, which built the ZR-1 Corvette's complex new LT5 V-8 under contract. Chevy chose the company for its experience in manufacturing high-quality aluminum engines.

▲ Corvette convertible production jumped 31.6 percent for 1989 despite a 5.6-percent price hike ($1965). All models got standard 17-inch wheels and the previously optional Z52 handling suspension, plus premium gas-charged shocks and quicker steering. Revised top latches enhanced convertible convenience.

▲ Chevy revived a tradition for 1989 by offering a detachable hardtop for the Corvette convertible. Tagged at $2000, the fiberglass cap included a full headliner and electric rear-window defroster. The hardtop was designed to fit previous C4 convertibles, and a fair number of owners likely splurged for one.

◄ ► The 1989 Cavalier lineup evidenced more fine-tuning of models and features. RS models were dropped in favor of a like-named package with similar content as an option for the base sedan, wagon, and coupe. Gas-charged shock absorbers were now standard for the Z24 convertible (*left*) and coupe (*right*), and all '89s adopted rear shoulder belts and a safer self-aligning steering wheel with large crash pad. As with Camaro, Cavalier posted higher sales this model year, up 16.6 percent to 376,626.

▲ Celebrity shed its slow-selling coupe and manual transmission for 1989, but its 4-cyl base engine added 12 horsepower via a number of internal refinements. The Eurosport option continued for the sedan (shown) and wagon. Total sales plunged 21.9 percent.

▲ Chevy expanded its Corsica compacts for 1989 with this four-door hatchback sedan, plus a sporty new LTZ notchback with standard 2.8-liter V-6. Despite these additions, though, Corsica's model-year sales declined a sharp 20.6 percent to 231,167 units.

► With its basic late-'70s design, the full-size Caprice was looking quite dated by 1989, yet model-year sales rose 4.2 percent to 197,044 units. Each one sold was a high profit-earner for Chevy dealers and pure gravy for the division, as tooling was long since paid for. Aiding the sales cause, air conditioning was newly standard for all models, which helped soothe a $2000 hike in base prices, and sedans came with a 5.0-liter V-8 instead of a base 4.3 V-6. This Brougham LS was again the costliest and best-equipped of four Caprice sedans, which also included base, Classic, and Classic Brougham models.

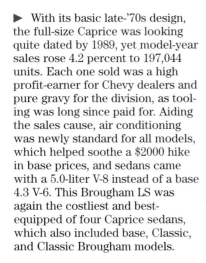

▲ S-10 pickups were always contenders in the annual 1000-mile off-road dash down the rugged Baja California peninsula. Capitalizing on the racing trucks' sucess was 1989's new "Baja" trim package for street S-10s, complete with rollover bar and auxiliary driving lights.

▲ Standard antilock brakes were an added safety feature for 1989 S-10 Blazers and pickups. Continued was "Insta-Trac" 4-wheel drive that allowed "on the fly" shifting between 2-wheel and 4WD High range. This 4×4 S-10 Blazer priced from $13,313.

◀ ▶ Truck lineups had become so broad that not even giant General Motors could afford to redesign all versions at once. This partly explains why Chevy's heavy-duty pickups like the Crew Cab "dooley" (twin rear wheels, *right*) retained old-look bodies for '89. Meantime, light-duty pickups offered a four-lamp front-end treatment as new option, shown (*left*) on a volume-selling ½-ton C1500 Fleetside conventional.

▶ If you're macho enough to drive a 4×4 pickup, why be shy? That may have been the reason for this bigger-than-life bodyside graphic as an option for Chevy's light-duty 4WD '89 pickups. Another extra on this extended-cab K1500 is upmarket LT trim, signified by small emblems on the rear roof posts. These larger 4×4s were usually ordered with a 5.7-liter gas V-8 or, for truly colossal towing torque, available 6.2-liter turbodiesel V-8. All new-wave Chevy pickups had a rather gimmicky dashboard that was roundly criticized by the press.

▲ Chevy's Suburban did see a few more changes for '89, but you'd never know it from outside. Then again, long-term design continuity helped maintain the big wagon's unusually high resale values.

▲ Rear antilock brakes were newly standard for '89 Astro mini-vans, as were power steering, front stabilizer bar, and a 27-gallon fuel tank, all options before. This Astro carries top-line CL trim.

Model Breakdown

Cavalier—355,075 built	Wght	Price	Prod
C37 cpe 2d, I-4	2,418	8,395	—
C69 sdn 4d, I-4	2,423	8,595	—
C35 wgn 5d, I-4	2,478	8,975	—
C35 wgn 5d, V-6	2,566	9,635	—
C37/			
WV9 VL cpe, I-4	—	7,375	—
F37 Z24 cpe, V-6	—	11,325	—
F67 Z24 conv cpe, V-6	2,729	16,615	—
Camaro—100,684 built			
P87 RS htchbk cpe 3d, V-6	3,082	11,495	—
P87 RS htchbk cpe 3d, V-8	3,285	11,895	—
P87/			
Z28 IROC-Z cpe, V-8	3,264	14,145	—
P67 RS conv cpe, V-8	3,116	16,995	—
P67/			
Z28 IROC-Z conv cpe, V-8	—	18,945	—
Corsica—370,741 built (includes Beretta)			
T69 sdn 4d, I-4	2,595	9,985	—

Corsica *(continued)*	Wght	Price	Prod
T69 sdn 4d, V-6	2,690	10,645	—
T68 htchbk sdn 5d, I-4	2,648	10,375`	—
T68 htchbk sdn 5d, V-6	—	11,035	—
Z69 LTZ sdn 4d, V-6	—	12,825	—
Beretta—370,741 built (includes Corsica)			
V37 cpe, I-4	2,631	10,575	—
V37 cpe, V-6	2,727	11,235	—
W37 GT cpe, V-6	—	12,685	—
W37 GTU cpe, V-6	—	—	—
Celebrity—70,365 built			
W19 sdn 4d, I-4	2,751	11,495	—
W19 sdn 4d, V-6	2,819	12,280	—
W35/			
B5E wgn 5d, 2S, I-4	2,888	11,925	—
W35/			
B5E wgn 5d, 2S, V-6	2,928	12,710	—
W35/			
AQ4 wgn 5d, 3S, I-4	—	12,175	—

Celebrity *(continued)*	Wght	Price	Prod
W35/			
AQ4 wgn 5d, 3S, V-6	—	12,960	—
Caprice—162,751 built			
L69 sdn 4d, V-6	3,693	13,865	—
N69 Classic sdn 4d, V-8	—	14,445	—
U69 Classic Brgm sdn			
4d, V-8	—	15,615	—
U69/			
B6N Classic LS Brgm			
sdn 4d, V-8	—	16,835	—
N35 Classic wgn			
4d, 3S, V-8	4,192	15,025	—
Corvette—25,279 built			
Y07 htchbk cpe 3d	3,229	31,545	—
Y67 conv cpe 2d	3,269	36,785	—
NA ZR-1 cpe	—	—	—

1990

- **New midsize Lumina introduced**

- **Corvettes get new dash as ZR-1 enters full production**

- **Larger base engines for many models**

- **Domestic car output plunges to 786,000**

▲ Arriving in spring 1989 as an early 1990 entry, the front-drive Lumina replaced the mid-size Celebrity coupe and sedan while introducing a related front-drive minivan (*at rear*) called APV, for "All-Purpose Vehicle." Celebrity wagons soldiered on.

▲ A 2.8-liter V-6 enlarged to 3.1 liters and upgraded to 135 horsepower was optional for the new Luminas. It replaced the 2.8 as either standard or optional for Beretta, Camaro, Cavalier, Celebrity, and Corsica.

▲ APV excepted, Luminas used the General Motors' W-body platform introduced with the 1988 Buick Regal, Olds Cutlass, and Pontiac Grand Prix. However, they had their own styling, as well as a clean-looking dashboard, shown here with standard instrumentation.

▶ The Lumina coupe and sedan shared not only front-drive powertrains but a 107.5-inch wheelbase platform. Even so, the sedan had its own, more conservative appearance, though it was quite attractive for a four-door. Each body style offered base and sporty Euro trim. As shown on this sedan, both Euro models wore a black-finish instead of bright-metal grille, rear spoiler, lower-profile tires, and 15-inch standard wheels instead of 14s. The 3.1 V-6 was also included— hence "Euro 3.1" badges—as were air conditioning and sportier chassis tuning. Options included alloy wheels and even beefier 16-inch tires. Despite its name, neither Euro was a true "sports sedan" in the BMW mold.

◄ Helped by a long debut model year, Lumina drew a strong 295,007 orders for 1990, though that was not enough to best the Ford Taurus, the new Chevy's main domestic rival. This sporty Euro 3.1 coupe was a spiritual replacement for the rear-drive Monte Carlo, which was dropped after '88. Exactly 33,703 were built. The Euro sedan proved more popular at 86,924. Coupe door handles were concealed in the B-posts.

▲ With its superior aerodynamics, the Lumina coupe was quickly adopted by Chevy racers in NASCAR. This black bullet carried Dale Earnhardt to the 1990 Winston Cup driver's championship.

▲ Lumina coupes claimed a dozen 1990 Winston Cup victories. Darrell Waltrip, always a threat, drove this and similar cars to claim the number-20 spot in the season point standings.

◄▲ Later nicknamed "Dustbuster" for its radically sloped nose (*above*), the Lumina APV also departed from non-GM minivans by using an internal steel "spaceframe" draped with metal and composite-plastic body panels (*left*). Only a single body style and powertrain were offered in uplevel CL (*shown*) and base models.

◄ With the introduction of the front-drive Lumina APV, the older rear-drive Astro became Chevy's "other" minivan for 1990. It wasn't forgotten, though. Added during the year was a roomier EXT body with an extra 10 inches behind the rear wheels. Also new was this "Dutch door" rear-end configuration, with dual center-opening panels that made for easier access to the cargo bay than a conventional drop-down tailgate. In addition, four-wheel antilock brakes became standard for all 1990 Astros, and a new 4-wheel-drive option automatically transferred power to the front wheels if the rears started to spin.

307

▲ Beretta was chosen as the pace car for the 1990 Indy 500, and Chevy offered a special Indy package for GT coupes. This ad details features that included special graphics, colors, and wheels.

▲ The actual Beretta pace car was a special yellow convertible. A showroom version (*foreground*) was announced, but was left stillborn by unexpected development problems.

◄► Chevy was serious enough about the ragtop Beretta to provide the press with the usual "glamour" shots like these. The new convertible was to replace the drop-top Cavalier as the most affordable open-air Chevy, but plans were changed when the Beretta prototype was judged unsuitable. The bulky upper "hoop" was used for structural strength and to preserve door handles inherited from the parent Beretta coupe.

◄▲ Replacing GTU as 1990's sportiest Beretta coupe, the new GTZ packed a high-tune 180-horsepower 2.3-liter twincam four.

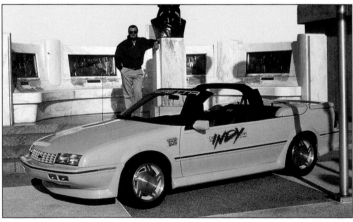

▲ Jim Perkins returned to Chevrolet in 1989 as division chief after 4 ½ years as senior vice president for Toyota's Lexus. Here he poses with the 1990 Indy 500 Beretta convertible pace car.

1990 Engine Availability

Engines	bore × stroke	bhp	availability
I-4, 133.0	3.50 × 3.46	95	S-Cav, Corsica, Beretta
I-4, 138.0	3.63 × 3.35	180	S-Beretta GTZ
I-4, 151.0	4.00 × 3.00	110	S-Celebrity wgn, Lumina
V-6, 191.0	3.50 × 3.31	135	S-Cav Z24, Beretta GT; O-Beretta, Cav wgn, Celeb wgn, Corsica, Lumina
V-6, 191.0	3.50 × 3.31	144	S-Camaro
V-8, 305.0	3.74 × 3.48	170	S-Camaro RS conv, Caprice; O-Camaro
V-8, 305.0	3.74 × 3.48	220	S-IROC-Z; O-Camaro RS cpe
V-8, 307.0	3.80 × 3.38	140	S-Caprice wgn
V-8, 350.0	4.00 × 3.48	230	O-IROC-Z
Corvette			
V-8, 350.0	4.00 × 3.48	245	S-base models
V-8, 350.0	3.90 × 3.66	375	S-ZR-1

◀ Corvette's cockpit became even more driver-focused for 1990 with this sweeping new dashboard. Improved ergonomics was the theme, with somewhat better placed switches and more legible instruments comprising a large digital speedometer, and analog dials for everything else. Like many other 1990 Chevys, the 'Vette offered extra safety in a standard driver's airbag mounted in the steering wheel. The new 'Vette dash was the key factor in the one-year delay of the ultra-performance ZR-1 coupe, of which 3049 were built for the model year. At a stiff $58,995, the ZR-1 cost $27,016 more than the regular coupe.

◀▶ The 1990 Corvette coupe (*left*) and convertible (*with hardtop, right*) looked little different outside, but boasted standard 17-inch wheels, as well as a new-design antilock brake system and improved cooling for their 245-hp 5.7 pushrod V-8. Total 'Vette sales were down 7.5 percent for the model year to 23,376, reflecting the start of another economic recession. As usual, the standard coupe outsold the ragtop, this year by a margin of 5607 units.

▲▶ New graphics and 16-inch alloy wheels spruced up the '90 Camaro IROC-Z, which also received a limited-slip differential. All Camaros added a driver's airbag. The base RS models switched to Chevy's new 3.1-liter V-6. Sales plunged 65.2 percent for the model year, though, to 34,986, the worst in Camaro history. The boxy Caprice (*right*) was set to be redesigned after '90. Sales decreased 44 percent as buyers awaited the new look.

▲ Designed at GM's recently opened Advance Concepts Center near Los Angeles, the 1990 California Camaro concept provided a slightly exaggerated preview of Chevy's next-generation ponycar styling. The swoopy, rounded shape was a big hit with auto show crowds.

▲ A blast from the past emerged as the new 454 SS for 1990. This time it was a short-box C1500 truck with special trim, sport suspension, and many features, including 230 big-block horses. Priced from just $18,295, the new pavement-pounding pickup appealed to 13,748 buyers.

▲ The big K1500 Blazer SUV saw no design change for 1990, but many previous options were now standard equipment.

▲ Chevy again offered many big 4×4 pickups in 1990. Here, a Sportside regular-cab (*right*) and Fleetside extended-cab square off.

▶ This big Bison conventional was one of many heavy-duty ("Class 8") Chevy truck models listed for 1990.

Model Breakdown

Cavalier	Wght	Price	Prod
C37 RS cpe, I-4	2,291	9,065	35,121
C69 RS sdn 4d, I-4	2,295	9,265	64,405
C35 RS wgn, I-4	2,295	10,270	13,812
C37/WV9 VL cpe, I-4	2,291	7,995	11,476
C69/WV9 VL sdn 4d, I-4	2,291	8,270	39,429
C35/WV9 VL wgn, I-4	2,295	9,225	8,234
F37 Z24 cpe, V-6	2,489	12,050	38,474
Total Cavalier			210,951
Camaro			
P87 RS cpe, V-6	2,975	10,995 ⌉	28,750
P87 RS cpe, V-8	3,142	11,345 ⌋	
P67 RS conv, V-8	3,270	16,880	729
P87 Z28 cpe, V-8	3,149	14,555	4,213
P67 Z28 conv, V-8	3,272	20,195	1,294
Total Camaro			34,986
Corsica			
T69 I-4/V-6			
T69 sdn, I-4	2,520	9,495 ⌉	170,545
T69 sdn, V-6	2,525	10,180 ⌋	

Corsica continuted	Wght	Price	Prod
T68 htchbk sdn 4d, I-4	2,540	9,895 ⌉	13,001
T68 htchbk sdn 4d, V-6	2,545	10,580 ⌋	
Z69 LTZ sdn, V-6	2,545	12,795	10,975
Total Corsica			194,521
Beretta			
V37 cpe, I-4	2,520	10,320 ⌉	46,082
V37 cpe, V-6	—	11,005 ⌋	
W37 GT cpe, V-6	2,676	12,500	35,785
W37 Indy GT cpe, V-6	—	—	4,615
W37 GTZ cpe, V-6	—	13,750	13,239
Total Beretta			99,721
Celebrity			
W35 wag 6P, V-6	2,809	12,395 ⌉	29,205
W35 wag 8P, V-6	—	12,645 ⌋	
Lumina			
L27 cpe, I-4	3,111	12,670	10,209
L69 sdn 4d, I-4	3,122	12,870	164,171
N27/ZV8 Euro cpe, V-6	—	14,795	33,703
N69/ZV8 Euro sdn 4d, V-6	—	14,240	86,924
Total Lumina			295,007

Caprice	Wght	Price	Prod
L69 sdn 4d, V-8	3,693	16,515	53,276
N69 Classic sdn 4d, V-8	—	18,470	15,679
U69 Classic Brgm sdn 4d, V-8	—	16,325	16,291
U69/B6N Classic LS Brgm sdn 4d, V-8	—	17,525	11,977
N35 Classic wgn, V-8	4,041	15,725	12,305
Total Caprice			109,528
Corvette			
V07 htchbk cpe, V-8	3,255	31,979	12,967
Y67 conv, V-8	3,301	37,264	7,630
Z07 ZR-1 cpe, V-8	3,479	58,995	3,049
Total Corvette			23,646

Note: No Cavalier C67 conv or Z34 Lumina in 1990

1991

NINETEEN NINETY-ONE   NINETEEN NINETY-ONE   NINETEEN NINETY-ONE   NINETEEN NINET

- **Caprice gets its first restyle in 14 years**

- **A minor facelift freshens Corvettes**

- **Lumina adds sporty Z34 coupe**

- **Domestic car sales rebound to nearly 936,000 units**

▲ Caprice was dramatically different for 1991, thanks to a thorough reworking of its basic 1977 design. The most obvious difference was a new "aero-style" body atop a reworked chassis with unchanged 115.9-inch wheelbase. Models were reduced to the base-trim wagon and Classic sedan seen here, plus base sedan. Buyers had a luke-warm response, as sales dipped 4.8 percent to 104,297 units.

▲ Not a line was shared between the '91 Caprice (*left*) and its 1977-90 predecessor, as this rear-flank view testifies. The new styling drew mixed reactions. Buyers seemed to like it well enough, but many journalists didn't, some terming it whale-like—or worse.

▲ The '91 Caprice featured a new, more "ergonomic" dashboard with simple instruments and handy controls. A large steering-wheel boss concealed a standard airbag, increasingly preferred over motorized seat belts for satisfying the government's requirement for "passive restraints."

▲ Though Chevy didn't break out 1991 Caprice sales figures, the Classic sedan (shown) was likely the most popular of the three models. The new B-body added two inches to overall length and width and about 200 pounds, which made a little more work for the 5.0-liter 170-horsepower V-8, which remained the only engine available.

▶ Fleet business had been a big chunk of Caprice sales for years, and Chevy didn't forget that in planning the redesigned '91 models. Of prime importance was a new Police Package, shown in this press photo with a "civilian" Classic sedan. Consumer Guide®, among many, lauded the newly standard four-wheel antilock brakes, but they bothered some law-enforcement officers, prompting Chevy to stage an educational campaign for them about the value of ABS.

311

▲ A subtle facelift gave a slightly sleeker look to all 1991 Corvettes. Total sales declined again, this time by 12.3 percent to 20,729. The convertible (shown) accounted for slightly more than a quarter of model-year volume with a modest 5762 orders.

▲ Corvette's 1991 facelift comprised a convex back panel and square taillights *a la* ZR-1; a slightly lower, smoother nose; and front-fender "strakes" instead of functional twin "gills." The curious result was that the rare, pricey ZR-1 was tough to distinguish from the standard coupe at a distance apart from its three-inch-wider rear haunches. Power ratings were unchanged.

▶ Long before the ZR-1, aftermarket tuner and former race driver Reeves Callaway conceived his own "super 'Vette" with a twin-turbo version of the veteran pushrod 5.7 V-8. Launched in 1986, his conversion, sold through Chevy dealers as a regular "option," also boasted unique styling and many functional upgrades. The 390-hp 1991 Callaway (shown) wasn't cheap at over $71,000, but it could blast through the quarter-mile in 13.4 seconds at 107.5 mph.

▲ Though in-plant PR photos were no longer in vogue, Chevy publicists wanted to re-emphasize the high-tech nature of the Bowling Green, Kentucky Corvette factory, hence this scene of a '91 coupe body about to meet its aluminum-intensive chassis.

▲ The racy Callaway Speedster bowed in 1991. The twin turbo V-8 pushed the car from 0 to 60 mph in 4.2 seconds.

▲ Callaway built only 12 individualized Speedsters at his Connecticut shop. Each customer chose the color.

▲ A revamped interior with driver's airbag was the main 1991 news for Beretta, here in GT trim with new "monochromatic" exterior. The even sportier GTZ returned with a 3.1 V-6 as a new option to the standard 2.3-liter "Quad 4" engine.

▲ Cavalier got another styling update for '91, plus revised interior. This RS was the sportier of two available wagon models.

▲ Total Cavalier sales rose 5.1 percent for 1991, helped by the midyear return of the RS convertible. Here, the RS sedan.

▲ The hottest '91 Camaros were again Z28s, as Chevy lost rights to the IROC name when the racing series turned to another brand. The revived Z (*left*) and base RS coupe and convertible were lightly restyled at each end; Zs wore a tall new spoiler and 16-inch wheels.

▲ With various state Highway Patrols running souped up Ford Mustangs, Chevy countered with a Police Package Camaro, here fronting a '91 Z28 coupe. Production is unknown but was probably very low—which must have pleased habitual speeders.

1991 Engine Availability

Engines	bore × stroke	bhp	availability
I-4, 133.0	3.50 × 3.46	95	S-Cav, Corsica, Beretta
I-4, 138.0	3.63 × 3.35	180	S-Beretta GTZ
I-4, 151.0	4.00 × 3.00	110	S-Lumina
V-6, 191.0	3.50 × 3.31	140	S-Cav Z24, Beretta GT, Camaro; O-Beretta, Cav wgn, Corsica, Lumina
V-6, 207.0	3.63 × 3.31	210	S-Lumina Z34
V-8, 305.0	3.74 × 3.48	170	S-Camaro RS conv, Caprice; O-Camaro
V-8, 305.0	3.74 × 3.48	230	S-Camaro Z28
V-8, 350.0	4.00 × 3.48	245	O-Camaro Z28 Corvette
V-8, 350.0	4.00 × 3.48	245	S-base models
V-8, 350.0	3.90 × 3.66	375	S-ZR-1

▲ The '91 Camaros, including this RS convertible, bowed in early 1990, which meant extra selling months. As a result, model-year sales almost doubled to just over 100,000 units.

313

◄▲► Lumina's big news for 1991 was the addition of a sporty Z34 coupe, named for its new 3.4-liter V-6 with dual overhead camshafts. A louvered hood, "ground effects" lower-body add-ons, subtle spoiler, and standard 16-inch wheels distinguished it from other models (*above and right*). The interior (*left*) featured unique sport front bucket seats and analog instruments, including tachometer.

◄► Suggesting that Chevy was mulling a new Monte Carlo was this like-named 1991 concept coupe. Based on the front-drive Lumina, it was fully drivable. Among its features: 18-inch wheels, Corvette-style clamshell hood, solar-reflecting glass windshield and rear window, and very ovoid styling.

Model Breakdown

Cavalier	Wght	Price	Prod
C37/WV9 VL cpe, I-4	2,480	7,577	
C37 RS cpe 2d, I-4	2,465	8,620	171,759
F37 Z24 cpe, V-6	2,688	11,505	
C67 RS conv, V-6	2,753	15,214	5,882
C69WV9 VL sdn 4d, I4	2,491	8,270	
C69 RS sdn 4d, I-4	2,444	9,265	125,713
C35/WV9 VL wag	2,587	9,225	
C35 RS wag	2,587	10,270	23,493
Total Cavalier			326,847
Camaro			
P87 RS cpe, V-6	3,103	12,180	
P87 RS cpe, V-8	3,263	12,530	92,306
P87 Z28 cpe, V-8	3,319	15,455	
P67 RS conv, V-6	3,203	17,960	
P67 RS conv, V-8	3,363	18,310	8,532
P67 Z28 conv, V-8	3,400	20,815	

Camaro *(continued)*	Wght	Price	Prod
Total Camaro			100,838
Corsica			
T69 sdn 4d, I-4	2,638	10,070	
T69 sdn 4d, V-6	2,742	10,755	187,981
T68 htchbk sdn 4d, I-4	2,706	10,745	
T68 htchbk sdn 4d, V-6	2,810	11,430	2,525
Total Corsica			190,506
Beretta			
V37 cpe, I-4	2,649	10,365	
V37 cpe, V-6	2,749	11,050	
W37 GT cpe, V-6	2,797	13,150	69,868
Z37 GTZ cpe, I-4	2,795	14,550	
Lumina			
L27 cpe, I-4	3,111	12,670	
L27 cpe, V-6	3,239	13,330	
N27 Euro cpe, V-6	3,239	14,795	36,345
P27 Z34 cpe, V-6	3,374	17,275	

Lumina *(continued)*	Wght	Price	Prod
L69 sdn 4d, I-4	3,192	12,870	
L69 sdn 4d, V-6	3,320	13,530	159,482
N69 Euro sdn 4d, V-6	3,321	14,995	
Total Lumina			195,827
Caprice			
L19 sdn 4d, V-8	3,907	16,615	
N19 Classic sdn, V-8	3,951	18,470	89,297
L35 wag, V-8	4,354	17,875	15,000
Total Caprice			104,297
Corvette			
Y07 htchbk cpe, V-8	3,223	32,455	12,923
Z07 ZR1 htchbk cpe, V-8	3,503	64,138	2,044
Y67 conv, V-8	3,263	38,770	5,762
Total Corvette			20,729

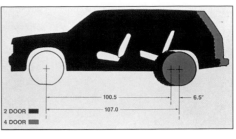

▲ Capitalizing on the popularity of the S-10 Blazer, Chevy added a four-door body style during 1990 as an early '91 debut. This dimensional comparison highlights the four-door's longer wheelbase and extra rear-seat room over the familiar two-door.

▲ The four-door S-10 Blazer (*foreground*) poses with its two-door sibling and their parent pickup in a press photo highlighting 1991 appearance changes, which were minor, as usual. The four-door was a very timely newcomer, arriving just months ahead of Ford's similar new Explorer SUV, which would soon reign as sales king among compact SUVs.

▲ Again aimed at fans of off-road racing in 1991 was the "Baja" cosmetic and suspension package for 4WD S-10 pickups. Note front "push bar" and rear "roller" bar.

▲ Introduced for 1990 and back for '91 was the full-size "W/T" or "Work Truck," a low-cost, no-frills C1500 Fleetside aimed at budget-minded light-duty users.

▲ The big 454 SS pickup had an improved big-block V-8 for '91 with 255 hp, up 20, and even more thumping torque. Even so, sales plunged to only about 1000 units.

▲ Big Chevy trucks still offered a torquey diesel V-8 option for '91. Many buyers chose it for towing in heavier-duty models like this "dooley" extended-cab.

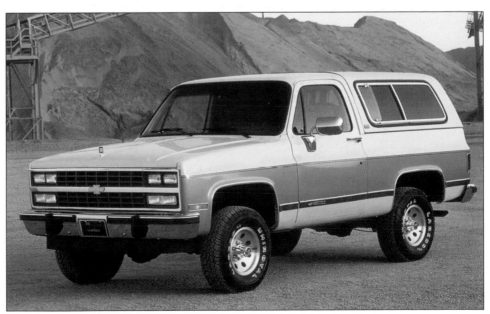

▲▶ Still consistently popular despite few year-to-year changes, the Suburban (*above*) and full-size Blazer (*right*) remained big, brawny sport-utility vehicles, yet could be optioned up to a surprising degree of luxury. Blazer offered two V-8s: 5.7-liter gasoline and optional 6.2-liter diesel. Suburban listed the same, plus the "Mark IV" 454 big block. New for '91 Suburbans was an advanced four-speed automatic transmission as standard equipment. Blazer continued with an older three-speed unit. As ever, each truck came in rear-drive and 4WD versions.

1992

- Corvette production passes 1 million

- New LT1 V-8 ups standard 'Vette power

- Camaro turns 25

- Lumina adds sporty Euro 3.4 sedan option

- Domestic car sales drop back to 833,655 units

▲ Though a more potent pushrod V-8 put the 1992 spotlight on standard Corvettes, all models offered added dynamic safety by adopting Acceleration Slip Regulation (ASR), which automatically applied the brakes and/or throttled back power to inhibit skidding.

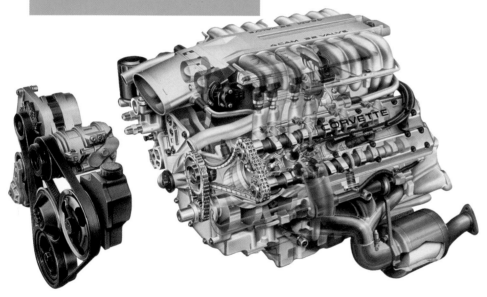

◄ Corvette's stalwart pushrod 5.7-liter V-8 was thoroughly reworked for 1992, giving standard models near ZR-1 performance. Horsepower climbed by 55 to 300 for the new LT1 engine, which also revved faster and higher than the predecessor L98.

▲ A big price gap still existed between the standard Corvette coupe (shown) and the ZR-1: this year a massive $31,683. That may be why ZR-1 sales plummeted 75 percent to just 502 units.

▲ Reengineered from top to bottom and making considerable use of lighter-weight components, the LT1 engine had slightly less torque than the L98 it replaced, and it peaked 800 rpm higher (at 4000). Even so, a standard '92 'Vette could run 0-60 mph in about 5.4 seconds. With that, some critics felt it rendered the costly ZR-1 almost superfluous.

▲ Corvette convertible production rose by 113 units from '91 to '92, but America's sports car suffered another fractional sales setback this year, declining 1.2 percent to 20,479 units. The ragtop now started at $40,145, a hefty $1375 hike from the previous year.

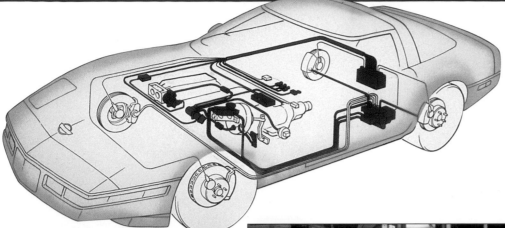

◄ This schematic shows the components of Corvette's new ASR antiskid system. Developed with Bosch of Germany, it used data from the antilock brake system's wheel-speed sensors to determine if one or more wheels were spinning faster than the others. In that event, an engine/chassis computer would brake the wheels involved and/or throttle back power until all wheels again rotated at the same rate. If desired, though, ASR could be switched off.

▲ Corvette engineer Zora Arkus-Duntov (*left*) and his successor, Dave McClellan, are all smiles over the 1-millionth Corvette.

▲▼ America's sports car passed a historic milestone on July 2, 1992, as Corvette number 1-million left the Bowling Green line (*above*). Fittingly, it was finished in Polo White with a Sportsman Red interior just like the very first '53 (*below*).

▲ Strictly for fun, Chevy commissioned Ryan Falconer Industries to build this aluminum V-12 based on the ZR-1 V-8.

▲ The huge 9.9-liter/601-cid Falconer made 580 hp in a long-nose ZR-1 rebadged ZR-12. Chevy called it Conan, as in the Barbarian. It was, with an 11.6-second 133-mph quarter-mile and 211-mph top speed.

▲▶ The rejuvenated full-size Chevy was little changed outside for '92, but a 5.7-liter V-8 option with 180 hp debuted for the Caprice wagon (*above*). Base, Classic (*right*), and LTZ sedans returned. The LTZ was actually a package option that included a heavy-duty frame and brakes, sports suspension, broad 235/70VR15 Goodyear Eagle performance tires, limited-slip differential, and analog engine gauges (but no tach) combined with the normal digital speedometer. Though fresh off being named *Motor Trend*'s '91 Car of the Year, the LTZ did nothing to help Caprice sales, which plunged nearly 50 percent. One likely factor in the decline was the advent of similar B-body models at sister GM divisions.

▲ With front "passive" restraints now required for all cars, automakers rushed to replace motorized seat belts with airbags, which buyers much preferred. Chevy issued these drawings to highlight the added safety of the "exploding" cushions, but emphasized that drivers were dummies if they didn't still buckle up, too.

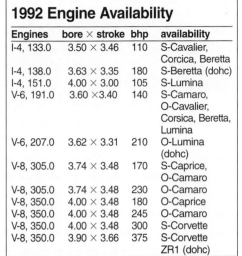

1992 Engine Availability

Engines	bore × stroke	bhp	availability
I-4, 133.0	3.50 × 3.46	110	S-Cavalier, Corcica, Beretta
I-4, 138.0	3.63 × 3.35	180	S-Beretta (dohc)
I-4, 151.0	4.00 × 3.00	105	S-Lumina
V-6, 191.0	3.60 ×3.40	140	S-Camaro, O-Cavalier, Corsica, Beretta, Lumina
V-6, 207.0	3.62 × 3.31	210	O-Lumina (dohc)
V-8, 305.0	3.74 × 3.48	170	S-Caprice, O-Camaro
V-8, 305.0	3.74 × 3.48	230	O-Camaro
V-8, 350.0	4.00 × 3.48	180	O-Caprice
V-8, 350.0	4.00 × 3.48	245	O-Camaro
V-8, 350.0	4.00 × 3.48	300	S-Corvette
V-8, 350.0	3.90 × 3.66	375	S-Corvette ZR1 (dohc)

▲ Hood/decklid stripes, body-color grille, and black headlamp nacelles characterized the Heritage Edition package that marked Camaro's 25th birthday. Here it graces a ragtop RS.

◄▲ Apart from the Heritage Edition birthday option, Camaro was a near-rerun for '92, mainly because a new generation was waiting in the wings. It was sorely needed, as suggested by the ponycar's 30.6-percent decline in total sales this model year. Camaro sales were down to 70,008 units.

▲ The Lumina sedan added a $1885 Euro 3.4 option for '92, a kind of four-door Z34. It had a bit less power, though, and came only with automatic transmission.

▲ The Z34 coupe returned with standard antilock brakes, which were a new option for other '92 Luminas. Five-speed manual shift was again standard.

▲ Lumina (Euro 3.1 coupe shown) posted 12-percent-higher sales for '92, one of the few Chevy car lines to manage a year-over-year increase this season.

▲ Cavaliers got standard ABS for '92, plus a new 110 hp 2.2-liter base 4-cyl. The top-line Z24 convertible (shown) and coupe again came only with a 3.1 V-6 making 140 hp.

▲ A new 165-hp 3.8-liter V-6 option provided welcome extra performance in 1992 Lumina APV minivans. Also new were standard antilock brakes and larger tires.

▲ The Lumina APV cargo van was the '90s equivalent of Chevy's old Panel Delivery models. It was not very popular, though. Most buyers preferred big brother Astro.

▲ The Sizighi concept, based on the Lumina minivan, showed Chevy's latest minivan ideas, including slit-style auxiliary lighting.

▲ Chevy outfitted a C1500 Fleetside pickup as a whimsical "Chuck Wagon," complete with a built-in stove, for 1992 auto shows.

▲ Standard four-wheel antilock brakes and 4WD with new electronic shift control headed a short list of major changes for 1992 S-10 Blazers (four-door shown).

▲ Again catering to those who needed maximum hauling space in a compact pick-up was this 1992 S-10 Long Bed, available only with 2-wheel drive.

▲ A revised suspension and more comfort and convenience options updated Chevy's full-size 1992 G-Series vans. This one shows off the available dual side cargo doors.

▲ The big Suburban finally adopted Chevy's latest big-pickup chassis and styling for '92. Here, the ½-ton 2WD C1500 version.

▲ Chevy's big '92 Crew Cabs also switched to the basic '88 light-duty design. This 1-ton K3500 4×4 has "Dooley" rear wheels.

Model Breakdown

Cavalier	Wght	Price	Prod
C37/WV9 VL cpe, I-4	2,509	8,899	126,117
C37 RS cpe, I-4	2,520	9,999	
F37 Z24 cpe, V-6	2,689	12,995	
F67 Z24 conv, V-6	2,826	18,305	9,045
C69/WV9 VL sdn 4d, I-4	2,520	8,999	70,786
C69 RS sdn 4d, I-4	2,520	10,199	
C35/WV9 VL wgn, I-4	2,617	10,099	19,685
C35 RS wgn, I-4	2,617	11,199	
Total Cavalier			225,633
Camaro			
P87 RS cpe, V-6	3,103	12,075	66,191
P87/Z28 Z28 cpe, V-8	3,319	16,055	

Camaro *(continued)*	Wght	Price	Prod
P67 RS conv, V-6	3,203	18,055	3,816
P67/Z28 Z28 conv, V-8	3,400	21,500	
Total Camaro			70,007
Corsica			
T69 LT sdn 4d, I-4	2,638	10,999	144,833
Beretta			
V37 cpe, I-4	2,649	10,999	52,451
W37 GT cpe, V-6	2,697	12,575	
Z37 GTZ cpe, I-4	2,795	15,590	
Lumina			
L27 cpe, I-4	3,115	13,200	38,037
N27 Euro cpe, V-6	3,256	15,600	
P27 Z34 cpe, V-6	3,447	18,400	

Lumina *(continued)*	Wght	Price	Prod
L69 sdn 4d, I-4	3,220	13,400	198,269
N69 Euro sdn 4d, V-6	3,361	15,800	
Total Lumina			236,306
Caprice			
L19 sdn 4d, V-8	3,907	17,300	103,381
N19 Classis sdn 4d, V-8	3,951	19,300	
N19/B4U Classic			
LTZ sdn 4d, V-8	4,080	20,125	
L35 wgn, V-8	4,354	18,700	13,400
Total Caprice			116,781
Corvette			
Y07 htchbk cpe 3d, V-8	3,223	33,635	14,102
Z07 ZR1 cpe, V-8	3,503	63,318	502
Y67 conv, V-8	3,269	40,145	5,875
Total Corvette			20,428

1993

- **All-new fourth-generation Camaro debuts, paces Indy 500**

- **Corvette observes 40 years with special Anniversary Package**

- **Caprice spruces up with a "taillift"**

- **Domestic model-year car sales slip again to 836,655 units.**

▲ Cavalier convertibles, both RS (shown) and Z24, got a glass rear window for 1993, which improved rear visibility with the top up. Another change was optional availability of the Z24's 3.1 V-6 for all RS models, not just the wagon. Despite few other changes, sales of Chevy's domestic subcompact turned up again, rising 11.1 percent for the model year, a fine showing considering that the basic J-body design had been around a lengthy 12 years.

▲ Caprice gained more conventional rear-quarter styling for '93. The top-line sedan (shown) was rebadged Classic LS.

▲ Electronic shift control for the optional automatic transmission was a new standard item on the '93 Lumina Z34 coupe.

▲ Still aggressively courting law-enforcement agencies, Chevy offered a special Police Package for the Lumina sedan (*above*) as well as for the big Caprice (*top*). As ever, though, officers greatly preferred the full-size Chevy for its superior strength, V-8 speed, roomier interior, and more familiar rear-wheel-drive handling traits. Even with a tuned engine and uprated chassis, the front-drive Lumina just wasn't in the same league, they said.

▲ If not so good for police work, the Lumina could be a dandy new-wave taxi. Chevy had a special package for that, too.

▲ The fully redesigned 1993 Camaro kept to a 101-inch wheelbase, but front lower A-arms returned and four-wheel antilock brakes debuted as standard equipment. Base models (no longer called RS) came with a new 3.4-liter pushrod V-6 with 160 horsepower, up 20 from the previous 3.1. Z28s got a version of the LT1 Corvette engine with 275 hp, up 30. It all added up to a more dynamically capable Camaro.

▲ Camaro's 1993 styling was fresh, yet bore many familiar cues as a muted version of the 1990 California Camaro concept theme. The new lines added only a half inch to length, but height gained 1 inch, width nearly 2 inches. Curb weight rose about 150 pounds despite the adoption of dent-resistant plasticlike composite materials for the front and rear ends, front fenders, door skins, roof, and rear hatch. This view of the Z28 coupe highlights the new design's pronounced wedge profile with sharply upswept beltline.

▲ Despite the new '93 body, the Camaro cockpit was as snug and low-slung as ever—arguably more so, thanks to a more steeply raked windshield.

▲ The new '93 Camaro dashboard earned plaudits for its more logical layout and easy-reach knobs and switches. Safety mavens hailed the newly standard dual front airbags.

▲ The new-generation Camaro was limited to a pair of coupes for the '93 model year. This base model came only with the new 3.4-liter version of Chevy's 1980-vintage 60-degree V-6.

▲ The Z28 again wore a standard rear spoiler, albeit a much lower, more smoothly integrated affair. Alas, total 1993 Camaro sales were the lowest in history at 40,224.

▶ Master "cutaway" artist Dave Kimble rendered this "inside look" at the 1993 Z28 coupe. Engines again mounted fairly far back in the chassis.

▲ The Z28's standard LT1 V-8 was even better for 1993, thanks to a new, more-precise sequential fuel-injection system and newly computerized ignition timing.

▲ Standard for '93 Camaros was this six-speed Borg-Warner gearbox, similar to Corvette's. The optional automatic was a new, electronically controlled four-speed.

▲ Camaro's new 3.4-liter base V-6 was essentially a bored-out 3.1 with higher compression and, like the V-8, sequential-port fuel injection.

◀ The new Camaro was a logical choice for 1993 Indianapolis 500 pace car. The actual pace cars—three were built—were Z28s outfitted with a Corvette automatic transmission, roll bar, strobe lights, safety harness, fire extinguisher, and special upholstery. Chevy offered 645 limited edition replicas for retail sale. Displaying a sense of history, Chevy PR photographers posed the '93 Camaro pace car with (background, from left) its '67, '69, and '82 forerunners.

▲ Internal improvements to the LT5 V-8 powerplant gave the 1993 Corvette ZR-1 an even 400 hp, plus 385 pound-feet of torque, up 15 from 1992. Despite these performance improvements, total sales for the pricey ZR-1 declined to just 448 units.

▲ This special emblem and Ruby Red paint were part of 1993's optional $1455 Corvette 40th Anniversary Package. Available for all three models, it also included unique wheel hubs and interior trim.

▲ A nifty new optional gimmick for any '93 Corvette was the Passive Keyless Entry System. This generated a low-level magnetic field that surrounded the car out to a few feet. As one carrying the fob left or approached, and passed through the field, the doors would lock or unlock automatically.

▲▼ Though not evident on this convertible (top and below), standard '93 Corvettes got inch-narrower front wheels and tires and slightly wider rear rubber for the sake of improved cornering. Cockpit (above) was untouched, but showed slightly better materials and workmanship than before.

1993 Engine Availability

Engines	bore × stroke	bhp	availability
I-4, 133.0	3.50 × 3.46	110	S-Cavalier, Corsica, Beretta, Lumina
I-4, 138.0	3.63 × 3.35	175	O-Beretta (dohc)
V-6, 191.0	3.60 × 3.40	140	O-Cavalier, Corsica, Beretta, Lumina
V-6, 207.0	3.62 × 3.31	160	S-Camaro
V-6, 207.0	3.62 × 3.31	210	O-Lumina (dohc)
V-8, 305.0	3.74 × 3.48	170	S-Caprice
V-8, 350.0	4.00 × 3.48	180	O-Caprice
V-8, 350.0	4.00 × 3.48	275	O-Camaro
V-8, 350.0	4.00 × 3.48	300	S-Corvette
V-8, 350.0	3.90 × 3.66	405	O-Corvette ZR1 (dohc)

◄ Priced at $34,595, an impressive 15,520 Corvette coupes left the showroom floors in 1993, up 10 percent from the prior year. Overall Corvette sales increased for the first time in four years. Perhaps the attention given to the 40th anniversary of America's sports car aided those sales. The base LT1 5.7-liter V-8 engine gained 10 pound-feet of torque for 1993, raising the total to 340. The slightly revised engine also ran more smoothly.

◄ A chrome grille was newly standard for all 1993 S-10 Blazers, including this four-door. Chevy's compact SUVs also received several minor trim and features changes, mostly to the interior. As in '92, the smaller Blazers offered two 4.3-liter V-6s: a 160-hp version with manual shift or an "enhanced" 200-hp unit with automatic transmission. A new vibration-quelling "balancer" shaft made both engines somewhat smoother for '93. Continued were two 4WD systems: "Insta-Trac" with conventional transfer-case lever, and an electronically controlled version with a dashboard button for shifting in and out of 4WD modes.

▲ The C1500 was the official truck of the 1993 Indy 500. Chevy offered an option package with the same paint scheme as the Camaro pace car.

▲ A year after taking on the full-size pickup platform, Chevy couldn't keep up with demand for its K1500 Blazer.

Model Breakdown

Cavalier	Wght	Price	Prod
C37WV9 VL cpe, I-4	2,509	8,520	
C37 RS cpe, I-4	2,515	9,520	127,229
F37 Z24 cpe, V-6	2,695	12,500	
C67 RS conv, I-4	2,678	15,395	
F67 Z24 conv, V-6	2,832	18,305	8,609
C69/WV9 VL sdn 4d, I-4	2,520	8,620	
C69 RS sdn 4d, I-4	2,526	9,620	96,545
C35/WV9 VL wag, I-4	2,623	9,735	
C35 RS wag, I-4	2,623	10,785	19,207
Total Cavalier			251,590
Camaro			
P87 cpe, V-6	3,241	13,339	
P87/Z28 Z28 cpe, V-8	3,373	16,799	39,103

Corsica	Wght	Price	Prod
T69 sdn 4d, I-4	2,665	11,395	
T69 sdn 4d, V-6	2,763	11,995	148,232
Beretta			
V37 cpe, I-4	2,649	11,395	
V37 cpe, V-6	2,749	11,995	
W37 GT cpe, I-4	2,749	12,995	
W37 GT cpe, V-6	2,797	13,595	42,263
Z37 GTZ cpe, I-4	2,795	15,995	
Z37 GTZ cpe, V-6	2,895	15,845	
Lumina			
L27 cpe, I-4	3,052	13,905	
L27 cpe, V-6	3,169	14,690	
N27 Euro cpe, V-6	3,193	15,600	30,166
P27 Z34 cpe, V-6	3,374	18,400	

Lumina (continued)	Wght	Price	Prod
L69 sdn 4d, I-4	3,180	13,400	
L69 sdn 4d, V-6	3,288	14,010	191,189
N69 Euro sdn 4d, V-6	3,312	15,800	
Total Lumina			221,355
Caprice Classic			
L19 sdn 4d, V 8	3,995	17,995	
N19 LS sdn 4d, V-8	3,988	19,995	90,041
L35 wag, V-8	4,471	19,575	10,607
Total Caprice Classic			100,648
Corvette			
Y07 htchbk cpe, V-8	3,309	36,785	18,788
Z07 ZR1 htchbk cpe, V-8	3,512	68,043	448
Y67 conv, V-8	3,383	41,195	5,712
Total Corvette			24,948

1994

- **New-generation Camaro convertibles arrive**

- **Impala SS reborn as hot-rod Caprice**

- **Stronger base engines for Beretta, Cavalier, and Corsica**

- **Domestic car sales slide again to just under 822,000**

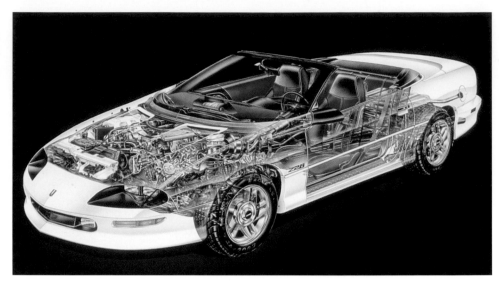

▲ After a year's hiatus, the ragtop Camaro returned for 1994 sharing the basic design of the new fourth-generation coupe. This cutaway illustration, again by Dave Kimble, highlights the construction and layout of the Z28 version. A power soft top with glass rear window was standard for both the base and Z28 models.

Lust

THE 1994 CHEVY CAMARO — CHEVROLET & GEO DEALERS

▲ The '94 Camaro convertible (Z28 *above*) presented an ultra-clean top-down profile with the top cover installed. The boot slipped under a perimeter lip molding and attached to the inner rear quarter panels with straps, all a bit tedious.

◄ Chevy's ad agency devised this series of 1994 Camaro billboards featuring the most affordable model, the base coupe. Though we can't be sure of their effectiveness, Camaro sales more than tripled for the model year. Manual-shift Z28s inherited the Corvette's Computer Aided Gear Selection feature that "forced" a change from first to fourth gears on light-throttle as a fuel-economy aid.

Envy

THE 1994 CHEVY CAMARO — CHEVROLET & GEO DEALERS

Passion

THE 1994 CHEVY CAMARO — CHEVROLET & GEO DEALERS

▲ The new ragtop Camaros (Z28 shown) were long on style but short on rear-seat and luggage space. Then again, nobody ever bought a Camaro for its practicality.

▲ Cavalier became a teenager with the 1994 models, which sported a base 2.2-liter four with 10 extra horsepower. Styling was little changed, as on this RS convertible.

▲ Despite a basic design now 13 years old, Cavalier posted a second consecutive sales gain for '94, up 9.1 percent. Three coupe models continued, including this RS.

▲ The Cavalier wagon came in only one nameless trim level for '94, though it was trimmed and equipped much like the previous RS model.

◄▲ Lumina saw little change for '94, as a redesigned replacement was a year away. Even so, sales rose fractionally. The Z34 coupe (*left*) and 3.4 Euro-package sedan (*above*) continued as the sportiest models.

▲► Like Cavalier, Corvette scored higher sales for a second straight year, up about 7 percent. Among several refinements were a modified dash incorporating knee bolsters and passenger-side airbag; electronic shift controls and safety interlock for the automatic transmission; softer damping for the FX3 Selective Ride Control option; a standard heated-glass rear window for ragtops; and new steering wheel, seats, and door panels. The ZR-1 (*right*) was slightly downpriced, but again found only 448 customers, versus 17,420 for the base coupe (*above*).

327

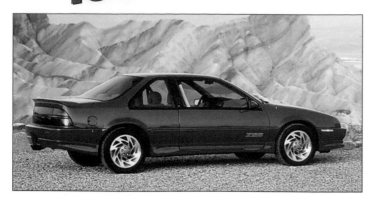

▲ The sportiest Beretta got a new name for '94: Z26. Replacing both the GT and GTZ, it offered the now-familiar 2.3-liter twincam "Quad 4" or an optional 3.1 V-6 with 160 hp, up 20.

▲ Corsica was still drawing decent sales despite having lost its hatchback body style after '91. For '94 came a stronger base 4-cyl engine and, with available V-6, a new four-speed automatic option.

▲ ► The hallowed Impala SS name made a surprise return in early '94 as a high-performance Caprice sedan. The idea allegedly came from one Chevy fan's custom Caprice, but wild response to Chevy's own concept model in 1992-93 convinced executives to build it. The car featured a 260-hp version of the Corvette's LT1 V-8 nestled within a much-modified Caprice with lower-riding Police Package suspension, big tires on handsome five-spoke alloys, four-wheel disc brakes with ABS, and snarky all-black exterior. The new Impala SS was a big-car performance bargain at $21,920 to start.

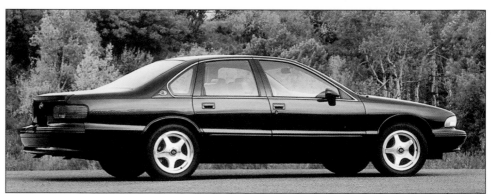

◄▲ Just like the good old days, the new Impala SS came with a sporty buckets-and-console interior (*left*), plus a full array of convenience features and power assists. A new iteration of the famous Impala logo (*above*) appeared inside and out.

▲ The three-model Caprice line got a new base engine for '94: a 200-hp 4.3-liter V-6 that replaced the 5.0 V-8. The Impala SS's 260-hp LT1 V-8 was also optional. Here, the Classic LS sedan.

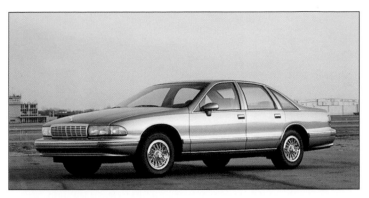

▲ This Caprice Classic sedan remained the most affordable full-size Chevy for 1994. Total Caprice sales, which had been falling since the '91 restyle, now reversed course, rising 4.8 percent.

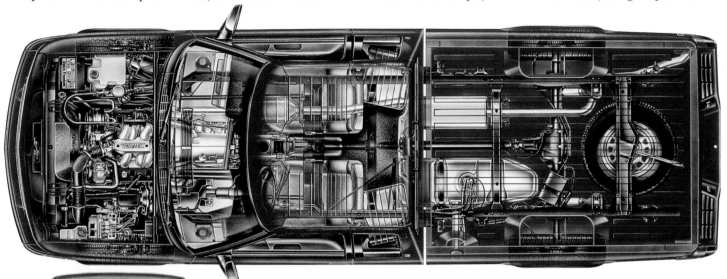

1994 Engine Availability

Engines	bore × stroke	bhp	availability
I-4, 133.0	3.50 × 3.46	120	S-Cavalier, Corsica, Beretta
I-4, 138.0	3.63 × 3.35	170	O-Beretta (dohc)
V-6, 191.0	3.60 × 3.40	140	S-Lumina, O-Cavalier
V-6, 191.0	3.60 × 3.40	160	O-Corsica, Beretta
V-6, 207.0	3.62 × 3.31	160	S-Camaro
V-6, 207.0	3.62 × 3.31	200	O-Camaro (dohc)
V-8, 265.0	3.74 × 3.00	200	S-Caprice
V-8, 350.0	4.00 × 3.48	260	S-Impala SS, O-Caprice
V-8, 350.0	4.00 × 3.48	275	O-Camaro
V-8, 350.0	4.00 × 3.48	300	S-Corvette
V-8, 350.0	3.90 × 3.66	385	S-Corvette ZR1 (dohc)

◀▲ After a dozen successful years, Chevy's S-10 compact pickups were fully redesigned for 1994, with smooth new styling, roomier extended (*left*) and regular cabs, and stronger bodies and chassis (*top*). Engines (*above left*) comprised a base 118-hp 2.2-liter 4-cyl and—more popular—a new "Vortec 4300" V-6 with 155-165 hp. Among many new options was a sporty ZR2 package for the short-box 4×4 (*above*) with elevated suspension, wider axles, off-road tires, and much more.

▲ Little changed after its 1993 redesign, the big Suburban SUV could seat up to nine passengers or haul up to 3480 pounds. Cargo capacity was colossal at 149.5 cubic feet.

▲ Suburbans offered a no-cost choice of center-opening rear cargo doors, shown here, or tailgate. Engines, still all V-8s, ranged from 5.7-liter gasoline to a stump-pulling 6.5-liter turbodiesel.

▲ Big changes were just around the corner for the S-10 Blazer, so virtually none were made for 1994. This two-door was priced from $15,438 with 2WD, $17,234 as a 4×4.

▲ Though the slow-selling 454 SS did not return for '94, its big-block V-8 was still available. Here, a short-box Sportside 4×4.

▶ Astro continued for 1994 in extended EXT (*right*) and regular-length models. Safety was highlighted this year with a standard driver's airbag (formerly optional), side-impact beams added to all doors, and a center high-mount rear stoplamp. This uplevel CS-trim EXT started at $16,580.

Model Breakdown

Cavalier	Wght	Price	Prod
C37/WV9 VL cpe, I-4	2,509	8,845	
C37 RS cpe, I-4	2,515	10,715	147,528
F37 Z24 cpe, V-6	2,695	13,995	
C67 RS conv, I-4	2,678	16,995	7,932
F67 Z24 conv, V-6	2,858	19,995	
C69/WV9 VL sdn 4d, I-4	2,520	8,995	98,966
C69 RS sdn 4d, I-4	2,526	11,315	
C35 RS wag, I-4	2,623	11,465	18,149
Total Cavalier			272,575
Camaro			
P87 cpe, V-6	3,247	13,399	112,539
P87/Z28 Z28 cpe, V-8	3,424	16,799	
P67 conv, V-6	3,342	18,745	7,260
P67/Z28 Z28 conv, V-8	3,524	22,075	
Total Camaro			119,799

Corsica	Wght	Price	Prod
D69 sdn 4d, I-4	2,665	13,145	143,296
D69 sdn 4d, V-6	2,763	13,865	
Beretta			
V37 cpe, I-4	2,649	12,415	
V37 cpe, V-6	2,749	13,690	64,277
W37 Z26 cpe, I-4	2,749	15,310	
W37 Z26 cpe, V-6	2,797	15,835	
Lumina			
N27 Euro cpe, V-6	3,269	16,875	3,860
P27 Z34 cpe, V-6	3,440	19,310	
L69 sdn 4d, V-6	3,333	15,305	82,766
N69 Euro sdn 4d, V-6	3,369	16,515	
Total Lumina			86,626

Caprice Classic/ Impala SS	Wght	Price	Prod
L19 Caprice sdn 4d, V-8	4,036	18,995	90,026
N19 Caprice			
LS sdn 4d, V-8	4,054	21,435	
L35 Caprice wag, V-8	4,449	21,180	7,719
N19/BN5 Impala SS sd 4d, V-8	4,218	21,920	6,303
Total Caprice Classic/ Impala SS			104,048
Corvette			
Y07 htchbk cpe, V-8	3,309	36,185	17,420
Z07 ZR1 htchbk cpe, V-8	3,512	67,443	448
Y67 conv, V-8	3,361	42,960	5,320
Total Corvette			23,188

1995

- Monte Carlo returns with front-wheel drive

- All-new Cavaliers, Lumina sedan debut

- Full-size Blazer redesigned as new two- and four-door Tahoe

- New-design Blazer compact SUV arrives

▲▼ The "King of the Hill" ZR-1 roared off into the sunset after 1995 and a final 448 examples. Happily, this year's coupe and convertible got its heavy-duty brakes. Ironically, the ZR-1's demise was announced just a few months after thousands of 'Vette fans converged on Bowling Green for the September 1994 opening of the National Corvette Museum.

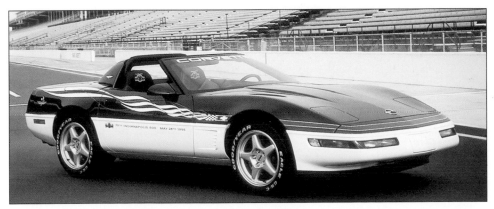

▲ 'Vette fans mourned the "King," then cheered as Corvette was named the '95 Indy 500 pace car. The pace car (shown) was a near-stock LT1 convertible. Chevy ran off 527 replicas, though without the rear roll bar, signal lights, and other track-required equipment.

▲ Hard to believe, but 1995 marked the 40th anniversary of Chevy's historic small-block V-8, the great-granddaddy of the modern LT1 Corvette engine shown here. And its story was far from over.

1995 Engine Availability

Engines	bore × stroke	bhp	availability
I-4, 133.0	3.50 × 3.46	120	S-Cavalier, Corsica, Beretta
I-4, 138.0	3.63 × 3.35	150	O-Cavalier (dohc)
V-6, 191.0	3.60 × 3.40	155	O-Corsica
V-6, 191.0	3.60 × 3.40	160	S-Lumina, Monte Carlo, O-Beretta
V-6, 207.0	3.62 × 3.31	160	S-Camaro
V-6, 207.0	3.62 × 3.31	210	O-Lumina, Monte Carlo (dohc)
V-8, 265.0	3.74 × 3.00	200	S-Caprice
V-8, 350.0	4.00 × 3.48	260	S-Impala SS, O-Caprice
V-8, 350.0	4.00 × 3.48	275	O-Camaro
V-8, 350.0	4.00 × 3.48	300	S-Corvette
V-8, 350.0	3.90 × 3.66	405	S-ZR1 Corvette

▶ The pairing of this 1995 Camaro Z28 convertible with a perky little 490 roadster illustrated how far automotive technology and styling had advanced in 80 years. Though very different, these cars share the bow tie badge and represented great value in their respectrive eras.

▲ After a premature announcement for '94, this year's Camaro Z28s (convertible *above*) got Corvette's traction control system (called Acceleration Slip Regulation) as a new option. Chevy's ponycar again notched higher model-year sales, improving by 8.5 percent.

◀ Call this a "top-down top-down" look at the 1995 Z28 convertible. Full "six-dial" instrumentation with tachometer and a convenient pull-up central handbrake lever were part of the sporty cockpit ambience in all fourth-generation Camaros. Note, too, the simple high-set climate controls just right of the steering wheel. The front seats were a lot more "buckety" than they appear from this angle.

▲ Chevy revived the Monte Carlo name for 1995 as a redesigned replacement for the Lumina coupe. There were still regular and sporty versions, the latter again called Z34 and pictured here.

▲ The 1995 Monte was much smaller than the last of the original line and the first with front drive, but it got a warm debut-year reception, racking up over 93,150 sales.

▲ Another first for Monte Carlo was the Z34's standard twincam 3.4-liter V-6. It delivered 210 horses via four-speed automatic transmission.

▲ Considering the NASCAR successes of earlier Monte Carlos, a sneak peek of the new 1995 model was accorded to race fans who saw it pace the first Brickyard 400 at Indianapolis on August 6, 1994.

▲ Much sleeker styling on a longer, 104.1-inch wheelbase highlighted the all-new 1995 Cavaliers like this sporty Z24 coupe.

▲ Cavalier offered two coupes, two sedans, and this LS convertible for 1995, but wagons were no more.

▲ Lumina was redesigned for '95 with new sedan-only styling and the same platform as Monte Carlo. This is the uplevel LS model.

◀ Car lovers tend to wince at scenes like this—except maybe those who are into "Demo Derby" smash fests—but crash testing was a literal auto industry fact of life by the mid 1990s. Per newer government regulations, cars now had to sustain various types of impacts at 30 mph without significant "injuries" to the high-tech, electronically monitored dummies inside. The government and some independent agencies also staged 35- and 40-mph collisions for consumer-information purposes. Here, a '95 Cavalier sedan gives up its life so people won't have to give up theirs should the unthinkable happen. Note how only the front end crumples under impact while the airbag deploys to protect the driver—who is fully belted in.

▲ The big, brawny Impala SS was available in Dark Cherry and Green-Gray for 1995, as well as all-black, but otherwise the car was unchanged. However, its "kinked" rear side windows showed up on this year's Caprice sedans.

◄► Though down 40 hp from Corvette tune, the LT1 Impala SS V-8 could vault the 2-ton sedan 0-to-60 mph in just 6.5 seconds on the way to 15-second, 92-mph quarter-mile, according to *Car and Driver*.

▲ Chevy's compact SUV was simply renamed Blazer for 1995—and it was all-new. This four-door 4×4 carries top-line LT equipment.

▲ An extra 4.4 inches in length and 2.4 inches in width added up to more cargo room in the redesigned 1995 four-door Blazers.

◄ Two-door Blazers gained 4.3 inches of length for '95, plus a sportier roof-line with a more sharply angled rear window. All the new Blazers shared their basic platform with the latest S-10 pickups.

▲ Detail changes were the only 1995 news for the big Suburban SUV, still on a king-size 131.5-inch wheelbase.

▲ If you had to tote a whole Little League team—and their coach—a '95 Suburban would do it in comfort and even style.

▲ Replacing the big Blazer for '95 was Tahoe, basically a shortened Suburban. This new four-door rode a 117.5-inch wheelbase.

▲ Chevy's full-size truck dashboard was much tidier and better organized by 1995. This one belongs to a new four-door Tahoe.

◀ Full-size trucks were racing in a highly popular NASCAR series by 1995. In response, Chevy provided a wild C1500 pace truck to work that year's Brickyard 400.

Model Breakdown

Cavalier	Wght	Price	Prod
C37 cpe, I-4	2,617	10,060	88,909
F37 Z24 cpe, I-4	2,788	13,810	
F67 LS conv, I-4	2,838	17,210	6,060
C69 sdn 4d, I-4	2,676	10,265	56,700
F69 LS sdn 4d, I-4	2,736	12,465	
Total Cavalier			151,669
Camaro			
P87 cpe, V-6	3,251	14,250	115,365
P87/Z28 Z28 cpe, V-8	3,390	17,915	
P67 conv, V-6	3,342	19,495	7,360
P67/Z28 Z28 conv, V-8	3,480	23,095	
Total Camaro			122,725
Corsica			
D69 sdn 4d, I-4	2,745	13,890	142,073
D69 sdn 4d, V-6	2,885	14,610	

Beretta	Wght	Price	Prod
V37 cpe, I-4	2,756	12,995	71,762
V37 cpe, V-6	2,896	14,270	
W37 Z26 cpe, V-6	2,990	16,295	
Lumina			
L69/Z7H sdn 4d, V-6	3,330	15,460	242,112
N69/Z7E LS sdn 4d, V-6	3,372	16,960	
Monte Carlo			
W27/Z7F LS cpe, V-6	3,276	16,760	93,150
X27/Z7G Z34 cpe, V-6	3,451	18,960	
Caprice Classic/Impala SS			
L19 Caprice sdn 4d, V-8	4,061	20,310	54,273

Caprice (continued)	Wght	Price	Prod
L35 Caprice wag, V-8	4,473	22,840	5,030
L19/BL5 Impala sdn 4d, V-8	4,036	22,910	21,434
Total Caprice Classic/ Impala SS			80,737
Corvette			
Y07 htchbk cpe, V-8	3,203	36,785	18,788
Z07 ZR1 htchbk cpe, V-8	3,512	68,043	448
Y67 conv, V-8	3,360	43,665	4,094
Total Corvette			23,330

1996

NINETEEN NINETY-SIX   NINETEEN NINETY-SIX   NINETEEN NINETY-SIX   NINETEEN NINET

- **Corvette offers special Grand Sports and Collector Editions**

- **Camaro gets larger, more potent base V-6**

- **Truck line introduces "3-door" cabs**

▲ Camaro became the only car to pace five races at Indianapolis when this special coupe did the honors at the 1996 Brickyard 400. Its covered headlamps, bold striping, 300-horsepower V-8, and other features were available through dealers in a limited-run F-1 package.

▲ Newly optional for '96 base Camaros were an RS dress-up kit and a Performance Package with Z28-style chassis upgrades.

▲ Base '96 Camaros also exchanged a standard 3.1-liter V-6 for General Motors' "3800" unit with 200 hp, up 40 from 1995.

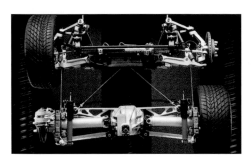

▲ Replacing Corvette's Selective Ride Control was a more responsive Selective Real Time Damping option. It, too, adjusted the firmness of the shock absorbers (*in red*), but more precisely with inputs from the traction control and ABS sensors.

► The fabled Grand Sport name returned for '96 on a new Corvette performance package featuring a new 5.7-liter LT4 V-8 with 330 hp, 30 more than the LT1. Available for the coupe (shown) and convertible, the GS also included broad dorsal stripes, special interior, engine dress-up, ZR-1 wheels and tires, rear-wheel flares, and black brake calipers with bright "Corvette" lettering. Grand Sport installations were limited to only 1000, but the LT4 was a $1450 option for other '96 'Vettes.

► Also available for the '96 Corvette convertible (shown) and coupe was a special Collector Edition package, which seemed to signal the imminent end of the C4 generation. Priced at $1250 (versus $2880/$3250 for the Grand Sport), this option delivered exclusive Sebring Silver paint, "Collector Edition" logos inside and out, leather upholstery, and the Grand Sport's black brake calipers. Corvette sales for calendar '96 totaled 21,018, down 7.7 percent from the previous 12-month period.

◄ Cavalier offered a twincam 4-cyl engine enlarged from 2.3 to 2.4 liters. Horsepower was unchanged, however, at 150. Simply called Twin Cam, the new engine was standard in the Z24 coupe and available for this ragtop LS.

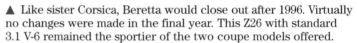

▲ The compact Corsica sedan was nearing the end of its road in 1996, so changes were confined to minor internal revisions aimed at making the optional 3.1-liter V-6 both quieter and thriftier.

▲ Like sister Corsica, Beretta would close out after 1996. Virtually no changes were made in the final year. This Z26 with standard 3.1 V-6 remained the sportier of the two coupe models offered.

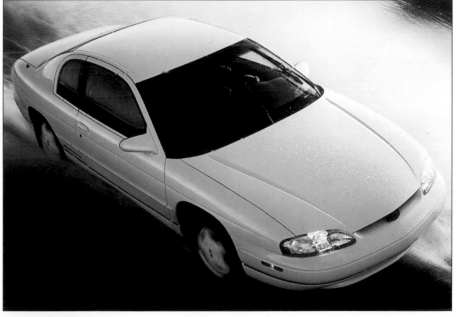

▲ Chevy's redesigned Lumina sedans were little changed for their sophomore year, but four-wheel disc brakes were newly included on the LS version (shown) with optional 3.4-liter V-6. Also new were optional leather upholstery, again reserved for LS, and an available child safety seat that folded down out of the rear seat backrest. Lumina sales improved nearly 5 percent over the prior year to 224,573.

▲ The front-drive Monte Carlo was also little changed for its second season, but the sporty Z34 (shown) now came with four-wheel disc brakes instead of rear drums. Antilock control remained standard on all Montes and Luminas. A total of 80,717 '96 Monte Carlos were sold, down 13 percent from '95.

◄ Lumina minivans got extra midrange muscle as a 3.4-liter V-6 replaced the previous 3.1. Horsepower swelled to 180, a healthy 60-hp gain. Also new for '96 were standard air conditioning, available seven-passenger seating, and an optional power sliding side door. Basic "Dustbuster" styling was little changed.

▲ The '96 Caprice Classic sedan (*above*) and wagon would be among the last traditional full-size Chevys.

▲ Big-Chevy calendar-year sales fell nearly 14 percent in 1996 to 69,581. Here, the woody-look Caprice Classic wagon.

▲ The Impala SS got a floorshift automatic, analog speedometer, and standard tachometer for '96. It, too, was in its final season.

▶ Law-enforcement officers still loved the Police Package Caprice, but this would the last year they could have a new one. Some agencies undoubtedly learned in advance of Chevy's decision to discontinue the big rear-drive sedan, and likely bought as many as they could before production ended, though exact sales are unavailable.

▶ Even after production ended, the Police Package Caprice (in "X-ray" view *above*) remained so popular among law-enforcement officers that one former Southern California deputy found a strong market for rebuilt used models. His restoration shop was busy and prosperous as late as 2001.

▲ Chevy devised this Police Package Tahoe to take over for the "John Law" Caprice, but officers didn't like it nearly as much.

▲ Tahoe's Police Package included the usual high-output "pursuit" V-8, uprated chassis, and custom law-enforcement equipment.

▲ Headlining improvements to the 1996 S-10 pickup line, the sole 4.3-liter V-6 was replaced by a "Vortec 4300." The new engine had extended service intervals and lowered torque peak for better midrange passing response, but no more horsepower. Here, a new "3-door" extended-cab Fleetside.

◄ This auxiliary left-side third door was a new option for 1996 extended-cab S-10s. Hinged at the rear, it was released from a flush "paddle" in the jamb, visible here, and thus couldn't be opened unless the front door was first. A power lift available through dealers enabled wheelchair-bound drivers to enter or exit the vehicle and stow the wheelchair, all without assistance.

▲ Blazer calendar-year sales rose 14.7 percent for 1996, reaching 247,307 units. A new "Vortec 4300" V-6 was standard for all models. This top-line LT four-door was again offered with permanently engaged 4WD drive as an exclusive option.

► Showing how diverse the compact-pickup market had become by 1996 is this pairing of identical but differently optioned S-10s. A 4×4 with the ZR2 off-road package stands behind a 2WD with an available SS group featuring body-color bumpers, lowered suspension, and other sporty touches.

▲ Full-size Chevy extended-cab pickups like this Fleetside 4×4 also offered an optional third door for '96, only it was on the right side, not the left as on S-10s. Otherwise, the design was the same and offered similarly improved entry/exit for rear-seat passengers.

1996 Engine Availability

Engines	bore × stroke	bhp	availability
I-4, 133.0	3.50 × 3.46	120	S-Cavalier, Corsica, Beretta
I-4, 146.0	3.54 × 3.70	150	O-Cavalier (dohc)
V-6, 191.0	3.60 × 3.40	155	O-Corsica, Beretta
V-6, 191.0	3.60 × 3.40	160	S-Lumina, Monte Carlo
V-6, 207.0	3.62 × 3.31	215	O-Lumina, Monte Carlo (dohc)
V-6, 231.0	3.80 × 3.40	200	S-Camaro
V-8, 265.0	3.74 × 3.00	200	S-Caprice
V-8, 350.0	4.00 × 3.48	260	S-Impala SS, O-Caprice
V-8, 350.0	4.00 × 3.48	285	O-Camaro
V-8, 350.0	4.00 × 3.48	305	O-Camaro
V-8, 350.0	4.00 × 3.48	300	S-Corvette
V-8, 350.0	4.00 × 3.48	330	O-Corvette

▲ Full-size trucks had their optional third door on the right, Chevy said, because buyers wanted better rear-seat access from the curb, not the street.

▲ Chevy's big-truck interiors could be almost luxury-car plush in '96, at least with top-line trim (shown).

▶ After 26 years, Chevy's big G-series vans were redesigned for '96. Retitled Express, the new line included a basic windowless Cargo van (*left*) and passenger models with long (*center*) or standard (*right*) bodies. All models pushed their front wheels 10 inches forward, making for a much more spacious front-seat area. Also featured was a first-ever seamless roof panel.

Model Breakdown

Cavalier	Wght	Price	Prod
C37 cpe, I-4	2,617	10,500	145,229
F37 Z24 cpe, I-4	2,838	14,200	
F67 LS conv, I-4	2,788	17,500	7,073*
C69 sdn 4d, I-4	2,676	10,700	116,447
F69 LS sdn 4d, I-4	2,736	12,900	
Camaro			
P87 cpe, V-6	3,306	14,990	54,525
P87 RS cpe, V-6	3,306	17,490	
P87/Z28 Z28 cpe, V-8	3,466	19,390	
P67 conv, V-6	3,440	21,270	6,837
P67 RS conv, V-6	3,440	22,720	
P67/Z28 Z28 conv, V-8	3,593	24,490	
Total Camaro			61,362

Corsica	Wght	Price	Prod
D69 sdn 4d, I-4	2,745	14,385	148,652
D69 sdn 4d, V-6	2,885	15,105	
Beretta			
V37 cpe, I-4	2,756	13,490	42,476
V37 cpe, V-6	2,896	14,765	
W37 Z26 cpe, V-6	2,990	16,690	
Lumina			
L69 sdn 4d, V-6	3,330	16,355	224,573
N69 LS sdn 4d, V-6	3,372	18,055	
Monte Carlo			
W27/Z7F cpe, V-6	3,306	17,255	80,717
X27/Z7G Z34 cpe, V-6	3,436	19,455	

Caprice Classic/ Impala SS	Wght	Price	Prod
L19 sdn 4d, V-8	4,061	19,905	27,155
L35 wag, V-8	4,473	22,405	485
L19/1SS Impala SS sdn 4d,	4036	24,405	41,941
Total Caprice Classic/ Impala SS			69,581
Corvette			
Y07 htchbk cpe, V-8	3,298	37,225	16,357
Y07 GS htchbk cpe, V-8	3,298	40,475	810
Y67 conv, V-8	3,360	45,060	4,179
Y67 GS conv, V-8	3,360	47,940	190
Total Corvette			21,536

*1996 Cavalier convertible sales figure.

1997

- All-new "C5" Corvette introduced

- Camaro offers 30th Anniversary and revived SS options

- Malibu returns as all-new front-drive sedan

▲ A limited-run '96 option, the Camaro SS became a full production package for 1997 Z28s. The $4000 price included a tuned 305-horsepower V-8 and functional hood scoop.

◄▲ Camaro began its third decade in 1997 with a 30th Anniversary Package inspired by the '96 Brickyard 400 pace car (*above*). Priced at just $575, the option included white paint (with matching wheels) set off by broad orange striping, a treatment first used on the '69 Z28 (*second from left, left, and above*). The birthday package could be combined with the SS option (*left, far left*). Spoiling all this fun, total Camaro sales dropped 10 percent for the calendar year to just under 55,000 units.

▲ Hailed as the best Corvette yet, the all-new 1997 "C5" put a slinky new body on a new more rigid perimeter frame. Wheelbase grew a massive 8.3 inches to 104.5, the longest in 'Vette history, and length was up by 1.2 inches, yet base curb weight actually fell some 80 pounds. This hatchback coupe was the only model for '97. Priced from $37,495, '97 Corvette sales reached only 9752 units in a shortened sales year.

▶ The C5 was ushered in by a Corvette team under chief engineer Dave Hill, here standing amidships of a prototype fixed-roof hardtop. This model, which wouldn't bow until 1999, was conceived as a lighter, no-frills 'Vette with a stronger performance orientation and a rumored $30,000 price tag. But it ended up being quite close to the debut hatchback in most every respect.

◀▶ A 5.7-liter pushrod V-8 remained the only powerplant for the C5, but was all-new like the rest of the car. With 345 horsepower, it was more potent than even the short-lived LT4. A costly but successful update of proven concepts, the LS1 boasted aluminum cylinder heads and block, plus a lightweight valvetrain and a more sophisticated electronic engine controller. With standard 6-speed manual shift, the new 'Vette vaulted 0-60 mph in just under 5 seconds in early major magazine tests.

▲ A wide tail provoked some debate but, overall, the C5 was a much more aerodynamic shape than the C4. Indeed, the drag factor was reduced to just 0.29. In 1997, no other production car was slipperier. Note the simple front-fender vents—functional, of course.

▲ The C5 was the first 'Vette with a rear transaxle, linked to the front-mounted engine via a stout longitudinal torque tube of 5-inch diameter. Fore/aft weight balance improved to an ideal 50/50.

▲ New suspension geometry, "hydroformed" frame rails measuring 6 inches across, and a welded-on rear steel roll bar combined to make the C5 a more rigid, even better-handling Corvette.

▲ The only exterior reference to Chevrolet on the new C5 Corvette was a small bow tie logo on the nose emblem.

◄ A new iteration of the traditional "twin cowl" Corvette dash dominated the C5's roomier cockpit. Improvements included lower door sills for easier entry/exit, wider footwells, easy-read analog gauges, and controls more logically placed.

▲ ▶ Replacing Corsica in Chevy's 1997 lineup was a new front-drive sedan reviving the Malibu name (*above*). Sized and priced between Cavalier and Lumina, it came with a 2.4-liter 4-cyl or optional 3.1-liter V-6, 107-inch wheelbase, and base or uplevel LS trim. *Motor Trend* named it 1997 Car of the Year (*right*).

◀▶ Lumina added a sporty GTZ model during 1997 (*left*), available with the Monte Carlo Z34's twincam V-6. The Monte itself was little changed, but remained a contender in NASCAR, where defending champ Terry Labonte campaigned in a new Hendricks Motorsports car. He posed with it before the '97 Brickyard 400 along with the race's Monte Carlo pace car (*right*).

▲ Headlining Chevy's three van series for '97 was the new front-drive Venture (*center*), which replaced the Lumina minivan and offered optional dual sliding rear doors. Here it poses with the little-changed full-size Express (*left*) and a newly restyled '97 Astro

1997 Engine Availability

Engines	bore × stroke	bhp	availability
I-4, 133.0	3.50 × 3.46	120	S-Cavalier
I-4, 146.0	3.54 × 3.70	150	S-Malibu, O-Cavalier (dohc)
V-6, 191.0	3.51 × 3.31	160	S-Lumina, Monte Carlo
V-6, 207.0	3.62 × 3.31	215	O-Lumina, Monte Carlo (dohc)
V-6, 231.0	3.80 × 3.40	200	S-Camaro
V-8, 350.0	4.00 × 3.48	285	O-Camaro
V-8, 350.0	4.00 × 3.48	305	O-Camaro
V-8, 350.0	3.90 × 3.62	340	S-Corvette

▲ Cal Ripken, Sr., former Baltimore Orioles manager, appeared at Chevy-sponsored baseball clinics for various youth groups. His son, Cal, Jr., was a spokesman for Chevy trucks.

▲ Off-road truck racers often get airborne. Here, Evan Evans flies his competition-prepped "Chevy Barrier Breakers" CK1500.

▲ Drag-prepped Chevy S-10s, like this, competed in the National Hot Rod Association's Pro Stock Truck Exhibition class in 1997.

▲ Chevy began building electric-powered S-10s for fleet use in 1997. This one was heavily customized for auto-show duty.

▲ This specially outfitted two-door Blazer was one of several support vehicles that Chevy donated to the U.S. Ski Team in '97.

▲ Chevy's U.S. Ski Team sponsorship also produced this custom Astro minivan as a support vehicle for the '97 ski season.

▲ Tahoe, Chevy's smaller big SUV, improved sales by 19 percent in 1997. A more durable standard automatic transmission was among the year's few changes.

▲ Chevy kept pushing the Police Package Tahoe for '97, but sales remained difficult, perhaps because law enforcement just couldn't get used to the idea of a high-speed "pursuit truck."

Model Breakdown

Cavalier	Wght	Price	Prod
C37 cpe, I-4	2,584	10,980	
C37/WP2 RS cpe, I-4	2,617	12,225	171,225
F37 Z24 cpe, I-4	2,749	14,465	
F67 LS conv, I-4	2,899	17,765	1,108
C69 sdn 4d, I-4	2,630	11,100	
F69 LS sdn 4d, I-4	2,729	13,380	142,803
Total Cavalier			315,136
Camaro			
P87 cpe, V-6	3,294	16,215	
P87 RS cpe, V-6	3,307	17,970	48,292
P87/Z28 Z28 cpe, V-8	3,433	20,115	

Camro continued	Wght	Price	Prod
P67 conv, V-6	3,446	21,770	
P67 RS conv, V-6	3,455	23,170	6,680
P67/Z28 conv, V-8	3,589	25,520	
Total Camaro			54,972
Malibu			
D69 sdn 4d, I-4	3,051	15,470	
D69 sdn 4d, V-6	3,077	15,865	100,266
E69 LS sdn 4d, V-6	3,077	18,190	
Lumina			
L69 sdn 4d, V-6	3,360	16,945	
N69/Z7H LS sdn 4d, V-6	3,388	19,145	234,626
— LTZ sdn 4d, V-6	—	19,455	

Monte Carlo	Wght	Price	Prod
W27/Z7F LS cpe, V-6	3,320	17,445	72,555
X27/Z7G Z34 cpe, V-6	3,455	19,945	
Corvette			
Y07 htchbk cpe, V-8	3,229	37,945	9,752

1998

- **C5 Corvette adds convertible, paces Indy 500**

- **Camaro, Lumina boast more power**

- **Fresh faces for Blazer, Camaro, S-10**

- **Cavalier revives Z24 convertible**

▲ As expected, Corvette added a C5 convertible (*foreground*) for 1998, even as Chevy continued making promises about a fixed-roof notchback hardtop (*background*). No matter, *Motor Trend* engraved "Corvette" on its 1998 Car of the Year trophy, here being presented to Chevy general manager John Middlebrook (*second from left*).

▶ The C5 was engineered to be rigid enough that a ragtop version (*foreground*) would need no additional bracing—and it worked beautifully. Priced from $44,425, the newest Corvette convertible also featured an external trunklid—the first since '62—and a manual-fold cloth top with heated glass rear window. The new hardtop (*background*), basically a convertible with a fixed roof, was shown in 1998, but was launched late that year as a 1999 model.

▼ The C5 hatchback had a $37,495 base price in 1998 form. The year-old design was basically unchanged, but lightweight magnesium wheels were a new option, and the standard automatic transmission could now be set to start in second gear for more controlled acceleration on slippery surfaces. Helped by the new ragtop, Corvette sales climbed to 31,083 units, the most since the mid 1980s.

▲ A mechanically stock C5 convertible paced the 1998 Indy 500, here taking time to pose with its predecessors. Exactly 1158 replicas were built. This was Chevy's 11th Indy Pace Car honor.

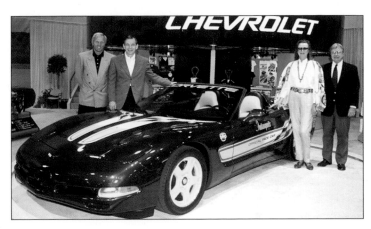

▲ The 1998 Indy pace car poses with (*left to right*) golfer Greg Norman, Chevy GM John Middlebrook, Indy Motor Speedway Chairman of the Board Mari H. George, and IMS Vice President Leo Mehl.

▶ The hatchback and other C5s came on "run-flat" tires that could be safely driven 200 miles without air pressure. Added during the 1998 season was an Active Handling option, basically an electronic stability control system with extra sensors. The result was more precisely modulated power delivery to counter skidding in hard cornering.

▼ NASCAR stockers ran the new Las Vegas Speedway in 1998, and this wildly painted Monte Carlo paced the field for that year's inaugural Las Vegas 400. Warner Bros. "Taz" character (*seen on rear fender*) was starting to appear in Monte advertising.

▲ Camaros got a more rounded nose for '98. Z28s (coupe shown) also got more muscle by adopting Corvette's aluminum LS1 V-8. Horsepower rose to 305 standard, 320 with the SS package.

▲ Chevy was still pushing a Camaro Police Package in 1998, but few such cars were likely delivered. Just as well, as no fast driver would want to see one of these missiles in the rearview mirror.

1998 Engine Availability

Engines	bore × stroke	bhp	availability
I-3, 61.0	2.91 × 3.03	55	S-Metro
I-4, 79.0	2.91 × 2.97	79	O-Metro
I-4, 109.5	3.11 × 3.60	120	S-Prizm (dohc)
I-4, 134.0	3.50 × 3.46	115	S-Cavalier
I-4, 146.0	3.54 × 3.70	150	S-Malibu, O-Cavalier (dohc)
V-6, 191.0	3.51 × 3.31	150	O-Malibu
V-6, 191.0	3.51 × 3.31	160	S-Lumina, Monte Carlo
V-6, 231.0	3.80 × 3.40	200	S-Camaro, O-Lumina, Monte Carlo
V-8, 346.0	3.90 × 3.48	305	O-Camaro
V-8, 346.0	3.90 × 3.48	320	O-Camaro
V-8, 346.0	3.90 × 3.62	345	S-Corvette

▲ Members of the U.S. Women's Olympic hockey team were presented with vehicles as part of Chevy's "The Team Behind the Team" program to support the training needs of Olympic hopefuls.

▼ Chevrolets again offered mainstream family sedans in three sizes for 1998 (*from left*): compact Malibu, subcompact Cavalier, and midsize Lumina, all shown here in uplevel LS trim.

▲ Ventures enhanced safety with standard front side airbags and GM's OnStar communications system as a new option.

▲ Formerly part of Chevy's Geo import line, the Toyota-based Prizm sedan got bow tie logos in a full 1998 redesign.

▲ Lumina still offered a Police Package for '98, though it was geared mainly for patrol work, not high-speed chases.

▲▶ Chevrolet tinkered with a couple of hot rod concepts in 1998. The Cavalier Technic (*top*), an answer to California pocket rockets, featured a 258-hp, supercharged, dohc I-4. The Malibu Sport (*right*) recalled Malibu SS days gone by. Modifications to its 3.4 liter V-6 boosted output to 238 hp. Neither car made it to market.

▲▶ With light-truck sales on a decade-long climb—and nearing 50 percent of the U.S. vehicle market—the annual Specialty Equipment Market Association (SEMA) show had more custom trucks than ever in 1998. All were designed to show how aftermarket accessories could be used to create uniquely personal vehicles, but they also enabled manufacturers to promote their basic wares. Chevy was naturally well represented. Its high-riding "Tonka" concept (*above*) had definite "big toys for big boys" exuberance. More down to earth—literally—was the custom "Tool Time" Express van (*right*) inspired by the character on TV's *Home Improvement* played by comedian and occasional Chevy racer Tim Allen.

▲ Hot trucks were also popular show vehicles. Horsepower reports for the brutish Chevy Xtreme Force S-10 ranged from 358 to 450, impressive either way for a V-6.

◀ The Greg Norman Hot Rod Silverado featured a 540-cu-in V-8 that put out 505 hp and 615 pound-feet of torque. According to the GM press release, it was "everything Greg Norman, the renowned golf professional, would want in a truck."

▲ General Motors' OnStar system came to Express passenger vans as a 1998 option, providing emergency assistance and information via cell phone and satellite links, plus a staff of operators.

▲ All Express models, including this basic Cargo Van, were little changed for their second season. Wheelbases were 135 or 155 inches except for the ½-ton chassis, which came only as 135.

▲ Like Prizm, the small Suzuki-based Geo Tracker SUV became a Chevrolet for 1998. This four-door 4×4 started at $15,605.

▲ A new "big Chevy truck" grille and standard dual airbags were featured on 1998 Blazers, like this two-door LS 4×4.

▲ GM OnStar and all-surface "AutoTrac" 4WD were new Tahoe options for 1998. Total sales rose 7.3 percent to 133,235 units.

▲ Not surprisingly, big-brother Suburban got Tahoe's AutoTrac 4WD and OnStar as new 1998 options. Sales of Chevy's biggest SUV rose 10 percent for the calendar year to near 109,000 units.

▲ Silverado featured few changes in the final year before its 1999 redesign. Among those changes were a new theft-deterrent system, new colors, and adjustments to the automatic transmission.

Model Breakdown

Metro	Wght	Price	Prod
R08 htchbk cpe, I-3	1,895	8,655	
R08/B4M LSi htchbk cpe, I-4	1,895	9,455	33,965
R69/B4M LSi sdn 4d, I-4	1,984	10,055	
Prizm			
K19 sdn 4d, I-4	2,359	12,045	49,842
K19/WP2 LSi dsn 4d, I-4	—	14,615	
Cavalier			
C37 cpe, I-4	2,584	11,610	
C37/WP2 RS cpe, I-4	2,584	12,870	
F37 Z24 cpe, I-4	2,749	15,710	
F67 Z24 conv, I-4	2,899	19,410	259,769
C69 sdn 4d, I-4	2,630	11,810	
F69 LS sdn 4d, I-4	2,630	14,250	

Camaro	Wght	Price	Prod
P87 cpe, V-6	3,331	16,625	
P87/Z28 Z28 cpe, V-8	3,349	20,470	48,806
P67 conv, V-6	3,468	22,125	
P67/Z28 Z28 conv, V-8	3,574	27450	
Malibu			
D69 sdn 4d, I-4	3,100	15,670	
D69 sdn 4d, V-6	—	16,165	221,405
E69 LS sdn 4d, V-6	—	18,470	
Lumina			
L69 sdn 4d, V-6	3,330	17,245	
L69/BV2 LS sdn 4d, V-6	3,372	19,245	176,505
N69 LTZ sdn 4d, V-6	3,420	19,745	

Monte Carlo	Wght	Price	Prod
W27 LS cpe, V-6	3,239	17,795	63,222
X27 Z34 cpe, V-6	3,452	20,295	
Corvette			
Y07 htchbk cpe, V-8	3,245	37,995	19,235
Y67 conv, V-8	3,246	44,425	11,849
Total Corvette			31,084

Model year sales includes cars sold between October 1 and September 30. May include cars produced in the previous model year. Corvette figures are model year production.

1999

- **Hardtop Corvette debuts after two years of previews**

- **Chevy begins rolling out redesigned full-size trucks**

- **For the fourth year running, Chevy sells more trucks than domestically built cars**

1999 Engine Availability

Engines	bore × stroke	bhp	availability
I-3, 61.0	2.91 × 3.03	55	S-Metro
I-4, 79.0	2.91 × 2.97	79	O-Metro
I-4, 109.5	3.11 × 3.60	120	S-Prizm (dohc)
I-4, 134.0	3.50 × 3.46	115	S-Cavalier
I-4, 146.0	3.54 × 3.70	150	S-Malibu, O-Cavalier (dohc)
V-6, 191.0	3.51 × 3.31	150	O-Malibu
V-6, 191.0	3.51 × 3.31	160	S-Lumina, Monte Carlo
V-6, 231.0	3.80 × 3.40	200	S-Camaro, O-Lumina, Monte Carlo
V-8, 346.0	3.90 × 3.62	305	O-Camaro
V-8, 346.0	3.90 × 3.62	320	O-Camaro
V-8, 346.0	3.90 × 3.62	345	S-Corvette

▲ Corvette's long-awaited notchback hardtop finally bowed for '99. The lowest-priced C5 at $38,197 base, it came only with the six-speed manual gearbox and Z51 handling suspension that were optional on other models, but was otherwise basically the same.

▲ The C5 ragtop (*above*) and hatchback got two new options for '99: a power adjustable telescopic steering column and a head-up display that projected speed and other data onto the windshield. Total 'Vette calendar-year sales rose 7 percent to 33,270 units.

▲ After some 20 years, factory-backed Corvettes would return to international racing in 2000. Heralding the historic move was this pair of specially equipped C5 hardtop pace cars for the 1999 running of the 24 Hours of LeMans in France.

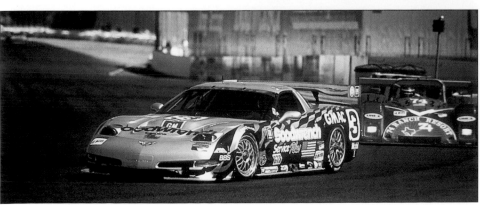

◄ Developed for LeMans and other world-class enduros at a cost of some $3.5 million, the new competition C5-R got a shakedown in several 1999 U.S. races. A unique 6.0-liter V-8 provided 600 horsepower. The aim was to beat GT-class Dodge Vipers.

351

▲ Lumina returned in base, LS (shown), and sporty LTZ models. Each made a few optional features standard for '99.

▲ Malibu got thicker windshield glass but few other changes for '99. Calendar-year sales rose 2 percent to 225,659.

▲ Cavalier was little changed for 1999 Even so, sales rose 4.3 percent for the calendar year to over 270,921.

◀▼ Representing the extremes of Chevy "carland" in 1999 are the little Suzuki-built Metro sedan (*left*) and a custom Monte Carlo (*below*) factory-built for this year's after-market-industry SEMA show. Note the Monte's reprofiled roofline, lower body skirts, and racing-style rear spoiler and under-bumper "ground effects" air channels.

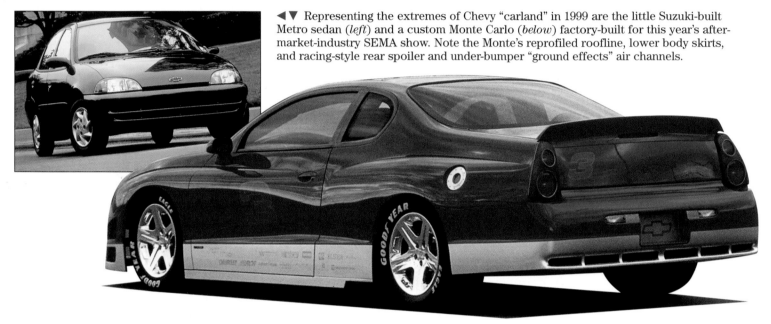

▲ Mia Hamm won the Chevrolet/U.S. Soccer Female Athlete of the Year award for 1998. Her prize was the use of a '99 Chevy Cavalier.

◀▼ Chevy's first new-design big pickups in 11 years began rolling off the assembly line in 1999 with ½-ton 1500s and light-duty ¾-ton 2500s, all called Silverado. Heavier-duty models would soon follow. A third door (*below*) was now standard on extend-ed-cabs like this short-bed Fleetside 4×4 (*left*).

▲ "Vortec" power was featured in all the new full-size Silverado pickups. The base engine remained a 200-hp 4.3-liter V-6 (*left*), but the 5.0- and 5.7-liter gas V-8s, respectively, gave way to a 255-hp 4.8-liter (*center*) and an equally new 270-hp 5.3 (*right*). Though smaller, the new pushrod V-8s delivered more power than their predecessors. Standard four-wheel disc brakes (with antilock) were a big pickup first, as was a mandatory four-speed automatic transmission with a "Tow/Haul" mode, which automatically adjusted shift points for best performance when towing or hauling heavy loads. Another class exclusive: optional shock absorbers with normal and firm modes to suit different roads and loads.

▲ Besides having a brawnier look, the new Silverados (*right*) were a bit wider than previous big-Chevy pickups (*left*). They also claimed more cab space and a somewhat smoother ride thanks to wheelbases stretched by 1.5-2.0 inches.

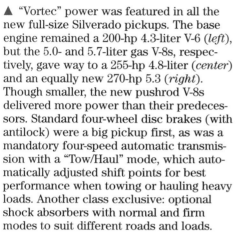

▲ Chevrolet Silverado won *Motor Trend* magazine's 1999 Truck of the Year award. Here, the trophy is presented to Chevrolet General Manager John G. Middlebrook (*second from right*).

▲ Silverado 4×4s switched from traditional 4WD to all-surface "AutoTrac," the only such system available. It was also the only 4WD in any pickup that could be used on dry pavement. Locked-in 4WD modes were provided for severe off-road use.

▶ This detailed "cutaway" illustration highlights the many features of the '99 Silverado and its all-new "GMT800" platform. Chevy claimed significant improvements in structural rigidity, ride comfort, handling and braking, as well as superior all-around performance

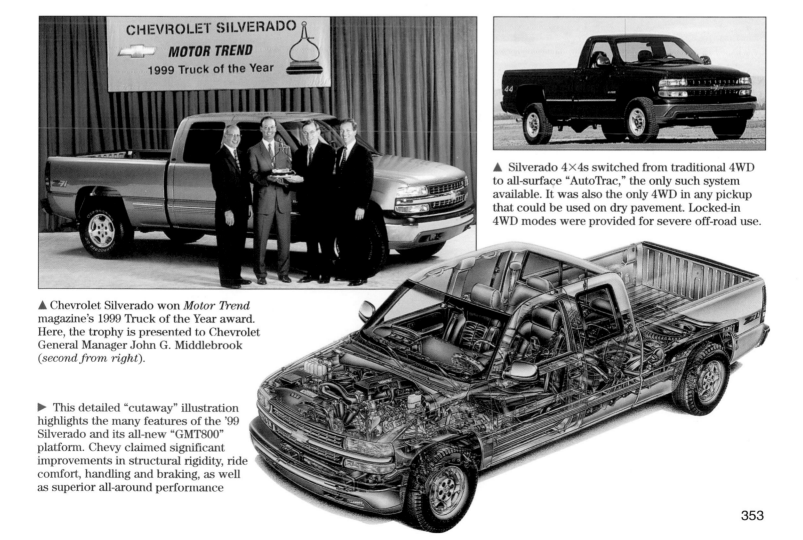

353

1999

▲▶ All-surface "AutoTrac" 4WD was a new alternative to "Insta-Trac" on 1999 Blazer 4×4s, which now included a spiffier top-line four-door called TrailBlazer (*above*). Meantime, the Suzuki-built Tracker convertible and wagon (*right*) got a thorough restyling to become slightly wider and longer, as well as looking more "grown-up."

◀ Ousting the sporty SS option for 2WD 1999 S-10s was a more extreme package called "Xtreme." Seen here on a long-box Sportside extended-cab, it featured "low-rider" suspension, big wheels, lower-body skirts, and vivid paint.

▲ Though all but unchanged for 1999, Suburban notched a healthy 27.6 percent gain in calendar-year sales to 138,977 units.

▲ Chevy continued most of its big C/K trucks in 1999. This ¾-ton C3500 carries an aftermarket stake body.

▲ Chevy still sold its StepVan in 1999, with a very old-fashioned body atop a big-pickup chassis. It hadn't changed much in decades.

Model Breakdown

Metro	Wght	Price	Prod
R08 htchbk cpe, I-3	1,895	8,993	
R08/B4M LSi htchbk cpe, I-4	1,895	9,790	29,272
R69/B4M LSi sdn 4d, I-4	1,984	10,402	
Prizm			
K19 sdn 4d, I-4	2,403	12,268	
K19/WP2 LSi sdn 4d, I-4	—	14,839	51,193
Cavalier			
C37 cpe, I-4	2,617	11,871	
C37/WP2 RS cpe, I-4	—	13,131	
F37 Z24 cpe, I-4	—	15,971	
F67 Z24 conv, I-4	2,838	19,571	270,921
C69 sdn 4d, I-4	2,676	11,971	
F69 LS sdn 4d, I-4	—	14,411	

Camaro	Wght	Price	Prod
P87 cpe, V-6	3,306	16,625	
P87/Z28 Z28 cpe, V-8	3,349	20,870	
P67 conv, V-6	3,500	22,125	41,412
P67/Z28 Z28 conv, V-8	3,574	27850	
Malibu			
D69 sdn 4d, I-4	3,051	15,950	
D69 sdn 4d, V-6	—	16,545	225,659
E69 LS sdn 4d, V-6	3,077	18,910	
Lumina			
L69 sdn 4d, V-6	3,330	18,190	
L69/BV2 LS sdn 4d, V-6	—	19,920	130,086
N69 LTZ sdn 4d, V-6	3,372	20,360	

Monte Carlo	Wght	Price	Prod
W27 LS cpe, V-6	3,306	18,510	
X27 Z34 cpe, V-6	3,436	20,535	69,845
Corvette			
Y37 hrdtp cpe, V-8	3,153	38,197	4,031
Y07 htchbk cpe, V-8	3,245	38,591	18,078
Y67 conv, V-8	3,246	44,999	11,161
Total Corvette			33,270

Model year sales includes cars sold between October 1 and September 30. May include cars produced in the previous model year. Corvette figures are model year production.

- Impala reborn as a front-drive sedan

- Monte Carlo, Tahoe, and Suburban are all fully redesigned

- Minor changes for other cars and trucks

- Domestic car sales up, truck sales flat

▲ Save revised pricing, the C5 Corvette convertible (*above*) and hatchback were all but unchanged for the last year of the 20th century. Sales of America's sports car remained strong, though, this time at 32,221 units.

▲ The 2000 C5 hardtop added several options already available on other 'Vettes: magnesium wheels, fog lamps, head-up instrument display, and dual-zone climate control.

▶ The editors spent some memorable seat time in this test 2000 C5 ragtop. The seats themselves were comfortable and support- ive, while cockpit ergonomics were arguably the best of any 'Vette since the original mid-'60s Sting Ray. Console switch- es controlled the firmness of this car's optional Continuously Variable Real Time Damping Suspension.

▲ As planned, the competition C5-R Corvette went to LeMans 2000 and finished 10th and 11th overall between a pair of GTS-R Dodge Vipers but ahead of a Porsche GT3R. It was a highly creditable per- formance for a brand-new enduro racer.

▲ Corvette raced in and paced the 2000 24 Hours of Daytona. The pace car wore a special paint scheme and polished alloy wheels, which were an $895 option on the production cars. Magnesium wheels could be had for $2000.

▲▼ Monte Carlo was redesigned for 2000 on a new front-drive platform shared with a reborn Impala sedan. Wheelbase was up three inches to 110.5, but overall length was down two inches. This sporty SS version came with General Motors' 200-horsepower "3800" V-6.

▼ A 180-hp 3.1 V-6 was standard for the new base Monte Carlo LS. Styling allegedly paid tribute to the first early-'70s Montes.

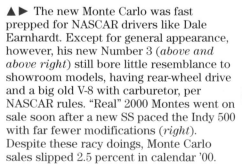

▲▶ The new Monte Carlo was fast prepped for NASCAR drivers like Dale Earnhardt. Except for general appearance, however, his new Number 3 (*above and above right*) still bore little resemblance to showroom models, having rear-wheel drive and a big old V-8 with carburetor, per NASCAR rules. "Real" 2000 Montes went on sale soon after a new SS paced the Indy 500 with far fewer modifications (*right*). Despite these racy doings, Monte Carlo sales slipped 2.5 percent in calendar '00.

356

▲▶ The Impala was back again in 2000, this time as a new front-drive sedan cousin to the redesigned Monte Carlo. Though technically a midsize on its shared 110.5-inch wheelbase, it was more space-efficient than the last rear-drive Impalas, offering as much interior space as some full-size cars. Critics divided on the styling, and Impala fans wondered about the two round taillights instead of the traditional three, but the car was widely judged a change for the better. There was no new SS, but options gave the uplevel LS (shown) a similarly sporty look. A 200-hp "3800" V-6 was standard for LS and available for the plainer base model.

▲ Lumina hung on in 2000 even though the new Impala was supposed to replace it. Sales fell by more than half to 44,358 units.

▲ Malibu shed its base 4-cyl engine and got a mild facelift for 2000. The surviving "3100" V-6 added 15 hp for a total of 170.

▲ The Toyota-designed subcompact Prizm had more standard features for 2000 in both uplevel LSi (shown) and base trim.

▲ Camaro's calendar-2000 sales rose 2 percent to 41,962 cars, but the market's big turn to trucks had Chevy's ponycar on a long general slide. All models, like this base coupe, changed only in a few details, such as new-design wheels.

357

2000 Engine Availability

Engines	bore × stroke	bhp	availability
I-3, 61.0	2.91 × 3.03	55	S-Metro
I-4, 79.0	2.91 × 2.97	79	O-Metro
I-4, 109.5	3.11 × 3.60	125	S-Prizm (dohc)
I-4, 134.0	3.50 × 3.46	115	S-Cavalier
I-4, 146.0	3.54 × 3.70	150	O-Cavalier (dohc)
V-6, 191.0	3.51 × 3.31	170	S-Malibu
V-6, 191.0	3.51 × 3.31	175	S-Lumina
V-6, 205.0	3.62 × 3.31	180	S-Impala, Monte Carlo
V-6, 231.0	3.80 × 3.40	200	S-Camaro, O-Impala, Monte Carlo
V-8, 346.0	3.90 × 3.62	305	O-Camaro
V-8, 346.0	3.90 × 3.62	320	O-Camaro
V-8, 346.0	3.90 × 3.62	345	S-Corvette

▲ Generating much interest at year-2000 auto shows was Avalanche, a clever SUV/pickup concept based on the big Suburban and offering lots of passenger/cargo carrying options. The concept was quite close to a production model that Chevy had already approved.

▶ Generating major buzz in 2000 was the concept SSR convertible pickup with a "retro" look taken from Chevy's late-'40s/early-'50s "Advance Design" pickups. The roof cleverly folded behind the cab for open-air jaunts. Built on a Blazer chassis but with a potent V-8 engine, the SSR prompted rabid pleas for a showroom model. Chevy soon said yes.

◀▶ Extended-cab 2000 Silverados (left) added an optional left-side back door to supplement the standard right-side rear portal, and all V-8 models gained 15 hp. Meantime, the full-size Suburban (right) and Tahoe adopted Silverado's basic styling and GMT800 platform for 2000. Buyers evidently approved, as both SUVs recorded higher calendar-year sales, even though Tahoe lost its two-door body style.

Model Breakdown

	Wght	Price	Prod
Metro			
R08 htchbk cpe, I-3	1,818	9,235	
R08/B4M LSi htchbk cpe, I-4	1,845	10,085	35,384
R69/B4M LSi sdn 4d, I-4	1,984	10,660	
Prizm			
K19 sdn 4d, I-4	2,403	13,960	
K19/WP2 LSi sdn 4d, I-4	2,431	16,010	48,168
Cavalier			
C37 cpe, I-4	2,584	13,160	
F37 Z24 cpe, I-4	2,749	16,365	
F67 Z24 conv, I-4	2,899	19,830	240,979
C69 sdn 4d, I-4	2,630	13,260	
F69 LS sdn 4d, I-4	2,729	14,805	

Camaro	Wght	Price	Prod
P87 cpe, V-6	3,317	17,040	
P87/Z28 Z28 cpe, V-8	3,424	21,615	41,962
P67 conv, V-6	3,454	24,340	
P67/Z28 Z28 conv, V-8	3,561	28,715	
Malibu			
D69 sdn 4d, V-6	3,051	16,535	
E69 LS sdn 4d, V-6	3,077	19,215	221,663
Lumina			
L69 sdn 4d, V-6	3,327	18,890	44,358
Impala			
F19 sdn 4d, V-6	3,389	18,890	174,962
H19 LS sdn 4d, V-6	3,466	22,790	

Monte Carlo	Wght	Price	Prod
W27 LS cpe, V-6	3,306	19,390	68,072
X27 SS cpe, V-6	3,436	21,935	
Corvette			
Y37 hrdtp cpe, V-8	3,173	38,705	
Y07 htchbk cpe, V-8	3,246	39,280	32,221
Y67 conv, V-8	3,248	45,705	

*Model year sales includes cars sold between October 1 and September 30. May include cars produced in the previous model year. Corvette figures are model year production.

2001

- **Corvette hardtop transformed into new high-performance Z06**

- **Racing C5-R gives Corvette its first outright win in the Daytona 24 Hours**

- **S-10, Silverado add full four-door cabs**

- **"Lowrider" Blazer Xtreme introduced**

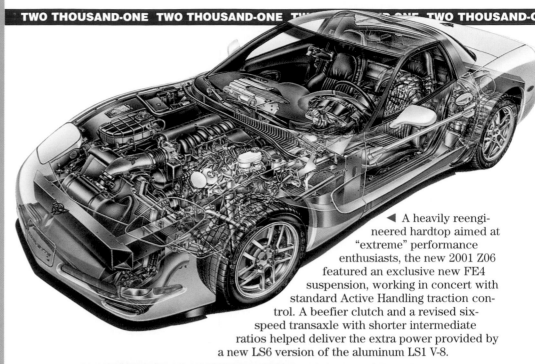

◄ A heavily reengineered hardtop aimed at "extreme" performance enthusiasts, the new 2001 Z06 featured an exclusive new FE4 suspension, working in concert with standard Active Handling traction control. A beefier clutch and a revised six-speed transaxle with shorter intermediate ratios helped deliver the extra power provided by a new LS6 version of the aluminum LS1 V-8.

► Base-priced at $46,855, $500 above the '01 Corvette convertible, the new Z06 wore unique mesh grille inserts, rear brake cooling ducts ahead of the wheel openings, wider new-design wheels, and specially developed Goodyear Eagle F1 SC tires. The last weren't "run-flats," but an emergency inflator kit was provided.

▲ Wearing red cylinder-head covers, the Z06's exclusive new LS6 V-8 made 385 horses, up 35 from the '01 LS1, and a stout 385 pound-feet of torque. Result: the fastest production 'Vette ever, besting even the storied ZR-1. Power-boosting enhancements included freer-flow intake and exhaust systems, revamped combustion chambers with higher compression, and a hotter, higher-lift camshaft.

◄▲ Though named for the famous '63 Sting Ray racing package, the new Z06 had the same conveniences as other '01 Corvettes. The cockpit (*above*) sported special black-and-red upholstery, more heavily bolstered seats, and Z06 logos. Red also adorned the brake calipers (*left*). The windshield and rear window used thinner glass, one of several weight-reducing modifications.

359

▲ The long line of "heritage" press photos from Chevy PR continued with this "there they go" portrait at the National Corvette Museum in Bowling Green, Kentucky. Bringing up the rear, ironically, is a prototype Z06.

▶ Corvette scored its first factory-backed win in big-league racing when a C5-R claimed the 2001 Rolex 24 Hours of Daytona. Running in the production-based GTS class, the C5-R, with lead drivers Ron Fellows and Chris Kneifel, outlasted a slew of more powerful prototype cars to finish an impressive eight laps ahead of the runner-up, a Porsche GT3RS.

◀▲ The 2001 Corvette hatchback (*above*) and convertible (*left*) weren't outwardly changed, but the Active Handling antiskid system now joined traction control as standard for both. In addition, their LS1 V-8 gained 5 horsepower—for 350 total—by adopting some of the improvements developed for the Z06's new LS6 version. That hp number is significant, as both 'Vette engines displaced 346 cubic inches, not the traditional 350, meaning each made more than the "1 hp per cu in" ideal touted way back in 1957.

▲ V-8 Camaros added 5 horses for '01, lifting the Z28 to 310 and the SS (*above*) to 325. But Chevy's ponycar continued losing sales ground to the rival Ford Mustang, which only intensified rumors of Camaro's imminent demise.

▲ Monte Carlo SS offered this new "High Sport Appearance" option for '01. Included were "ground effects" lower-body skirts, trunklid spoiler, special wheels, and unique trim.

▲ The Impala LS got GM's OnStar communications system as a new standard for '01.

▲ Minor equipment changes were the only news for 2001 Malibus. This base model was outwardly identical with the uplevel LS.

▲ Cavaliers like this base coupe boasted only upgraded radios for 2001. The slow-selling Z24 convertible was dropped.

▲ Venture got Consumer Guide®'s "Best Buy" nod in 2001, but was still handily outsold by rival minivans. Options expanded to include a third-row seat that folded into the floor and a Rear Parking Assist system that warned of obstacles when backing up.

▲ Echoing the S-10 Xtreme was this new 2001 package option for two-door 2WD Blazers. This one was mostly for show, too, but did include a lowered handling-oriented suspension, 16-inch alloy wheels (versus 15s), and body-color bumpers and perimeter skirts.

▲ The small Suzuki-built Tracker SUV added this sporty ZR2 wagon for 2001 with standard 2.5-liter V-6 instead of a 2.0 four.

▲ Tracker's V-6, which Suzuki had kept to itself, was also standard on this midrange LT wagon. Side steps were standard too.

▼ This view of the S-10 Crew Cab shows why buyers were flocking to four-door trucks by 2001. Besides much easier rear entry/exit, the Crew Cab was longer than a conventional extended cab, which meant more rear-seat passenger and cargo space. Making up for the short box, Chevy offered an accessory bed extender that folded out onto the lowered tailgate for longer loads.

◄ Crew Cab pickups with four regular-size front-hinged doors were fast becoming popular, and the S-10 belatedly joined in for 2001. Unlike extended-cab models, the Crew offered only an abbreviated Fleetside box measuring 4.6 feet long. Initial sales were hampered by a slow production ramp-up. Ironically, Chevy had sold an S-10 Crew Cab in Brazil for some years before this.

2001 Engine Availability

Engines	bore × stroke	bhp	availability
I-4, 109.5	3.11 × 3.60	125	S-Prizm (dohc)
I-4, 134.0	3.50 × 3.46	115	S-Cavalier
I-4, 146.0	3.54 × 3.70	150	O-Cavalier (dohc)
V-6, 191.0	3.51 × 3.31	170	S-Malibu
V-6, 205.0	3.62 × 3.31	180	S-Impala, Monte Carlo
V-6, 231.0	3.80 × 3.40	200	S-Camaro, O-Impala, Monte Carlo
V-8, 346.0	3.90 × 3.62	310	O-Camaro
V-8, 346.0	3.90 × 3.62	325	O-Camaro
V-8, 346.0	3.90 × 3.62	350	S-Corvette
V-8, 346.0	3.90 × 3.62	385	S-Z06 Corvette

▲ The full-size Express vans showed little outward change for '01. This one is a standard-length 1500 with top-line LT trim.

▲ The '01 Express one-upped the rear-seat entertainment systems of many minivans with this new twin-screen setup.

▲ Chevy's brawniest pickups switched to the basic Silverado platform for '01 and were renamed HD for "Heavy Duty."

▲ Tahoe was Consumer Guide®'s 2001 "Best Buy" choice among full-size SUVs. This 4×4 carries luxury LT trim.

▲ Like Tahoe, the big-rig Suburban was little changed for '01. Not that changes were really needed, as the design was just a year old.

◄► Two new V-8 options provided extra muscle for Chevy's "big rig" 2001 pickups. The previous 7.4-liter gasoline unit gave way to a "Vortec 8100" (*left*) with 300 hp and a stump-pulling 520 pound-feet of torque. Replacing the old 6.5-liter turbodiesel was a new Isuzu-designed 6.6-liter "Duramax" (*right*), the first U.S.-available truck engine with direct fuel injection. It delivered 455 hp and 455 pound-feet of torque.

Model Breakdown

Prizm	Wght	Price	Prod
K19 sdn 4d, I-4	2,403	14,155	—
K19/WP2			
LSi sdn 4d, I-4	2,431	16,220	—
Cavalier			
C37 cpe, I-4	2,617	13,260	—
F37 Z24 cpe, I-4	2,676	16,465	—
C69 sdn 4d, I-4	2,676	13,360	—
F69 LS sdn 4d, I-4	2,729	14,955	—
Camaro			
P87 cpe, V-6	3,306	17,305	—

Camaro *(continued)*	Wght	Price	Prod
P87/Z28			
Z28 cpe, V-8	3,439	21,875	—
P67 conv, V-6	3,500	24,600	—
P67/Z28 Z28 conv, V-8	3,574	28,980	—
Malibu			
D69 sdn 4d, V-6	3,051	17,150	—
E69 LS sdn 4d, V-6	3,077	19,410	—
Impala			
F19 sdn 4d, V-6	3,466	19,269	—
H19 LS sdn 4d, V-6	3,466	23,345	—

Monte Carlo	Wght	Price	Prod
W27 LS cpe, V-6	3,340	19,690	—
X27 SS cpe, V-6	3,391	22,520	—
Corvette			
Y07 htchbk cpe, V-8	3,214	39,830	—
Y37 Z06 hrdtp cpe, V-8	3,116	46,855	—
Y67 conv, V-8	3,210	46,355	—

- Corvette Z06 powers up to 405 horses

- Camaro marks its 35th birthday—and its final season

- Unique Avalanche SUV/pickup debuts

- New TrailBlazer replaces four-door Blazers

▲ Replacing four-door Blazers for 2002, the new midsize TrailBlazer bowed as five-passenger wagon standing 10 inches longer and five inches wider and higher on a six-inch longer wheelbase. This LTZ was the premium model, priced above LT and base LS versions.

▲ TrailBlazer's only engine was this new twincam "Vortec 4200," Chevy's first inline-six in many years. With 270 horsepower, it out-muscled the V-8s of most rival SUVs.

▲▼ Critics generally judged TrailBlazer a big improvement over Blazer (which continued), especially for room, comfort, and ergonomics (below). Seven-seat models with a 16-inch longer wheelbase were scheduled to debut at mid-model year.

2002 Engine Availability

Engines	bore × stroke	bhp	availability
I-4, 109.5	3.11 × 3.60	125	S-Prizm (dohc)
I-4, 134.0	3.50 × 3.46	115	S-Cavalier
I-4, 134.0	3.38 × 3.72	140	O-Cavalier (dohc)
I-4, 146.0	3.54 × 3.70	150	O-Cavalier (dohc)
V-6, 191.0	3.51 × 3.31	170	S-Malibu
V-6, 205.0	3.62 × 3.31	180	S-Impala, Monte Carlo
V-6, 231.0	3.80 × 3.40	200	S-Camaro, O-Impala, Monte Carlo
V-8, 346.0	3.90 × 3.62	310	O-Camaro
V-8, 346.0	3.90 × 3.62	325	O-Camaro
V-8, 346.0	3.90 × 3.62	350	S-Corvette
V-8, 346.0	3.90 × 3.62	405	S-Z06 Corvette

▲ Topside checkered-flag stripes and painted 16-inch wheels marked 2002 SS Camaros equipped with a new limited-edition 35th Anniversary Package. But Camaro fans mourned when Chevy ended speculation with word that 2002 would be Camaro's last year.

▲ Cavalier reached out to "sport compact" fans for '02 with a first-ever Z24 sedan as a new limited edition.

◄▲ Racy styling add-ons, including a tall rear spoiler (*above*) marked Cavalier's new 2002 LS Sport coupe (*left*) and sedan. A twincam 2.2 four with 140 hp was standard.

▲► Monte Carlo SS (*above*) was little changed for '02, but Chevy offered a Dale Earnhardt Signature Edition, honoring the veteran NASCAR ace killed at the very end of the 2001 Daytona 500. Done mostly in black like Dale's Number-3 racing Montes, the special was limited to 3333 copies. Meanwhile, engine tweaks added 20 hp to the Z06 (*right*) for 405 in all. The hottest 'Vette also boasted new cast-alloy wheels, uprated chassis, and other enhancements.

2002

▲ Plugging a gap in the big-truck field, the new 2002 Avalanche was part Suburban, part pickup, and loaded with clever features.

▲ Looking much like the earlier concept vehicle, Avalanche offered 5.3-liter 1500 and 8.1-liter 2500 V-8 models with 2- or 4-wheel drive.

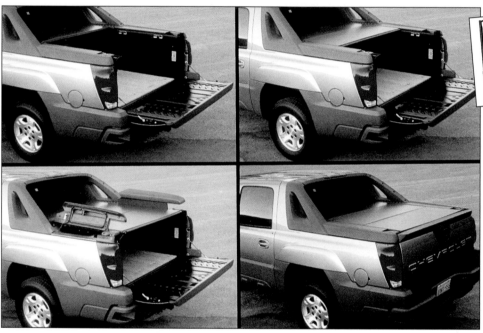

▲ Chevy utilized its Avalanche Ultimate Challenge debut tour to raise awareness of charity partner Students Against Violence Everywhere (S.A.V.E.).

▲ Besides handy sidewall storage boxes (*above left*), Avalanche came with a three-piece hard cover for enclosing its 5.3-foot cargo box. Lowering both the rear seats and a unique "midgate" extended cargo length to 8 feet with the tailgate raised.

▲ Blazer offerings were pared for '02, but the sporty 4×2 Xtreme two-door became a separate model, priced from just $21,360.

Model Breakdown

Prizm	Wght	Price	Prod	Cavalier (continued)	Wght	Price	Prod	Malibu (continued)	Wght	Price	Prod
K19 sdn 4d, I-4	2,403	14,330	—	H69 LS Sport sdn 4d, I-4	—	16,380	—	E69 LS sdn 4d, V-6	3,077	19,740	—
K19/WP2 LSi sdn 4d, I-4	2,431	16,395	—	H69 Z24 sdn 4d, I-4	2,809	16,580	—	**Impala**			
Cavalier				**Camaro**				F19 sdn 4d, V-6	3,389	19,960	—
C37 cpe, I-4	2,617	13,860	—	P87 cpe, V-6	3,323	18,080	—	H19 LS sdn 4d, V-6	3,389	23,660	—
S37 LS cpe, I-4	2,617	14,910	—	P87/Z28 Z28 cpe, V-8 3,524	22,495	—		**Monte Carlo**			
H37 LS Sport cpe, I-4 2,676	16,280	—		P67 conv, V-6	3,524	26,075	—	W27 LS cpe, V-6	3,340	20,060	—
F37 Z24 cpe, I-4	2,749	16,480	—	P67/Z28 Z28 conv, V-8	3,577	29,590	—	X27 SS cpe, V-6	3,395	22,860	—
C69 sdn 4d, I-4	2,676	13,960	—	**Malibu**				**Corvette**			
F69 LS sdn 4d, I-4	2,729	15,010	—	D69 sdn 4d, V-6	3,053	17,535	—	Y07 htchbk cpe, V-8	3,214	41,005	—
								Y37 Z06 hrdtp cpe, V-8 3,116	49,705	—	
								Y67 conv, V-8	3,210	47,530	—

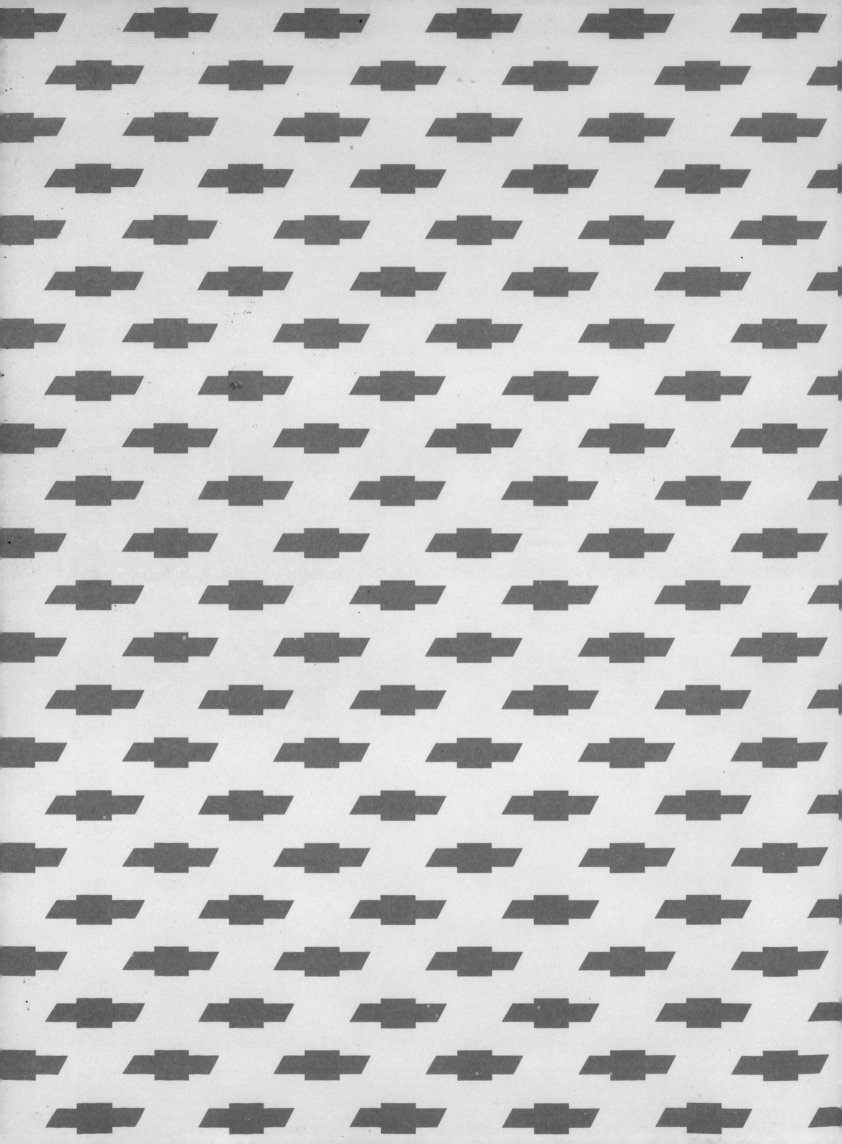